POLITICS, LIES AND VIDEOTAPE

3,000 Questions and
Answers on
the Mideast Crisis

Yitschak Ben Gad

SHAPOLSKY PUBLISHERS, INC.
NEW YORK

For any additional information, contact:
Shapolsky Publishers, Inc.
136 West 22nd Street
New York, NY 10011
(212) 633-2022

10 9 8 7 6 5 4 3 2

ISBN 1-56171-015-6

Design and Typography by Owl Graphics, New York

Printed and Bound by Book Press, Brattleboro, Vermont

Manufactured in the United States of America

To my wife, Judith Ann . . .

> *Many woman are the best, but you*
> *excellest them all.*
>
> Proverbs 29

**The book is dedicated to you for your help,
patience, and advice. Without all of these, the
book could not have become a reality.**

CONTENTS

INTRODUCTION

> *You should love truth and peace.*
>
> Zachariah 8:19
>
> ---
>
> *True peace is not merely the absence of tension; it is the presence of justice.*
>
> MARTIN LUTHER KING, JR.

Propaganda is the continuation of warfare by other means. The Arab war of propaganda against Israel is never-ending. On this front, the Arabs have never agreed to a ceasefire, truce, or compromise. They have consistently and systematically done their utmost to damage Israel's favorable image, trying to depict her as an evil – deserving condemnation and annihilation.

Arab propaganda has made Israel the only country which must strive to justify her right to exist. There are around 20 Arab countries in the world and no one is questioning the legitimacy of their existence. The Arabs make up 3 percent of the human race, hold 13 percent of the vote in the United Nations and have a virtual hold over 30 percent more, and control 15 percent of the earth's land surface and 60 percent of the world's oil resources. Tiny Israel's existence, on the other hand, according to "Arab justice," is illegitimate. The famous author Elie Wiesel has put it thus: "As long as the Jew has existed, he has been judged. At first by God. Then by men who, one after the other, using different titles and pretexts, insisted on substituting themselves for God. Finally, each Jew had to justify himself in the eyes of the entire world for each day, each hour that he was still alive. And the game goes on. He is rebuked for his nationalism and his universalism, his wealth and his poverty, his submissiveness and his revolt. We have not yet finished pleading on behalf of the Jews who during the Holocaust acccepted death without a fight, and already we are forced to defend other Jews who, one generation later, do fight and fight well because they refuse to die."

Abba Eban expressed this absurdity by the following: "There is certainly no other state, big or small, young or old, that would consider mere recognition of its 'right to exist' a favor, or a negotiable concession."

Since her inception, Israel has had to fight for her existence. Israel won all her wars on the battlefields, yet lost all the battles of propaganda. In the field, the battle is fought with machine guns, cannons, warplanes, missiles, etc. The target is to capture a piece of land, a city, or a desert. In the war of propaganda, the means of warfare is the media and proper, timely reactions. The target is to capture public opinion.

The late David Ben-Gurion once said: "It is more important what the Jews do than what the non-Jews think." The traditional Israeli policy was to relate to Israel's public relations as a subject of minor importance. As a result of this traditional policy, and because of the Arabs' huge economic power coupled with highly effective Arab PLO propaganda, especially since the 1967 war, Israel was neither treated fairly in the world media in general nor in the United Nations in particular. Today, sophisticated Arab propaganda against Israel endangers her very existence. Israel and her few friends must act now in order to let the world know the truth about the Arab-Israeli conflict. Israel should be the prosecutor, not the defendant.

The Palestinian refugee problem is a very effective Arab propaganda weapon against Israel. Considering the total number of the world's refugees, the problem of Palestinian refugees is neither the largest nor the most difficult. Yet despite this fact, the impression is that the Palestinian problem is one of the major problems facing the world. In the last generation, tens of millions of refugees the world over (1,400,000 of them Jews) have been integrated into hospitable countries. The exception is the 600,000 Palestinians who fled from Israel in 1948 and have since troubled world peace.

The PLO, superb master in double talk and the big-lie technique, has adopted many of the ideas of the notorious Adolf Hitler, who said: "A definite factor in getting a lie believed is the size of the lie. The broad mass of people, in the simplicity of their hearts, more easily fall victim to a big lie than a small one."

Apologists for Arab terrorism and supporters of the PLO constantly explain the need to draw the world's attention to Palestinian national homelessness. Israel, they claim, has robbed the Arabs of Palestine, their country. However, it is a fact that the overwhelming majority of Palestinians – over 80 percent – are still living within the confines of the former mandate territory of Palestine, and that even today 77 percent of this area is purely Arab and is administered by an Arab government: Jordan.

King Hussein of Jordan, as well as PLO chairman Yassir Arafat and many other Palestinian leaders, have specified time and time again that Jordan is Palestine and Palestine is Jordan. Jordanians and Palestinians are one nation and share one destiny. The Palestinians are not stateless. They control today more than three-quarters of mandatory Palestine.

People tend to forget that the Arab-Israeli conflict was neither about refugees nor about occupied land. The conflict is about tiny Israel's right to survive. If one needed a reminder of this fact, the president of Iraq supplied it in March 1990. In his hostile speech towards Israel, Saddam Hussein warned that Iraq may destroy half of Israel with chemical weapons. The PLO in Tunis hailed the Iraqi president's speech. We must remember that the size of Israel's territory (with Judea, Samaria, the Gaza Strip, and the Golan Heights), is less than one-sixth of a percent of the huge Arab world, which is, in territory, double the size of the United States of America. The absurdity is that, since her establishment, Israel – who fought and is still fighting for her right to breathe – is considered today "Goliath," while the immense, extremely powerful Arabs and Palestinians are the small "David." Tiny Israel is a mere drop in the Arabs' virtual oceans of land stretching over two continents – "from the Atlantic Ocean to the Persian Gulf." The Arabs call the Persian Gulf the Arab Gulf.

PLO leaders are international champions of double talk. Recent peaceful declarations of the PLO are one thing, reality is quite another. Yassir Arafat holds the olive branch for the West to see, while launching terror attacks throughout Lebanon and guiding the violent uprising in Judea, Samaria, and the Gaza Strip, killing innocent Jews and Arabs indiscriminately. No propaganda campaign can erase the criminal record of Yassir Arafat.

Moreover, while the world is over-occupied with the dilemma of the Palestinian problem, nothing is heard about the Jewish refugees from Arab countries, most of whom now reside in Israel while others remain dispersed among other nations, some still without citizenship. The number of Jews who have left the Arab states since 1948 is almost equal to the number of Palestinians who fled Israel in the same year. However, the combined value of the property left by the Jews in their Arab countries of origin is over five times that of the Palestinians'.

The Jews, who in 1948 constituted 1.5 percent of the total population of the Arab lands in which they had been living for generations, evacuated approximately 100,000 square kilometers. That amounts to five times the terrritory of Israel prior to the 1967 Six-Day War. Moreover, if the 38,000 Jews of Libya (where the author of this book was born) alone were to receive their portion in territory in their country of origin, according to their percentage in the Libyan population, they would be entitled to a piece of land more extensive than Israel with Judea, Samaria, and the Gaza Strip.

The famous UN Security Council Resoultion 242 of November 22, 1967, speaks about a "just settlement of the refugee problem." According to Lord Caradon, a British ambassador to the United Nations in 1967, and his American counterpart, the late Arthur Goldberg, the resolution refers to Jewish as well as Arab refugees. The world remains uninformed about the plight of the Jews from Arab countries – their rights, suffering, persecutions, and even executions by cruel Arab leaders and citizens.

Massive Arab propaganda and its distortion of the facts is dangerous to Israel's very existence. The writer of this book believes that peace is inevitable. However, in order to strengthen the chances for peace between Israel and her neighbors and to keep Israel strong, the world must know the facts. Peace may be achieved when the Arabs understand that in the field of propaganda they cannot win *all the time*. The facts are stronger than Arab propaganda.

This book is based on a great collection of material from different sources in a number of languages, and especially from the material of the Israeli Foreign Office and PLO publications (see detailed list in the Bibliography at the end of the book). The approach of the book is unique. It is composed of thousands of short questions, answers, comments, and quotations from various sources dealing with subjects concerning the Middle East. This is not meant to be a history book.

The goal is to enable the average reader, who may show some interest in our troubled area, to get an idea about most of the subjects without having to strive or to read at great length. The questions and subjects are based upon my selective and subjective discretion. I have no intention of dealing with *all* aspects of the conflict. The idea is to deal with either forgotten issues or with subjects that may demonstrate the absurdity of the conflict and the great injustice inflicted upon the Jewish people. The quotations are meant to strengthen the points dealt with in each chapter.

I would like to thank all the people who have helped to make this book a reality: my wife, Judith; Mr. Dan Abraham – a man of peace and vision; Mr. Elie Gridish; Mr. Ian Shapolsky – the publisher; Mr. Abe Foxman – Chairman of the ADL; the Weisenthal Institute; Mr. Benjamin Netanyahu – Israel's Vice Minister of Foreign Affairs; and Mr. David Bedein. I thank them all and the many others who have helped me in one way or another.

Last but not least, I hope this book will help to put history in its proper perspective. I believe that only when the facts are known will the chances for peace in our troubled area, based upon justice, be enhanced. Our prophet, Zachariah, said: "You should love truth and peace." This comes to show that truth precedes peace.

Yitschak Ben Gad
Netanya, Israel
1991

PART I

THE PLO TERROR, DOUBLE TALK, AND BRILLIANT PROPAGANDA

CHAPTER ONE

PLO PROPAGANDA –
TACTICS AND STRATEGIES

At first a small state; and with the help of Allah, it will be made large and expand to the east, west, north and south . . . I am interested in the liberation of Palestine, step by step.

ABU IYAD, second in command
to PLO Chairman Yassir Arafat,
Al-Anba, Kuwait, December 18, 1988

The CIA, if it were wise, would equip Afghan rebels with video cameras as well as rifles. In the modern world, TV tape is mightier than a cannon . . . The American media still has the sense not to glorify a gunman who uses hostages to shield himself from the police, but every day they are making Yassir Arafat out to be a plucky little hero, even as he hides behind the innocent civilians of West Beirut.

MORTON KONDRACKE,
Wall Street Journal,
July 22, 1982

The Palestine Liberation Organization (PLO) has learned that, without any military action, they can exert fantastic pressure on Israel through diplomatic means. There is an Arab proverb which says: "On words one does not pay duties." The PLO, veritable artists in the use of words, has elevated the diplomacy of words to new heights. Israel's position can be weakened by cleverly using all kinds of hazy terminologies and special words which ring well in Western ears. Through "word diplomacy" the PLO has achieved much more than it has achieved on the battlefield.

> *And let us bathe our hands in . . . blood up to the elbows, and besmear our swords. Then walk we forth, even to the market place, and waving our red weapons o'er our heads, let's all cry "peace, freedom, and liberty!"*
>
> SHAKESPEARE,
> *Julius Caesar*, III, i, 106-10

Yassir Arafat, the murderer of innocent children in Ma'alot and Nahariya (northern Israel), likes to pose before the world media kissing children in order to demonstrate his "humanity." Encounters with Israeli troops in which PLO terrorists were killed were described by the PLO propaganda machine as a "fantastic victory over the Zionist enemy," minor clashes were transformed into fierce battles and incidental fires claimed as well-planned sabotage. Quite often three or four different factions of the PLO would boast and claim responsibility for such minor incidents.

The PLO has managed to continuously focus world opinion on itself, gaining the image of an army and giving the world's foremost architect of terror, Yassir Arafat, the status of a head of state. The tremendous media coverage of the PLO exceeds any proportion to its size: an organization of diverse groups numbering some 15,000 claiming to represent some 3,000,000 Palestinians.

> *If President Reagan thinks that we will stop attacks against Israeli military targets, then I tell him to stop the dialogue now.*
>
> spoken at a rally in Abu Dhabi,
> December 17, 1988
>
> ---
>
> *Neither military attacks nor our heroic* Intifada *will stop. We will carry on our struggle until the Palestinian flag is hoisted over Jerusalem.*
>
> SALEH KHALEF (Abu Iyad),
> Arafat's deputy in Fatah

PLO "Ideology and Practice" was sent to Palestinians on Fatah stationery dated July 18, 1981, and signed by Arafat. It was entitled "Document 5: Shelling Safed and Other Towns," and read:"Greetings for the Revolution! I am strengthening your hands! Thus you will prove your worth as heroic sons of your people and your revolution! We expect Safed and Ja'un[1] to be shelled with heavy rockets tonight due to the extreme importance we attach to this. You also have to shell the settlements in the vicinity of the border with 120mm and 160mm mortars. Proceed immediately. You must also dispatch battle patrols, either from your troops or from the joint forces,[2] to set ambushes along the border and deep into the occupied territory."[3]

1. The Israeli town of Rosh Pina, a major crossroads in the Galilee.
2. The joint command of the PLO in southern Lebanon.
3. In the PLO lexicon, the term "occupied territory" includes Israel proper, not only the territories administered by Israel since the 1967 war.

THE PLO: MASTER OF THE BIG LIE TECHNIQUE

The partitioning of Palestine in 1947 and the establishment of Israel is fundamentally null and void.

Article 10, PLO National Covenant

He whose argument is unsound seeks to cover it with many words.

The Talmud

After the Six-Day War, the Arab world understood that their slogan, "To throw the Jews into the sea," was very damaging to the Arabs. In light of this realization, the Arabs switched from a hard line to a softer approach, thereby creating their new image as the underdog.

Q: What change occurred?
A: Instead of speaking outright about destroying Israel, the PLO now speaks of the "homeless Palestinians." The fact that the Palestinian and Arab leaders were themselves the reason behind this human problem is never mentioned.

For non-Arabs the PLO used the "underdog approach" as in this booklet from the 1970s:

The rabbit has a home.   The horse has a home.   A Palestinian has no home.
Its home is the burrow.   Its home is the stable.   The tents and houses he
                                               lives in are not his home.

> *For every evil, silence is the best remedy.*
> The Talmud

Q: What are some other means?

A: An awful irony runs through PLO publicity: Arafat kissing babies in front of television cameras in beseiged Beirut or well-groomed boys appearing on the same screen vowing to carry on the "Palestinian revolution" around the world. What a cynical use of the child by an organization that does not shun deliberately attacking nurseries and schools in Israel.

> *All wisdom is not new wisdom, and the past should be studied if the future is to be successfully encountered.*
> WINSTON CHURCHILL

Q: What about exaggeration?

A: During the "Peace for Galilee" campaign, the PLO succeeded in misleading all the world. The notorious axiom that the greater the lie, and the more often it is repeated,the more credible it will be worked very well in the Lebanon war. The news was flashed: 10,000 Lebanese and Palestinians dead, 40,000 wounded, 600,000 home-less, in the Israeli bombardment of southern Lebanon. When the actual civilian casualty figures were released by the International Committee of the Red Cross, the PLO "estimate" of 10,000 killed came down to several hundred.

> *Arab observers, too, have noted the Arab tendency to exaggerate and have attacked it with sharp words of criticism. Indeed, Salim al-Luzi, the editor of the Beirut weekly* Al-Hawadith, *in an article published in the June 16, 1972, issue of his paper on the occasion of the fifth anniversary of the Six-Day War of 1967, reproached the Arab press and radio with feeding the Arab consciousness with futile imaginings, lies, and exaggerations.*
> RAPHAEL PATAI,
> *The Arab Mind*

Q: Who was the person who lied to the world with grossly exaggerated and dramatic numbers of casualties?

A: The man is no less than Dr. Fathi Arafat, Yassir Arafat's brother and head of the PLO-affiliated Red Crescent.

Q: Can another example be cited?

A: When Lebanese President-elect Bashir Gemayel was murdered on September 14, 1982, Arafat, master of the big lie technique, claimed that the Israelis killed him. He claimed this when it was well-known that Bashir Gemayel was friendly with Israel and as such, he raised the opposition of the Syrians and the PLO, who very probably were the ones who murdered him.

> *We are dealing with exaggerations of anywhere up to 2000 - 3000 percent.*
> MAX LERNER,
> *New York Post,*
> July 21, 1982

Q: How could the PLO explain its expulsion from Lebanon?

A: Arafat's defeat in Lebanon and the PLO's humiliating expulsion from Beirut, were carefully portrayed as a story of PLO success. Arafat boasted that his men bravely faced the Israeli army for 80 days, longer than any other Arab army in the past.

Q: How did the PLO terrorists fight in Lebanon in 1982?

A: The number of PLO casualties in the Lebanon war was not high. The reason is very simple: In most cases, these terrorists preferred to run away, to hide, or to surrender rather than fight back.

Q: How did the PLO terrorists fight under siege in Beirut in 1982?

A: Most of the PLO "freedom fighters" were probably busier looting some 25,000 Beirut apartments evacuated by their owners than actually fighting the "Zionist enemy."

7

Q: What else can be said of Arafat's big bluff?

A: The PLO chairman has told the world time and again the story of his childhood in Jerusalem, where he claims his home was destroyed by the Israelis. In reality, Arafat was neither born in Jerusalem nor did he ever live there. According to his biographer, Thomas Kirnan, Arafat was born in Cairo on August 27, 1929, and grew up in Gaza.

> *The Arabs have a proclivity of substituting words for actions (pp.61-62)...*
>
> *In the Arab mentality words often can and do serve as substitutes for acts (p.64) and that verbal utterance achieves such importance that the question of whether or not it is subsequently carried out becomes of minor significance (p.65).*
> RAPHAEL PATAI,
> *The Arab Mind*

Q: What helps the PLO promote its propaganda?

A: Besides using effective methods in order to attract world public opinion, including murder and sabotage, Arafat also spends huge amounts of money to achieve PLO goals. The PLO, as a very rich terrorist organization, uses its finances to promote the Palestinian cause with films, exhibitions, books, shows, ads in papers across the globe, with bribery, etc.

> *To lie during a war is permitted in order to encourage the Moslems.*
>
> IBN ALARABI,
> devout Moslem

Q: Can an example be cited?

A: Yes. During the Lebanon war, an 800-word ad was published in seven leading American papers at a cost of $120,000. The ad called upon American citizens to write to their congressmen and demand that they put a stop to the "merciless killing of Lebanese and Palestinians by insensitive Israel with American-made weapons."

Q: What are the other methods?

A: Arafat and the other PLO leaders are unquestionably masters of double talk. To their own people while speaking in Arabic, they say one thing. To the world in other languages they say something different. (See Chapter Four on PLO double talk.)

> *When the PLO desperately needed a ceasefire [in June 1982],*
> *it turned for help to moderate Egypt, whose peace process it had*
> *vilified and at the death of whose leader [the late Anwar Sadat]*
> *Palestinians had danced in the streets.*
>
> HENRY KISSINGER,
> *Washington Post*,
> June 19, 1982

Q: What is the pattern?

A: The pattern is very simple – making moderate statements for the consumption of certain audiences and denying it the very next day. For example, Arafat fooled U.S. congressmen who visited Beirut in August 1982 with a signed piece of paper, supposedly recognizing Israel, only to disavow the statement the next day, after it had gained worldwide coverage.

Q: What makes these lies effective?

A: Any given denial is usually printed in small print on an inside page, whereas the big news is printed on the front page. The PLO's propaganda uses this trick often.

> *To lie is a sin unless used to serve the interests of a Moslem or*
> *save him from a disaster.*
>
> ATTABARANI,
> Arab historian

Cranes retrieve bodies from the Savoy Hotel, Tel Aviv, which was attacked by Fatah in March 1975.

Mussa Juma, member captured during the attack on the Savoy – in which eight civilians were killed and six wounded.

ARAFAT – PLO LEADER: PROUD OF HIS FRIENDS

ARAFAT: CONVINCING BY THE BULLET

> *Whoever thinks of stopping the* Intifada *before it achieves its goal, I will give him ten bullets in the chest.*
>
> YASSIR ARAFAT,
speaking in Riyadh, Saudi Arabia,
January 1, 1989
>
> *(The threat was directed at Elias Freij, Mayor of Bethlehem, who had suggested a few days prior to Arafat's threat that the PLO should end the uprising in order to start an Israeli-Palestinian dialogue.)*

Arafat is by no means a liberal democrat. He believes that the pistol should be used in order to convince any "rebels." For Arafat, the life of a human being is like the life of a fly. In order to achieve PLO goals, all means are justified. The shocking but true accounts of thousands of crimes committed by the PLO against different people – Jews and non-Jews alike – is good proof. Threats, intimidation, and murder were even applied against journalists. Most of these journalists understood the message. Those that did not listen paid a very high price.

Q: Can an example be cited?

A: Salim Lawzi, age 54, owner of the prestigious Lebanese weekly *Al-Hawadith*, was apprehended at a PLO checkpost in July 1978. He was taken to Aramoun village where he was tortured. His eyes were gouged out and his body cut to pieces. Photos of his mutilated body were distributed among the press community of Beirut as a warning. Lawzi, of course, had refused to write pro-PLO articles.

Q: Is there another example?

A: Yes. Edouard Sa'eb, age 46 and editor-in-chief of the daily *L'Orion le Jour* and local correspondent of *Le Monde,* was shot to death in September 1976 while crossing Beirut's Green Line.

It is an ugly irony but a historic inevitability. Give instruments of murder to fanatics who live to kill, make heroes of them and one day, if you cross them, they will look at you and decide that you too must die.

A.M. ROSENTHAL,
New York Times,
March 25, 1990

Q: What happened to Riadh Taha?

A: The murder that totally shocked the media community in Beirut was that of Riadh Taha, president of the Lebanese newspaper publisher's union and an influential Moslem leader. At the end of 1980, he met with Bashir Gemayel in an effort to solidify an anti-PLO front. Coming out from this meeting, he was gunned down by PLO terrorists at the entrance of the Beirut Carlton Hotel.

Intimidation of the foreign press was directed at those who presented the PLO in a negative light. One example was the German television network, ZDF, which was threatened by the PLO terror in Lebanon.

In 1978, an *Album of Terrorist Atrocities* was published in Lebanon. The study detailed in photographs and documents the years of suffering under PLO domination. A senior editor of the French language daily *L'Orion le Jour* said that the PLO murdered his editor-in-chief, Edouard Sa'eb, in 1976. George later said that he and his wife had received death threats.

On August 27, 1982, George told the Israeli daily *Ma'ariv* that the PLO killed seven foreign journalists in West Beirut between 1976 and 1978. Those listed: Larry Buchman, correspondent for ABC Television;

Mark Tryon of Free Belgium Radio; Robert Pfeffer, correspondent for the weeklies *Der Spiegel* of West Germany and *Unità* of Italy; Italian journalists Tony Italo and Graciella Difaco; Sean Toolan, ABC correspondent; and Jean Lougeau, correspondent for French TV-1.

George listed as well numerous examples of Lebanese papers whose offices were bombed and destroyed by the PLO: *Al-Jamhou* weekly, April 1975; *Al-Mouharer* daily, May 1975; *Abi Sadr* printing plant, May 1975; *Al-Moustaqbal* daily, closed under bomb threats and moved to Paris, August 1975; and *A-Safir* daily, November 1981.

> *Three months ago I supported the idea to liberate Palestine at once. I was stupid. Now I am interested to liberate Palestine by stages. This is the art of liberation.*
>
> ABU IYAD, Arafat deputy,
> *Al-Anba*, Kuwait, December 18, 1988

In the biggest hijack so far, passengers and crew of this Swissair plane pose for their PFLP captors in Zarka, Jordan, before the plane is blown up along with two others from BOAC and TWA, on September 6, 1970.

THE PLO "DEMOCRATIC STATE": THE BIG LIE

> *Now I understand why Israel is refusing the suggested "democratic Palestine" where the Israelis and the Palestinians would live together. The outstanding example the Palestinian people are giving now in Lebanon is, I believe, more than enough to warn Israel of such a trap-state. I am a Lebanese citizen whose brother and two cousins have been coldly shot down by the Palestinians in their own homes in Hitlerian style. I can already see the day when, in order to survive, our people will join Israel, being bound to the same fate: Survival.*
>
> ELISS MARVUN, Beirut,
> *Time*, July 14, 1975

> *If the slogan of a democratic state is only designed to reply to the contention that we aim to throw the Jews into the sea, then it is a successful slogan and an effective political propaganda tool, but if we wish to see it as the final strategical aim, then I am convinced that it demands continued consideration.*
> SHAFIQ AL HUT of the PLO,
> *Al-Anwar,* Beirut, March 8, 1970

The PLO idea of a democratic secular state in which Jews, Christians and Moslems will live together in one state was used after the Six-Day War of 1967. The PLO realized then that the slogan to throw the Jews into the sea was not successful since it was rejected by most of the world community. The PLO had to change its tactics, yet not its goal: the destruction of Israel. The terrorist organization attempted to convince the world that a democratic state is the best solution since it enables all the people of Palestine to live in peace and harmony.

> *We have in the Lebanese experience a significant example that is close to the multi-religious state that we are trying to achieve.*
> YASSIR ARAFAT,
> *The Economist,* April 12, 1974

However, propaganda is one thing, reality is quite another. The PLO intervention in Lebanon and its support of the Moslems against the Christians in the bitter civil war proved that the PLO slogan about a democratic state is not serious. The civil war erupted in the spring of 1975, proving that the Moslems would not accept Christian supremacy in Lebanon. Democracy, according to Arafat, is when the Palestinian Moslems will rule the country.

> *The principle of secularism, fully accepted by Turkey, has not yet been finally adopted by any Arab country.*
> MAJID KHADDURI,
> *Political Trends in the Arab World*

Q: How democratic are the Arab states?
A: In all the Arab world, Islam is the state religion. There is no reason to believe that the PLO in their "state" would deviate from this policy. The treatment of the Jews in Arab countries, arising out of

their Dhimmi status, does not augur well for Jews who might find themselves in a PLO state.

Q: The PLO has masked its ideology in a single formula: "a secular democratic state." What does the PLO mean by this?

A: There is no "democratic secular" state in any part of the Arab world, unless the PLO means "democratic" like Qaddafi's Libya or "secular" like Saudi Arabia.

> *Land of tolerance, human synthesis, fraternal and peaceful.*
> *This Lebanon, thus made by the grace of God and the merit of*
> *its people, is it not a symbol of what the world could be,*
> *delivered from the reign of violence and undertakings inspired*
> *by religious or racial exclusivism?*
>
> SULEIMAN FRANJIEH,
> former Lebanese president,
> UN Assembly, November 14, 1974

Q: Is the PLO democratic in its own structure?

A: Not at all. Within its own institutions, the PLO has all the characteristics of a centralized bureaucracy wherein ordinary Palestinians have no say.

Q: Will the Palestinians be able to establish a Palestinian democratic state?

A: No. The Palestinians would not succeed where all the other Arabs have failed. No democratic Arab state (in the Western sense of democracy) exists in the Middle East.

Q: What is the meaning of "democracy" and "secular" in Arabic?

A: In Arabic the words "democracy" and "secular" do not exist as understood in the West. For example, the concept of "secular" in Arabic is translated *Ilmani,* which derives from the word *Ilm,* meaning religious science. The Western concept of a "secular state" is totally foreign to the Arab mind.

> *A 45-year-old Christian Arab woman from Tyre (Lebanon) told*
> *foreign correspondents about the fate of her two teenage*
> *daughters. The two girls, 16 and 17, were repeatedly raped and*
> *brutalized by local PLO men. Resistance would have meant a*
> *bullet in the head. Finally, after being gang-raped one night by*
> *a dozen PLO men, the girls killed themselves in despair.*
>
> Israeli television,
> July 13, 1982

Q: Is the PLO moderate?

A: Dr. Henry Kissinger, former U.S. Secretary of State, provides the answer in an article published in the *Washington Post* on June 19, 1982. He wrote: "One of the principal casualities of the Lebanese crisis has been the Western illusion – especially prevalent in Europe but rife, too, in the Middle East – that peace is to be found in PLO-Israeli negotiation based on various formulas to 'moderate' the PLO."

> *We shall fight together as one Moslem nation, under one flag.*
>
> YASSIR ARAFAT, in Teheran,
> *Voice of Fatah*, Beirut,
> February 19, 1979

ARAB COUNTRIES: ISLAM IS STATE RELIGION

> *Islam is always superior and never inferior.*
>
> Islamic saying

Excerpts from Constitutions of Arab States:

Algeria: "Islam is the religion of the State."
Article 4, September 8, 1963
Egypt: "Islam is the state religion and Arabic its official language. Islamic jurisprudence is a chief source for legislation."
Article 2, September 11, 1971
Iraq: "Islam is the religion of the State."
Article 4, July 16, 1970 (provisional)
Jordan: "Islam is the religion of the State."
Article 2, January 8, 1952
Kuwait: "The religion of the State is Islam, and Islamic jurisprudence shall be a chief source for legislation."
Article 2, November 11, 1962
Libya: "Islam is the religion of the State."
Article 2, December 11, 1969 (provisional)

Morocco: "Islam is the religion of the State."
Article 6, March 10, 1972
Qatar: "The State shall endeavor to instill proper Islamic
religious principles in society."
Article 7, April 2, 1970 (provisional)
South Yemen: "Islam is the state religion."
Article 46, November 30, 1970
Sudan: "In the Democratic Republic of Sudan there is the
Islamic religion. Society is rightly guided by Islam, the
religion of the majority."
Article 16, April 14, 1973
Tunisia: "Islam is the religion of the State."
Article 1, June 1, 1959
United Arab Emirates: "Islam is the religion of the
State and Islamic jurisprudence is a chief source
for legislation."
Article 6, December 2, 1971

Convert to Islam, you will be saved.

Islamic saying

Q: What is Israel?
A: Israel is the only free, democratic state in the entire Middle East. To
wit: "The State of Israel will insure complete equality of social and
political rights to all its inhabitants irrespective of religion, race or
sex; it will guarantee freedom of religion, conscience, language,
education and culture; it will safeguard the holy places of all religions;
and it will be faithful to the principles of the Charter of the United
Nations." (Excerpt from the Declaration of Independence of Israel,
May 14, 1948.)

The conclusion is very simple: the slogan about a Palestinian secular
democratic state is merely a catchy slogan. The reality proves that
"secularism" and Islam are two different contradictory terms.

The Lebanese civil war affects the Arab-Israeli equation in a disastrous way. The Palestine Liberation Organization has weakened, perhaps irreparably, its argument that Jews, Moslems, and Christians could live in harmony side by side in a future greater Palestine. It can now be seen that Arabs themselves, citizens of the same country, not only cannot coexist but collide day and night.

Jordan's KING HUSSEIN,
interview with *Newsweek*
senior editor Arnaud de Borchegrave

The following cartoons appeared on February 21 and 20, 1974, respectively, in the PLO newspaper *Al-Anwar*. They represent the Democratic State, Arafat-style. In the first, the Arabic may be translated: "Hold it tight, so I can dismantle it." In the second, "Arafat was elected Man of the Year in Spain."

PROFESSIONAL PRESS RELATIONS AND STRATEGIES

One wonders how the PLO has succeeded in overwhelming the media over the past several years. Its success has little to do with petro-dollars, anti-Semitic correspondents, or any other subjective phenomena. The PLO has simply and cleverly pioneered a systematic and professional press relations strategy in Jerusalem where thousands of journalists have visited over the last few years and where approximately 200 news bureaus maintain full-time or part-time foreign correspondents. Israel's adversaries wisely concluded that Jerusalem, Israel's capital, is one of the few places where journalists can freely operate, following the demise of media centers such as in Teheran, Beirut, Damascus, Baghdad, and other Arab capitals.

The PLO press strategy works as follows:

1. Personal lobbying at the American Colony Hotel in East Jerusalem, where a "welcome wagon" is provided for all correspondents, wherever they stay. The PLO offers a wide range of personalized services for the newly arrived correspondents, including tours of refugee camps, meetings with Arab political leaders, and visits with Arab "victims."

2. Databases are provided, which are accessible to any journalist anywhere in the world, beginning in Jerusalem, concerning alleged Israeli human rights abuses. These are presented as "documented." Arab land claims in Judea and Samaria are entered into these databases, also seemingly factual and "documented."

3. The PLO publishes timely newsletters and daily press releases, which are then distributed to the foreign press corps in Jerusalem and to editorial offices throughout the world. These publications cannot be published in any Arab country for reasons of press censorship, but they can be published in Israel, where freedom of the press is allowed.

4. Activation of world-renowned and internationally respected human rights organizations, as the Palestinian state demands, is presented as an "inalienable and fundamental" human right. PLO organizations have renamed several of their terrorist groups to sound like human rights organizations.

5. The PLO collaborates with the United Nations Relief and Works Agency (UNRWA), which continues to administer the Arab refugee camps after 40 years. The hopes of the Arabs – that they will return

to Haifa, Ramle, and 300 other places now within Israel proper – is consequently kept alive. UNRWA hires pro-PLO leadership to run these camps and provides necessary support services at the time of strikes. Meanwhile, UNRWA restricts Israel from improving health, educational, and welfare services, and reinforces United Nations resolutions that veto Israeli improvements in housing, sanitation, etc.

Registered as a Newspaper at the Post Office

AL-QABAS INTERNATIONAL EDITION

Friday, 27 September 1985, 1st. Year, No. 128

No peace
No recognition
No negotiations
LARNACA

Above: a Kuwaiti commentary on the murder by PLO "Force 17" killers of three Israelis (1 woman, 2 men) on their yacht, moored in the marina at Larnaca, Cyprus, on September 25, 1985.

CHAPTER TWO

THE PLO NATIONAL COVENANT (ALMITHAQ AL-WATANI AL-FILASTINI)

> *The popular revolution in Palestine will continue the struggle to expel the Zionist occupation from all the Palestinian Arab soil, from the (Jordan) river to the (Mediterranean) sea.*
> PLO leader NOYEF HAWATMEH,
> quoted by Jamahiriya News Agency, Libya,
> April 19, 1989
>
> *We are on the Iranian side and agree to what Khomeini agrees to.*
> YASSIR ARAFAT

Q: What is the Palestinian National Covenant?

A: A very radical and fanatic document that seeks Israel's destruction and the establishment of an Arab Palestinian state.

Q: Why is it so important?

A: (1) The covenant is the platform for all the terrorist factions under the umbrella of the PLO.

(2) It is the official document of the PLO.

(3) What is written in the covenant carries more weight and importance than the declarations of any given Palestinian spokesman.

Q: How many versions are there of the PLO covenant?

A: There are two versions. The first was adopted at the first Palestinian Congress which convened in Jerusalem in May 1964 at the time of the establishment of the PLO. The amendment to the covenant was written during the session of the Palestinian National Congress in Cairo, Egypt, July 10 – 17, 1968.

Q: Why was it called a "covenant"?

A: The document was called a "covenant" in order to emphasize its national sanctity and the introductory words to the covenant conclude with an oath to implement it. The Palestinians claim that the covenant was written in blood to demonstrate its holiness.

Q: How many articles are in the covenant?

A: There are 33 articles.

Who would dare ask for an amendment of the PLO Charter? Arafat himself would kill him.

PLO leader HANI EL-HASSAN,
March 16, 1977

DOCUMENT OF HATRED AND FANATICISM

Q: What are the most important articles of the covenant?

A: The most important articles are 3, 6, 9, 18, 19, and 21.

Q: What was written in article 6?

A: "Jews who were living permanently in Palestine until the beginning of the Zionist invasion will be considered Palestinians."

Q: When was "the beginning of the Zionist invasion?

A: The beginning of the Zionist invasion was at the time of the Balfour Declaration on November 2, 1917.

Q: What about the Jews who came after 1917 – the year of the Balfour Declaration?

A: Jews who are not recognized as Palestinians are therefore considered aliens who have no right of residence and must leave.

Your children shall come back to their own country.

Jeremiah 31:17

Q: What kind of a state would the PLO like to establish?

A: Palestinian Arabs speak about creating a secular state as opposed to Israel, which they condemn as an anachronistic state based upon religious principles.

Q: Are there any Arab states that can be considered secular?

A: No. In all the constitutions of the Arab states, Islam is stated as the state religion. (Lebanon, due to its unique nature is not considered a pure Arab state.) In most constitutions it is also specified that the *Shari'a* (Islamic law) is the source for the laws of the state.

> *We shall never permit Israel to live in peace . . . each Israeli should feel that behind each wall there stands a guerilla aiming at him.*
>
> FAROUK KADDOUMI,
> head of the PLO Political Department,
> *Stern* (West Germany), July 1981

Q: Does the PLO, in policy, follow the principles of a secular state?
A: No. The Fatah appealed to a congress held in Al-Azhar University in September 1968 to consider contributions to the fedayeen Zakat (a religious alms tax) and warfare against Israel, Jihad (Islamic holy war).
Q: What is written in article 3 of the covenant?
A: "The Palestinian Arab people possesses the legal right to its homeland, and when the liberation of its homeland is completed it will exercise self-determination solely according to its own will and choice."
Q: Article 3 speaks about legal rights for Palestinian Arabs alone. What about the Jews?
A: Only Palestinian Arabs have rights in this article.

> *In some of those Galilean villages – such as Kfar Alma, Ein Zeitim, Biria, Pekiin, Kfar Hanania, Kfar Kana, and Kfar Yassif – the Jews against all logic and in defiance of the pressures, taxations, and confiscations of generations of foreign conquerers had succeeded in clinging to the land for fifteen centuries.*
>
> YITZCHAK BEN-ZVI,
> *Shear Yashuv*, Jerusalem, 1927
>
> ---
>
> *He who hides hatred uses lying lips, and he that utters a slander, is a fool.*
>
> Proverbs 10:18

> *I want to tell Carter and Begin that when the Arabs set off their volcano, there will only be Arabs in this part of the world . . . Our people will continue to fuel the torch of the revolution with rivers of blood until the whole of the occupied homeland is liberated, not just part of it.*
>
> YASSIR ARAFAT,
> Beirut, March 12, 1979,
> after the signing of the Camp David Agreement

Q: What does article 19 say?

A: Article 19 declares the Balfour Declaration, the Mandate for Palestine, the 1947 UN partition plan, and the establishment of the State of Israel "illegal."

Q: What is written in article 21?

A: "The Palestinian Arab people, in expressing itself through the armed Palestinian revolution, rejects every solution that is a substitute for a complete liberation of Palestine, and rejects all plans that aim at the settlement of the Palestine issue or its internationalization."

Q: What are the main points of article 21?

A: (1) The article rejects any settlement based on compromise; Security Council resolution 242 of November 22, 1967.
(2) The article rejects the establishment of a Palestinian state in Judea and Samaria as a settlement based on compromise.
(3) The article states clearly that any solution cannot be political but military.

> *There are no moderates in the PLO . . . we never allow any party to interfere in our affairs, especially in two major matters, our non-recognition of Israel, and our refusal to amend our national covenant in any way. I hope I am making myself clear to everyone everywhere . . .*
>
> FAROUK KADDOUMI, PLO leader,
> *Monday Morning Magazine,*
> April 6-12, 1981

Q: What is written in article 9?

A: "Armed struggle is the only way to liberate Palestine, and is therefore a strategy and not tactics. The Palestinian Arab people affirms its absolute resolution and abiding determination to pursue the armed struggle and to march forward toward the armed popular revolution, to liberate its homeland and return to it, (to maintain) its right to a natural life in it, and to exercise its right of self-determination in it and sovereignty over it."

Q: What is written in article 18?

A: "The liberation of Palestine, from an international viewpoint, is a defensive act necessitated by the requirements of self-defense. For this reason, the people of Palestine, desiring to befriend all peoples, look to the support of the states which love freedom, justice, and peace in restoring the legal situation to Palestine, establishing security and peace in its territory, and enabling its people to exercise national sovereignty [*Wataniyya*] and national freedom [*Qawmiyya*]."

Q: What are the main points in article 18?

A: Since Israel's existence is illegal, therefore war against her is very legal. Moreover, since Israel's existence is illegal, the Jews' right of self-defense is illegal.

Q: What is written in article 21?

A: "Palestine with its boundaries that existed at the time of the British mandate is an integral regional unit."

Q: What is the main point of article 21?

A: The main point is that Palestine should not be divided into Arab and Jewish states.

> *Not a weapon forged against you will succeed. Every tongue that accuses you in judgment will be refuted. Such will be the lot of the lord, the vindication I award them. It is the Lord who speaks.*
>
> Isaiah 54:17

Q: What are the boundaries of the British mandate?

A: Article 4 is subject to two interpretations: (a) the Palestinian State includes also Jordan and thus supersedes it, and (b) the West Bank is detached from Jordan.

PALESTINIAN UNITY AND SACRIFICE: THE ROAD TO LIBERATION

Q: What is a Palestinian according to the covenant?

A: Article 7 of the covenant puts it thus: "The Palestinians are the Arab citizens who were living permanently in Palestine until 1947, whether they were expelled from there or remained. Whoever is born to a Palestinian Arab father after this date, within Palestine or outside it, is a Palestinian.

Q: How do the Palestinians intend to settle their own controversies and contradictions?

A: Article 8 of the covenant supplies the answer: "The contradictions among the Palestinian national forces are of a secondary order which must be suspended in the interest of the fundamental contradiction between Zionism and colonialism on the one side and the Palestinian Arab people on the other . . ." The PLO, therefore, deems it necessary to postpone internal disputes among its ranks in order to concentrate on warfare against Israel.

Q: Who will carry the bulk of the burden against Israel?

A: The answer is in article 10 which reads: "Fedayeen action forms the nucleus of the popular Palestinian war of liberation. This demands its promotion, extension and protection, and the mobilization of all the mass and scientific capacities of the Palestinians . . ." That the Palestinians would carry most of the burden is mentioned as well in articles 14 and 15 of the covenant.

Q: How can the Arabs achieve Arab unity?

A: Article 13 reads: "Arab unity and the liberation of Palestine are two complementary aims. Each one paves the way for realization of the other. Arab unity leads to the liberation of Palestine, and the liberation of Palestine leads to Arab unity. Working for both goes hand in hand."

"JEWS ARE NOT A NATION AND HAVE NO NATIONAL RIGHTS"

Q: How do the Palestinians relate to the partition plan?

A: The answer is given in article 19: "The partitioning of Palestine in 1947 and the establishments of Israel is fundamentally null and void . . . "

Q: How do the Palestinians view the Balfour Declaration and the mandate over Palestine?

A: Article 20 supplies the answer: "The Balfour Declaration, the mandate document, and what has been based upon them are considered null and void . . ."

Q: How does the convenant relate to the Jewish peoples' connection with Palestine?

A: The convenant clearly denies any rights. Article 20 states: ". . .The claim of a historical or spiritual tie between Jews and Palestine does not tally with historical realities nor with the constituents of statehood in their true sense. Judaism, in its character as a religion of revelation, is not a nationality with an independent existence. Likewise, the Jews are not one people with an independent personality, they are rather citizens of the states to which they belong."

> *Again I will build you, and you shall be built. O maiden of Israel . . . And you shall replant vineyards on the Samarian hills . . . For thus says the Lord: Sing out joyouslyand exult among the great nations . . . and give praise and say: God has rescued His people, the remnant of Israel.*
>
> Jeremiah 31: 4, 5, 7

Q: How does the convenant view Zionism – the Jewish national movement?

A: Article 22 reads: "Zionism is a political movement organically related to world imperialism and hostile to all movements of liberation and progress in the world. It is a racist and fanatical movement in its formation; aggressive, expansionist and colonialist in its aims; and fascist and Nazi in its means."

> *Zionism is the embodiment of the millennial longing of a people driven out of its country by the Roman conquest and dreaming of a return to Zion -- an authentic movement of national liberation.*
>
> ANDREI GROMYKO,
> United Nations, Minute No. 70,
> May 20, 1948

Q: How do the Palestinians view themselves?

A: Article 24 speaks for itself: "The Palestinian Arab people believe in the principles of justice, freedom, sovereignty, self-determination, human dignity and the right of peoples to exercise them."

Q: What is the position of the PLO towards the other Arab states?

A: According to Article 27: "The Palestine Liberation Organization will cooperate with all Arab states, each according to its capacities, and will maintain neutrality in their mutual relations in the light of, and on the basis of, the requirements of the battle of liberation, and will not interfere in the internal affairs of any Arab state."

Q: In turn, how does the PLO expect the Arab states to relate to it?

A: Article 28 reads: "The Palestinian Arab people insists upon the originality and independence of its national revolution and rejects every manner of interference, guardianship and subordination."

Q: How can the covenant be altered?

A: The final article of the covenant, number 33, reads: "This covenant cannot be amended except by a two-thirds majority of all the members of the National Council of the Palestine Liberation Organization in a special session called for this purpose."

Q: Has any member of the PLO ever criticized the radical content and spirit of the covenant?

A: To the best of my knowledge, no PLO member has done so to date.

Q: Should the covenant be taken seriously?

A: Yes. People with a long historical memory, such as the Jews, know why. In 1924, Adolf Hitler was in jail in Landsberg, Germany, dictating his book *Mein Kampf,* which called for the liquidation of the Jews. At that time this call was ignored. We know the results. If the PLO does not attach too much importance to its own covenant why then don't they denounce it?

We and the Iranian revolution are in the same boat. From the beginning we have maintained close contacts with the Iranian revolution, on the basis of the principle that Iran is a friend of the Palestinian revolution.

YASSIR ARAFAT,
Al-Shab, Algeria,
November 19, 1979

Cuba, the Cuban leadership, the Cuban people, the Commmunist Party and the government, especially dear comrade Fidel Castro, who supports us . . . they are on the side of all just causes, with the cause of the Palestinian people at the top of the list.

YASSIR ARAFAT,
Gramna, Cuba, August 23, 1981

The Palestine Liberation Organization is the closest to the heart of the Islamic Resistance Movement. It contains the father and the brother, the next of kin and the friend. The Moslem does not estrange himself from his father, brother, next of kin or friend. Our homeland is one, our situation isone, our fate is one and the enemy is a joint enemy to all of us.

Article 27, Covenant of the
Islamic Resistance Movement

"We shall fight together, as one Moslem nation, under one flag." (Yassir Arafat, in a speech in Teheran, *Voice of Fatah,* Beirut, February 19, 1979.)

"WE ARE ANTI-ISRAEL, NOT ANTI-JEWISH"

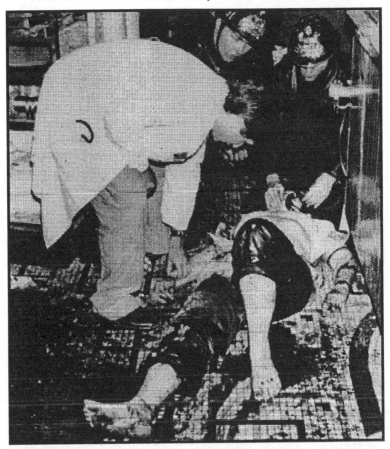

One of the victims of the shooting spree inside Goldenberg – Paris' best-known Jewish restaurant, on August 9, 1982. The attacking PLO terrorists killed 6 and wounded 22.

CHAPTER THREE

PLO CRIMES IN
LEBANON

The PLO began to establish itself in Lebanon in late 1968. From that time until June 1982, when the Israeli army entered Lebanon, it gradually set up a Palestinian state within a state, assuming sovereignty over a large part of its host country despite Lebanese protests.

The inherently weak Lebanese government could do nothing to limit PLO activities, and pressure from other Arab countries led to the Cairo Agreement of 1969. This granted the PLO territorial rights over the Palestinian refugee camps and a degree of freedom to conduct terrorist activities against Israel from within Lebanon. After the final expulsion from Jordan in 1970, the PLO transferred the center of its operations to Beirut. Armed terrorists began to take over the cities of Southern Lebanon, bringing the PLO into conflict with the Lebanese army, which tried to protect civilians from harassment. The PLO succeeded in defying the Lebanese government, and under the Melkart Agreement of 1973, further concessions to PLO demands for autonomy were made.

> *My best friend, a woman doctor, was dragged from her car three years ago while making a night trip to the hospital. She was brutally beaten and raped and hasn't been able to practice since. The PLO have practiced terror for terror's own sake. There is no military objective to be achieved by that kind of thing. It got to the point that a trip to the supermarket had to be planned like a sortie into enemy territory.*
> SUSIE ASSALAN, a Beirut widow,
> *Jerusalem Post*, August 20, 1982

A visit to Sidon's Granada cinema turned into a nightmare for a local doctor and his wife. During the show they were seized and taken outside by three PLO gunmen. The physician was thrown out into the street while his wife was dragged to the lavatory where the men took turns raping her. Because of the frequency of such incidents, most Lebanese women stopped going out after dark.

Ma'ariv,
July 26, 1982

The prison was built in 1973 and many families were locked up there. At night they would bring young girls to the office. In a special room used for the purpose, the girls could be heard screaming, "Allah, leave us alone; Allah, protect your women, please do not let our honor be defiled." After a while there was only silence.

HASSAN ABED AL-HAMID,
Israeli television, July 13, 1982

It is not yet a very little while, and Lebanon shall be turned into a fruitful field.

Isaiah 19:17

The PLO began to conduct itself like a separate government within Lebanon. Its territory stretched from south Beirut to Tyre and from the Mediterranean Sea in the west to the Syrian border in the east. It established its own army of 15,000 men, armed with sophisticated modern weapons; it set up its own legal system and PLO courts its own radio network and its own entry and exit system to the territory it controlled, without reference to Lebanese regulations.

In fact, the PLO altogether ignored Lebanese law and all directives from the Lebanese government. Worst of all, it turned Southern Lebanon into a training ground for international terrorism.

The wall of the church where the cross once hung is pock-marked by bullets. Below where the altar once stood lies a pile of greasy engine casings and spare parts. Oil stains spot the floor of the church, which evidently had been turned into a garage. In another part of town, the large St. Elias Church is in similar disarray. The Palestinians had apparently found a

> *new use for this church as well: the pews inside have long since been removed and a volleyball net stretches across the interior between two pillars.*
>
> International Herald Tribune,
> July 7, 1982
>
> ---
>
> *The PLO came [in 1976] and looted our houses, which were beautifully furnished, and took our money. They were the PLO and the other wretched ruffians they brought from the Arab countries. They cut men and women to pieces with hatchets. We fled to the palace of President Chamoun and from there we were taken by ship to Jounieh. We left Damur ablaze behind us. For years I was told, "You will be back." Now, thank God, we have returned home.*
>
> UM ATTALA,
> Israeli television, July 23, 1982

LEBANON'S MODERN HISTORY

Q: Why was it easy for the PLO to function in Lebanon?

A: The ethnic, cultural, and religious make-up of Lebanon is so varied as to defy the conventional definitions of nationhood. The lack of unity among the Lebanese enabled the PLO to establish a state within a state.

Q: What increased the division among the Lebanese?

A: Each ethno-cultural-religious group is not only subdivided among itself – Sunnis and Shiites among the Moslems; Maronites, Greek Orthodox, and Greek Catholic among the Christians – but these subdivisions tend to be further exacerbated by family and clan rivalries and controversies, which at times take on the appearance of political differences (for example, the "socialist" Druze led by the Jumblat clan as against the conservative Druze led by the Arselan clan).

Q: What adds to the antagonism?

A: Constant clashes, bickering, competition, and one-upmanship has been caused by regional antagonism (south against north, Mt. Lebanon against the coastal cities) compounded by the Palestinian influx in 1948 and then again in 1970, and the amazingly complex

32

residential patterns (Druze within Christian areas, Christians within Moslem areas, etc.).

Q: When did Lebanon gain its independence?

A: Lebanon gained its independence from the French in 1945.

Q: Did it succeed in becoming independent?

A: Yes. Between the years 1945 and 1975, successive Lebanese governments were able, more or less, to preserve the country's independence and territorial integrity. Lebanon joined the Arab league.

Q: What was Syria's reaction?

A: Syria is the only Arab country that has never established regular diplomatic relations with Beirut. Its claims to "Greater Syria" have limited its contact with the Lebanese to talks between leaders of the two countries or to military occupation.

Q: What characterized Lebanon until 1975?

A: The Lebanese channeled their energy, creativity, and enterprising spirit into business, trading, and banking. The country became a major clearing house for Arab oil money. Lebanon continued to survive as an island of free political discourse in the Arab world, while attempting to maintain the delicate, uneasy balance between its various communities.

Q: When was Lebanese tranquillity first shaken?

A: In 1958, Nasserist sentiment led to public support among some Lebanese Moslems for the incorporation of Lebanon into the United Arab Republic of Egypt and Syria. President Camille Chamoun felt incapable of toning down Moslem fervor. He then called in the United States Marine Corps, which eventually left Lebanon when a new president, Fouad Chihab, was elected. Stability seemed to be restored.

Mrs. Carol Ghamloush, 38, from Barnes, is married to a Lebanese gold merchant. She left London to live in Sidon, a city in which, she said, the only "government" was the Palestine Liberation Organizations. "They ruled the streets with their guns," she said. Trucks with recoilless rifles mounted on the back patrolled everywhere. Whenever they wanted money they held up a shop and robbed it. We always stayed in at night. It was far too dangerous to go out. All I can say is, thank goodness the Israelis invaded. They have destroyed parts of the city with their bombardment, but we welcome them.

Daily Telegraph,
June 17, 1982

On page 10 of a document that provided guidelines for PLO terrorist activities inside Israel was found that was called "Document 6: Guidelines for Attacking Civilian Targets in Israel, Section 6: Target Selection and Timing of the Operation." In contained the following five instructions:

1. The blow must be directed at the enemy's weak point. His greatest weakness is his small population. Therefore, operations must be launched which will liquidate immigration into Israel. This can be achieved by various means: attacking absorption centres for new immigrants; creating problems for them in their new homes by sabotaging their water and electricity supply; using weapons in terrifying ways against them where they live and using arson whenever possible.
2. Any installation which is designated as a target must meet the criterion of importance to the civilian population. Blows directed at secondary or isolated targets, whose impact passes unnoticed, are of no use.
3. Attacks can be made to multiply their impact. For instance, attacking a tourist installation during the height of the tourist season is much more useful than dealing the same blow at another time. If fuel tanks are set on fire during an energy crisis, this can be much more useful than at another time. Likewise, dealing a blow to the enemy immediately following his own attack constitutes an excellent reprisal which is beneficial to our morale.
4. Density of the population in the streets and market places of cities tends to increase on special occasions like holidays and vacations. One ought to bear this in mind in order to better select the place of action and improve the impact of the blow.
5. Attention should be given to the safety of our people. The type of action should take their safety into consideration.

PALESTINIAN INTERVENTION

> *To the world Yassir Arafat is the leader of the organization that is the sole legitimate representative of the Palestinian people. To the Palestinians of Saida, Yassir Arafat is the leader of a gang of thieves.*
>
> The Village Voice,
> New York, June 7, 1983

Until the 1967 Six-Day War, at least some of the 200,000 or so Palestinian refugees in Lebanon were well on their way to assimilating into the existing political system. The refugees' presence both within and outside their camps hardly posed a problem to the Lebanese authorities. After the mid-1960s, however, when the Fatah group began to take the lead in the PLO, the Palestinian refugee camps in Lebanon became the setting for paramilitary training, political propaganda, mass mobilization, social radicalization and arms stockpiling.

> *Life was terrible. They [the PLO] never used their brain (sic). They used their Kalachnikovs. Even in the car they used a machine gun to open the road for them.*
>
> KHALIL HAMDAN,
> *New York Times*, July 25, 1982
>
> ---
>
> *Every junior officer zipped in our city streets in a new Mercedes, armed with a machine gun, or in a Range Rover with the barrel of a gun sticking out.*
>
> DR. RASN HAMMUD,
> owner of the largest hospital in Sidon,
> *Ma'ariv*, July 16, 1982

Q: What did the Syrians do in this period?

A: The Syrians, who had grudgingly witnessed the Lebanese state grow and prosper outside their grip, now saw a golden opportunity to arm, train, finance, and dominate the PLO armed groups as possible surrogates in Lebanon.

Q: Why didn't the Lebanese government end the deterioration?

A: Despite their discontent at the sight of growing PLO power in Lebanon, the Lebanese felt impotent to arrest the process, much less undo it, for fear of Syrian intervention or renewed civil disturbances or both. PLO groups began to surface in Lebanon's major cities and

35

towns, to operate in the full light of day, and use their Lebanese base to launch worldwide acts of terror, such as plane hijackings, bombings, and killings.

Q: What characterized the situation in Lebanon in the 1970s?

A: By the 1970s, a PLO state within a state had emerged in Lebanon, with its own administrative and military services. The PLO systematically encroached upon Lebanese sovereignty and provoked Israel reprisal raids against its forces inside Lebanon. The Lebanese had no choice but to provide it with political and diplomatic shelter.

Q: What was the Lebanese government's dilemma?

A: Lebanon desperately sought to accommodate PLO wishes while preserving what remained of its sovereignty, but all attempts to limit Palestinian raids against Israel from Lebanese territory ended in failure.

Q: What was the Israeli reaction to the PLO attacks?

A: At times, Israel reacted violently against attacks on its civilian population centers, airlines, and embassies, as when it raided the Beirut airport in December 1968, or launched the April 1973 commando operation against PLO headquarters inside the Lebanese capital.

Q: What was the style of terror of the PLO in this period?

A: The PLO began to cultivate "revolutionary" myths and symbols drawn from a wide range of communist and anti-Western ideologies from Mao to Castro, Guevara, and Ho Chi Minh. "Guerilla warfare," "Arafat trail," and the "revolution growing from the barrel of the gun" became household words in the PLO.

Q: What is the character of the PLO terrorist activities?

A: Since 1967 the PLO have been engaged in a continuous ruthless worldwide terror campaign against Israeli, Jewish, and Western targets. Three major factors ought to be remembered:
(1) Almost all the PLO terror is directed against innocent helpless civilians and civilian targets. That alone disqualifies the PLO from being regarded as a guerilla national movement.
(2) Although the PLO has claimed that its struggle has been anti-Zionist, many PLO attacks have been aimed at Jewish targets outside Israel.
(3) The PLO conducts a policy of terror against moderate Arabs and Palestinians, effectively eliminating any moderate voice in the Arab world.

Q: Why is the year 1970 considered a crucial year for Lebanon?

A: After "Black September" in 1970, when the main base of PLO activity was eradicated in Jordan, Lebanon became the one country where the

Palestinian squads could secure a political, military, and logistic base. The Lebanese Army desperately attempted to prevent the PLO military takeover of southern Lebanon and even ventured, at the price of all-out military clashes, to disarm PLO militants traveling outside their camps.

> *At first they kidnapped Sister C. and raped her. Then they beat the rest of us. We hid in the cellars of the monastery for 18 months. Food was brought at night by the local Christians. For seven years the bells of our monastery did not ring.*
>
> *At* magazine, August 1982,
> about a Christian school north of
> Nabatiye taken by the PLO

Q: Who backed the PLO in 1970?

A: The Syrians openly backed the PLO, both politically and logistically, until the Beirut government resigned itself to a new "agreement" with the PLO.

> *For nearly seven years, until the Israel army attacked and captured it last week, the town was inaccessible to its own people; the Palestine Liberation Organization made it a strong-hold, using the churches as firing ranges and armories. A huge new church, left unfinished by the fleeing Maronite Christians in 1976, is covered with spray-painted Palestinian nationalist slogans and plastered with posters.*
>
> DAVID SHIPLER,
> *New York Times,*
> June 21, 1982

> *The PLO attacked our village like ants. They shot my elder son, my soul, on the doorstep . . . Then they killed the younger boy. I prayed to Santa Maria: "Give me courage!" They wanted to take the bodies away and burn them. I cried: "Don't touch the dead. It is forbidden!" Before leaving, they looted the house and also took the sheep with them.*
>
> ZAKIEH ABU-MARAI,
> in an Arabic program on
> Israeli television, July 23,1982

37

LEBANON: THE CIVIL WAR OF 1975

A long string of skirmishes, negotiations, and compromises followed one another during the years 1970-75. However, they could not stabilize the situation for any length of time. Any such "agreement" to yield authority and sovereignty to a foreign body was, by definition, detrimental to the central government.

The presence of the "PLO state" in Lebanon added to the existing tensions between Moslem and Christian sects, leading directly to the civil war that commenced in 1975 in which almost 100,000 people were killed and a quarter of a million injured. Syria, which had always regarded Lebanon as part of "Greater Syria," moved in during 1976, on the pretext of being a "peacekeeping" force. It proceeded to occupy large areas of the country. Any hopes that the Lebanese governnment might have had of regaining control of its own country were finally dashed and were not resuscitated until the Israeli operation "Peace for Galilee."

Q: When did civil war break out?

A: Open clashes erupted in Sidon in April 1975 between the PLO and the Christian forces, who could no longer bear the central government's impotence. They soon spread all over Lebanon.

Q: Who was fighting whom?

A: Although the fighting took place mainly between Lebanese Christians (now dubbed "rightists" or "conservatives" by the media) and a coalition of the PLO and the Moslems (who won the new epithets of "leftists" and "progressives"), it also exposed destructive quarrels between various factions within each major division.

Q: What happened to the Lebanese Army?

A: The Lebanese Army was dismantled, with its various communal components joining their respective coreligionists, or simply deserting.

On the first day of the war, the PLO broke into the village. They fired at the Israeli planes from the roofs, saying they would now pay us back by attracting Israeli fire to the village, and thus destroying it. The Israeli pilots are clever: they dropped one bomb, which hit the cannon right on the nose!

MUKHTAR SALAH SHAFRO,
Los Angeles Herald Examiner,
July 13, 1982

Q: What happened to the Lebanese government?

A: The Lebanese government could no longer function, despite the election in 1976, under Syrian guns, of a new president, Elias Sarkis, by the quickly convened parliament. The president and his cabinet barely controlled the vicinity of the presidential palace, while the rest of the country was carved up between the belligerent groups. Many attempts were made by various Arab conferences to settle the Lebanese crisis, but all they yielded were dozens of ceasefire agreements which were violated as soon as they were signed.

THE MURDER OF TOP POLITICAL LEADERS

+ March 1977: Kamal Jumblat, the Druze leader, was murdered.
+ June 1978: Tony Franjieh, son of the former president of Lebanon, was murdered in his home.
+ September 1978: Imam Musah Sadr, religious leader, disappeared in Libya.
+ September 1982: Bashir Gemayel, president-elect of Lebanon, was murdered.
+ June 1987: Rashid Karame, Prime Minister of Lebanon, was murdered.
+ November 1989: René Awwad, president-elect of Lebanon, was murdered.

While searching a citizen of the town, the PLO found on him Israeli money and a pair of shoes made in Israel. He was sentenced to death. The execution took place in the square in the following manner: His hands and legs were chained to the fenders of 4 vehicles. When a Fatah officer signalled with his pistol, the 4 cars raced away, tearing his body apart while the horrified spectators screamed.

Los Angeles Herald Examiner,
July 16, 1982

THE SYRIAN CONTROL OF
LEBANON IN 1976

> *But politics here was much more than patronage and debate.*
> *The major tool of persuasion was the gun, according to those*
> *who lived through it.*
>
> DAVID SHIPLER,
> *New York Times,*
> July 25, 1982

In 1976, the Arab League decided to intervene in order to end the killing and achieve some kind of compromise between the sides involved. The "all-Arab" troops brought to Beirut in June 1976 to supervise the ceasefire, in accordance with the resolutions of a conference in Cairo, soon proved inadequate for the task, while the internal Lebanese conflict, in which the PLO now took an increasingly crucial part, kept raging.

Once Syria decided to move in directly and to stop the pretense that it was merely implementing "all-Arab" resolutions, events in Lebanon took a new turn in the summer of 1976. While, in April 1975, Syria had made no secret of its support for Muslim PLO and other pro-Syrian elements in Lebanon, a year later it attempted to create a new order in Lebanon, which would perpetuate the communal divisions in Lebanese politics and would place the Lebanese state under a de facto Syrian protectorate. The Christians, who feared extermination at the hands of the PLO and other "leftists," reluctantly consented to the proposed arrangement, thus pulling the rug out from under the "natural allies" of the Syrians: the PLO and the left. The latter rejected the offer as no longer reflecting the new demographic balance in Lebanon and renewed the fighting. Syria, fearing that the PLO-leftist coalition would take over Lebanon and set it onto a separate course, sent in troops in May 1976 to take over the major cities and roads. The Christians joined in the fighting on the Syrian side and, in August 1976, conquered Tel al-Za'tar, the PLO stronghold in Beirut, thus signaling what they thought would be the beginning of the end of PLO domination in Lebanon.

Q: What was the result of the new round of fighting?
A: By late summer, Lebanon was divided into three de facto areas of control: the Syrians in the north and east controlled some 2/3 of the country; the Christians in the north now dominated East Beirut, the

northern part of Mt. Lebanon, and parts of the littoral around the port of Jounieh; and the PLO-Moslem coalition now ran West Beirut, the Tripoli area, and southern Lebanon.

> *. . . the PLO resisted, as it had previously aggressed, from the midst of civilian life, and of Lebanese as well as of Palestinians civilian life. With excruciating consistency, the PLO's commanders seemed to favour for the anti-aircraft batteries the courtyards of schools, for their tanks and artillery the environs of hospitals, apartment buildings, and – easiest for them and most devastating for their families – the labyrinthine alleys of the refugee camps, Rashidiye at Tyre and Ain-el-Hilwe at Sidon.*
>
> *The New Republic,*
> August 2, 1982

Q: What was the most important decision of the Summit of October 1976?

A: At the Cairo Conference of October 1976, it was agreed that the Syrians would henceforth make up the bulk of the "all-Arab" peace-keeping force in Lebanon. The Syrians also proceeded to disarm the various parties. In short, the summit made Syrian presence in Lebanon legal.

The Syrians supported or resented certain factions at different times in Lebanon according to their own interests at that time. In 1976 they supported the Christians against the Moslems and the PLO. In July 1978 they launched massive attacks on the Christian strongholds in both East Beirut and Mt. Lebanon, slaughtering thousands of Christians. Another attack was in April 1981 when their attack was against East Beirut and the city of Zahleh in the Lebanese Valley (the Beka'a). The Christians were on the verge of losing their strongholds. Israel intervened on their behalf and shot down two Syrian helicopters. The Syrians introduced their SAM ground-to-air missiles into Lebanon in an attempt to limit Israel's freedom of action in the air.

This camp did not have to be destroyed. It could have remained intact. In leaflets dropped by Israeli planes, we were requested to leave the camp, but the PLO would let nobody out. My neighbor, Saleh, tried to escape. They shot him in the back and tied him to a pillar in the square until he bled to death. Three hundred people were killed in our camp. Who is to blame for their death? Write down – only the PLO.

ABBAS AL-HAJ,
resident of a refugee camp in Lebanon,
Ha'aretz, August 20, 1982

It was when they broke into the operating theater and forced us to stop surgery and treat their wounded instead – and badly beat one of our doctors who refused to obey them – that I realized they were beasts from the jungle.

DR. GHASSEN HAMOUD,
owner-director of Sidon's largest hospital,
Ma'ariv, July 16, 1982

Ali Bader al-Din, the Imam of Arouf, refused to inject Palestinian nationalist themes into his sermons at the village mosque. He resisted until the 19th day of the Moslem fast month of Ramadan, when he disappeared. A few days later his body was found by a shepherd under a bridge. In an attempt to forestall a possible protest, the PLO ordered his funeral to be held at night, even though this is contrary to Islamic practice.

New York Times,
July 25, 1982

"OPERATION LITANI," 1978

> *To say that Arafat did not personally run Black September, even if it is postulated that he did not approve of their more horrific deeds, and to argue from this that he is moderate, is pure sophistry. If Arafat had disapproved of Black September, it was open to him to have Khalaf, Salameh and Najjar expelled from the organizations under his direct control, or at least to denounce their deeds. He did neither.*
>
> BRIAN BROZIER,
> *Now,* April 3, 1981

In the meantime, PLO activities against Israel from southern Lebanon continues to escalate, reaching a climax on March 11, 1978 when two Israel civilian buses were intercepted by Palestinian terrorists and 35 passengers were killed and another 80 wounded. Responsibility was claimed by Yassir Arafat's Fatah organization.

Q: What was Israel's reaction?
A: The Israeli army marched across the border on March 15, 1978 in order to mop up the PLO bases in Southern Lebanon, in what became known as "Operation Litani." The goal was to destroy the PLO's logistic and support network up to the Litani River and to prevent its future regrouping in that area.
Q: Under what conditions did Israel withdraw its forces?
A: Israel withdrew her forces under United Nations and American assurances that the UN Interim Force in Lebanon (UNIFIL) would frustrate any PLO attempt to retake its bases and launch further attacks against Israeli population centers.
Q: Did the UN forces keep their promises?
A: No. It quickly became evident that neither UNIFIL nor other international "guarantees" would prevent renewed PLO deployment in many parts of southern Lebanon.
Q: What was Israel's reaction now to PLO attacks?
A: In 1979, Israel adopted a policy of hitting the PLO directly within southern Lebanon and strengthening local Lebanese opposition to the terrorists. The three enclaves now acquired territorial contiguity in a 5- to 8-by-50-mile belt with a mixed population of Christians and Shi'ites,

Q: What is the concept of "Free Lebanon?
A: In April 1979, Haddad declared his territory to be "Free Lebanon."
   He professed to have no separation aspirations. His declaration was
   meant to be a protest against Syrian and PLO occupation of the rest
   of Lebanon and a statement that genuine Lebanese sovereignty, free
   of any foreign yoke, existed only in the territory held by his militias.

The PLO continued to use southern Lebanon as a launching pad against
Israel. It also consolidated its hold on large areas of Beirut and other
coastal cities, which became logistic centers, equipment and ammunition
depots, training bases for infantry and naval forces, supply ports and
launching grounds for terrorist missions against Israel or Israeli or Jewish
interests abroad.

---

*I want to say that the only way for peace is to erase completely
the cancerous presence of Zionism.*

PLO leader GEORGE HABASH,
Reuters, Beirut,
March 28, 1980

Q: What was the PLO's power in southern Lebanon?
A: In the south alone, some 6,000 PLO people were encamped in dozens
   of different locations, 700 of them within UNIFIL-controlled territory. They openly operated jeeps, mortars, and artillery including
   130mm Russian-made guns; 155mm French-made guns, 122mm,
   130mm, and 240mm Katyusha rockets made in the Soviet Union; and
   107mm Katyushas made in North Korea.

For the first time, at the beginning of 1980, the PLO introduced large
quantities of T-34 tanks – 500 in all – to reinforce its forces and to
challenge both the area under Haddad and Israeli towns and villages in the
Galilee. Following a particularly intensive exchange of fire between the
PLO and Israel, in July 1981, when the PLO military array seemed to be
on the verge of collapse, a ceasefire was arranged under the United States'
auspices.

Q: What happened between July 1981 and June 1982?
A: From July 1981 to June 1982, the PLO, under cover of the ceasefire,

pursued its acts of terror against Israel, resulting in 26 deaths and 264 injured.

Q: What was Israel's reaction?

A: When Israeli warnings went unheeded, air raids were mounted against the PLO on April 2, May 9, and on June 4 and 5, 1982. The PLO responded with a full range of artillery, tank, and mortar fire on the Israeli population of the Galilee, forcing Israel to launch Operation Peace for Galilee on June 6, 1982.

> *Several residents told the same story, although one middle-aged middle-class woman, the owner of some orange orchards, expressed her plight most dramatically: "When the Israelis came . . . the Palestinian fighters took their guns and placed them next to our homes, next to apartment blocks and hospitals and schools. They thought this would protect them. We pleaded with them to take their guns away but they refused. So when they fired at the Israelis, the planes came and bombed our homes." The woman was telling the truth. At their own Ein Hilwer camp, the Palestinians actually put their guns on the roof of the hospital.*
>
> *The Times,* London,
> June 19, 1982

Mahmet Ali Agca, who shot Pope John Paul II on May 13, 1981, is a graduate of a PLO training course in Lebanon, CBS-TV reported in September 1982. Following PLO training, Agca was held for the murder of a newspaper editor in Turkey, but escaped.

He was helped both by communist Bulgaria's secret police and the fascist Grey Wolves of Turkey, before attacking the pope with a pistol provided by a notorious neo-Nazi, Horst Grimayer.

> *We could see buildings damaged that had undamaged buildings on either side. Obviously it was a very selective use of fire-power.*
>
> U.S. Major General HUGH HOFFMAN,
> *Washington Post*, August 11, 1982,
> reporting on Israel acting "extremely
> cautious" in southern Lebanon

THE PLO'S FULL CONTROL OF SOUTHERN LEBANON

> *The Palestinians increased the influx of arms into Lebanon
> . . . They transformed most of the refugee camps, if not all, into
> military bastions . . . common law criminals fleeing from Leba-
> nese justice found shelter and protection in the camps . . .*
> Ambassador EMIL GHORA,
> Lebanese Permanent Representative
> to the United Nations,
> October 14, 1976

After Syria's takeover of Lebanon in 1976, and more so following its alignment with the PLO in 1977, the terrorist organization was able to reinforce its bases in southern Lebanon without incurring the risk of intervention on the part of the practically non-existent Lebanese Army.

Q: What was the condition in the south?

A: The south was not only beyond the reach of both the the Lebanese and the Syrians, but it was also heavily populated by Palestinians on the outskirts of Tyre and Sidon. Moreover, it was conveniently located along the southern border so as to facilitate PLO operations and acts of terror against Israel.

Q: What was the purpose of the "Good Fence"?

A: Thousands of Lebanese villagers began to receive treatment in Israel's clinics at the Good Fence and to seek work in and do business with Israel, now that their ties with Beirut and other war-torn cities were all but severed.

Q: What kind of relationship developed between Israel and the Lebanese Christians?

A: As a de facto state of peace grew between Israel and its Lebanese neighbors in the Haddad enclave, the Christian and Shi'ite militias asked for and obtained military assistance from Israel to defend themselves against continued PLO harassment.

A few months prior to PLO chairman Arafat's enthusiastic reception at the United Nations in November 1974, the Palestine National Council declared on June 8, 1974 that (1) the PLO would struggle against any plan . . . whose price is recognition, conciliation, secure borders . . . and that (2) the Palestinian national authority will struggle for the unity of the confrontation states for the sake of completing the liberation of all Palestinian soil . . .

THE PLO, CENTER OF INTERNATIONAL TERROR: AID AND ENCOURAGEMENT

Over the years, the PLO has developed an extensive network of active relations with the violent groups which have been terrorizing much of the world. Most prominently, these include the Japanese Red Army, Baader-Meinhof in Germany and the IRA in Ireland. These and other movements rely on the PLO for weapons and training. In exchange, they give cover to PLO terrorists in Europe and Africa, sometimes even supplying manpower for terrorist operations.

The target: a group of children on a street in 1980. Jewish children about to go on holiday were attacked by the PFLP as they boarded a bus in Antwerp. One child was killed, nine children and seven adults were injured.

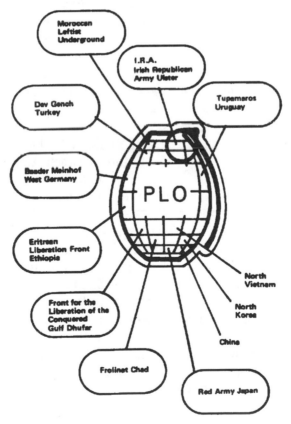

THE PLO AND INTERNATIONAL TERROR

◆ December 12, 1969: U.S. Army installations and the El Al office in West Berlin were bombed.

◆ December 21, 1975: The OPEC convention in Vienna is held for ransom by the PFLP, Carlos, and the Japanese Red Army.

◆ January 25, 1976: Baader-Meinhof gang members Brigitte Schulz and Thomas Reuter are arrested during an unsuccessful attempt to hit an El Al plane at Nairobi Airport with Soviet-made Strella ground-to-air missiles; with PLO associate Wadia Haddad.

◆ January 5, 1982: Brigitte Bergendham of Baader-Meinhof and Nasser al-Tamimi of the Popular Front for the Liberation of Palestine (PFLP) were arrested in the Rome Airport carrying fake passports and explosives meant for the Israel Embassy in Bonn.

◆ Verona, March 1982: At the trial of Red Brigades kidnappers of U.S. Brig. General James Dozier, it was established that the arms used had been smuggled from Fatah via diplomatic pouch.

> *Terrorism is not the accidental killing of civilians that accompanies every war. It is not guerilla warfare in which irregular forces focus on military targets. Terrorism is the deliberate and systematic attack on civilians . . . The terrorists target the innocent precisely because they are innocent, In assaulting them, he tells us that for him no atrocity is out of bounds, that he is prepared to pursue any means to achieve his goal, which is to frighten us into submission.*
>
> BENJAMIN NETANYAHU,
> former Israeli Ambassador
> to the United Nations,
> expressing his opinion about world terror

There is evidence of links between the PLO and the world's major terrorist organizations, which collaborate in training, the exchange of weapons, organizational aid, and the granting of asylum. Backed by totalitarian regimes, terrorist organizations throughout the world direct their violence against the free countries of the West.

The PLO is the main center of international terror and the reason for this is simple. The PLO has a unique position in the international terrorist community. It is the world's major terrorist organization. It is the only one which operates openly, and it has offices in more than 70 countries. It does not hide its destructive intentions, and its members do not hide.

It runs or has run camps in Libya, Algeria, Iraq, Syria, South Yemen, and other countries, where people from all over come to train and to which they can return after they have attacked their target. Arab countries supply the PLO with arms and refuge, and its leader, Arafat, is applauded by the United Nations when he appears before the General Assembly with a gun at his side.

The PLO has the best of both worlds; while it threatens, blackmails, attacks and kills civilians throughout the world, it is granted legitimacy by the various countries in the world.

Q: What does the PLO offer its fellow terrorists?
A: (1) The PLO is a very rich organization as a result of massive Arab aid. It can thus purchase public opinion through its sophisticated propaganda machine, which buys respectability not only for itself but for terrorism in general.

(2) Until June 1982, PLO camps in Lebanon provided training for terrorists from many organizations, including the Japanese Red Army, the Baader-Meinhof gang and the Turkish People's Liberation Front. One sixth of the terrorists captured by Israel in Lebanon were not Palestinians.

(3) Logistics and financial aid from Arab states mean that the PLO can operate an intelligence network, buy arms, forge papers, and help with escape and asylum. Diplomatic passports provided by some Arab countries give the PLO immunity and allow easy movement for its members from one country to another.

(4) The PLO is not troubled by the ideological affiliation of those who seek its support, and co-operates with Marxists-Leninists as easily as with Fascists. It rationalizes links with the leftist Red Army and Baader-Meinhof gang because they purport to be against imperialism and reaction. It also has no problem in providing training and financial support for neo-Nazis, such as the Karl-Heinz Sports Gruppe in West Germany.

The hand of the PLO is evident in the growing number of joint operations undertaken by the terrorist community. Between January 1968 and October 1980 literally thousands of terrorist incidents have been recorded throughout the world, according to the United States State Department. Of these, over 38 percent took place in Western Europe. There were virtually no attacks in Libya, Algeria, Iraq, Syria, the Soviet Union, or the Eastern Bloc. These are countries that support the PLO.

Two tour buses carrying families returning from vacation were hijacked by PLO terrorists on the Haifa-Tel Aviv highway on March 11, 1978. 35 passengers were killed and 80 wounded. Responsibility was claimed by Yassir Arafat's Fatah organization.

Fear God and fear people who are not afraid of God.
Arab saying

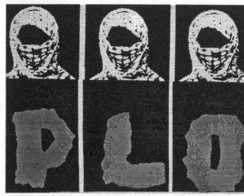

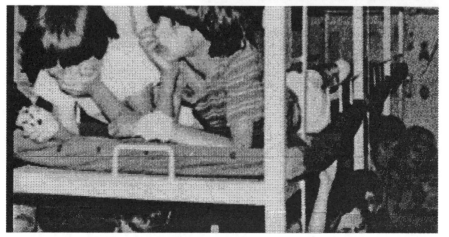

A generation of children in northern Israel has had to spend nights sleeping in bomb shelters to escape repeated Katyusha rocket and artillery barrages from PLO guns.

PLO INTERNATIONAL TERROR: Kozo Okamoto, one of the Japanese Red Army terrorists responsible for the massacre at Ben-Gurion Airport on May 30, 1972, is brought to trial. Most of the 26 passengers killed were pilgrims from Puerto Rico. There were 76 wounded. *(Israel Sun)*

Q: Who financed the PLO to establish an empire of terror in the world?

A: The answer is found in the book *Inside the PLO,* by N. Livingstone and D. Halevy. Arafat and the PLO are credited with amassing a financial empire built partly on contributions from oil-rich Arab countries and what the writers contend were payments from oil companies and airlines to protect themselves from attack by the PLO.

A document, below, dated July 18, 1981, and written on the stationery of the PLO's Supreme Military Council, was found in PLO headquarters in Sidon. It was entitled "Document 3: PLO Plan to Destroy Israeli Towns," and read: "To: El-Haj Ismail, Greetings for the Revolution! The Supreme Military Council has decided to concentrate on the destruction of Kiryat Shemona, Metulla, Dan, She'ar Yashuv, and Nahariya and its vicinity. Kirat Shemona will be distributed among all the platoons and will be shelled with improved "Grad" shells. Metulla will be shelled with 160mm mortars (Palestinian Liberation Front – As-Sa'iqa). Nahariya and its vicinity will be shelled with 130mm guns – Artillery Battalion 1."

WHO IS FIGHTING WHOM IN LEBANON?

> *There are six things which the Lord hates . . . a proud look, lying tongue and hands that shed innocent blood, a heart that devised wicked thoughts, feet that are swift in running in mischief, a false witness that breathes us lies and one that sows discord among brethren.*
>
> Proverbs 6:15-19

The civil war in Lebanon broke out in April 1975. Since that time, hundreds of thousands of Lebanese have died, have been wounded, or forced to flee their homes. Lebanon, the Switzerland of the Middle East, has become a land of misery, death, torture, and hatred.

Two external main forces have caused this condition: the PLO on the one hand, the Syrians on the other. Both forces have created in Lebanon a kind of state within a state, brutally crushing the sovereignty and independence of Lebanon.

Who are the warring groups? There are two groups of forces: one in support of Syria, the other against it.

ANTI-SYRIAN FORCES

1. *The forces of General Michel Aoun, the Christian Prime Minister of Lebanon.* Aoun's own forces are mainly comprised of Maronite Christians from the Lebanese army and number about 20,000 soldiers. They are the main forces that defend eastern Beirut – the location of the Christian districts. The forces of Michel Aoun were defeated by Syria in the first week of September 1990.
2. *The Falangia forces.* The Christian Lebanese forces are known as the Falangiamilitias and their commander is Samir Ja'-ja'. These forces were, in the past, equipped by Israel. They cooperated with Israel before, during, and after operation "Peace for Galilee" in 1982.
3. *The South Lebanon Army.* This army is supported, trained and equipped by Israel. Its units are mainly Christian yet include Shi'ite Moslem soldiers. It numbers about 2,500. The main task of this army is to guard the 50-mile border with northern Israel. The depth of this area is approximately 6 miles and it is commonly referred to as the security zone. In the past, the fence that separated Israel and Lebanon was known as the "Good Fence." The commander of this force is Colonel Antoine Lahad. His predecessor was Saad Haddad.

THE PRO-SYRIAN FORCES

1. *The Syrian Army.* The Syrian troops number approximately 40,000 in Lebanon. The Syrians entered Lebanon in 1976 and today control an estimated 70 percent of Lebanese territory. In 1976, the Syrians helped the Christians against the Moslems. In the years that followed, they supported the Moslems, the PLO, and the leftist elements in their fight against the Christians.

2. *The Druze forces.* The Druze forces are under the leadership of Walid Jumblat leader of the Progressive Socialist party. The Druze forces number around 4,000 and are mainly equipped by Syria. The Druze are located in the Shuf mountains southeast of Beirut.

3. *The Amal forces.* The Amal forces are under the leadership of Nabih Berri and are mainly located in southern Lebanon. Their forces number between 6,000 and 7,000.

4. *The Palestinians.* The Palestinians that support Syria in Lebanon are the forces of Ahmed Jibril leader of the Popular Front for the Liberation of Palestine General Command and the forces of Abu Musa. Abu Musa heads the PLO forces that rejected Arafat's leadership after the PLO defeat in Lebanon in 1982.

5. *The Moslem section of the Lebanese Army.* These forces number around 20,000 and are Druze, Shi'ite, and Moslem soldiers. The commander of these forces is Major General Sami Alkhatib.

6. *The Hizballah forces.* These forces are pro-Iranian Shi'ite Moslems and are located in southern Beirut and the Ba'albek area of eastern Lebanon. Their number is estimated at 3,500 and they are supported and trained by Iran.

The Syrians are killing thousands in Lebanon and no one really cares; the world pays virtually no attention. No protest demonstrations, no denunciatory resolutions, none. The Syrians hold down 70 percent of the country and are free to murder as many Lebanese as their shells can reach. Nobody seems to mind very much.

a Western journalist

Travelers: The charred wreckage of one of the two excursion buses hijacked by a Fatah gang on the Haifa-Tel Aviv coastal road on March 11, 1978, in which 35 passengers were killed and 82 wounded. *(Israel Sun)*

Passers-by: Victims of a bombing in Jerusalem's Zion Square on July 4, 1975. The massive bomb hidden by Fatah in an old refrigerator killed 15 civilians and wounded 62. (Government Press Office)

CHAPTER FOUR

PLO DOUBLE TALK – SINCE 1988

To lie during a war is permitted in order to encourage the Moslems.

IBN ALARABI, devout Moslem

To lie is a sin unless used to serve the interests of a Moslem or to save him from a disaster.

ATTABARANI, Arab historian

The PLO has established a priori the use of the armed struggle in the liberation of Palestine. It cannot be abandoned even if there is a political settlement . . .

FAROUK KADDOUMI,
head of the PLO Political Department,
Al-Ittihad, December 13, 1988

The PLO has deliberately built a dual image. By saying different things to different people, the organization has gained a reputation for being both radical and moderate, according to the interpretation of its audience.

To its fellow Arabs, the PLO leadership has always made extremist and uncompromising statements about its desire for the destruction of Israel. From its establishment to the present day, it has continually repeated its aims, which have been borne out by its actions.

To the West, the PLO makes "moderate" statements, which are accepted at face value and are featured prominently in the media. The PLO's refusal to amend its charter calling for Israel's destruction, and its constant denial to the Arab world of any moderation, are given very slight attention by an anxious West, determined to see a change of attitude which does not exist.

From the Arabs, the PLO wants not only recognition as the sole legitimate representative of the Palestinian people, but as the leading protagonist in the struggle against Israel. To maintain its image, it must be seen to be continually harassing Israel.

From the West, and from the United States in particular, it wants more recognition. It needs, too, to be regarded as an essential partner in any peace negotiation. It also hopes to persuade American and European governments to put pressure on Israel to accept a Palestinian state, ostensibly in the West Bank and Gaza, but finally – if the PLO has its way – extending over the whole of Israel.

It has, therefore, become important for the PLO to change its image from that of terrorists to one of an organization willing to accept a political solution to the Palestinian problem.

The obvious and big difference between its stated aims and its desired image had to be overcome. In order to obscure the fact that its Charter remains unchanged, the PLO has resorted to deception, evasion, and subterfuge. All the means are justified.

Gannett Westchester Newspapers/Tuesday, April 4, 1989

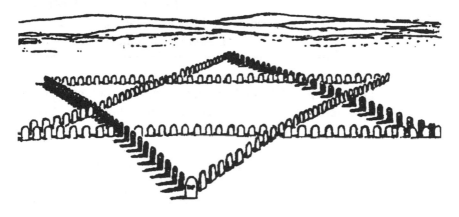

MIDDLE EAST PEACE PLAN ACCORDING TO THE P.L.O. CHARTER...

> *The establishment of a Palestinian state in any part of Palestine has as its goal the establishment of a Palestinian state in all of Palestine.*
>
> SALEH KALEF, Arafat deputy,
> *Al-Siyassa*, Kuwait,
> December 12, 1988

On December 14, 1988, Arafat supposedly met the requirements of the United States in order to begin a dialogue. He said that the PLO now accepts Security Council Resolution 242; it renounces terrorism and will follow the road to peace. Moreover, at a later date during a visit to Paris, he said that the Palestinian Covenant is null and void.

The facts, however, prove that Arafat is not serious in his promises and declarations. He did not accept Resolution 242. He did not end terror, and he could not cancel the PLO Covenant. According to the Covenant, paragraph 33, it can be amended only by a two-thirds majority vote of the total membership of the National Congress of the PLO at a specially convened session.

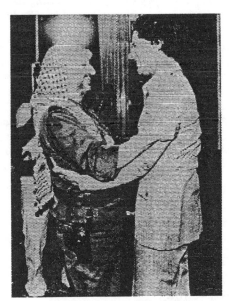

Partners: Arafat and Qaddafy

HAS ARAFAT CHANGED?

> *Four shall not enter paradise: the scoffer, the liar, the hypocrite and the slanderer.*
>
> The Talmud
>
> ---
>
> *If you tell the truth you don't have to remember anything.*
> MARK TWAIN
>
> ---
>
> *The partition of Palestine in 1947 and the establishment of the State of Israel are entirely illegal, regardless of the passage of time.*
>
> PLO Covenant, Article 19

Arafat speaks . . .

To the world:	*To his people:*
Come and bury the hatchet. (*Paris press conference, May 3, 1989*)	*Nothing and nobody can deter the PLO from attacking its main enemy, Israel.* (*Quoted by AP, June 8, 1989*)
We are bent on peace, come what may, come what may. (*Geneva press conference, December 14, 1988*)	*The PLO offers . . . the peace of Saladin [a heroic arab leader who kicked the crusaders out of the Middle East].* (*Saudi Press Agency, January 2, 1989*)
We totally and absolutely renounce all forms of terrorism. (*Geneva press conference, December 14, 1988*)	*I did not mean renounce . . . I am still committed to what I said in Cairo in 1985 [when he retained the right to attack Israel and the occupied territories].* (*Vienna television interview, December 19, 1988*)
As for the Covenant [which called the State of Israel illegal], I believe there is an expression in French, "C'est caduque" (null and void). (*Paris statement, May 2, 1989*)	*I haven't the authority to effect changes in the Covenant by myself.* (*Le Figaro, April 29, 1989*)
These [Palestine National Council] resolutions constitute a firm, unambiguous response to all arguments. (*Address to UN in Geneva, December 13, 1988*)	*I can always come back to our PNC and declare that moderation does not pay.* (*During Algiers summit, November 15, 1988*)

[The Palestinians'] human dignity shall be safeguarded under a democratic parliamentary system of government built on freedom of opinion. (Address to UN General Assembly, December 13, 1988)

Whoever thinks of stopping the Intifada [uprising] before it achieves its goals, I will give him ten bullets in the chest. (Speaking in Riyadh, Saudi Arabia, January 1, 1989)

The military struggle will not stop as a result of the Algeria declaration. We will start with a little Palestinian state as a first stage and, God willing, it would grow and get wider, to east, west, north and south. Three months ago I supported the idea to liberate Palestine at once. I was stupid. Now I am interested to liberate Palestine by stages. This is the art of liberation.

ABU IYAD, Arafat deputy,
Al-Anba, Kuwait,
December 18, 1988

ARAFAT: WHAT DOES HE SAY?
WHAT DOES HE BELIEVE?

The Palestinian uprising will in no way end until the attainment of the legitimate rights of the Palestinian people, including the right of return.

YASSIR ARAFAT,
Qatar News Agency, January 13, 1989

Q: What does Arafat say?

A: "Our desire for peace is a strategy and not an interim tactic . . ." (Geneva press conference, December 14, 1988).

Q: What does Arafat believe?

A: "An escalated struggle, an intensification of the uprising, continued martyrdom, and an expansion of the confrontation will bring us our final victory" ("Voice of Palestine" radio, Baghdad, December 15, 1988). "I didn't change my policy and didn't surrender to the American demands and conditions. The U.S. has changed its policy" (*Al-Qabas*, Kuwait, December 23, 1988).

Q: What does he say?

A: "We totally and absolutely renounce all forms of terrorism" (Geneva press conference, December 14, 1988).

Q: What does he believe?

A: "I did not mean to renounce . . . Actually, I only repeated what our Palestine National Council had accepted . . . I am still now committed to what I said in Cairo in 1985" (Viennese television interview, December 19, 1988).

Q: What does he say?

A: "I also made reference to our acceptance of Resolutions 242 and 338 as the basis for the negotiations with Israel within the framework of the international conference" (Geneva press conference, December 14, 1988).

Q: What does he believe?

A: "The acceptance of resolution 242 by the PNC is conditional upon these three principles – a Palestinian state, self-determination, and the right of return" (speaking in Abu Dhabi, Middle East News Agency, January 5, 1989).

Q: What does he believe?

A: In a press conference on Jordanian television on August 20, 1989, Arafat justified the killings of Arab collaborators. "Any Palestinian leader who suggests ending the *Intifada* exposes himself to the bullets of his own people and endangers his own life. The PLO will know how to deal with him" (*Al-Anba*, Kuwaiti daily, January 3, 1989).

"I know of cases," the doctor said, *"of people being thrown into acid tanks by PLO terrorists and reduced to unrecognizable masses of porous bone. Numerous young girls came to me for abortions after being raped by PLO mobsters, I think you call them in the states . . ."*

FRANK GERVASI,
Los Angeles Herald Examiner,
July 13, 1982

Q: What does he say and believe?

A: "Look at the Israeli flag: the two blue stripes bordering the 'Star of David' are meant to symbolize the Nile (in Egypt) and the Euphrates (in Iraq). This illustrates the 'Empire of Israel' " (*Le Figaro*, April 29, 1989).

Q: What is the reality?

A: The following account of the symbolism of the Israeli flag was given by the flag's designer, David Wolfsohn, after it first appeared at the Zionist Congress in Basel in 1897: ". . . Then an idea struck me. We have a flag – and it is blue and white. The 'tallit' [prayer shawl] with which we wrap ourselves when we pray: that is our symbol. Let us take this 'tallit' from its bag and unroll it before the eyes of Israel and the eyes of the nations. So I ordered a blue and white flag with the Shield of David painted on it. That is how our national flag came into being. And no one expressed any surprise or asked whence it came or how."

Q: What does Arafat say and believe?

A: "For more than 15 years, a sign has been hanging over the entrance to the Israeli parliament which reads 'The Land of Israel extends from the Nile to the Euphrates' " (*Le Figaro*, April 29, 1989).

Q: What is the reality?

A: It is a fact that the Israeli Knesset is open to the public, and the entrance is in full view of the visitors, No such sign exists nor has it ever existed.

> *I treated people with arms severed by PLO shelling and men whose testicles had been cut off in torture sessions. The victims, more often than not, were not Christians but Moslems.*
> KHALIL TORBEY,
> prominent Lebanese surgeon,
> *Los Angeles Herald Examiner*, July 13,1982

Q: What does he say?

A: In an April 29, 1989, interview in *Le Figaro*, Arafat was asked: "And the hijackings, which stained the 70s with blood – do you not feel that these were mistakes?" He answered: "I was against this from the very beginning, and there are documents to prove it."

Q: What is the reality?

A: Arafat became chairman of the PLO and commander of its armed units in early July 1968. Very soon thereafter, on July 23, 1968, a PLO terror group carried out the organization's first hijacking – against an El Al plane which was forced to land in Algeria. Numerous PLO hijackings have since taken place. As late as April 1, 1986, a unit of the Hawari Apparatus detonated a bomb aboard a TWA plane, killing four persons, including a mother and her infant daughter who were sucked out of the aircraft. The Hawari Apparatus has been identified by the U.S. Defense Department (*Terrorist Group Profiles*, U.S. Government Printing Office, 1988) as a Fatah unit under Arafat's command.

Q: Were Arafat and the PLO ever directly involved in terror against Americans?

A: Yes. One example is when members of Black September, a covert unit of the PLO, executed two American diplomats in Khartoum, Sudan, in March 1973. Then-American Secretary of State Henry Kissinger responded by dispatching Lieut. Gen. Vernon Walters on a still-secret meeting with two top PLO figures in Rabat, Morocco, calling for an end to such acts. At that time, the United States had sufficient evidence of Arafat's and the PLO's direct involvement in the slayings. However, the Nixon administration was preoccupied with the growing Watergate scandal and wanted to prevent another crisis. Therefore, there was no American response.

[The PLO is] . . . opposed to a Zionist state . . . Zionism is a racist movement [and] we don't want a racist state in this area.
ARAFAT, speaking one week before the
November PNC meeting in Algiers,
Los Angeles Times,
December 19, 1988

Hypocrisy is like a woman who is in the apartment of her lover and swears by the life of her husband.
The Talmud

If a lie is the only way to achieve good results, it is allowed.
AL-GHAZZALI, famous Arab theologian

WHAT DO THE PLO LEADERS SAY?

On December 14, 1988, Yassir Arafat, at a press conference in Geneva supposedly met the requirements of the United States to begin a dialogue. At the same time, his closest associates, while speaking to the Arab press, expressed their views on Middle East peace.

Q: Do the new moderate policies of the PLO truly mean the abandonment of violence as a tactic for achieving its goals?

A: "Neither military attacks nor the heroic *Intifada* will cease. We will continue our struggle until the Palestinian flag waves over Jerusalem " (Abu Iyad [Saleh Khalef], Arafat deputy, Qatar News Agency, December 17, 1988).

Q: The PLO's goal, according to its National Covenant, is the total elimination of Israel. Has this been amended, revoked, or changed in any manner?

A: "We in the PLO draw a clear distinction between the charter and political programs, since the charter contains the permanent strategic policy, while the political programs contain the phased policy" (Ahmed Sadki al-Dejani, high-ranking PNC deputy, *Ukaz*, November 22, 1988).

> *I want to release a part of this Arab territory and this cannot be released by war . . . Afterwards we would liberate all the rest.*
> NABIL SHA'AT, Arafat's chief advisor,
> *Al-Anba*, Kuwait, March 28, 1989

Q: Is the PLO willing to accept the establishment of a Palestinian state in Judea and Samaria and the Gaza Strip alone, leaving Israel to live in peace within the pre-1967 borders?

A: "If we succeed in gaining a part of Palestine upon which we will establish a state, we will later be able to demand from the entire world, while positioned upon Palestinian soil, to act to enable us to get our rights as a state and a nation...We must take, and continue to ask for more, yet, without offering concessions" (Abd el-Hamid Sayekh, chairman of the PNC, *Al-Siyassa*, December 21, 1988).

Q: Doesn't the PLO's recognition of Israel, along with the desire to establish an independent Palestinian state, imply that the PLO is willing to live in peace and security with Israel?

A: "The territory exists, Israel exists, and I am opposed to it, but I cannot deny its existence. The Arabs and the world stand by our side in the restoration of the '67 lands. Let us restore these lands and afterwards we will fight for a restoration of the rest. We will continue in this process . . ." (Samir Ghosha, leader of the Popular Struggle Front, *Al-Qabas*, December 15, 1988).

> *The proclamation of the Palestinian state is the first step toward obliterating the new Zionist-fascist state.*
> ABADALLAH AL-KHOURAN,
> PLO Executive Committee member,
> *Washington Post,* December 22, 1988

Q: Do Yassir Arafat's statements concerning the recognition of Israel and the renouncement of terrorism represent a new PLO policy?

A: "The statements made by the PLO chairman at his press conference in Geneva were incompatible with the resolutions of the latest PNC meeting, and he [Arafat] expressed only his personal opinion . . ." (Abu Ali Mustafa [Mustafa el-Zibri], Deputy Secretary General of the

PFLP, member of PLO Executive Committee, Radio Monte Carlo, December 18, 1988).

Q: If a solution to the Israeli-Palestinian conflict is reached through negotiations, will Israel then, after conceding land, be free to live in peace and security?

A: "The PLO has established a priori the use of the armed struggle in the liberation of Palestine. It cannot be abandoned even if there is a political settlement . . ." (Farouk Kaddoumi, *Al-Ittihad*, December 13, 1988).

Q: Will the PLO ever turn away from its policies of violence to rely on the policies of diplomacy for achieving its goals?

A: "There is no alternative to defending the political communiqué through powerful armed activity . . . the armed struggle will not stand out from among the pages of the communiqué, but will escalate and grow . . . at first, a small state, and with Allah's will, it will be made large, and expand to the east, west, north and south . . . the liberation of Palestine, step-by-step" (Abu Iyad, *Al-Anba,* December 18, 1988).

The Palestinian state would be a skipboard from which we would be able to release Jaffa, Acre and all Palestine.

ABU IYAD,
Al-Sakra, PLO organ,
Kuwait, January 6, 1988

The stage plan still exists, Its purpose is to serve the present interests yet it does not contradict the Palestinian National Covenant.

FAROUK KADDOUMI,
Al-Sakra, Kuwait, October 18, 1988

We in the PLO distinguish between the PLO National Covenant and the political plans. The first includes the final political aim the second includes the step-by-step road.

ABU IYAD,
Ukaz, Saudi Arabia,
November 22, 1988

"WE WANT JAFFA, LYDDA, AND HAIFA"

> *He who strives to attain that which is not for him loses that which was intended for him.*
>
> The Talmud

When Arafat states that the PLO acceptance of UN Security Council Resolution 242 is conditional upon the implementation of three conditions, one of which is the "right of return," it makes his statement meaningless and shows that Arafat continues to be committed to the destruction of Israel. No PLO demand exemplifies its aim for the liquidation of the State of Israel more than its repeated calls for the "right of return." The PLO views the "right of return" as a key element in its strategy to ultimately destroy Israel.

> *I want to go back to Lydda.*
>
> GEORGE HABASH,
> head of the PLO's PFPL,
> January 26, 1989

The "right of return," if it were to be implemented, would enable hundreds of thousands of Palestinians to enter Israel, overwhelm it from within and thereby bring about its dissolution. It is noteworthy that most PLO leaders do not come from the West Bank, but from towns and villages in the areas of Israel within the pre-1967 lines, which are more important to them than towns and villages like Nablus, Ramallah, and Jenin in the West Bank.

Q: If a Palestinian state were established, would the PLO accept the legality of Israel?

A: No. Arafat's second-in-command, Abu Iyad, stated in the Saudi newspaper *Ukaz* on January 3, 1989, that the PLO does not accept demands that it abolish the "right of return" and article 19 of the PLO Covenant which terms the establishment of Israel as "entirely illegal, regardless of the passage of time."

Q: What does Arafat say about the "right of return"?

A: "The Palestinian uprising will in no way end until the attainment of the legitimate rights of the Palestinian people, including the 'right of return'" (Arafat to Qatar News Agency, January 13, 1989).

> *The establishment of an independent Palestinian state on the West Bank and in the Gaza Strip does not contradict our ultimate strategic aim, which is the establishment of a democratic state in the territory of Palestine, but rather is a step in that direction.*
>
> PLO leader ABU IYAD,
> *Al-Safir,* Lebanon, January 25,1988

Q: Will the Palestinians be satisfied with an independent Palestinian state in Judea and Samaria?

A: "Impossible, impossible, impossible, impossible. Bush, Gorbachev, Thatcher, all should know that this will not be the solution. They think it will be a solution. But those people living in Shatila and Rashidiyeh (two camps in Lebanon) will not regard it as a solution. What about the Palestinians living in Lebanon, Syria and Kuwait? What about them? You know, five years from now there will be another revolution against Israel" (George Habash, *The Independent*, London, January 26, 1989).

Q: Do other Palestinians say the same?

A: "Our return to Palestine and our victory will be possible only with Allah's help and with our return to Faluja, Jaffa and Haifa" (Rafik al-Natshe, PLO representative in Saudi Arabia on Radio Riyadh, January 1, 1989).

> *Our first objective is to return to Nablus, and then move on to Tel Aviv. The day that we achieve independence will signify the defeat of Israel as a state.*
>
> LEILA KHALED, Secretary General,
> PLO General Union of Palestinian Women,
> *The Middle East Monthly*, London, January 1989
>
> ---
>
> *Armed struggle is the only way to liberate Palestine.*
>
> PLO covenant, Article 9

The PLO's actions over the last 30 years have defined the term: the kidnapping and murder of civilians, the bombing of civilian aircraft in flight, the massacre of athletes, tourists, passengers, pilgrims, men, women, children and babies – murder unlimited in time, place, or in the choice of victims.

> *I shall make it very perfectly clear to you. We shall never recognize Israel, never accept the usurper, the colonialist, the imperialist. We shall never allow Israel to live in peace.*
>
> FAROUK KADDOUMI,
> head of the PLO Political Department,
> *Stern*, West Germany,
> July 30, 1981

WHOM SHOULD ISRAEL BELIEVE?

> *Given the history of threats against Israel, the initial burden of proof has to rest on the Palestinians. To hint otherwise treats that history unfairly. It also encourages the PLO to resist . . .*
>
> New York Times, editorial,
> May 24, 1989

> *Mr. Moshe Arens said today: "Some of these people [Palestinian Arabs] I have talked to have told me that , as things are right now, anybody that would put forth his candidacy if he did not have the endorsement of the PLO would probably be dead in 24 hours. And they say, 'So you can't have free elections under such circumstances.' "*
>
> New York Times,
> July 18, 1989

Q: Does Arafat mean it when he says he renounces terrorism?

A: If so, why does he insist that the military operations against Israeli civilians are not covered by his statement?

Q: Why is Arafat silent whenever member groups of the PLO send terrorists into Israel?

A: If he cannot stop them, does he have the right to speak for the PLO?

Q: Does Arafat believe in political negotiations?

A: If so, why does he threaten any Palestinian that negotiates with Israel expressing his free opinion?

> *I may disagree with what you say, but I will defend with my life your right to say it.*
>
> VOLTAIRE

Q: Has Arafat truly had a change of heart?

A: If so, why does he refuse to call for a repeal of the Palestinian National Covenant which calls for Israel's destruction?

Q: How does Arafat consider the American-PLO dialogue?

A: In an interview with a Kuwaiti newspaper Yassir Arafat responded thusly to this question: "It was the U.S. that changed its policy and not the PLO."

Q: Would the PLO recognize Israel if a Palestinian state were established?

A: "The PLO will not recognize Israel even if an independent Palestinian state is established" (Farouk Kaddoumi, *Al Watan*, Kuwait, October 28, 1979).

> *I saw men – live men – dragged through the streets by fast-moving cars to which they were tied by their feet. All this was motivated in the early years by a desire to create the impression that a civil war was going on.*
>
> MAY EL-MURR, Lebanese poet,
> *Los Angeles Herald Examiner*,
> July 13, 1982

Q: What is the PLO stages policy?

A: In June 1974, the National Palestinian Congress convened in Cairo and the debate was between moderates and radicals in the PLO. The position of the radicals was the continuation of warfare with no concessions whatsoever, not even losing time with diplomatic negotiations. The moderates said that the PLO should participate in the Geneva Conference and accept political authority over the West Bank and the Gaza Strip after Israeli withdrawal to the 1967 borders. After this stage, that Palestinians will demand Israeli withdrawal to the 1947 borders. "Once we have Israel back at the 1947 borders," the moderates said, "we will gain the final victory by a war on three fronts."

> *The condition of the inhabitants of the camp was very bad, but the commanders of the PLO did wonderfully well for themselves. They drove expensive cars, some of which were stolen. For years the Arab states gave millions for us, the Palestinians. But there was never money to build a sewage system for our camp.*
>
> ABASS AL-HAJ,
> longtime resident of Ein Hilwe camp,
> *Ha'aretz*, August 20, 1982

The following story is meaningful: A farmer was once requested by his neighbor to lend him his goat for a day. The following day, when the neighbor failed to return the goat, the farmer came to claim it. However, the neighbor described how the goat had died soon after he had borrowed it. Just then, the goat began to bleat. When the owner said he could hear his goat's voice, the neighbor demanded angrily: "Do you believe your goat and not me?"

The story reflects the PLO. When will the world believe the goat?

On February 22, 1989, in Jerusalem, at a public meeting of Israeli peace groups, a videotape was played that had been made by Abu Iyad, Yassir Arafat's deputy. For the first time, a leading PLO figure with a terrorist background spoke to an audience in Jerusalem.

Abu Iyad impressed his listeners. He called for two states – Israel and Palestine – to live in peace. He said the PLO no longer insisted that the land belonged only to the Palestinians.

Yet at the same Abu Iyad was reported by the Qatar News Agency on December 21, 1988 as declaring that one of the PLO's new goals is to "develop the armed struggle in those areas within Palestine where it is not presently active."

The chairman of the Palestine National Council, Abd Al-Hamid El-Sayekh, told the Kuwaiti newspaper *Al-Siyassa* on December 21, 1988: "If the PLO succeeds in establishing a state in the West Bank and Gaza, it would not prevent the continuation of the struggle until the liberation of all of Palestine is achieved."

Nabil Sha'ath, the head of the PLO delegation to a conference in New York in mid-March, told the same Kuwaiti newspaper on January 29: "If we will gain independence on part of our land, we will not relinquish our dream of establishing a single democratic state over all of the Palestinian land."

These statements were made after Arafat's declaration at a press conference in Geneva on December 14, 1988, that he recognized Israel's right to exist, accepted UN Resolution 242 (which speaks of secure boundaries for all of the states in the region), and renounced terrorism.

Whom shall Israel believe?

The PLO is now actively engaged in a campaign of intimidation and assassination against any Palestinians who wish to live in peace with Israel or even to talk with American negotiators. Scores have been murdered. Only four Palestinians dared to show up at a meeting with a U.S. State Department team in Jerusalem in May 1989 and their lives were threatened for doing so.

Q: What are the implications of American-PLO dialogue?
A: The issue goes beyond the conflict between Israelis and Palestinians. It mocks the credibility of the United States as a fighter against terrorism. It consequently strengthens the confidence and power of the terrorist forces around the world.

> *The establishment of a Palestinian state in any part of Palestine has as its goal the establishment of a Palestinian state in all of Palestine.*
>
> SALAH KHALEF (Abu Iyad),
> *Al-Siyassa*, Kuwait,
> December 17, 1988

THE ABORTIVE PLO OPERATION OF MASS MURDER, MAY 1990

> *The land of Palestine is the homeland of the Palestinians, and the homeland of the Arab nation from the Ocean to the Gulf . . . The PLO offers not the peace of the weak, but the peace of Salah Aldin.*
>
> Saudi News Agency,
> January 2, 1989
>
> *(Note: In 1192, Salah Aldin [Saladin] concluded a peace treaty with the Crusaders. Soon thereafter, the Moslems attacked the Crusaders and drove them out of the Holy Land.)*

On May 30, 1990, six PLO boats were sent by the Abu Abbas section of the PLO on a mass murder mission on Israel's shores.

Q: What was the purpose of the attack on Israel's coastline?

A: The purpose of the raid was to indiscriminately murder Israelis vacationing at the shoreline at the height of the Shavuoth holiday on May 30.

Q: Where were the terrorists trained?

A: The attackers were trained, outfitted, and transported by Libyan officers.

Q: Who is Abu Abbas?

A: Abu Abbas, whose full name is Abbas Muhammed, is a member of the PLO Executive Committee, is a leader of the Palestine Liberation Front, and is the hijacker of the cruise ship *Achille Lauro,* on the Mediterranean Sea in 1985. On that ship, Abu Abbas murdered an American citizen, Leon Klinghoffer, then threw his body into the sea.

A cartoon that appeared in the Saudi paper *Al-Riad* on May 23,1990, depicting the victory of the Palestinians in Judea and Samaria. Israel's Prime Minister Shamir is the fallen bull and the matador is a Palestinian holding a stone in one hand and the Palestinian flag in another.

Muhammed Ahmad Youseph, deputy commander of the Abu Abbas aborted operation in Israel, spoke to the Israeli media in an interview on June 5, 1990. The following is an English translation of the interview:

Q: Do you belong to an organization?

A: Yes. I belong to the Palestine Liberation Organization [Abu Abbas' organization]. Before that, I was affiliated with Fatah [Arafat's organization].

Q: What was your task in this operation?

A: The purpose was to kill civilians. We were supposed to shell the Tel Aviv hotel area . . . after shelling to get off the boats and to attack. My personal task was to enter the Sheraton Hotel in Tel Aviv and to kill every person I saw there.

Q: And in case you saw civilians, unarmed, what was to have been their fate, according to your orders?

A: To kill every person we see.

Q: Where were you trained for this operation?

A: In Libya. Libyan instructors supervised our training. One colonel from the Libyan Navy, Mr. Ali, taught us naval tactics. We maneuvered together. We were accompanied by a frigate that joined our maneuvers. After this exercise, Mr. Ali told us: "Now you can destroy any boat you come across."

Q: Whom did you see before going to the operation?

A: We met Abu Abbas . . . we kissed one another and separated.

Q: Who were with you on board the ship?

A: Colonel Zuhayr from the Libyan Navy and Abu Alazz, Abu Abbas' deputy.

Q: What were your instructions, in the event you fell prisoners?

A: The instructions were that no one would admit by whom we were trained, who helped us, who supplied us with weapons and boats. We were told to admit that we were trained in Libya, but not to say that we got our weapons and boats from Libya.

The above interview was carried by ITIM, the Israel News Agency.

Q: What was the main U.S. condition in 1988 for negotiating with the PLO?

A: The condition was that the PLO stop terror. The Americans accepted at face value Arafat's promises that the PLO would end and then renounce terrorism.

Q: What was the American reaction after the abortive 1990 operation?

A: The United States demanded that the PLO expel Abu Abbas from the PLO ranks and condemn the action.

Q: Did the PLO accept the American demands?

A: No. The PLO neither condemned the operation nor expelled Abu Abbas from its ranks.

It was not just another random raid by Arab zealots. The Palestinian terror teams intercepted by Israeli forces as they tried to land on civilian beaches Wednesday were part of a carefully planned, elaborately equipped attack. That blunt fact forces Yassir Arafat to make a fundamental choice: Take strong action against the responsible terrorist faction of his Palestine Liberation Organization or forfeit direct dialogue with the United States, thus his best chance to advance the Palestinian cause.

New York Times, editorial,
June 1, 1990

Reacting to the American demands, [PLO leader] Hani el-Hassan said: "The PLO did not beg for a dialogue with the U.S. but forced it on Washington through the Intifada.*"*

Al-Kabas, Kuwait,
June 3, 1990

Q: What was the PLO reaction?

A: Arafat's chief deputy, Abu Iyad, said: "The PLO never committed itself to anyone in the world to stop its armed struggle . . . The term 'terror' does not embrace armed struggle against Israel." (The quote is from the BBC in Arabic, June 3, 1990.)

Section 1302 (b) of the International Security and Development Cooperation Act of 1985 (Public Law 99-83) reads: "No officer or employee of the United States government shall negotiate with the Palestine Liberation Organization or any representatives thereof (except in emergency or humanitarian situations) unless and until the Palestine Organization recognized Israel's right to exist, accepts United Nations Security Council Resolutions 242 and 338 and renounces the use of terrorism."

This means that the PLO's refusal to renounce the terrorist bid to attack Tel Aviv beaches makes American contacts with its representatives a violation of Federal Law. But it is doubtful

---

> *whether such contacts were legal even before Arafat refused to renounce the raid and expel Abu Abbas. The law does not refer to declarations of an individual, but to the PLO as an organization. And Arafat's December 14, 1988, press statement in Geneva does not reflect official PLO positions, and the PNC never satisfied the conditions that would allow legal American contacts with the organization.*
>
> *Jerusalem Post,* editorial,
> July 3, 1990

Q: What did the chairman of the Political Department, Farouk Kaddoumi, say?

A: "It is the Palestinian people's right to choose its methods of struggle, suitable for the liberation of its land . . . The American veto [in the United Nations] proved that the U.S. is at the head of the terrorist countries." (The quote is from *Al-Watan,* Kuwait, June 3, 1990.)

Q: What was the Libyan reaction?

A: As expected, the Libyans denied any involvement. Moreover, the Libyan Foreign Ministry expressed sympathy for the motives of the attack. The Libyans added: "This commando operation was not the first and will not be the last . . . "

Q: What is the conclusion?

A: The conclusion is very simple: The PLO has not stopped its terror, it did not renounce terrorism, and it did not keep its promise to the United States. The PLO was and remains a terrorist organization. The term "double talk" is very characteristic to the nature of the PLO.

> *As an organization, the PLO has never recognized Israel's right to exist. It has not changed its charter, which calls for Israel's destruction, nor has it disavowed the ten resolutions of the "policy of phases" adopted by the PNC in Cairo in June 1974. Resolution Eight states that, after the establishment of a national independent fighting authority on any part of the Palestinian territory that will be liberated, "the Palestinian national authority will struggle to unite the confrontation countries to pave the way for the completion of the liberation of all the Palestinian territory." All letterheads, maps, and emblems of the PLO, including those on official documents submitted to the UN, show the State of Palestine as covering the whole area from the Jordan to the Mediterranean. Israel, whose*

right to exist Arafat is presumed to recognize, does not exist on these maps.

Jerusalem Post, editorial,
July 3, 1990

Some of the findings in a report submitted to the U.S. Congress by the nation's State Department on March 19, 1990, are that:

1. PLO statements and actions continue to pursue a course of terrorism and the rejection of Israel's legitimate existence (pp. 2-13).
2. The PLO Covenant stands as the ideological credo of the PLO, and the statements of PLO leaders point out that no attempt has been made by the PNC to repeal the Covenant or change any of its provisions advocating the elimination of Israel (pp. 16-19).
3. The PLO's "Phased Plan" remains the key PLO strategy for implementing its Covenant, and PLO leaders reaffirm that the establishment of a Palestinian state in the territories would be just a prelude to expanding such a state in "all of Palestine" (pp. 20-23).
4. All of the PLO factions which participated in the November 1988 PNC have engaged in infiltration attempts since December 1988, and Arafat, instead of trying to halt the terror operations, has endorsed them (pp. 27-32).
5. The PLO has opposed the extradition and prosecution of PLO terrorists wanted for attacks abroad (p. 38).
6. The PLO has refused to acknowledge its responsibility for PLO terrorism, and has not compensated American victims (pp. 38-39).

Shortly after the events of May 1990, cartoonist Margulies produced the following, in the *Houston Post:*

CHAPTER FIVE

A PALESTINIAN STATE –
MORTAL DANGER TO ISRAEL

Such a state would control strategic mountainous terrain on the West Bank overlooking the coastal plain . . . This means the width of Israel's coastal plain (where two-thirds of the Jewish population lives) would, on average, shrink to about 14 miles. This would constitute a death sentence for Israel's main infrastructure . . .

GENERAL ARIEL SHARON,
New York Times, March 5, 1990

Q: Do you think Arab governments want a Palestinian state? A: Frankly, no. Syria and Jordan are most opposed. If there were a Palestinian state, there would be no logical reason for Jordan to exist.

ABU IYAD, second in command
to Arafat, *U.S. News and World Report,*
December 15, 1986

The way to Tel Aviv goes through Amman.
PLO leader GEORGE HABASH

Some honest people the world over believe that the solution to the Arab-Israeli conflict is based on the establishment of a Palestinian state in Judea, Samaria, and the Gaza Strip. They reason that once the Palestinians achieve such a state, they would accept Israel as a reality.

Israel is fully prepared to take risks to achieve peace. The creation of a Palestinian Arab state in Judea, Samaria, and the Gaza district would, however, expose the State of Israel to mortal danger. No country can be expected to take a risk that, in effect, would jeopardize its very existence.

> *Peace, peace, yet there is no peace.*
> Jeremiah 6:14

Israel includes only about one-fifth of Palestine. The other four-fifths form the Palestinian State of Jordan. Thus, the Palestinians are not a people without a land. Fewer in number than the Israelis, they hold four times more land than Israel.

ISRAEL'S DANGEROUS STRATEGIC DEPTH

> *A Palestinian state, with all the elements of a state and with the ambition to destroy Israel, would make it very difficult to protect the State of Israel with the borders of 1967 and the power of 1990.*
> General NATAN VILNAY,
> commander of Israel's southern front,
> *Ma'ariv*, February 26, 1990

Israeli withdrawal to the June 4, 1967, borders would place Israel under constant, severe danger to her very existence. It is impossible to speak about real peace and at the same time Israeli withdrawal to the June 5, 1967, borders in order to establish a Palestinian state in Judea and Samaria.

The accompanying map vividly shows the ridiculous and highly dangerous borders of June 4, 1967. Tel Aviv, Israel's largest metropolitan area with over a million inhabitants was only 11 miles from the border. Netanya is even less: 9 miles from the border. The Ben-Gurion International Airport is only 4 miles from the border. Jerusalem, Israel's capital, was split in half by barbed wire. These borders were one of the factors that encouraged Arab aggression that led to the 1967 war.

> *I announce from here . . . that this time we will exterminate Israel.*
> President GAMAL ABDEL NASSER of Egypt,
> July 26, 1959

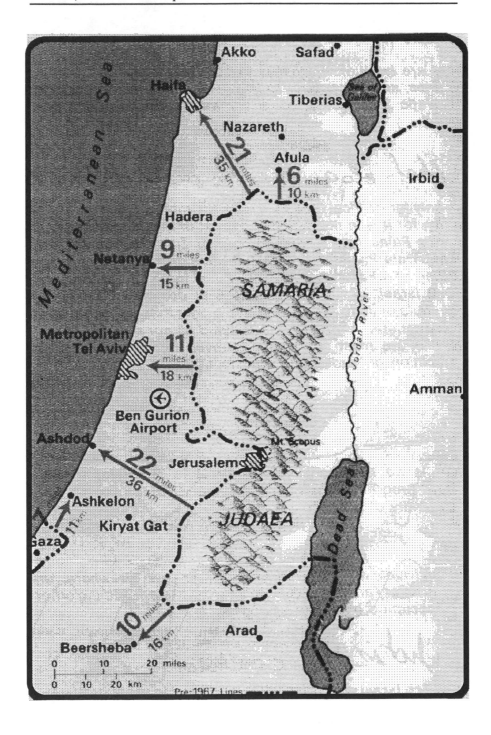

It is said that in this era of rockets, borders are no longer important. Yet had the Yom Kippur War of 1973 been triggered from the borders existing prior to June 1967, it would not have been fought in the sands of Sinai and on the Golan Heights, but in the streets of Jerusalem and Tel Aviv instead.

> *The Zionist in our homeland is one of those errors which human history is witness to. This error cannot continue and is bound toward demise.*
>
> Al-Ba'ath, Damascus, May 2, 1975

The threat posed by the advancing Egyptian and Syrian forces was neutralized, to a large extent, by their distance from the heartland of Israel, which allowed the Israel Defense Forces the time necessary to call up its reserves, consolidate its forces, and prepare its counter-offensive.

People may mistakenly presume that in this era of sophisticated missiles that can reach very distant targets the value of borders is insignificant. This presumption is incorrect. Bombs and missiles can cause severe damage should they reach their target; however, they would not be the crucial factor if the country attacked – in this case Israel – is willing and able to fight back. In order to defeat a country, you have to capture territory and here lies the importance of strategic depth.

There is wide agreement among Israeli leaders and strategists, in both major political camps, that the Jordan River now represents Israel's "security border" to the east. It is a designation not very difficult to accept, considering that the distance from that ancient river to Israel's western border, the Mediterranean seaboard, is a scant 50 miles.

> *Libya's aid to us amounted to hundreds of millions of dollars.*
> PLO leader AHMED JIBRIL,
> *Al-Safir,* Beirut, July 18, 1982

WHAT ARE THE MAIN DANGERS POSED BY A PALESTINIAN STATE?

> *Our people will continue to fuel the torch of the revolution with rivers of blood, until the whole of the occupied homeland is liberated . . . not just part of it.*
> YASSIR ARAFAT,
> Associated Press, Beirut, March 12, 1979

> *I hope I am making myself clear to everyone everywhere . . . We have said it over and over again that we refuse to recognize Israel. This is an unchangeable, permanent policy.*
> FAROUK KADDOUMI,
> head of the PLO Political Department
> Reuters, Beirut, April 9, 1981

> *The fulfillment of Palestinian aspirations will be achieved only by the gun. The PLO will never recognize Israel.*
> IBRAHIM SOUSSE, PLO representative in Paris,
> *Le Monde,* November 30, 1982

The great majority of the Israeli people consider the establishment of a Palestinian state as a mortal danger to Israel. Most Israelis believe that the national aspiration of the Palestinian people has been fulfilled in Jordan, which is an integral part of Palestine and a Palestinian state.

The PLO leaders in the past and today have declared at various times that the establishment of a state in Judea and Samaria is not the end of the struggle against Israel. They intend to continue the struggle until a Palestinian state is established on all the territory of Palestine.

Q: Who would control such a state should it be established?
A: A Palestinian state would be a PLO terrorist-controlled state.
Q: Why would such a state endanger Israel and others?
A: (1) It would place Israel's major centers of population and the country's industrial infrastructure under perennial threat of the gun.
(2) Israel's entire airspace could be fully controlled from these areas.
(3) It would serve as a launching pad for attack by radical and uncompromising Arab states, and as a base for attack by the various terrorist factions operating independently of centralized, responsible government.

(4) It would lack political and economic stability and thus would lead to general regional destabilization.

(5) Demilitarization is not a viable expectation at this time.

(6) It would inevitably become a radical satellite on Israel's doorstep.

Q: What conditions would such a state create?

A: Due to the short warning times available to Israeli decision makers, if military control over Judea and Samaria were to be relinquished, Israel would have to respond pre-emptively even if only the probability of a threat is evident.

Q: Is there a danger that Israel would find herself cut in half?

A: Absolutely. For Israel, there would be very little room for error, no grey areas or time to reconsider. The possibility of Israel finding herself cut in half, with the bulk of its population and factories concentrated in a highly vulnerable 11-mile-wide strip, is a very real threat.

Q: What are the true intentions of the PLO?

A: Let the PLO speak for itself:

> *There are two (initial) phases to our return: the first phase to the 1967 lines, and the second to the 1948 lines . . . the third stage is the democratic state of Palestine. So we are fighting for these three states.*
>
> FAROUK KADDOUMI, head of the PLO
> Political Department,
> *Newsweek*, March 14, 1977

Q: How does the PLO view Jordan and Israel?

A: Once again the PLO answers this question. In the words of Zuheir Muhsin, head of the PLO Military Operations Department, in *Trouw*, a Netherlands daily, on March 31, 1977: "It is only for political reasons that we carefully stress our Palestinian identity, for it is in the national interest of the Arabs to encourage a separate Palestinian identity to counter Zionism. Yes, the existence of a separate Palestinian identity serves only tactical purpose. The founding of a Palestinian state is a new tool in the continuing battle against Israel . . . Jordan is a state with defined borders. It cannot claim Haifa or Jaffa, whereas I have a right to Haifa, Jaffa, Jerusalem, and Beersheba. After we have attained all our rights in the whole of Palestine, we must not postpone, even for a single moment, the reunification of Jordan and Palestine."

Q: What about de-militarization of Judea and Samaria?

A: Demilitarization is not the answer. It may work in a vast, nearly empty region like the Sinai peninsula. However, it will not work in a small, populated area bordering directly on Arab countries from which arms can be shipped in, surreptitiously or otherwise.

Q: Then what is the conclusion?

A: The situation in which Israel would therefore find itself if a Palestinian state were to rise upon the ideologies expressed above would be intolerable. Needless to say, there would be no chance of any modicum of agreement being reached towards a peaceful future, given the parameters of its principles as stated above.

Q: Who are the allies of the PLO in the Arab world?

A: The PLO has for years been, and will continue to be, a convenient political tool of the Rejectionist Arab states and the Soviet Union in their perennial quest to destabilize the region. The Rejectionist Arab states have repeatedly referred to the PLO as the "sole legitimate representative of the Palestinians" and it can be assumed that a PLO state will continue to serve the goals of Arab extremism as faithfully as has the terrorist movement.

> *The struggle with the Zionism enemy is not a struggle about Israel's borders, but about Israel's existence. We will never agree to anything less than the return of all our land and the establishment of the independent state.*
> PLO leader BASSAM ABU SHARIF,
> Kuwait News Agency, May 31, 1986

Q: What is the policy of the United States?

A: The traditional American policy rejects the establishment of a Palestinian state in Judea, Samaria, and the Gaza Strip.

Q: What is the American military view?

A: A study of the defensive characteristics of the Judean-Samarian region was carried out by the United States Joint Chiefs of Staff in June 1967. The study concluded that Israel's minimum defense line should be drawn down the middle of Judea and Samaria.

Q: What advantage would such demarcation provide?

A: This line would widen the narrow portion of Israel and would provide additional terrain for the defense of Tel Aviv. The Joint Chiefs of Staff noted that the hills of "West Jordan [northern Judea] overlook Israel's narrow midsection.'' and if held by Jordan, would present it with ''a route for a thrust to the sea,'' enabling it to split Israel in half. The pre-1967 borders would not enable the containment of an enemy thrust, when the latter has the initiative and could utilize the sector of its choice for the direction of its attack.

The following is material published by Palestinian Arabs in Judea and Samaria:

''Palestine is yours . . . Go there with your blood.''

''March, the month of bounty, the month of the land, the monthof honor, the month of pampering.''

''Fatah says . . . Palestine, all of Palestine.''

''We are here . . . We will stay here . . . We will plant almond and olive trees so that blossoms will return to the land.''

A PALESTINIAN STATE:
ECONOMICALLY UNFEASIBLE

> *The liquidation of Israel is one of the means we adopt to achieve unity and freedom in the Arab world . . .*
> PLO leader HANI AL-HASSAN,
> *An Nahar*, Beirut, January 9, 1982

Q: What would be the economic chances of a Palestinian state?

A: Given the fact that a Palestinian state composed of Judea, Samaria, and the Gaza Strip would have no natural resources, extremely limited farmland, an underdeveloped industrial infrastructure, an extremely high population density, and a basically unskilled work force, there is little chance of immediate or foreseeable economic independence.

Q: What would be the size of such a state?

A: The area in question is a total of 6,200 square kilometers.

Q: What is the estimated population of this area?

A: The area in question is populated by an estimated 1.5 million people and it can be assumed that an independent Palestinian state would attract Palestinians currently living under refugee conditions in other parts of the Arab world.

> *There are two different approaches in the Arab world: that Israel can be overwhelmed militarily or that a military victory is impossible. The power struggle between Israel and the Arabs is a long-term historical trial. Victory or defeat are for us questions of existence or annihilation.*
> *Al-Riyadh*, Saudi Arabia, July 11,1986

Q: Would such a state be economically feasible?

A: With the expected increase in population density and, as a result the increase in human needs such as housing, education, social services, water, electricity, etc., the Palestinian state can, by no means, be economically feasible.

Q: Is it possible that such a state could absorb the Palestinians in exile?

A: Anyone who imagines that extensive investment and modern technology can serve to maintain the existing population of Judea and Samaria and Gaza – about 1.5 million – and the Palestinians in exile is indulging in fantasy.

Q: What is the population density in Judea, Samaria, and the Gaza Strip in comparison to Israel?

84

A: Even today, without the returnees, the population density in these areas is greater than that in Israel.

Q: What increases the difficulties even more?

A: In addition, local sources of livelihood are few and far between, and a substantial part of the local manpower is employed in Israel, Jordan and in the oil-rich Arab countries. The territories have no raw materials, no sources of energy, no industry. The water supply is meager and there is very little by way of the transportation and communications systems needed to develop industry.

Q: Can huge financial investment solve the problem?

A: Even if the investment required to establish a rudimentary industrial base were available – and the recent economic setbacks suffered by several oil-rich states make this rather unlikely – it would take years to train the required local professional personnel, acquire equipment and secure adequate markets.

Q: However, isn't the size of the state of Luxembourg only 998 square miles?

A: Luxembourg has highly developed heavy industry, nourished by rich strata of iron ore, that is the envy of much larger states. Yet its population is no more than 350,000, fewer than the number of inhabitants in the Gaza district alone.

Q: How does the population density of Judea, Samaria, and Gaza compare to some states in Europe?

A: The population density in these areas is greater than that of Switzerland, Austria, France, Italy, and a long list of other industrial countries.

Q: Would a Palestinian state solve the problem of all the Palestinians?

A: Not at all. It might pose a solution for one-third of the Palestinians, yet it would ignore the remaining two-thirds.

Q: What would the Arab states do, should such a state be established?

A: The Arab host countries could be expected to invite the refugees to pack their bags and "go home." This, of course, would be mockery, for no such "home" exists.

The Reagan plan attempts to contain and to extinguish the Palestinian revolution . . . unfortunately, it does not deal with refugees of 1948, and it limits the rights of return to the West Bank and Gaza and not to their fundamental place of Jaffa, Haifa, and Safed.

FAROUK KADDOUMI,
Al-Hadaf, January 17, 1983

Q: Whom would the international community blame if such a state would be unable to absorb the returning refugees?

A: The Israelis would be considered the guilty ones, and would be expected to correct this "injustice." Israel would be required to prove her dedication to true peace in the Middle East by opening her gates to the refugees who have nowhere to go. Israel would be exposed and subjected to pressures, censure, and sanctions if she claimed that the price had already been paid and all the possible sacrifices had been made.

Q: Which country can absorb all the Palestinians?

A: Jordan, which is more than three times the size of Israel, can readily absorb all of them. Jordan has the space and the potential ability to absorb all the Palestinians.

Q: What else makes Jordan a natural place in which to solve the problem?

A: Only in Jordan is there now a majority of Palestinians, linked by family ties to the Palestinians dispersed in the neighboring countries. And thus there the local Arabs can be expected not to give a cold shoulder to their brothers who come to join them.

> *When we talk about an armed struggle, the legality of which has been acknowledged by the UN, we are talking about all the occupied areas of Palestine . . .*
>
> PLO leader FAROUK KADDOUMI,
> *Quotidien de Paris*, November 11, 1985

Q: Who would be the likely patrons of such a state?

A: Economic dependence by definition means political dependence and it is logical to assume that the main financial backers of a Palestinian state would be those Arab states which have a correlation of ideology with the Palestinians and defined anti-Israel policies.

PALESTINIANS AND A PALESTINIAN STATE

> *Our activities will continue in Tel Aviv and elsewhere, until we achieve victory and hoist our flag over Jerusalem and the other cities in the occupied homeland.*
>
> YASSIR ARAFAT,
> Reuters, May 12, 1978

The PLO vehemently opposes any political settlement regardless of boundaries or conditions, because its opposition is to the principle of a Jewish state in any size or shape. The PLO formulated this opposition to a political settlement in their National Covenant in its new version adopted by their congress in Cairo of July 1968 and reinforced with explicit resolutions.

Q: Do the Palestinians want a Palestinian state?
A: If they wanted a Palestinian state, why didn't they establish one in 1948, according to the United Nations Partition Plan of November 29, 1947?
Q: What did the Palestinians desire at that time?
A: The Palestinians in 1948 did not want to establish a Palestinian state. Instead, they wanted to prevent the establishment of a Jewish state, according to the Partition Plan.

> *[I have] never met an Arab leader that in private professed a desire for an independent Palestinian state. Publicly, they all espouse an independent Palestinian state – almost all of them – because that is what they committed themselves to do at Rabat [the 1974 Arab League summit conference]. But the private diplomatic tone of conversations is much more proper . . .*
>
> U.S. President JIMMY CARTER,
> 1979 press conference

Q: Did the Palestinians seek statehood between the years 1948 and 1967?
A: Not at all. Between the years 1948 and 1967, Judea and Samaria were under Jordanian control and the Gaza Strip was under Egyptian control. Not even one single Palestinian spoke of such a state in these territories.

Q: Isn't it true that the PLO, which was established in 1964, did want an independent Palestinian state?

A: Not at all. Like other Arabs, the PLO started its fight against Israel before 1967, when Judea, Samaria, and the Gaza Strip were in Arab hands.

Q: Did the PLO give clear expression to its rejection of such a Palestinian state and to the existence of Israel?

A: Yes. The following articles of the Palestinian Covenant express this rejection:

Article 15: The liberation of Palestine . . . aims at the elimination of Zionism in Palestine.

Article 19: The partition of Palestine in 1947 and the establishment of the State of Israel are entirely illegal . . .

Article 21: The Arab Palestinian people . . . reject all solutions which are substitutes for the total liberation of Palestine . . .

We in the PLO totally reject to cancel article 19 of the Palestine National Covenant.

ABU IYAD,
Ukaz, January 1989

(Article 19 says that partition is illegal.)

If we achieve part of our territory, we will not relinquish our dream to establish one democratic state on all of Palestine.
Arafat advisor NABIL SHA'AT,
Al-Siyassa, Kuwait, January 29, 1989

Q: Where was the center of Palestinian nationalism?

A: During the Jordanian occupation of Judea and Samaria (1948-67), some 400,000 Arabs from those areas moved to the area east of the Jordan River – mainly because of the political centrality of Amman as the kingdom's capital, and for economic reasons. The west-to-east movement continued during the 1970s, though at a reduced rate.

The Palestinian struggle must be directed to establish a Palestinian state in the West Bank and Gaza. This will not stop us from achieving our final goal to liberate all Palestine.
PLO leader NOYEF HAWATMEH,
The French News Agency, January 1989

Q: Why was such movement so natural?

A: The ethnic-social-religious-linguistic affinity between the populations on the two sides of the river, and the short distance (only 45 miles from Nablus to Amman) made these migrations not so much an uprooting as a move from one part of Palestine to another.

Q: If Israel agrees to offer you a Palestinian state on the West Bank and the Gaza Strip, will you sign a peace treaty with Israel?

A : You are asking me a hypothetical question. Until now, we are not aware of such a proposal made by Israel. However, such a state would probably be accepted by our organization in the short run. But in the long run, it would not be an economically feasible state. It must ultimately include what is now Israel. We believe that only a democratic state, in which all can live in peace, should exist.

PLO spokesman Dr. NABIL SHA'AT,
in an interview, *Philadelphia Inquirer,*
December 1, 1974

THE PALESTINIAN NATIONAL COUNCIL OF JUNE 8, 1974

On June 8, 1974, the Palestinian National Council met in Cairo, Egypt. The major organizations belonging to the PLO were divided in their views, as follows:

The "moderates" were those who held that the PLO will gain tactical advantage by participating in the Geneva conference, and establishing a Palestinian state without renouncing the final objective, which is the destruction of Israel and Jordan. These organizations include the Fatah (Fatah means "occupation" in Arabic) of Yassir Arafat.

The "radicals," led by George Habash, were against any settlement and participation in Geneva. They believe that the only way to solve the problem is by constant war.

The ultimate aims, therefore, of both groups are identical. They differ only in the timing of their tactics and strategies. While the moderates want to achieve their goal in stages, the radicals want the same goal at once.

The main points of the Palestinian National Covenant of June 1974 were that the PLO:

1. should declare an independent Palestinian state on any territory evacuated by Israel. (Article 2)
2. should use the Palestinian state as a base for war against Israel. (Article 4)
3. should act in order to cause a war between Israel and the Arab states in order to put an end to Israel. (Article 8)

WHY ISRAEL SHOULD NOT NEGOTIATE WITH THE PLO

The great majority of citizens in Israel reject any negotiations with the PLO. People do not consider the PLO a partner in any peace talks in the future between Israel, on the one hand, and the Arabs and Palestinians on the other. Israel's denial of the PLO is based on different and various reasons:

◆ The main goal of the PLO is to destroy Israel. No country is willing to negotiate with any adversary seeking its destruction.

◆ The PLO has made killing a way of life, intimidation a method, and fanaticism a policy. All these not only will not guarantee peace, but will frustrate any peace efforts. Peace and the PLO are two contradictory terms.

◆ The notorious PLO Covenant, which calls for Israel's demise, claims that the Jews are not a nation, that Zionism is racism, and that the solution to the conflict can only be military. This covenant is still in force today.

◆ The PLO has murdered thousands of innocent people all over the world in general and in Israel in particular. The "sin" of these innocent victims was simply that they happened to be Jews, or were Arabs who rejected PLO violence, or others who accidentally found themselves in the line of fire of PLO gangs on their murder missions.

◆ All the existing PLO theories and strategies are based on Israel's destruction. These beliefs do not change overnight.

◆ The PLO is an outsider. Peace should be negotiated with the Palestinian Arabs residing in Judea, Samaria, and the Gaza Strip, and not with PLO outsiders living in Tunisia.

◆ The PLO threats to any Palestinian in Judea, Samaria, and Gaza who dares to talk peace with Israel is another reason why Israel will not negotiate with the PLO.

◆ The PLO is a terrorist movement. No sovereign state would make peace with terrorists.

> *What is there to talk about? If you agree to hold political negotiations with the PLO you are essentially coming to terms with a third state between the Mediterranean and Jordan. Such a state will be a cancer in the heart of the Middle East.*
>
> YITZHAK RABIN,
> Israeli Minister of Defense, September 1989
>
> ---
>
> *There is no new policy by the PLO to recognize Israel . . . The declared program of the PLO is to bring about the destruction of the Zionist entity of Israel.*
>
> PLO Information Office,
> Oslo, Norway, May 5, 1977

Q: Isn't a war of liberation always a war against the innocent?

A: The greatest oppression in the annals of mankind was the Nazi occupation of Europe. Yet none of the resistance movements fighting against the Nazis resorted to terrorism against German children. The French resistance, for example, directed its attacks against German soldiers even though German wives and children were well within its reach.

Q: What can be said for PLO terror?

A: PLO terror, like any other terror, is not the "inevitable" result of oppression. It is not the inevitable result of anything. It is a choice, an evil choice, to pursue the conflict through violence. Violence against the innocent – men, women, and children.

Q: Is there a connection between oppression and terrorism?

A: No. It is a fact – the liberal democracies have borne the brunt of the attack of international terrorism. What "oppression," for example, engendered the Red Brigades of Italy or the Baader Meinhof gang in West Germany or the Red Army in Japan? Terrorism has concentrated its attacks on the very societies which enjoy full democracy and observe human rights.

> *In the Middle East, terror is an endemic feature of local politics. Most of the terror is not anti-Israel or even anti-West, but intra-Arab and intra-Muslim. It is a way for Syria to check Jordan, for Syria to subvert Iraq (and vice versa), for Lebanese factions to deal with one another, and for Libya to tame its enemies everywhere.*
>
> a Western observer

91

THE PLO TERROR AGAINST
THE HELPLESS AND INNOCENT

A PLO attack on a school in the northern town of Ma'alot, on May 15, 1974, resulted in 16 teenagers killed and 62 others wounded. Responsibility was claimed by Noyef Hawatmeh's Popular Front for the Liberation of Palestine.

Nine schoolchildren and three teachers were killed and 19 children wounded when a PLO terror squad ambushed a school bus carrying children from Moshav Avivim to their school in northern Galilee on May 20, 1970. Responsibility was claimed by Ahmed Jibril's Popular Front for the Liberation of Palestine – General Command.

The children's house of Kibbutz Misgav Am on the Lebanese border was attacked by a PLO terror unit on April 7, 1980. A two-year-old boy and one kibbutz member were killed and four small children wounded. Responsibility was claimed by the Arab Liberation Front.

92

THE PLO, THE FLN, AND THE MAU MAU

World history is full of examples of national movements that succeeded in achieving independence for their countries. These movements fought bravely against different colonial powers and removed them from their countries. In most cases, the leaders of these national movements went on to become the leaders of the newly established states following the withdrawal of the colonial powers.

The Front de Libération Nationale, or FLN, was the Algerian national movement headed by Ahmed Ben Bella. The FLN fought bravely against the French. After constant bitter struggles, the French admitted defeat, left Algeria in the hands of the Algerians, and returned to their own country – France.

The Mau Mau was the Kenyan national movement headed by Jomo Kenyatta. The Mau Mau fought against the British colonial power in Kenya. After a long struggle, the British forces gave up and returned to Britain.

We have, however, never heard of any movement that wanted to kick out the British from Britain or the French from France. Yet it is the PLO that wants to kick the Israelis out of Israel.

> *The victory march will continue until the Palestinian flag flies in Jerusalem and in all of Palestine – from the Jordan River to the Mediterranean Sea and from Rosh Hanikra to Eilat.*
>
> YASSIR ARAFAT,
> *Saut Filastin*, Beirut, December 7, 1980

The conclusion is very simple: The PLO, neither by its theories, tactics, and strategies, nor by its actions, can claim to be a national movement. The PLO is in reality a terrorist movement. On May 15, 1974, Radio Damascus proclaimed: "Today is the day of Palestinian nationalism." The PLO declaration on Radio Damascus followed the slaying of schoolchildren and others in Ma'alot, in northern Israel. Sixteen teen-agers were killed, and 62 others were wounded.

93

CHAPTER SIX

THE PLO – LEADERS
AND ORGANIZATIONS

> *In the Middle East it is hard to draw the line between terrorism
> and diplomacy. Without the terrorists' power, the threatened
> nations would not be very afraid of Mr. Arafat.*
> A. M. ROSENTHAL,
> *New York Times*, March 25, 1990

THE LEADERS

Arafat, Yassir (Abu Ammar): Chairman of the PLO's Executive
Committee, head of the PLO's Military Department, leader of Fatah.
Fatah is the largest and most significant organization in the PLO and
accounts for nearly 70 percent of the strength of the Palestinian terrorists.
Fatah has thousands of members based in a number of Arab states –
mainly Lebanon, Iraq, Algeria, and Tunisia. Arafat established Al-Fatah
together with his colleague Abu Iyad in Kuwait in 1959.

Abbas, Mohammed (Abu Abbas): Member of the PLO Executive
Committee, leader of the PLO's Palestine Liberation Front (PLF). One
of the hijackers of the cruise ship *Achille Lauro* in 1987.

Abd Rabbo, Yassir: Member of the PLO Executive Committee, head
of the PLO's Information Department, Deputy General – Secretary of the
Democratic Front for the Liberation of Palestine (DFLP).

Abu Jihad (Khalil Alwazir): Assassinated in his home in Tunisia in
April 1988 by what is generally believed to have been an Israeli
commando team. He was the main organizer and planner of terror actions
against Israel in Israel and abroad. He was responsible for the military arm
of Fatah, including seaborne attacks. Among the most notorious attacks
was the coastal road massacre in Israel in March 1978. The attack left 35
civilians dead and 80 wounded. In June 1974, Fatah carried out an attack
in the northern coastal city of Nahariya, murdering an Israeli civilian and
his two babies.

Abu Iyad (Saleh Khalef): Deputy to Arafat, member of Fatah Central Committee, head of PLO's unified security apparatus. Together with Arafat founded Al-Fatah in Kuwait in 1959. He has been the leader of Black September. For decades he has been a key planner and organizer of PLO terror activities. His record includes the murder of 11 Israeli athletes at the 1972 Munich Olympics and the killing in Sudan of Ambassador Cleo A. Noel, Jr., of the United States and his counselor, George C. Moore.

Abu Lughod, Ibrahim: PNC member, American citizen.

Abu Mazen (Mahmoud Abbas): Member of PLO Executive Committee, head of the PLO's Arab and International Relations Department, member of Fatah Central Committee, Fatah representative in Gulf.

Abu Musa (Said Musa): Leader of the Fatah dissident faction: ''Fatah Uprising.'' Split from the Fatah in 1983 and is supported by Syria.

Abu Nidal (Sabri Al-Banna): Leader of Fatah – Revolutionary Council. According to a Western diplomat, Abu Nidal's base is in Libya. He also has a base and followers in Lebanon's Beka'a Valley.

The Balfour Declaration, the Mandate Document, and everything based upon them are deemed null and void. The claim of historical or religious ties between Jews and Palestine does not tally with historical realities nor with the constituents of statehood in their true sense.

PLO National Covenant, Article 20

Abu Sharif, Bassam: Arafat's spokesman and media advisor.

Ahmed, Abd El-Rahim: Member of PLO Executive Committee, leader of PLO's Arab Liberation Front (ALF), head of PLO's Labour and Popular Organizations Departments.

Arafat, Fathi: President of the PLO's Palestine Red Crescent, brother of Yassir Arafat.

Balawi, Khakem: PLO representative in Tunis.

Darwish, Mahmoud: Member of PLO Executive Committee, chairman of PLO's Supreme Council for Culture, Heritage and Information.

Al-Dejani, Ahmed Sidki: Senior PNC member, PLO Educational and Cultural Council.

Ghosheh, Samir: Leader of the PLO's Popular Struggle Front (PSF).

Al-Ghusayn, Jawid: Member of PLO Executive Committee, head of the PLO's Palestine National Fund Department.

Habash, George: Leader of the PLO's Popular Front for the Liberation of Palestine (PFLP). He is a Christian and is known for his leftist views.

Hillal, Jamal: Director, PLO Information Bureau.

Al-Hassan, Hani: Senior advisor to Arafat, member of Fatah Central Committee.

Al-Hassan, Khaled (Abu As-Said): Senior advisor to Arafat, member of Fatah Central Committee, chairman of PNC Foreign Relations Council.

> *The Palestinian Arab people, in expressing itself through the armed Palestinian revolution, rejects every solution that is a substitute for a complete liberation of Palestine.*
> PLO National Covenant, Article 21

Hawatmeh, Noyef: Leader of the PLO's Democratic Front for the Liberation of Palestine (DFLP). He is known for his leftist views.

Jibril, Ahmed: Leader of the Popular Front for the Liberation of Palestine – General Command (PFLP-GC). He is anti-Arafat and is supported by Syria. Western reports have linked Jibril to the bombing of Pan Am Flight 103 over Lockerbie, Scotland, in December 1988. In that bombing 270 people lost their lives.

Kaddoumi, Farouk (Abu-Luft): Member of PLO Executive Committee, head of the PLO's Political Department, Secretary General of Fatah.

Kamal, Said: PLO representative in Cairo, Egypt.

Khourani, Abdullah: Member of the PLO Executive Committee, head of the PLO's Cultural Affairs Department.

Khuri, Bishop Ilya: Member of the PLO Executive Committee.

Milhem, Muhammed: Member of the PLO Executive Committee, head of the PLO's Occupied Homeland Affairs Department.

Mustafa El-Zibri, Abu Ali: Member of the PLO Executive Committee, head of the PLO's Repatriates' Affairs Department, Deputy Secretary General of PFLP.

Najab, Suleiman: Member of the PLO Executive Committee, head of the PLO's Social Affairs Department, leader of Palestine Communist Party (PCP).

Al-Natshe, Rafik (Abu-Shakir): PLO representative in Saudi Arabia, member of Fatah Central Committee.

El-Rahman, Ahmed Abd: PLO spokesman, editor of *Filastin Al-Thawrah*.

Said, Edward: PNC member, American citizen.

Al-Sayeh, Sheik Abd El-Hamid: Speaker of the PLO's "Palestine National Council" (PNC).

Sha'ath, Nabil: Senior political advisor to Arafat, chairman of PNC Political Committee.

Souss, Ibrahim: PLO representative in Paris.

Surani, Jamal: Member of the PLO Executive Committee, head of the PLO's Administrative Affairs Department.

Terzi, Zehdi Labib: PLO representative at the United Nations.

Al-Yahya, Abd Al-Razzaq: Member of PLO Executive Committee, head of the PLO's Economic Affairs and Education Departments, PLO representative in Amman, Jordan.

Zaanoun, Salim (Abul Adib): Deputy Chairman of PNC, member of Fatah Central Committee.

Fuzi Salim Ali Mahdi: Senior activist in Fatah "Force 17." His code name is Abu Hitler. His two sons are named Eichmann and Hitler.

U.S. Ambassador to Sudan Cleo Noel is laid to rest following his assassination along with the Embassy First Secretary and the Belgian Chargé d'Affaires by the Black September gang in Khartoum on March 5, 1973. Arafat was the commander of Black September. (AP)

THE PLO ORGANIZATIONS

The PLO, or Palestine Liberation Organization, was established in June 1964 as the umbrella organization for Palestinian Arab terrorist organizations. Its prime purpose was to seek, "by all available means, including armed struggle," to bring about the liquidation of Israel. Yassir Arafat heads the PLO.

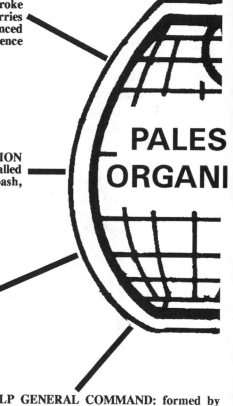

PFLP: a splinter group created by Wadia Haddad, former PFLP chief of foreign operations, when he broke with Habash in 1975. Based in South Yemen, it carries out terrorist acts mainly in Europe. Strongly influenced by Libya, Haddad was poisoned by Iraqi intelligence agents in 1978.

PFLP – POPULAR FRONT FOR THE LIBERATION OF PALESTINE: known as the strongest of the so-called "rejection front" organizations. Led by George Habash, it categorically rejects any dialogue with Israel.

PDFLP – POPULAR DEMOCRATIC FRONT FOR THE LIBERATION OF PALESTINE: created out of another split from the PFLP in 1969 by Noyef Hawatmeh. Has a Marxist orientation.

PFLP GENERAL COMMAND: formed by Ahmed Jibril when he broke from the PFLP in 1968. Heavily influenced by Libya, it is also pro-Syrian and maintains training facilities in Syria.

PLF – PALESTINE LIBERATION FRONT: the product of a split from Jibril's General Command. Led by Ibn Mahmoud Zaidan and close to Libya and Iraq.

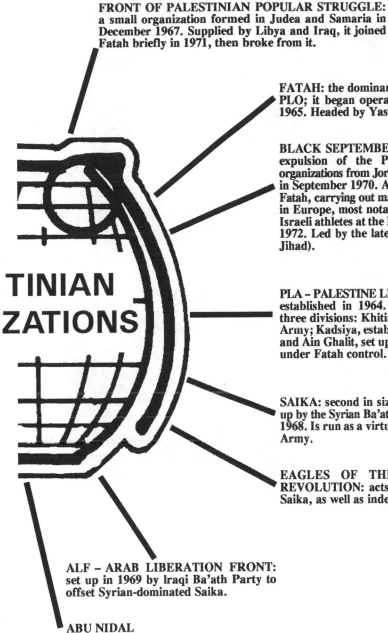

FRONT OF PALESTINIAN POPULAR STRUGGLE: a small organization formed in Judea and Samaria in December 1967. Supplied by Libya and Iraq, it joined Fatah briefly in 1971, then broke from it.

FATAH: the dominant component of the PLO; it began operating on January 1, 1965. Headed by Yassir Arafat.

BLACK SEPTEMBER: named after the expulsion of the Palestinian terrorist organizations from Jordan by King Hussein in September 1970. Acts as surrogate for Fatah, carrying out many acts of terrorism in Europe, most notably the massacre of Israeli athletes at the Munich Olympics in 1972. Led by the late Khalil Wazir (Abu Jihad).

PLA – PALESTINE LIBERATION ARMY: established in 1964. It is composed of three divisions: Khitin, within the Syrian Army; Kadsiya, established by the Iraqis; and Ain Ghalit, set up by Egypt, and now under Fatah control.

SAIKA: second in size to Fatah. Was set up by the Syrian Ba'ath Party in December 1968. Is run as a virtual unit of the Syrian Army.

EAGLES OF THE PALESTINIAN REVOLUTION: acts as a surrogate for Saika, as well as independently.

ALF – ARAB LIBERATION FRONT: set up in 1969 by Iraqi Ba'ath Party to offset Syrian-dominated Saika.

ABU NIDAL

As his companion considers the damage caused by a Katyusha rocket attack, this young resident of Kiryat Shmona picks up a trowel, ready to help with the rebuilding. This north Galileean town was a favorite target of the PLO and sustained heavy civilian casualities prior to "Operation Peace for Galilee." *(Israel Sun)*

WHAT IS THE PLO REALLY AFTER?

George Habash, leader of the Popular Front for the Liberation of Palestine (PFLP), the second-largest faction in the PLO: "We seek to establish a state which we can use in order to liberate the other part of the Palestinian state" *(Al-Hadaf,* PFLP organ, Damascus, April 9, 1989).

Noyef Hawatmeh, leader of the Democratic Front for the Liberation of Palestine (DFLP), the third-largest faction in the PLO: "The popular revolution in Palestine will continue the struggle to expel the Zionist occupation from all the Palestinian Arab soil, from the [Jordan] River to the [Mediterranean] Sea" (Jamahiriya News Agency, Libya, April 19, 1989).

Rafik al-Natshe, member of the Central Committee of Fatah: "Our return to Palestine and our victory will be possible only with the help of Allah. We shall return to Faluja, Jaffa, and Haifa" (Saudi News Agency, January 2, 1989).

Saleh Khalef (Abu Iyad), second to Arafat in the PLO hierarchy: "At first a small state, and with the help of Allah, it will be made large, and expand to the east, west, north, and south . . . I am interested in the liberation of Palestine, step by step" (*Al-Anba*, Kuwait, December 18, 1988).

The Palestinian emblem in a slightly different form: depicting the PLO's goal to liberate the entire west side of Palestine, including all of Israel. Fatah is the main branch of the PLO. The chairman of Fatah is Yassir Arafat. (Fatah, or "occupation," means the occupation of the whole of Palestine.)

PLO recruit tramples the Star of David underfoot in this poster found in Beirut, in August 1982. (Government Post Office)

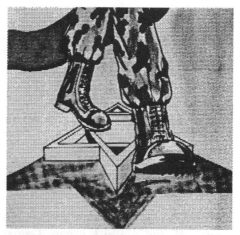

SCHOOL CHILDREN

Victims of the PLO attack on the bus carrying the children of Moshav Avivim to school in northern Galilee on May 20, 1970. Nine pupils and three teachers were killed and nineteen children wounded. The Ahmed Jibril front claimed responsibility. *(Israel Sun)*

PART II

JEWISH AND PALESTINIAN ARAB STATES EXIST IN PALESTINE

CHAPTER SEVEN

JORDAN IS PALESTINE

> *Palestine is Jordan and Jordan is Palestine; there is one people and one land, with one history and one and the same fate.*
> PRINCE HASSAN,
> Jordanian National Assembly,
> February 2, 1970

> *There should be a kind of linkage because Jordanians and Palestinians are considered by the PLO as one people.*
> FAROUK KADDOUMI,
> head of the PLO Political Department,
> *Newsweek*, March 14, 1977

THE PALESTINIAN COMPONENTS OF JORDAN

Culturally, linguistically, religiously, demographically, geographically, and historically, Jordan is a Palestinian Arab state in every respect.

All non-Jewish inhabitants in the area conquered by Jordan in 1948 were granted Jordanian citizenship, and there was free and unhampered movement between the areas on the two sides of the river. Over 400,000 Palestinian Arabs from Judea and Samaria moved east of the Jordan River – mainly to be closer to Amman, Jordan's capital, and the improved social and economic opportunities offered there. Ethnic, social, religious and linguistic similarities between the Arab populations on both sides of the river, and the extremely short distance, made these migrations merely a "change of address" as one writer put it.

◆ Do you know that Jordan occupies almost 77 percent of the original Palestine mandate?

◆ Do you know that more than two-thirds of Jordan's people – nearly 2 million citizens – are Palestinians?

◆ Do you know that the majority of citizens residing in Amman, the Jordanian capital, are Palestinians?

◆ Do you know that King Hussein sent a delegation to the Geneva Conference in December 1973, two-thirds of which were Palestinians?

◆ Do you know that the Jordanian citizenship law number 6 of February 4, 1954, granted Jordanian nationality to residents of Judea and Samaria which had been illegally annexed to Jordan?

◆ Do you know that Paragraph 3 of this law states: "Any man will be a Jordanian subject . . . if he is not Jewish?"

◆ Do you know that three-fourths of Jordan's government appointments, including Cabinet posts, are held by Palestinians?

> *The partitioning of Palestine in 1947 and the establishment of Israel are fundamentally null and void . . . the liberation of Palestine will destroy the Zionist and imperialist presence . . .*
> PLO National Covenant, Articles 19 and 22

◆ Do you know that half of Jordan's prime ministers since 1950 have been Palestinian?

◆ Do you know that a majority of Jordan's army and other security forces are Palestinian?

> *The Palestinians here constitute not less than one half the members of the armed forces. They and their brothers, the sons of Transjordan constitute the members of one family who are equal in everything, in rights and duties.*
> KING HUSSEIN, Amman Radio,
> February 3, 1973

◆ Do you know that Palestinians have invigorated Jordan's economy and control 70 percent of its businesses?

◆ Do you know that the *New York Times* has called Jordan's capital "the greatest Palestinian city in the world"?

◆ Do you know that with a population density of less than 61 per square mile, it has ample room for all of those who choose to live among their own people in their own homeland?

◆ Do you know that the ethnic-social-religious-linguistic affinity between the populations on the two sides of the river, and the short distance (only 45 miles from Nablus to Amman), made these migrations not so much an uprooting as a move from one part of Palestine to the other?

One additional historical point illuminates the special role of Jordan as a homeland for the Palestinians. Between 1948 and 1967, when Jordan held the area known as the West Bank, massive emigration took place from that area to the East Bank. As a result of this movement, the West Bank population was reduced from 62 percent of the population of the Kingdom of Jordan in 1948 to 38 percent on the eve of 1967. This was natural, of course, because Transjordan was part of Palestine – its land, its environment, its language, its culture and its religion.

PALESTINE: BRITISH MANDATE AND THE FIRST PARTITION

Following the First World War, the Palestinian Arabs exerted severe pressure on the British government and the League of Nations. The Arabs called upon Britain to cancel the Balfour Declaration and the establishment of a national home for the Jews in Palestine. The Palestinian Arabs used arms to prove their intentions. Forgotten Palestine became a subject of hot debate between the British, the Jews and the Palestinian Arabs.

Q: What is Palestine?
A: The geopolitical entity to which the Romans in the second century CE gave the name "Palestina" entered history as the sovereign homeland of the Jewish nation more than 3,800 years ago. Since that time, Jews have continually lived there, though often under foreign conquerors.
Q: What has been the common denominator in Palestine?
A: For over 3,800 years the one common demographic denominator in Palestine has been the Jews. No other ethnic or national community, except the Jews, has claimed Palestine/Israel as its distinctive home.

> *My heart is in the East [Jerusalem], yet I am in the West [Spain].*
> *How can I chew my food or enjoy it?*
> YEHUDA HALEVI,
> Jewish poet (1080–1140)

Q: What is the meaning of the name "Palestine"?

A: Until the early twentieth century, Palestine was considered a geographic concept, covering the area both west and east of the Jordan River. The term "Palestinian" must therefore refer to all the inhabitants of this area.

Q: So who is considered a Palestinian?

A: The "right of self-determination for the Palestinians" is a right to which Palestinian Jews as well as Palestinian Arabs are entitled and which both, in fact, have attained, the Jews in Israel and the Palestinians in Jordan.

Q: Why did the League of Nations grant the mandate over Palestine to Great Britain?

A: In 1922, recognizing the "historical connection of the Jewish people with Palestine" and "the grounds for reconstituting their national home in that country," the League of Nations decided to grant Britain a mandate over Palestine, pending the establishment there of a Jewish national home.

Q: What did Britain do then?

A: One of Britain's first acts was to divide Palestine, giving over 77 percent to the Emir Abdullah. In 1946, Britain granted independence to Transjordan, later renamed Jordan. King Abdullah originally had wanted to call his country "Palestine" but was persuaded that the name "Jordan" would emphasize the King's rule over both banks of that river.

> *Those fishing in troubled waters will not succeed in dividing our people, which extends to both sides of the [River] Jordan, in spite of the artificial boundaries established by the Colonial Office and Winston Churchill half a century ago.*
> YASSIR ARAFAT to Eric Roleau

Q: What was the meaning of the Jewish claim?

A: The Jewish claim to Palestine, after the First World War, was universally understood to encompass the territory that now comprises Israel, the West Bank, and Jordan.

Q: What was the size of the Jewish national home in comparison to the territory given to the Arabs?

A: The territory given to the Arabs was more than 100 times greater in area and hundreds of times richer in resources than the Palestine designated for the Jewish national home.

Q: What was the meaning of the division of Palestine?

A: The division meant that in the greater part of Palestine – the area east of the Jordan River – the right of Palestinian Arabs to self-determination was realized.

Q: What happened to the remaining 23 percent of Palestine?

A: The Jews' right to self-determination in the remaining 23 percent of Palestine was not to be granted so readily. Arab militants, through terror and intimidation, opposed the fulfillment of Jewish national aspirations in any part of Palestine whatsoever.

A STATE FOR PALESTINIAN ARABS?

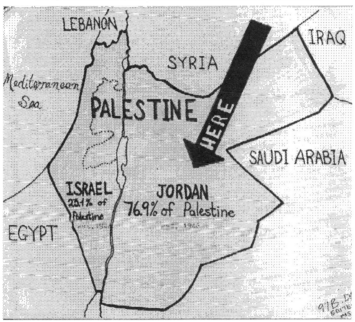

Jordan is Palestine and Palestine is Jordan. There is one people and one land, a common history and a common fate.
PRINCE HASSAN,
Jordan's National Assembly,
February 2, 1970

Let's not forget that the east bank of the Jordan River [Jordan], where 70 percent of the residents are Palestinians, belongs to the Palestinian nation.
Shuon Filastinya, PLO journal,
February 1970

> *Palestinian Arabs control over 75 percent of the Jordanian economy*
>
> *Al-Ahram*, Egyptian daily,
> March 5, 1976
>
> ---
>
> *Palestine, with its British mandate boundaries on both banks of the Jordan, is one unit that is inseparable.*
>
> Palestinian Covenant, Article 2
>
> ---
>
> *The two nations [the Jordanian and the Palestinian] are, in fact, one.*
>
> KING HUSSEIN,
> Jordanian television,
> October 10, 1977

THE MIDDLE EAST NEEDS PEACE, NOT A SECOND PALESTINIAN STATE

Q: What was Palestine prior to the Balfour Declaration?

A: Mark Twain, who visited Palestine in 1867, wrote, in *The Innocents Abroad*: " . . . [a] desolate country whose soil is rich enough, but is given over wholly to weeds – a silent mournful expanse . . . A desolation is here that not even imagination can grace with the pomp of life and action . . . We never saw a human being on the whole route . . . There was hardly a tree or a shrub anywhere. Even the olive and the cactus, those fast friends of a worthless soil, had almost deserted the country."

Q: Are the Arabs correct in their claim that the Jews usurped the land from the Arabs in Palestine?

A: No. The British Royal Commission, which came to Palestine at the end of 1936, published its findings in July 1937: "The Arab charge that the Jews have obtained too large a proportion of good land cannot be maintained. Much of the land now carrying orange groves was sand dunes or swamp and uncultivated when it was purchased . . . there was at the time at least of the earlier sales little evidence that the owners possessed either the resources or training needed to develop the land."

According to figures from a 1948 British *Survey of Palestine*, the lands that made up the State of Israel included: 8.6 percent land owned by resident Jews; 3.3 percent land owned by resident Arabs; 16.9 percent abandoned by Arabs told to leave by Arab leaders; and 71.2 percent Crown Lands inherited by the Mandatory Government from Turkey. In 1948, it passed to the Government of Israel as its legal heir.

> *I wish to explain to the delegates that the claim just made by the representative of Israel, in speaking about the union between people of Jordan and Palestine, is true in the sense that we form part of the same nation and that the historical links between the Palestinian people in Jordan and those in Palestine go back very far . . .*
>
> K. OBEIDAT, Jordan's representative
> to the United Nations, November 29, 1979

PALESTINE, THE UNITED NATIONS, AND THE SECOND PARTITION

> *The Palestinians and the Jordanians have created on this soil since 1948 one family – all of whose children have equal rights and obligations.*
>
> KING HUSSEIN,
> to the U.S. delegation in Amman,
> February 19, 1975

The first partition of Palestine of 1922 was not the end. The Palestinian Arabs opposed the establishment of the Jewish Homeland on any part of Palestine. They demanded that Palestine be an Arab state. They called upon the League of Nations in general and Great Britain in particular to nullify the Balfour Declaration and the mandate over Palestine. They called upon Britain to stop the sale of land to the Jews, to end Jewish immigration to Palestine and to allow the establishment of an Arab government in Palestine.

When their demands were not met, the Palestinian Arabs started to oppose the Jewish national home by force. There were riots against the Jews in Palestine in 1920, 1921, 1929, 1933, 1936-39, and 1947-48.

The riots of 1936-39 are referred to by the Palestinian Arabs as "The big Arab revolt" – *Altawra Alarabiyya Alkubrah*. Thousands of people were killed or wounded, mostly Palestinian Arabs – victims at the hands of other Palestinian Arabs. The British government sent a Royal committee, the Peel Committee, to Palestine in order to study the situation and to make its recommendation. The committee published its recommendations on July 7, 1937. The Peel Committee proposed the partition of the west side of Palestine into two states, one Jewish and the other Arab. The Jews accepted the partition; the Arabs rejected it.

Q: When did the riots of 1936-39 end?
A: They ended when World War II broke out.
Q: What happened during the war?
A: The leader of the Palestinian Arabs, Haj Muhammed Amin al-Husseini, cooperated with Hitler. The Jewish national home helped the Allies to defeat the Nazis.

> *The Palestinian Arabs . . . demand for a separate Arab state in Palestine is . . . relatively weak. It would seem as though, in existing circumstances, most of the Palestinian Arabs would be quite content to be incorporated into Transjordan.*
> FOLKE BERNADOTTE,
> United Nations mediator in Palestine,
> in *To Jerusalem*

Q: What happened during the war?
A: The Palestine arena was quiet. Both sides awaited the results of the war. The Jews wanted an Allied victory, the Palestinian Arabs preferred the Nazis.
Q: What happened after the war?
A: The Palestine issue gained momentum. The liquidation of European Jewry raised sympathy for the Jews and the Jewish national home. The United Nations sent a delegation to Palestine to investigate the situation, and to make recommendations. The committee recommended the partition of Palestine. Once again the Arabs rejected partition and the Jews accepted.
Q: When was the second partition?
A: On November 29, 1947, the United Nations sought to settle the conflict by another division (this time of western Palestine) into Jewish and Arab states.
Q: When was Israel established?
A: In May 1948 Jewish Palestine (Israel) proclaimed its independence.
Q: What was the Arab reaction?
A: The neighboring Arab states joined in a massive assault on the newly established State of Israel.

112

> *Palestine and Transjordan are one, for Palestine is the coast-*
> *line and Transjordan the hinterland of the same country.*
>
> KING ABDULLAH,
> Arab League meeting,
> Cairo, April 12, 1948
>
> ---
>
> *Let us not forget the East Bank of the [River] Jordan,*
> *where seventy percent of the inhabitants belong to the Palestin-*
> *ian nation.*
>
> GEORGE HABASH,
> leader of the PFLP of the PLO,
> *Shuon Filastinya*, PLO publication,
> February 1970

Q: What is the composition of the majority of Jordan's population?

A: Today, Jordan's population – even without the western area it lost in its abortive attack on Israel in 1967 – is still composed mostly of Arabs of west-Palestinian origin (the rest are Arabs of east-Palestinian origin).

Q: Is Jordan Palestine, according to King Hussein?

A: Yes. As Jordan's King Hussein said in an interview for the Paris-based *An-Nahar Al Arabi W'al-Daouli* on December 26, 1981: "The truth is that Jordan is Palestine and Palestine is Jordan."

In days of old, Samaria became the capital of the northern kingdom, Israel, as Jerusalem was the capital of the southern kingdom, Judah or Judea. *Shemer* means "guard," "preserve," or "watch." The mountain ridges of Samaria, named after Shemer, geographically guard western Israel, as well as the Jordan rift valley to the east. They form the geographic heart of the Jewish homeland.

A typical manifestation of the prevalent feelings of the Palestinians about the connections between the two banks of the Jordan River can be found in the words of Ishaq El-Dazdar, a candidate for the House of Representatives who, during the election campaign in 1962, said: "It is said that we joined the east bank, but the truth is that it is the east bank which has joined us. We are Palestinians and the Jordanian is Palestinian whether he likes it or not."

THE ARABS THEMSELVES SAY
JORDAN IS PALESTINE

Jordan is 76.9 percent of historic Palestine and the majority of its population are Palestinian Arabs. Doesn't that make Jordan a Palestinian homeland? Today the territory of Palestine consists of: (a) an Arab state called Jordan, 76.9 percent; (b) a Jewish state called Israel, 17.8 percent; and (c) a disputed area called Judea, Samaria, and the Gaza Strip, 5.3 percent.

President Bourguiba of Tunisia said in a public statement in July 1973: "With all respect to King Hussein, I suggest that the Emirate of Transjordan was created from whole cloth by Great Britain, which for this purpose cut up ancient Palestine. To this desert territory to the east of the Jordan [River], it gave the name Transjordan. But there is nothing in history which carries this name, While since our earliest time there was Palestine and Palestinians. I maintain that the matter of Transjordan is an artificial one, and that Palestine is the basic problem. King Hussein should submit to the wishes of the people, in accordance with the principles of democracy and self-determination, so as to avoid the fate of his grandfather, Abdullah, or of his cousin, Feisal, both of whom were assassinated."

From a commentary broadcast by Radio Amman, June 30, 1980, came this: "Along these lines, the West German *Der Spiegel* magazine cited Dr. George Habash, leader of one of the Palestinian organizations, as saying that 70 percent of Jordan's population are Palestinians and that the power in Jordan should be seized."

The Egyptian newspaper *Al-Ahram* on March 5, 1976, reported: "Palestinian Arabs control over 75 percent of Jordan's economy."

King Hussein was quoted in *An-Nahar,* Beirut, August 24, 1972: "We consider it necessary to clarify to one and all, in the Arab world and outside, that the Palestinian people with its nobility and conscience is to be found here on the East Bank, the West Bank and the Gaza Strip. Its overwhelmingly majority is here and nowhere else."

> *[The PLO] will struggle with the Jordanian national forces for the establishment of a Jordanian Palestine national front whose aim is the establishment of a national democratic government that will be established as a result of our struggle.*
>
> Article 5 of the ten-point program
> of the Palestine National Council,
> reconvened in Cairo, June 6-8, 1974

Article 2 of the PLO Covenant states: "Palestine with the boundaries it had during the British mandate is an indivisible unit."

> *We cannot think of recognition [of Israel] because this would mean conceding a part of our lands. Our intermediate goal is the creation of an independent Palestinian state on all parts of our land that will be liberated. There have been similar developments in the world. In Vietnam for example, the Vietnamese decided on the creation of North Vietnam, and after ten years they liberated South Vietnam.*
>
> FAROUK KADDOUMI,
> head of the PLO Political Department,
> Voice of Palestine, July 2, 1977

The Arab claim was satisfied when 12 Arab states, including two Yemens – North Yemen and South Yemen – and one Palestinian Arab state, Jordan, were created in the aftermath of the First World War. Eight more were created after World War II.

> *Jordan is ours, Palestine is ours, and we shall build our national entity on the whole of this land after having freed it of both the Zionist presence and the reactionary traitor's [i.e., King Hussein's] presence.*
>
> YASSIR ARAFAT,
> "A Letter to Jordanian Student Congress
> in Baghdad," as reported in the
> *Washington Post*, November 12, 1974

Abu Iyad, Arafat's deputy, also confessed, in Jordan's *Al-Rai* on December 11, 1989, that Jordan is Palestine: "I say that as soon as the Palestinian state is proclaimed on the very next day that state will unite with Jordan . . . That is because we are one people with one history. You cannot differentiate between a Jordanian and a Palestinian . . ."

THE SOLUTION: CAMP DAVID

Judea, Samaria, and the Gaza Strip being integral parts of the historic Jewish homeland, as recognized by the League of Nations in 1922, Israel reserves the full right to claim sovereignty over these areas. In consideration, however, of the negotiating process set forth in the Camp David Agreements, it has not exercised this right by incorporating them into the state or applying Israeli law to them. Israel offers a ray of hope – the Camp David Agreements.

Q: What is the problem?
A: The problem is not the absence of a homeland for the Palestinians. The homeland exists and in it both Arabs and Jews have found national self-expression. The problem now focuses on a 2,200-square-mile area called Judea and Samaria, whose political future is yet to be determined. And that is where the two-part Camp David Agreements come in.
Q: What is the Camp David solution?
A: The Camp David autonomy plan, negotiated by Israel, Egypt, and the United States in 1978, is an interim measure – a transition stage between the present situation and the permanent status of Judea, Samaria, and the Gaza district to be worked out in negotiations towards the end of the five-year transitional period.
Q: Why is a transition stage necessary?
A: With over 70 years of hostility between the parties, this interim period is extremely important to build up mutual confidence, tolerance, and understanding, as well as to try out new political arrangements.

> *The war of attrition against the Zionist enemy will never cease . . . It is in my interest to have a war in the region, because I believe that the only remedy for the ills of the Arab nation is a true war against the Zionist enemy.*
> YASSIR ARAFAT,
> *Al-Destour,* Lebanon, December 26, 1983

Q: What did Israel do to prove its desire for peace?
A: So far, it has been Israel that has made the lion's share of material, social, economic, and strategic concessions in order to make the realization of the Camp David Agreements possible. In April 1982, Israel voluntarily gave Egypt the entire strategic 150-mile-wide Sinai Peninsula, for an Egyptian-Israeli peace based on those agreements.

Q: Can Israel give up the Camp David Accords?

A: No. Having staked everything on a settlement based on the Camp David peace package, which includes the autonomy plan, Israel cannot now be expected to re-negotiate its future and that of the region on the basis of new "peace plans" containing provisions that had been deliberately excluded from the Camp David Agreements.

"Israel stands by its right and its claim of sovereignty to Judea, Samaria and the Gaza district. In the knowledge that other claims exist, it proposes, for the sake of the agreement and the peace, that the question of sovereignty in these areas be left open." The preceding proposal of Israel in December 1977 was for the establishment of autonomy for the Arab inhabitants of the areas in question. This proposal later became part of the understanding central to the Camp David Agreements, concluded in September 1978.

Q: What is the spirit of the Camp David Accords?

A: The formula for a peaceful resolution of the conflict is there. Its principle ingredients are mutual recognition, direct negotiation, and the determination to abandon war as an instrument of policy and to embark on the road to peace. It is a formula that works: it has worked for Israel and Egypt.

Q: Can the Camp David Accords apply to other sides as well?

A: Yes. With a measure of good will and a genuine aspiration for peace, it can be adapted – with changes as appropriate in each case – to other states in the region, states that so far have shown no inclination to join the peace process.

Q: Who will negotiate the ultimate disposition of Judea, Samaria, and the Gaza Strip?

A: Under Camp David, the final disposition of Judea, Samaria, and Gaza is to be made, after a three-year "running in" period for the autonomy, through negotiations conducted among representatives of Israel, Egypt, Jordan, and the inhabitants of those areas.

Q: Did Egypt and Israel reach any progress in their negotiations to establish such an autonomy?

A: Yes. The words of PLO leader Yassir Arafat will supply the answer. In a PLO document of November 13, 1979 (a talk between Andrei Gromyko and Arafat in Moscow), he said: "We have to admit that the talks held between Burg [representative of Israel] and Mustafa Khalil [representative of Egypt], resulted in Khalil's agreement, according to Sadat's instructions, to the autonomy plan. So they reached some almost final agreements except for Jerusalem, state land and natural resources. These subjects were left for a later date."

Q: What is Israeli Prime Minister Shamir's initiative of May 1989?

A: Mr. Shamir's approach calls for talks with the Palestinians to set up elections for local officials in Judea, Samaria, and the Gaza Strip. Once elected, these officials would then negotiate with Israel the terms for limited autonomy. Later, the two sides would address the final status of the areas in question.

In concluding peace with Egypt, Israel sacrificed the strategic depth afforded by the Sinai Peninsula. It also gave up the Sinai oil fields, which provided a substantial proportion of the country's energy needs, and a number of vital airfields. The enormous risks thus taken indicate the lengths to which Israel was prepared to go for peace.

Dry Bones

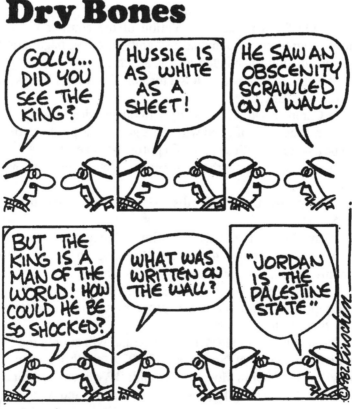

Copyright © 1982 Kirschen, *Jerusalem Post*

CHAPTER EIGHT

JEWS – THE LEGAL OWNERS OF PALESTINE

يَٰقَوْمِ ادْخُلُوا الْأَرْضَ الْمُقَدَّسَةَ الَّتِي كَتَبَ اللّٰهُ لَكُمْ

وَلَا تَرْتَدُّوا عَلَىٰ أَدْبَارِكُمْ فَتَنْقَلِبُوا خَٰسِرِينَ

And Moses said to his people . . . "O my people, enter the Holy Land which Allah has ordained for you and do not turn back, for then you will turn losers."

The Koran, *Sura el-Maida*,
Chapter 5, Verse 20

PALESTINE: TO WHOM DOES IT BELONG?

◆ Do you know that for over 3,800 years, the Jewish people have continually resided in Palestine? The Jews called it Eretz Yisrael – the Land of Israel.

◆ Do you know that neither Palestinians, Arabs, nor any other nation, except the Jews, claimed Palestine to be their national home?

◆ Do you know that the name "Palestine" was a Roman invention? The Romans did so in order to eradicate the close ties of the Jewish people with the Land of Israel.

I was glad when they said to me, let us go into the house of the Lord. When our feet stood within the gate of Jerusalem. O, Jerusalem built as a city that is compact together.

Psalms 122:1-3

✦ Do you know that since that time, the Jews have never forgotten the Land of Israel? They come from all over the world to visit the land, to live, and then to die in it. Other people also lived in it, but none of them ever claimed that the land was theirs or Jerusalem their capital.

> *I really wish the Jews in Judea, an independent nation.*
> U.S. President JOHN ADAMS,
> in a letter to M. Noah, Washington, D.C., 1818

✦ Do you know that the name "Jerusalem" is mentioned 628 times in the Bible?

> *Pray for the peace of Jerusalem. They who love thee should prosper, peace be with thy walls and prosperity within your palaces.*
> Psalms 122: 6-7

✦ Do you know that according to Islam, Jerusalem is only third in its holiness after Mecca and Medina – *"Awwal Alqiblatany Wataleth Alharamayny"*? For the Jews, Jerusalem is the holiest city and is the very soul of the Jewish people.

> *If I forget thee, oh Jerusalem, let my right hand forget its cunning, let my tongue cleave to the roof of my mouth.*
> Psalms 137: 5-7

✦ Do you know that Palestine is both banks of the Jordan River?
✦ Do you know that the East Bank is a Palestinian state and is called today Jordan?
✦ Do you know that Emir Abdullah, former ruler of Jordan and the late grandfather of Jordan's present king, Hussein, wanted to call his state Palestine? Only under British pressure did he agree to name it Jordan.
✦ Do you know that the Palestinian State – Jordan – is about 77 percent of mandatory Palestine?

> *It is only for tactical reasons that we carefully stress our Palestinian identity, for it is in the national interest of the Arabs to encourage a separate Palestinian identity to counter Zionism: The founding of a Palestinian state is a new tool in the ongoing battle against Israel.*
> ZOHAIR MOHSIN,
> PLO Executive Council member,
> *Trouw* (Netherlands), March 31, 1977

> *After being forcibly exiled from its Land, the people kept faith with it throughout its dispersion, and never ceased to pray and hope for its return to it and for the restoration in it of its political freedom.*
>
> Declaration of the Establishment of
> the State of Israel, May 14, 1948

THE INTERNATIONAL COMMUNITY'S RECOGNITION OF JEWISH RIGHTS TO PALESTINE

> *The establishment in Palestine of a national home for the Jewish people in recognition of the historical connection of the Jewish people with Palestine and to the grounds for reconstituting their national home in that country.*
>
> Preamble to the
> British Mandate for Palestine
> given to England by the League of Nations (1920)

◆ Do you know that the Balfour Declaration recognized the rights of the Jewish people to Palestine? The Balfour Declaration reads: "His Majesty's Government views with favour the establishment in Palestine of a national home for the Jewish people, and will use their best endeavours to facilitate the achievement of this object." (November 2, 1917)

◆ Do you know that the term "Arab" is not mentioned at all in the declaration?

◆ Do you know that while for the Jews the declaration speaks of national rights, for non-Jews it speaks of civil and religious rights alone?

◆ Do you know that after the First World War the League of Nations adopted the Balfour Declaration and asked Great Britain to agree to have the mandate on Palestine in order to fulfill the Balfour Declaration?

◆ Do you know that Palestine, which was promised to the Jews, was merely a very small portion of the area that was taken from the Ottoman Turks and given to the Arabs?

◆ Do you know that the aspirations of the Arab national movement were fulfilled in Cairo, Baghdad, Damascus, Riyadh, etc.?

✦ Do you know that there are 21 Arab states and only one tiny Israel?

✦ Do you know that Israel's area totals 8,299 square miles while the 21 Arab states total 5,300,000 square miles? The Arab states are 640 times the size of Israel with Judea, Samaria, and the Gaza Strip.

✦ Do you know that the Arab world in combined territory is twice as big as the United States?

✦ Do you know that after the First World War, the Palestinian Arabs declared that Palestine is Southern Syria – *Surya Algianubyya*?

✦ Do you know that the term "Palestinian" applies not only to Palestinian Arabs, but to Palestinian Jews as well?

✦ Do you know that in 1922 Britain gave 77 percent of Palestine to Emir Abdullah to establish the Emirate of Jordan?

✦ Do you know that the rights of self-determination in Palestine applies to Jews and Arabs? Both nations have attained it – the Jews in Israel and the Palestinian Arabs in Jordan. Jordan and Israel are mandatory Palestine.

✦ Do you know that the Emirate of Jordan gained its independence in 1946 and became the Palestine state of Transjordan?

The Land of Israel is intertwined far more intimately into the religious and historical memories of the Jewish people; for their connection with the country . . . has been continuous from the second millennium BCE up to modern times – and their religious literature is more intimately connected with its history, its climate and its soil. The Land, therefore, has provided an emotional centre which has endured through the whole of their period of "exile" and has led to constant returns or attempted returns culminating in our own day in the Zionist Movement.

Dr. JAMES PARKES,
British historian and theologian,
Whose Land?

✦ Do you know that Judea, Samaria, and Gaza are only 5,720 square kilometers or 2,200 square miles?

✦ Do you know that Jordan's King Hussein, Yassir Arafat, and all the PLO leaders have declared time and again that Jordan is Palestine and that Palestine is Jordan?

✦ Do you know that the only English-language daily newspaper in Israel today, the *Jerusalem Post,* was known as the *Palestine Post* prior to the establishment of the state in 1948?

> *[Judaism is] tied to the history of a single people and the geographic actuality of a single land.*
>
> Dr. JAMES PARKES,
> British historian and theologian,
> *Whose Land?*

◆ Do you know that in 1950 the independent Palestinian state of Transjordan became known as the Hashemite Kingdom of Jordan and that it consists of about 77 percent of mandatory Palestine?

◆ Do you know that the majority of citizens in Jordan are Palestinians?

Q: What are the roots of the name "Falastin"?

A: The term "Falastin" was related to the Philistines, one of a series of conquerors of part of the Land of Israel. The Romans revived the memory of the Philistines by referring to parts of the Land of Israel as "Palestina." This was a deliberate attempt on the part of the Romans to obliterate any sign of Jewish attachment to a homeland. Following the Ottoman-Muslim occupation in 1517, Falastin was the name given to parts of the country. It was late in the nineteenth century that the whole western side of the country was referred to as Falastin.

> *This right was recognized in the Balfour Declaration of 2 November 1917, and reaffirmed in the Mandate of the League of Nations, which, in particular, gave international sanction to the historic connection between the Jewish people and the Land of Israel and to the right of the Jewish people to rebuild its national home.*
>
> Declaration of the Establishment of
> the State of Israel, May 14, 1948

ARAB RESISTANCE TO THE
JEWISH PRESENCE IN PALESTINE

> *. . . Jews strove in every successive generation to re-establish themselves in their ancient homeland. In recent years they returned in their masses . . .*
>
> Declaration of the Establishment of
> the State of Israel, May 14, 1948

The Arab-Israeli conflict was neither about what is called Arab refugees nor about Arab occupied territories. The Arabs refused to accept Israel in their midst long before the Arab refugee problem was created and when Israel was outside the "Arab occupied territories." The Arabs' refusal to accept Israel as a sovereign state is the reason for all the troubles and bloodshed, with the subsequent death and injury of many tens of thousands – Jew and Arab alike.

The Arabs did not hide their intentions to destroy Israel.

> *The conflict with the Zionist enemy goes beyond the struggle of the countries whose territories were occupied in 1967 and involves the entire Arab nation in view of the military, political, economic and cultural danger which the Zionist enemy represents to the entire Arab nation, its fundamental nationalist interests, its civilization and destiny.*
>
> Declaration of the Baghdad Conference
> in November 1978

The Arab Palestinian refusal to face reality, and to behave accordingly, has caused hatred, enmity, and various destructive wars. Moreover, it caused severe damage to the Palestinian Arabs.

> *We, the Palestinians, lost the possible because we always demanded the impossible.*
>
> MUHAMMAD ABU SHILBAYA,
> Palestinian journalist, 1975

The leaders of the Jewish National Home between the First and Second World Wars made different and various attempts to reach a kind of compromise with the Palestinian Arabs. However, all the efforts failed. The Palestinian Arabs, under the notorious Mufti Haj Muhammed Amin al-Husseini, refused to compromise.

> *We extend our hand to all neighbouring states and their peoples in an offer of peace and good neighbourliness and appeal to them to establish bonds of cooperation and mutual help with the sovereign Jewish people settled in its own land. The State of Israel is prepared to do its share in a common effort for the advancement of the entire Middle East.*
>
> Declaration of the Establishment of
> the State of Israel, May 14, 1948

Immediately after the First World War, it appeared that the Palestinian Arabs' undisputed leader tended to recognize the Jewish rights to Palestine. In a letter that Emir Faisal wrote to Felix Frankfurter on March 3, 1919, Faisal said: "The Jewish movement is nationalist and not imperialist, our movement is nationalist and not imperialist and there is room in Syria for us both." (Palestine was known as Southern Syria.)

The honest words of Emir Faisal with regard to the Jews' right to Palestine were immediately rejected by the other Palestinian leaders. After World War I, the Palestinian radicals, who rejected any compromise, became the speakers for the Palestinian Arabs.

> *. . . Palestine which, desolate for centuries, is now renewing its youth and vitality through enthusiasm, hard work, and self sacrifice of the Jewish pioneers who toil there in a spirit of peace and social justice.*
>
> U.S. President HERBERT HOOVER

Despite the fact that 77 percent of Palestine (Jordan) promised to the Jews was given to the Arabs, the Palestinian Arabs of the West Bank of Jordan resisted the establishment of the Jewish national home in Palestine (the remaining 23 percent).

In Genesis 29:35 it is written that Leah bore four sons to Jacob (whose name was to be changed to Israel): "And she conceived again, and bore a son. And she said, 'Now will I praise the Lord': Therefore she called his name Judah . . ." The Hebrew root of "praise" and "Judah" is the same. The name Judah, Judea, or Yehuda in Hebrew comes from the same linguistic root as the word "odeh," which means "I will praise." The word "todah," meaning "thank you," has the same root. Thus the root of the name of the land of Judea, and its people, Judeans, means something close to "praise" or "thanks" and relates to the birth of Jacob and Leah's fourth son.

125

✦ Do you know that the Palestinian Arabs, under the leadership of the pro-Nazi collaborator Haj Amin al-Husseini, conducted a policy of hatred and hostility against the British forces in general and the Jewish national home in particular in the years between the two World Wars?

> *The Palestinian people will achieve an independent Palestinian state which will be the start of the liberation of the entire homeland. This is the beginning of liberation and not its consummation; there will be no halt along the borders of that state. The rise of the Palestinian state shall be the beginning of the end of Israel.*
>
> ABU IYAD, Arafat's deputy
> in Fatah, November 1984

✦ Do you know that the Palestinian Arab opposition to the Jewish national home caused the death and injury of many thousands of Jews and Arabs in Palestine?

✦ Do you know that the Palestinian Arabs rioted against the Jews in Palestine in the years: 1920, 1921, 1929, 1933, 1936-39, and 1948? The Arabs demanded the end of Jewish immigration to Palestine, to stop the sale of land to the Jews, and the establishment of an Arab Palestinian State.

✦ Do you know that in the riots of 1936-39 more Palestinian Arabs killed Palestinian Arabs than Jews were killed by Palestinian Arabs?

JUDEA AND SAMARIA AND INTERNATIONAL LAW

> *There is, I think, an open question as to who has legal right to the West Bank.*
>
> CYRUS VANCE,
> Secretary of State, at a Washington
> press conference, July 28, 1977
>
> *The West Bank clearly was not and is not the sovereign territory of Jordan, from whom Israel took it in a war of self-defense in 1967. The West Bank is an integral part of the Palestine mandate within which a Jewish national home was to be created. In this sense, the territory must be considered today to*

> *be unallocated territory.*
>
> WILLIAM O'BRIEN,
> *Washington Star,*
> November 26, 1978
>
> *And he bought the hill Samaria from Shemer for two talents of silver and built on the hills, and called the name of the city which he built after the name of Shemer, owner of the hill Samaria.*
> Kings I 16:24

With regard to the legal status of Judea, Samaria, and the Gaza Strip, three points should be made clear:

1. Israel does not recognize any foreign sovereignty, whether Jordanian or Egyptian, over these areas.
2. Israel maintains that these areas are no-man's land in dispute and are open for negotiation.
3. Israel does not consider these areas to be occupied.

Israel's former ambassador to the United Nations, Professor Yehuda Blum, has explained the legal basis for Israel's attitude thusly: (a) Jordan and Egypt illegally occupied the areas in question as a result of a war of aggression waged against Israel in 1948, and therefore did not acquire any right of sovereignty over these areas, (b) Israel acted in self-defense, and (c) since no state can produce a legal claim to these areas that is equal to that of Israel, this relative superiority of claim may be sufficient, under international law, to make Israel's possession of these areas virtually indistinguishable from that of an absolute sovereign.

However, in practical terms, and despite these legal considerations, Israel established a military government in Judea, Samaria, and Gaz, which has functioned in accordance with all internationally accepted rules.

> *The only possible geographic, demographic, and political definition of Palestine is that of the [League of Nations] Mandate, which included what are now Israel and Jordan as well as the West Bank and the Gaza Strip. The term "Palestine" applies to all the peoples who live or have a right to live in the territory – Jews, Christians, and Moslems alike. Thus the West Bank and the Gaza Strip are not "Arab" territories in the legal sense, but territories of the Mandate which have been recognized as belonging to Israel or to Jordan.*
>
> Dr. EUGENE V. ROSTOW,
> Professor of Law and Public Affairs, Yale University,
> Under-Secretary of State (1966-69),
> *Yale Studies in World Public Order*, Vol. 5, 1979

International law requires the peaceful settlement of disputes through negotiations. A country cannot perpetually violate this precept and at the same time make claims against the other party to such a dspute. Moreover, international law does not require a state to retain the status of an occupying power indefinitely, in order to accommodate the destructive policies of the state which formerly governed the disputed territory. This is especially so if the territory had changed hands as a result of a war of aggression initiated by the state which is unwilling to negotiate peace.

> *Where the prior holder of territory had seized that territory unlawfully, the State which subsequently takes that territory in the lawful exercise of self-defense, has, against that prior holder, better title.*
>
> United Nations International Law Commissions,
> *American Journal of International Law*, 1970
>
> ---
>
> *. . . and the desire of all nations shall come, and I will fill this house with glory . . . and in this place will I give peace, saith the Lord of Hosts.*
>
> the prophet HAGGAI

✦ Do you know that except for 18 years (between 1949 and 1967), when Judea and Samaria were under Jordanian control, these areas were always an integral part of the Land of Israel?

✦ Do you know that cities such as Jericho, Hebron, Bethel, Shechem, and Bethlehem in Judea and Samaria are a part of Jewish history and are as famous as Jerusalem, Jaffa, etc.?

◆ Do you know that Samaria became the capital of the northern kingdom – Israel – and Jerusalem was the capital of the southern kingdom – Judah or Judea?

> *For God will save Zion and rebuild the towns of Judah (Judea); they will be lived in, owned, and handed down to his servants's descendants.*
>
> Psalms 69:35
> _____
> *It is impossible for one who has studied at all the services of the Hebrew people to avoid the faith that they will one day be restored to their historic national home and there enter on a new and yet greater phase of their contribution to the advance of humanity.*
>
> WARREN G. HARDING,
> U.S. President, 1921-23

◆ Do you know that the sons of Jacob, one of our patriarchs, herded his flocks near the city of Shechem?

> God speaking to Abraham at Hebron: *"Look all around from where you stand, toward the north and the south, toward the east and the west. All the land you see I will give to you and your descendants forever."*
>
> Genesis 13:14-17

◆ Do you know that Judea and Samaria never belonged to Jordan? They were designated to be the second Palestinian state by the United Nations Partition Plan and were captured by the Jordanian Army in a war of aggression against Israel.
◆ Do you know that Jordan's occupation of Judea and Samaria nullified the Partition Plan?
◆ Do you know that Jordanian occupation of Judea and Samaria and its annexation of these territories in 1950 were rejected by the international community? (Only England and Pakistan recognized the annexation.)
◆ Do you know that even the Arab League rejected Jordan's annexation of Judea and Samaria?
◆ Do you know that since this territory is not Jordanian, its ultimate status remains to be determined?

> God speaking to Abraham at Shechem: *"It is to your descendants I give this land."*
>
> Genesis 12:7

✦ Do you know that Jordan, in blatant violation of the 1949 Israel-Jordan agreement and the United Nations charter, launched an attack on Israel in June 1967?

> *I had faith in Israel before it was established, I have faith in it now. I believe it has a glorious future before it – not just another sovereign nation, but as an embodiment of the great ideals of our civilization.*
>
> HARRY S. TRUMAN,
> U.S. President, 1945-53

✦ Do you know that in a legal counter-attack, Israeli forces kicked out the Jordanian forces from Judea and Samaria in the Six-Day War of 1967?

✦ Do you know that the armistice lines that divided Judea and Samaria from the rest of Israel between the years 1949 and 1967 were never meant to be permanent borders?

✦ Do you know that the armistice agreement stated that the armistice demarcation line had no standing with regard to any political settlement in the future?

✦ Do you know that Judea and Samaria are only about 30 to 35 miles wide and little more than 2,000 square miles in total area?

> *. . . as between Israel, acting defensively in 1948 and 1967, on the one hand, and her Arab neighbours, acting aggressively in 1948 and 1967, on the other, Israel has better title in the territory of what was Palestine, including the whole of Jerusalem, than do Jordan and Egypt . . .*
>
> STEPHEN SCHWEBEL,
> former legal advisor to the U.S. State Department,
> *The American Journal of International Law,*
> May 1970

> *Israel's claims to the territory are at least as good as those of Jordan, since Jordan held the territory for 19 years after a war of aggression, whereas Israel took the area in the course of a war of self-defense, so far as Jordan was concerned.*
> Dr. EUGENE ROSTOW,
> former U.S. Under-Secretary of State (1966-69),
> in a letter to the *New York Times,*
> September 15, 1983
>
> *Yes, we do want a state; every nation on earth, every normal nation, beginning with the smallest and humblest who do not claim any merit, any role in humanity's development, they all have a state of their own. That's the normal condition for a people.*
> ZEEV JABOTINSKY,
> before the Palestinian Royal Commission, 1937,
> *The Zionist Idea,* New York, 1970

THE SINAI VIS-A-VIS JUDEA AND SAMARIA

> *What we hold in common are the bonds of trust and friendship – qualities that in our eyes make Israel a great nation. No people have fought longer, struggled harder, or sacrificed more than yours in order to survive, to grow, and to live in freedom.*
> RONALD REAGAN,
> U.S. President, 1981-89
>
> *Grass withers, flowers wilt, but the word of our God remains forever. Go up on a high mountain, you who bear good tidings of Zion. Lift up your voice forcefully . . . lift it up, be not afraid, you who bear good tidings of Jerusalem. Tell the cities of Judah: Your God is here.*
> Isaiah 40:8-9

People ask why, if Israel, for the sake of peace, withdrew her forces from Sinai and returned it to Egypt, wouldn't she do the same with Judea and Samaria – i.e. return the land for the sake of peace?

One can imagine the results of the October 1973 War had the fighting erupted from the borders of June 4, 1967. In that case, the war would have been fought in Tel Aviv, Jerusalem, and other cities in Israel proper. Very probably Israel would have had no chance to repulse the Arab aggression. What saved Israel were her secure borders. The fact that the Egyptian forces were on the Suez Canal, the Jordanians were along the Jordan River, and the Syrians were deep on the Golan Heights, prevented catastrophic results. These borders are the result of Israel's war of defense of June 1967. These same borders perhaps saved Israel from annihilation in the October War of 1973.

✦ Do you know that the Sinai desert is more than ten times the size of Judea and Samaria? Sinai is desert land, almost uninhabited, thereby enabling Israel to mobilize her forces in case Egypt decides to go to war against Israel in the future.

✦ Do you know that although the Israelites wandered through the Sinai desert for forty years, Sinai was never considered part of the Land of Israel?

✦ Do you know that Judea and Samaria are an integral part of Israel?

✦ Do you know that Judea and Samaria are the bottleneck of Israel? Arab control over these areas can pose mortal danger to Israel's very existence.

> *Jewish settlements on the West Bank is an issue today only because the existence of Israel is an issue . . . The issue of Jewish settlements in the West Bank today is simply one thin layer that emanates from and partially conceals the core of the conflict, namely, the non-recognition by the Arab states of Israel's right to exist.*
>
> FRED GOTTHEIL, University of Illinois,
> to U.S. House of Representatives Committee
> on International Relations, September 12, 1977

✦ Do you know that Judea and Samaria are about 2,200 square miles and this tiny area is populated by over 870,000 Palestinians, most of whom are hostile to Israel?

✦ Do you know that before the 1967 war, the coastal strip, in which 75 percent of Israel's population and industry are located, was not wider than 9 to 15 miles?

✦ Do you know that Judea and Samaria served as a base for Jordanian aggression against Israel in 1948 and again in 1967?

✦ Do you know that whoever controls the mountainous area in Judea and Samaria also has control over the coastal strip?

◆ Do you know that Israel fulfilled the contents and spirit of United Nations Resolution 242 by giving up the entire Sinai Peninsula to the Egyptians? Sinai is the great bulk of the areas captured in Israel's defense war of 1967. Therefore, Israel has already given up most of the territories.

THE UNITED NATIONS IN THE SERVICE OF THE PLO

The following cartoons are from the Lebanese newspaper *Al-Muharrer*. The editor of the paper is Shafik Al-Hut, one of Yassir Arafat's advisors. Both cartoons date from February 1974.

The United Nations has stated: "All member states shall settle their international disputes by peaceful means." And, further: "All members shall refrain from the use of force against the territorial integrity or political independence of any state."

The PLO also has a charter, Benjamin Netanyahu, former Israeli ambassador to the UN, has reminded us. Article 19 of the Palestine National Covenant states the PLO's overall objective: "The establishment of the State of Israel is null and void, regardless of the passage of time." Article 9 reads: "Armed struggle is the only way to liberate Palestine."

The U.N. Assembly affirms the Palestinians' rights

> *There are no devout men left. Fidelity has vanished from mankind. All they do is lie to one another flattering lips, talk from a double heart.*
>
> Psalms 12:2

SETTLEMENTS IN
THE ADMINISTERED TERRITORIES

> *The charge by the [Carter] Administration at the time those settlements first started that they were illegal is false . . . All people – Moslems, Jews and Christians – are entitled to live on the West Bank.*
>
> U.S. President RONALD REAGAN,
> October 1980 press conference

Q: How many settlements are there in Judea, Samaria, and the Gaza Strip?

A: Since 1967, over 130 Jewish settlements have been established in Judea, Samaria, and the Gaza Strip.

Q: What is their population?

A: The population was approximately 70,000 as of the end of 1988. This number constitutes only 5 percent of the total population of Judea, Samaria, and the Gaza Strip.

Q: Why did Israel establish these settlements?

A: After the 1967 war, the Israeli government began to establish settlements in order to strengthen her security. Populating these areas was a reaffirmation of Jewish rights to live in all parts of the Land of Israel. This view is accepted mainly by religious and nationalistic parties in Israel, as well as by some segments of the Labor Party.

Q: What is the difference in views between the Likud and Labor Parties in this respect?

A: The Labor Party stands for confining Jewish settlements to only those areas expected to remain in Israel's hands after the conclusion of a peace treaty with the Arab states. The Likud bloc, and most of its religious allies, stand for the unqualified right of the Jews to live anywhere in these territories.

> *You will plant vineyards once more on the mountains of Samaria.*
>
> Jeremiah 31:5

Q: Why can't Israel stop the settlements?

A: William Safire supplies the answer to this question in an article in the *New York Times* of May 24, 1979. He wrote: "Sovereignty – who owns the land – is the key. Jordan claims it, the PLO claims it, and Israel, through its continued settlement policy, asserts its own claim. The moment Israel gives up its right to settle, it gives up that claim to sovereignty. If Israel were to admit it is not at least part owner, an independent Palestinian state would be born which – in this decade, at least – would be an intolerable threat to Israel's security."

There will be no confiscation or requisitioning of any private land whatsoever. Any expansion of the settlements or allocation of land to them will be done from state-owned land, after strict and detailed scrutiny by the Attorney-General.

decision adopted by the Government of Israel, October 14, 1979, to expand seven existing settlements

---

Q: What is the meaning of 130 settlements in these territories?

A: Some people are of the opinion that the rapid increase of Jewish settlements in the territories has created an irreversible situation; namely, there is no way now in which any Israeli government would give up the territories even if it would wish to do so. Others have made it clear that the final borders will be determined in negotiations between Israel and her neighbors, rather than by the location of Jewish settlements in the territories.

Q: How many new immigrants have settled in Judea and Samaria?

A: Their number is very small. "Well, in my opinion this is a side issue," said the late Egyptian president, Sadat, in reference to the Jewish settlements, on ABC-TV, August 4, 1977.

Q: Will the Jewish settlements pose an obstacle to peace in the future?

A: Not at all. Whenever people live together, in this case Jews and Arabs, they come to know and understand one another. This can only increase the chances for peace between them. On the western side of Palestine – from the Jordan River to the Mediterranean Sea – Jews and Arabs live together almost everywhere, including Judea and Samaria.

Q: Will Israel, in the long run, annex these territories?

A: No. Israel is committed to the Camp David Accords, which call for the establishment of autonomy in Judea, Samaria, and the Gaza Strip.

Q: Would the Palestinian Arabs vote for the Israeli Parliament?

A: No. The Palestinian Arabs are Jordanian citizens and they would exercise their right to vote for the Jordanian Parliament. The Jewish settlers are Israeli citizens and they would, therefore, vote for the Israeli Parliament.

Q: What will be the final status of Judea and Samaria?

A: Judea and Samaria will be neither a Palestinian state nor be annexed by Israel. They will remain autonomous areas which will be agreed upon by the Palestinian Arabs and the government of Israel.

> *The relationship between the settlements and the principle of self-determination cannot be discussed in isolation, because the settlements are but a single factor involved in negotiating peace.*
>
> U.S. Asst. Secretary of State ALFRED ATHERTON,
> before a House committee in
> Washington, D.C., October 1977

Q: Can these territories be anything other than an autonomy?

A: Yes, if the parties involved would agree on a status different from autonomy.

> *The [Benedictine] monastery owned, and still owns, land on the East Bank. One of these was, before my time, sold to Jewish pioneers. One of my confreres told me that he saw a photo of the stripped and partly mutilated bodies of the young settlers after an attack by Arabs. Now the Jews have resettled Hebron, and the above-mentioned piece of land became the nucleus of what is now the Gush Etzion. Are those settlements "illegal"?*
>
> Abbot LEO RUDLOFF, former head of
> Benedictine Monastery
> on Mount Zion in Jerusalem,
> *New York Times,* July 17, 1979
>
> ---
>
> *Zionism is the embodiment of the millennial longing of a people driven out of its country by the Roman conquest and dreaming of a "Return to Zion" – an authentic "movement of National Liberation."*
>
> ANDREI GROMYKO,
> at the United Nations, May 20, 1948

Q: Is the statement correct that the Jewish settlements in Judea and Samaria are illegal?

A: No country today has any claims of sovereignty over what used to be

Mandatory Palestine that are better than or even equal to Israel's claims.

> *Israel has an unassailable legal right to establish settlements in the West Bank. The West Bank is part of the British Mandate in Palestine which included Israel and Jordan as well as certain other territories not yet generally recognized as belonging to either country. While Jewish settlement east of the Jordan River was suspended in 1922, such settlements remained legal in the West Bank.*
>
> EUGENE V. ROSTOW of Yale University,
> *New York Times,* September 13, 1983
>
> ---
>
> *There have always been Jewish settlements on the West Bank. Hebron, a city with many ancient historical ties with Israel, had a prospering Jewish community until most of them were slaughtered during the Arab riots of 1929-1936; the rest fled.*
> Abbot LEO RUDLOFF, former head of Benedictine
> Monastery on Mount Zion in Jerusalem,
> *New York Times,* July 17, 1979

In any event, however, the rules of conduct laid down in the Geneva Convention contain no restrictions on the freedom of persons to take up residence in the area involved. It bars forcible transfers, not voluntary acts of individuals or groups. Moreover, not a single Arab resident of Judea and Samaria has been evicted as a result of the establishment of Jewish settlements.

> *Let me make one point clear: The settlements will not decide the final borders between Israel and its neighbors. The borders will be decided upon in negotiations between Israel and its neighbors.*
>
> MOSHE DAYAN, late Foreign Minister
> of Israel, United Nations General Assembly,
> October 10, 1977

Q What can be said of the claim that the settlements are an obstacle to peace?

A: According to Chaim Herzog, then-Israeli ambassador to the United Nations, in an address before the General Assembly, October 26, 1977:"For 19 years from 1948 to 1967 we were not establishing settlements in Judea, Samaria, Gaza, Sinai and the Golan, because we were not there. There was no such 'obstacle' from 1948 to 1967. Did the Arabs talk about peace, or negotiate peace?''

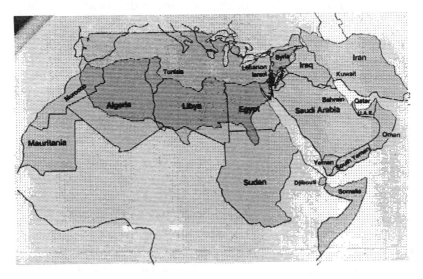

◆ THE SIZE OF THE ARAB STATES, IF WE INCLUDE IRAN, IS 5.3 MILLION SQUARE MILES.
◆ THAT'S ALMOST DOUBLE THE SIZE OF THE UNITED STATES.
◆ THE SIZE OF THE ARAB STATES IS LARGER THAN ALL EUROPE BY ONE-THIRD.
◆ THE SIZE OF ISRAEL IS 8,299 SQUARE MILES, WHICH IS ABOUT THE SAME SIZE AS NEW JERSEY – ONE OF THE SMALLER STATES IN THE UNITED STATES.
◆ THE JEWISH POPULATION IN ISRAEL IS ABOUT 3.6 MILLION. THE ARAB POPULATION IN THE ARAB STATES IS 188 MILLION. THE ARAB POPULATION IS MORE THAN 50 TIMES THE ISRAELI POPULATION.
◆ ISRAEL IS 640 TIMES SMALLER THAN THE ARAB WORLD.
◆ DEMONSTRATING ITS WILL FOR PEACE, ISRAEL TRANSFERRED THE SINAI DESERT TO EGYPT.
◆ THE SINAI DESERT ALONE IS 3 TIMES LARGER THAN ISRAEL.

THE MILITARY BALANCE IN
THE MIDDLE EAST 1988-89

Country	Population (millions)	GNP US$ Billions	1987 Defense Budget 1987 US$ Billions	Armed Forces Active	Reserves	Planes	Tanks
Syria	11.35	20.05	3.95	404,000	272,500	600	4050
Jordan	2.53	4.1	0.83	85,250	35,000	140	980
Iraq	16.28	17.7	11.58	1,000,000	650,000	500	6250
Saudi Arabia	13.1	82.4	16.23	72,300	–	182	550
Libya	4.3	18.8	1.29	71,500	40,000	525	1980
Algeria	23.76	69.1	1.24	139,000	150,000	320	950
TOTAL	71.22	212.6	35.12	1,772,050	1,147,500	2267	14,760
Israel	4.46	33.5	5.14	141,000	504,000	650	3,850
Ratio	1:16	1:6.4	1:7	1:12.6	1:2.3	1:3.5	1:4

Source: *The Military Balance 1988-1989*, International Institute for Strategic Studies, London.

PART III

ABOUT ZIONISM, ANTI-SEMITISM, AND JEWISH RIGHTS

CHAPTER NINE

IF I FORGET THEE,
O JERUSALEM!

> *If I forget thee, O Jerusalem, let my right hand lose its cunning, let my tongue cleave to the roof of my mouth.*
>
> Psalms 137:56

> *When the lord brought back the captivity of Zion we were like men in a dream. Then was our mouth filled with laughter and our tongue with singing.*
>
> Psalms 126:1-2

The opening words of Israel's Declaration of Independence in 1948 are: "ERETZ YISRAEL was the birthplace of the Jewish people. Here its spiritual, religious and political identity was shaped. Here it first attained to statehood, created cultural values of national and universal significance and gave the world the eternal Book of Books."

As these words indicate, the birth of Israel in 1948 was in fact a rebirth. The historical connection of the Jewish people with the Land of Israel goes back about 3,800 years, to the time of the Hebrew Patriarchs Abraham, Isaac, and Jacob. The longing for the land of Israel is an integral part of the Jewish spirit and history. Jews the world over dreamt about the Land of Israel, prayed for the safety of Jerusalem, and expressed in their prayer the wish to be in it.

> *Palestine is not primarily a place of refuge for the Jews . . . but the embodiment of the re-awakening corporate spirit of the whole Jewish nation . . . the Zionist movement today shows history has assigned to us the task of taking an active part in the economic and cultural reconstruction of our native land.*
>
> ALBERT EINSTEIN,
> *New York Times,* April 5, 1929

143

> *American policy toward Jerusalem is that it should remain undivided with free access to the holy sites.*
>
> U.S. President RONALD REAGAN

> *The President said that he preferred for Jerusalem to remain under Israel's sovereignty.*
>
> Official White House statement,
> September 1980, November 1981

> *Whoever mourns for Jerusalem will be privileged to see its rejoicing.*
>
> The Talmud

Q: Do the Jews mention Jerusalem in Jewish celebrations?

A: The well-known act of breaking a glass as part of the ceremony of Jewish weddings is the way in which to remember Jerusalem – namely, there can never be complete joy for the Jews as long as the Jewish Temple is not rebuilt in Jerusalem.

> *The link between a land and a people is determined not by the rule of the people over the land but the rule of the land over the people.*
>
> BENZION DINUR

> *Jewish history is a history of the land of Israel and for the land of Israel.*
>
> YEHUDA HALEVI (1075-1147),
> celebrated Jewish poet

✦ Do you know that the Jewish religion combines universal values and a particular relationship to the Jewish people and the Jewish homeland – the Land of Israel?

✦ Do you know that on Tisha B'av – the ninth day of the month of Av – the destruction of the Temple is mourned?

✦ Do you know that the burial prayer says: "May the Lord comfort you among all those that mourn for Zion and Jerusalem"?

> *You [the Jews] have prayed for Jerusalem for 2,000 years, and you shall have it.*
>
> WINSTON CHURCHILL,
> *The Times*, London, May 5, 1983

Q: How do the Jews express their commitment in prayer?

A: Three times a day the religious Jew says: "Have mercy, O Lord, and return to Jerusalem, Thy city." On Passover he says: "Next year in Jerusalem." After the meal he says: "Build Jerusalem the Holy City, speedily in our days," and during a wedding: "May Zion rejoice as her children are restored to her in joy."

Q: Does the longing find expression in literature?

A: Absolutely. Hebrew and Jewish literature in exile is imbued with a longing for the Land of Israel symbolized by Jerusalem. An example is expressed by the great poet Yehuda Halevi, who wrote: "Would that I have wings that I could wend my way to Thee, O Jerusalem."

Q: Did other nations maintain their special connection with Palestine?

A: No. Only the Jews, although in exile, maintained a special relationship to the Land of Israel, seeing it as their national home and not as a province in an Empire. The Arabs saw it as a province of Syria.

Q: How holy is Jerusalem for the Moslems?

A: For the Moslem, Jerusalem is third in holiness after Mecca and Medina.

Q: When did Jerusalem become an integral part of Israel?

A: The Israeli Knesset passed the Law and Admimistration Ordinance (Amendment No. 11), immediately upon entering the territories. Contained in this ordinance are the following words: "The law, jurisdiction and administration of the State of Israel shall extend to any area of Eretz Yisrael designated by the government by order." Under this provision, the government issued an order dated June 28, 1967, which applied the law, jurisdiction, and administration of Israel to East Jerusalem, establishing it as an integral part of the State of Israel.

Praise be unto him who transported his servant (the prophet) by night from the sacred temple of Mecca to the farther temple of Jerusalem, the circuit of which we have blessed, that we might show him some of our signs, for Allah is he who heareth, and seeth.

The Koran, *The Night Journey*, Verse 1

When the Lord brings his people home, what joy for Jacob, what happiness for Israel.

Isaiah 44:23

ZIONISM: JEWISH NATIONALISM

> *They who trust in the Lord shall be like Mount Zion which cannot be removed but abides forever.*
>
> Psalms 125:1

Simply put, Zionism is the national liberation movement of the Jewish people. Freed from Egyptian bondage, the Jewish people established the first nation-state based on the principle of ethical monotheism. Since the destruction of the second Jewish commonwealth about 1,930 years ago in Jerusalem, the fall of the Temple on Mount Zion, and the subsequent expulsion of the people from their homeland, Jews have wandered to the four corners of the earth. In the diaspora, their statelessness was translated into powerlessness, and they fell victim to crusades, pogroms, and eventually to the devastating Holocaust only forty-five years ago. Yet through it all, Zion continued to be at the center of Jewish hope and belief. In the literature, liturgy, and religious ceremonies of Judaism, Zion has always been the focus of Jewish prayer and longing.

> *The growth and progress of the new State of Israel are a source of great satisfaction to me. I had faith in Israel even before it was established. I knew it was based on the love of freedom which has been the guiding star of the Jewish people since the days of Moses.*
>
> U.S. President HARRY S. TRUMAN, 1952

Q: What is Zion?
A: Zion, actually a hill in Jerusalem, is one of the names by which Jews have always referred to their homeland, the Land of Israel (in Hebrew, Eretz Yisrael).
Q: What is the biblical meaning of "Zion"?
A: Zion is a term used in the Bible both for the Land of Israel and for its national and spiritual capital, Jerusalem.

> *For Christians to acknowledge the necessity of Judaism is to acknowledge that Judaism presupposes inextricable ties with the Land of Israel and the City of David, without which Judaism cannot be truly itself. Theologically, it is this dimension to the religion of Judaism which leads us to support the reunification of the city of Jerusalem . . .*
>
> from a statement of 16 leading U.S. theologians,
> *New York Times*, July 12, 1967

Q: What is the connection between Zion and the Jews?

A: Simply put, Zion is the birthplace of the Jewish nation. Here, this nation was politically sovereign or, at least, culturally autonomous for 1,500 years, creating and developing what has come to be known as the Judaic civilization.

Q: What is unique about Zion?

A: Zion has had a continuous Jewish population for thousands of years. It is the only country on earth that is inhabited today by the same nation, with the same religion and culture and speaking the same language as that which lived in it 3,800 years ago.

Q: What kept the Jewish people tied to Zion?

A: For many centuries, the majority of the Jewish people have lived dispersed in countries all over the world. Yet, powerful national, spiritual bonds, expressed mainly in liturgy and literature, have constantly linked these Jewish communities with their ancestral homeland.

Q: What is Zion today?

A: After centuries of decline and neglect under foreign occupation, Zion is flourishing once again, with the large increase in its Jewish population over the last 100 years, and the restoration of its political independence in 1948.

> *The people of Israel have labored long and hard to make of their ancient land a highly developed nation. Their achievements are remarkable.*
> U.S. President LYNDON B. JOHNSON, 1964

Q: What is Zionism?

A: Zionism is the national liberation movement of the Jewish people.

> *If you will it, it is no dream.*
> THEODOR HERZL, *Altneuland*, 1902

Q: What is the expression of Zionism?

A: Zionism is the modern expression of the 1,920 year old dream of rebuilding Israel, after Rome put an end to Jewish independence in the Land of Israel.

Q: What else can be said of Zionism?

A: Zionism is the conviction that the Jewish people has the right to freedom and political independence in its homeland.

Q: What is the implication of Zionism for the Jewish people?

A: Zionism is the ongoing effort, through political means, to develop and secure the Jewish people's national existence in the Land of Israel.

Q: What are the values of Zionism?

A: Zionism recognizes that Jewish peoplehood is characterized by certain common values relating to religion, culture, language, history, and basic ideals and aspirations.

Q: Are all Jews Zionists?

A: Jews are Zionists in the sense that the restoration of the Jewish people in its homeland is a fundamental tenet of Judaism. Most Jews support the State of Israel – the basic realization of Zionism. Some Jews, however, do not accept Zionism as a political movement.

Jerusalem has never been the capital of any people except the Jewish people . . . we are struck by the fact that since the Six-Day War [1967] all people are free to worship in their place of choice, unlike the situation during 1948-1967. The unity of Jerusalem must be preserved . . . internationalization is an idea which never worked in history.

statement by Evangelical Christians,
and Rev. Douglas Young, Jerusalem, 1971,
Institute of Holy Land Studies

Q: How did Zionism become an organized political movement?

A: Zionism developed into an organized political movement, in a period marked by growing recognition of national movements in Europe, when Jews felt the time was ripe for the reassertion of Jewish national identity as well.

Q: What are the other reasons that helped Zionism become realized?

A: Zionism was further spurred by growing anti-Semitism in Europe in the latter part of the nineteenth century.

Q: When was Zionism declared a national movement?

A: Zionism was formally organized into a national movement in 1897 at the First Zionist Congress in Basel with the call for the restoration of the Jewish national home.

Q: Are there different kinds of Zionism?

A: Since Israel represents many different things, there are many forms of Zionism. Each is associated with outstanding modern personalities. Theodor Herzl is the founder of political Zionism; Rabbi Samuel Mohilever of religious Zionism; Ahad Ha'am of cultural Zionism; and Nachman Syrkin of Labor Zionism.

Q: Do diaspora Jews support Zionism?

A: Diaspora Jews, on the whole, support Zionism in one way or another through active participation in aspects of the movement itself or through public or financial support of Israel.

Q: Does Zionism mean immigration to Israel?

A: Some diaspora Jews realize their belief in Zionism by immigrating to the Land of Israel in order to participate in the task of rebuilding the nation.

> *I'm actually in the illustrious old city where Solomon dwelt . . . everywhere precious remains of Solomon's temple. That portion of the ancient wall . . . which is called the Jew's Place of Wailing and where the Hebrews assemble every Friday to kiss the venerated stones and weep over the fallen greatness of Zion.*
> MARK TWAIN, *The Innocents Abroad*
>
> *As the mountains are round about Jerusalem, so the Lord is round about his people from henceforth and forever.*
> Psalms 125:1-2

Q: What is the relationship between diaspora Jews and Israel?

A: Diaspora Jews, whether or not associated with Zionist activities, have been enriched culturally, socially and spiritually by the re-establishment of Israel in its ancestral homeland.

Q: Did Zionism complete its task with the re-establishment of the State of Israel?

A: The re-establishment of the State of Israel meant the realization of the major element of Zionist ideology: the restoration of Jewish sovereignty in the Land of Israel.

> *About Zion I will not be silent, about Jerusalem I will not be still.*
> Isaiah 62:1

Q: What are the other goals and purposes of Zionism?

A: The Zionist ideal contains facets that are still in the process of being realized. The Zionist ideal aspires to: (a) an Israel at peace with all its neighbors; (b) an Israel enjoying full political and economic independence; and (c) the social and economic well-being of all citizens and communities residing in Israel.

More specifically, the aims of Zionism are:

+ the unity of the Jewish people and the centrality of Israel in its life
+ the ingathering of the Jewish people in its historical homeland, Eretz Yisrael, through *Aliyah* (immigration), from all lands
+ the strengthening of the State of Israel, founded on the prophetic ideals of justice and peace
+ the preservation of the identity of the Jewish people through the fostering of Jewish and Hebrew education and of Jewish spiritual and cultural values
+ the protection of Jewish rights everywhere

> *Christians and Jews alike in Jerusalem lived in great poverty and in conditions of great deprivation. There are not many Christians but there are many Jews, and these the Moslems persecute in various ways. The Moslems know that the Jews think and even say that this is the Holy Land which has been promised to them and that those Jews who dwell there are regarded as holy by Jews elsewhere, because . . . they refuse to leave the Land.*
>
> MARTIN KABTANIK,
> Christian pilgrim from Bohemia,
> *A Journey to Jerusalem*, 1491

Q: Are anti-Zionism and anti-Semitism the same thing?
A: There is a dangerous confluence between anti-Zionism and anti-semitism, even though the two concepts are not always identical.
Q: What exactly is anti-Zionism?
A: Anti-Zionism is directed today against the political realization of Zionism – the State of Israel.
Q: What else can be said of anti-Zionism?
A: This term has also become a modern catchword for old-fashioned anti-Semitism. It has provided anti-Semites with a convenient cloak behind which to conceal their hatred of Jews. Anti-Zionism, in the sense that it seeks to deny the right of national self-expression to the Jewish people, is a kind of anti-Semitism.

> *A definite factor in getting a lie believed is the size of the lie. The broad mass of the people, in the simplicity of their hearts, more easily fall victim to a big lie than to a small one.*
> ADOLF HITLER

Q: Is Zionism racism?
A: Definitely not. Zionism is the antithesis of racism. In fact, modern Zionism grew in part as a response to anti-Semitism.
Q: Didn't the United Nations equate Zionism with racism?
A: Anti-Zionists in 1975 succeeded in passing a UN resolution determining that "Zionism is a form of racism."

> For the United Nations General Assembly to pass a resolution branding Zionism as "racism and racial discrimination" is the rankest hypocrisy yet perpetuated by that discredited forum. Anti-Zionism at the UN can do little harm to Israel and nothing to help a peaceful settlement between Arab and Jew in the Middle East. All it will do is to debase what remnant of international authority the UN may still lay claim to.
> *Daily Mail*, November 12, 1975

Q: How could such a resolution pass?
A: Though opposed by the Western democracies, the resolution was approved by virtue of the automatic majority of the UN's controlling Arab/Third World/Communist bloc which, in recent years, has been able to pass any anti-Western, anti-democratic or anti-Israel resolution proposed, regardless of merit or basis in fact.
Q: So what is Israel today?
A: In point of fact, far from being racist, the State of Israel is a pluralistic and open society, comprising many ethnic and religious groups, all free to practice their faiths and traditions, develop their cultures and participate in the country's democratic processes.

> Go through Zion, walk around her, counting her towers, admiring her walls, reviewing her palaces. Then tell the next generation that God is here . . . for ever and ever.
> Palms 48:12-14

Q: Doesn't the "Law of Return" grant immediate citizenship to Jews alone?
A: Israel was founded as a haven from oppression for the Jewish people, and therefore, any Jew who immigrates to Israel is granted immediate citizenship under the Law of Return. This does not mean that others are excluded. On the contrary, citizenship requirements for non-Jews who immigrate to Israel – Christian, Moslem, Bahai or

others – are in fact more liberal than those of the United States and of most other Western countries.

Q: What are the roots of Arab opposition to Zionism?

A: Arab opposition to Zionism is based on issues concerning:

(1) National rights: Most Arab states demand Arab sovereignty over the entire Middle East, to the total exclusion of Jewish rights.

(2) Religion: Historically, Islam has not recognized the right to sovereignty of any non-Moslem people in any part of the Islamic world. Jews, like Christians, have been relegated to the position of Dhimmis – protected subject peoples under Moslem dominion. Islam, therefore, rejects the idea of a Jewish state in what it regards as the Islamic-Arab world.

(3) Socio-economics: Many Arab leaders feel that their positions would be jeopardized if there were free interchange between their traditional and conservative countries and Israel – an open, democratic and rapidly developing society.

Q: Can Zionist and Arab aspirations coexist?

A: Coexistence, through mutual recognition, direct negotiation, and a genuine desire to set out on the road to peace, is the key to the reconciliation of Zionist and Arab aspirations. The Israel-Egypt peace treaty, signed in 1979, provides a working model for such coexistence.

Q: Did the Zionist movement seek peaceful relations with the Arabs?

A: The Zionist movement, both before and since the establishment of the State of Israel, has always advocated and striven for peaceful and mutually beneficial relations among the peoples and the states of the region.

Q: How can peace be achieved?

A: Only a strong determination, and patience on the part of all concerned, to achieve this goal in a spirit of goodwill and tolerance will bring real peace for the peoples of the Middle East.

Who ever heard of such a thing, who ever saw anything like this? Is a country born in one day? Is a nation brought forth in one moment, that Zion only just in labor has brought forth sons? Shall I bring the birth and not cause to bring forth? It is the Lord who speaks.

Isaiah 66:8-9

Patience is bitter, yet it helps.

Egyptian saying

THE HISTORICAL CONNECTION

> *I made my covenant with them to give them the Land of Canaan, the land they lived in as strangers, and I have heard the groaning of the sons of Israel . . . and have remembered my covenant . . . With my arm outstretched and my strokes of power I will deliver you . . . bringing you to the land I swore to Abraham, Isaac, and Jacob. I the Lord will do this.*
>
> Exodus 6:5-8

Q: When did the Jews settle in Palestine?

A: Palestine became a distinct geographical, historical and political entity for the first time when the Jews settled there 3,800 years ago.

Q: Who populated the area prior to the establishment of the ancient Jewish commonwealth?

A: Before the foundation of the Jewish commonwealth in Palestine, a conglomeration of tribes, which no longer exist, lived there.

Q: For how many years was Palestine ruled by the Jews?

A: For more than 2,000 years Palestine was ruled by the Jewish people.

Q: When was the first Temple destroyed and the second built?

A: The return to Zion has a precedent in ancient times. In 586 BCE the Kingdom of Judea was destroyed by the Babylonians and its people exiled. In 516 BCE they returned and founded the second Temple.

Q: When was the second Temple destroyed?

A: In 70 CE the Jewish state was destroyed by Roman imperialism. The Jews continued to fight in a kind of guerilla war and in 132 CE succeeded in restoring Jewish independence under Bar Kochba for a short period. Even afterwards, the Jews remained a majority in Palestine for many centuries.

> *Israel and the United States have an affinity not only for each other, but for basic principles of democratic self-government which distinguish these two nations from most of the other countries of today's world.*
>
> U.S President GERALD R. FORD, 1976

Q: Did the Arabs at any time have their own state in Palestine?

A: No, Judea was the last independent state to exist in Palestine until the rebirth of Israel in 1948. There was never an Arab state there.

Q: Who ruled Palestine in the last thirteen centuries?

A: During the last 2,000 years, Palestine was ruled by a succession of foreign conquerors. For all of them, Palestine was a remote province in a huge empire. For none of them was Jerusalem the capital.

Q: Did the foreign conquerors recognize the connection of the Jews to Palestine?

A: Without exception, all the conquerors recognized the special relationship between the Jewish people and the Land of Israel:

(1) The Persians returned Jerusalem to the Jews.

(2) The Arab Caliph Omar allowed the Jews to resettle in Palestine and recognized the link between the Jews and the land.

(3) The Crusaders' leader Godfrey of Bouillon wrote to the Pope from "Terra Israel."

(4) The Ottoman Sultan Beyazit called on the Jews to return to their homeland.

(5) The British accepted the Jewish claim to Palestine in the Balfour Declaration.

(6) A sizeable Jewish population existed until the eleventh century.

I mean to deliver them out of the hands of the Egyptians and bring them up to a land rich and broad, flowing with milk and honey.

Exodus 3:17

Zion, will you not ask if peace will be with your captives . . . Of the return of your captivity, I am a harp for your songs . . . Zion, perfect in beauty! . . . Your God has desired you for a dwelling place. . . .

YEHUDA HALEVI (1075-1147), celebrated Jewish poet

ISRAEL: NEVER AN ARAB LAND

> *I really wish the Jews again in Judea an independent nation for,*
> *as I believe, the most enlightened men of it have participated in*
> *the amelioration of the philosophy of the age.*
> former U.S. PRESIDENT JOHN ADAMS, 1818

One of the myths related to the Arab-Israeli conflict is that Israel and the whole of Mandatory Palestine before it, was stolen from the Arabs as a result of imperialist machinations and settled by alien Jews.

The fact is that until the defeat of the Ottoman Turkish Empire during World War I, there was no geopolitical entity called Palestine, no Arab nation lived on this soil, and no national claim was ever made to the territory by any group other than the Jews.

Between the expulsion of the Jews by Rome in 70-132 CE and the defeat of the Ottoman Empire in 1918, Palestine was occupied by fourteen conquerors over thirteen centuries. The following table shows the approximate historical periods of the various rulers of Palestine:

Israel rule (Biblical period)	1350 BCE	to	586 BCE
Babylonian conquest	587 BCE	to	538 BCE
Israel autonomy (under Persian and Greco-Assyrian suzerainty)	538 BCE	to	168 BCE
Revolt of the Maccabees	168 BCE	to	143 BCE
Rule of the Hasmoneans and their successors	143 BCE	to	70 CE
Jewish autonomy (under Roman and Byzantine suzerainty)	70 CE	to	637 CE
Rule of Arab Caliphates	637 CE	to	1072 CE
Mecca	637 CE	to	661 CE
Umayyides	661 CE	to	750 CE
Abbasides	750 CE	to	870 CE
Fatimides	969 CE	to	1071 CE
Seljuks' rule	1072 CE	to	1096 CE
Crusaders' rule	1099 CE	to	1291 CE
Ayyubids	1175 CE	to	1291 CE
Mamelukes' rule	1291 CE	to	1516 CE
Ottomans' (Turks') rule	1516 CE	to	1918 CE
British Mandate	1918 CE	to	1948 CE

> *By the rivers of Babylon, we sat down and wept, when we remembered Zion. There we hung our harps upon willows. Our captors demanded "Sing to us one of the songs of Zion." How can we sing the Lord's song in an alien land? If I forget you, O Jerusalem, may my right hand forget its cunning, may my tongue cleave to the roof of my mouth, if I do not remember you, if I do not set Jerusalem above my highest joy.*
>
> Psalms 137:1-6
>
> ---
>
> *From now on you shall be named not Jacob but Israel . . . I give you this land, the land I gave to Abraham and to Isaac, and I will give this land to your descendants after you.*
>
> Genesis 35:9-13

JERUSALEM: 8 NEIGHBORHOODS WITH 124,000 PEOPLE SINCE 1967

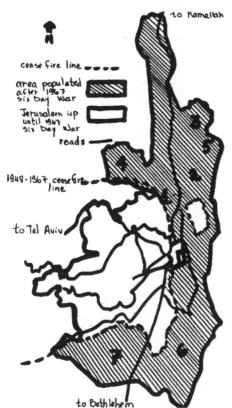

cease fire line ━ ━ ━

area populated after 1967 six Day War

Jerusalem up until 1967 six Day War

roads ━

1848-1967 cease fire line

to Tel Aviv

to Kamallah

to Bethlehem

1. RAMAT ESHKOL	11,600
2. THE FRENCH HILL	9,600
3. NEVE YAACOV	17,000
4. RAMOT	29,000
5. PISGAT ZEEV	6,500
6. TALPIOT	15,000
7. GILOH	28,000
SANHEDRIA	4,500
THE JEWISH QUARTER (in the OLD CITY)	3,000
	124,200

Since 1967, approximately 70,000 new apartments were built in these areas. In this same period, the Arabs built approximately 11,000 new apartments.

156

CHAPTER TEN

THE BALFOUR DECLARATION – NATIONAL HOME OR A JEWISH STATE?

> *I see the creation, in our lifetime, by the banks of the Jordan, of a Jewish State under the protection of the British crown.*
> WINSTON CHURCHILL,
> *Illustrated Sunday Herald*,
> February 1920

The outbreak of World War I in 1914 seemed at first disastrous for Zionism. The Jewish community in Palestine underwent acute economic hardship, repression by the Turkish authorities, expulsion of active Zionists, and dwindled in numbers. As an international body straddling the opposing combatant powers, the Zionist organization was virtually paralyzed, and was able to remain intact only by shifting its headquarters from Berlin to neutral Copenhagen.

Dr. Chaim Weizmann had settled in England, and been drawn into scientific work connected with munitions production. It was realized that, with Turkey in the war on the other side, an Allied victory would open up the question of the future of Palestine. With the help of Zionist colleagues and gentile friends, Dr. Weizmann gained support for recognizing Zionist aspirations in a postwar settlement.

The Balfour Declaration was given by the British government to the British Jewish leader Lord Rothschild. The declaration, named after the then-British Foreign Minister Arthur Balfour, was given on November 2, 1917.

The Balfour Declaration, in the form of a letter, reads: "I have much pleasure in conveying to you, on behalf of His Majesty's Government, the following declaration of sympathy with Jewish Zionist aspirations, which has been submitted to and approved by the cabinet. His Majesty's

Government views with favour the establishment in Palestine of a national home for the Jewish people, and will use their best endeavours to facilitate the achievement of this object, it being clearly understood that nothing shall be done that may prejudice the civil and religious rights of existing non-Jewish communities in Palestine, or the rights and political status enjoyed by Jews in other countries.''

Q: What was the meaning of a "national home"?

A: The Balfour Declaration endorsed the basic Zionist thesis that the Jews were a separate people, that they were entitled to a national home, and that it would be established in their ancestral homeland. The exact form and status of the proposed "national home" were left implicit. The authors of the declaration contemplated that, with immigration and settlement, the national home would in due course become an independent state with a Jewish majority.

Q: Did the British government fully intend the establishment of a Jewish state?

A: Yes. This was the original expectation, later confirmed by the two British leaders most directly concerned – Lloyd George and Balfour – by Winston Churchill, who as Colonial Secretary had to deal with the Near East settlement after the war; and by the South African statesman General Smuts, a member of the British War Cabinet at the time the declaration was issued. In 1937, the Palestine Royal (Peel) Commission reviewed all the evidence and came to the same conclusion.

The Allied nations with the fullest concurrence of our government . . . are agreed that in Palestine shall be laid the foundations of a Jewish commonwealth.
U.S. President WOODROW WILSON,
March 3, 1919

Q: Where was the Jewish state meant to be located?
A: On both banks of the Jordan River.
Q: What is mentioned about the rights of the Arabs?
A: The term "Arab" is not at all mentioned in the declaration. It speaks instead about the "non-Jewish communities."
Q: What kind of rights would the non-Jewish population be entitled to?
A: Not national – only civil and religious rights.
Q: Then where would the Arabs have national rights?
A: The national rights of the Arabs were never meant to be fulfilled in Palestine. Their rights were to be realized in Damascus, Cairo, Baghdad, etc., not in Jerusalem.

Q: Why did the British government give the declaration to the Jews?
A: The most important reason was the British recognition of the Jewish peoples' right to nationhood. The Land of Israel is the historic homeland of the Jewish people where, over nearly 4,000 years, it became a nation and developed its distinctive language, law and culture,
Q: Were the rights of the Jews recognized only by the Balfour Declaration?
A: No. Israel's international "birthright" was recognized in the Balfour Declaration of 1917, the League of Nations Mandate of 1922, the United Nations Partition Plan of 1947, and Israel's subsequent admission to the United Nations in 1949.
Q: Is there another reason why the British recognized Israel's birthright?
A: Yes. The British thought that since the Arabs could enjoy independence in huge states, justice requires that the Jews should have a tiny state.

> *. . . Why not give Palestine back to the Jews again? According to God's distribution of nations, it is their home – an inalienable possession from which they were expelled by force . . .*
> petition to U.S. President
> Benjamin Harrison, 1891,
> signed by foremost U.S. personalities

Q: What was the percentage of Palestine from the territory liberated by the British and given to the Arabs after the First World War?
A: About 3 percent.
Q: What is the size of Israel today in comparison to the Arab world?
A: Israel is less than 1/6 of one percent of the Arab world.
Q: Did the Arabs accept the international community's decision?
A: No. Six times since attaining its independence Israel has had to defend itself against Arab aggression in wars, some of which ended in border arrangements reflecting the outcome of battle.
Q: How did the Arabs justify their rejection of a Jewish state?
A: The Arabs developed an entire theory about the rights of the Palestinians to the land while negating the Jews' right to the land.
Q: What is the PLO's reaction?
A: In its national "Covenant," Paragraph 20 reads: "The Balfour Declaration, the Mandate for Palestine and everything that has been based upon them, are deemed null and void."
Q: Why?

A: Paragraph 20 of the PLO covenant continues: ". . . Judaism being a religion, is not an independent nationality nor do the Jews constitute a single nation with an identity of its own; they are citizens of the states to which they belong."

Q: How did the Palestinians express their opposition to the declaration?

A: Since 1917 and every year thereafter on November 2, the Palestinians have expressed their opposition to the Balfour Declaration by strikes, demonstrations, and verbal and literary opposition. The Palestinian Arabs believe that the Balfour Declaration was the greatest injustice ever inflicted upon them.

The Jews of America are profoundly interested in establishing a National Home in the ancient land for their race. Indeed, this is the ideal of the Jewish people everywhere, for, despite their dispersion, Palestine has been the object of their veneration since they were expelled by the Romans. For generations they have prayed for the return to Zion. During the past century this prayer has assumed practical form . . .

Committee of Foreign Affairs of
the U.S. House of Representatives,
approving the joint resolution of
the 67th Congress, 1922

I am glad . . . to express again my sympathy with the deep and intense longing which finds such fine expression in the Jewish National Homeland in Palestine.

U.S. President CALVIN COOLIDGE

CHAPTER ELEVEN

ABOUT ZIONISM, ANTI-SEMITISM, AND RACISM

> *There is of course no difference whatever between anti-Semitism and the denial of Israel's statehood. Classical anti-Semitism denies the equal rights of Jews as citizens within society, Anti-Zionism denies the equal rights of the Jewish people to its lawful sovereignty within the community of nations. The common principle in the two cases is discrimination.*
>
> ABBA EBAN, *New York Times*

On November 10, 1975, the United Nations shamelessly passed a resolution equating Zionism to a kind of racism. Seventy-two countries voted in favor of this notorious resolution. Of the 72 members voting for the resolution, only 14 were true democracies. The remaining 58 were countries ruled by dictators, strongmen, or an elite group.

Of the 35 members voting against the resolution, 27 were democracies and only eight countries were ruled by dictators or strongmen. Among those voting against the resolution was the United States. Thirty-two states abstained and three were not present at the time of the vote.

> *The attempt now being made by certain Arab governments to strike at the very roots of Israel, by trying to denigrate Zionism, its ideological basis, is nothing but ruthless and cynical political warfare . . . namely, a renewed effort by the enemies of the Jewish people to deprive it of its homeland.*
>
> CHAIM HERZOG, Israel's ambassador
> to the United Nations, UN Third Committee,
> October 16, 1975

Q: Is Zionism a form of racism?

A: Zionism is the national movement of the Jewish people.

> *Anti-Semitism made the Jewish people a better nation.*
> THEODOR HERZL,
> leader of political Zionism

Q: When and why did Zionism develop?

A: Zionism developed in response to anti-Semitism and was part of the great movement of nationalism that arose in the eighteenth century. Zionism became the first of the anti-colonial, anti-racial movements in the Middle East. Its roots lay in Jewish history and it is the response to a long record of persecution.

Q: Does Zionism consider all people to be equal?

A: Yes. Israel has endeavored to create a society which strives to implement the highest ideals of society for all its inhabitants irrespective of religion, race and sex. The Arabs who live in Israel are equal citizens before the law, sharing in the general progress and prosperity of the country since 1948.

> *And it shall come to pass that everyone that is left of all the nations which came against Jerusalem shall go up from year to year to worship before the King, Lord of Hosts, and celebrate the feast of tabernacles.*
> Zachariah 14:16

Q: Is Zionism concerned only about the Jewish people?

A: If it is argued that Zionism is racism because it is a Jewish national movement concerned to establish an autonomous state for the Jewish people, then all national movements must be racist.

> *In the prophetic spirit of Zionism all free men today look to a better world and in the experience of Zionism we know that it takes courage . . . to achieve it.*
> U.S. President JOHN F. KENNEDY

Q: When was the term "anti-Semitism" used for the first time?

A: The term "anti-Semitism" was first coined and used in 1879 by Wilhelm Marr, a German anti-Semite. Marr used the term in the sense of hostility towards Jews.

Q: Can all those who criticize Zionism be considered anti-Zionist and/or anti-Semitic?

A: It is true that many who criticize Israel are not necessarily anti-Zionist nor are all anti-Zionists anti-Semitic. However, it is equally true that many anti-Semites use anti-Zionism as a cover for their racism. Also, while many anti-Zionists are not intentionally anti-Semites (in that they do not believe Jews to be inferior), the outcome of their anti-Zionism would be that Israel would not exist and thus one of the central factors of Jewish life would be denied to the Jews.

> *And I will establish my covenant between me and you and your descendants . . . the entire land of Canaan for an everlasting possession.*
>
> Genesis 17:7, 8

Q: Is the denial of national rights for the Jews anti-Semitism?

A: Given the premise that the Jews are a people, the argument is very simple: those who deny the Jews what they seek which other peoples have are discriminating against them. So to deny the national rights of the Jews while seeking them for the Palestinians is collective anti-Semitism.

Q: Can the Arabs, who are themselves Semitic people, be anti-Semitic?

A: Arab apologists claim that since they are a Semitic people, it is impossible for them to be anti-Semitic. But "anti-Semitism" is a term invented to give anti-Jewish feelings a scientific label. Consequently, anti-Semitism means nothing else but anti-Jewish.

> *Israel has always opposed racism and racial discrimination including apartheid . . .*
>
> YEHUDA BLUM, Israeli
> ambassador to the United Nations,
> November 30, 1981
>
> ---
>
> *The Jewish people achieved their republic of Israel, striking a further blow at imperialist domination in the Middle East . . . the reactionary governments of the Arab countries were thrown against the young Israeli state, to prevent the Jewish people from building their free, independent and democratic state.*
>
> *The British Labour Monthly,*
> September 1949

Q: What is the distorted view of Zionism by Arab propaganda?

A: The Arabs view Zionism as a supremely rich, powerful, and malevolent international conspiracy, bent on world domination with its tentacles ready to crush whatever lies in its path.

Q: What strengthens the Arab belief?

A: From a Moslem point of view, it is clear that Zionism can represent a great deal more than a simple nationalist movement. Israel won its War of Independence in 1948. An area which had traditionally (and certainly since the time of the Crusades except for the brief period of British rule) been part of Dar Ul-Islam (the territory of Islam) was lost to a Dhimmi nation.

Mein Kampf – popular edition of Hitler's book in Arabic, distributed throughout the Arab world by the PLO.

Q: What strengthened Arab anti-Semitism?

A: European anti-Semitic ideas were increasingly introduced into the repertoire of anti-Israel polemic which was also informed by the anti-Jewish traditions and prejudice of the Islamic world. Blood libels were alluded to; grossly anti-Semitic caricatures were propagated in the Arab press and even in school text books, and Arab translations of the classic texts of European anti-Semitism were disseminated.

Q: When did the Arabs start to produce anti-Semitic literature for the world?

A: Until after the 1973 Yom Kippur War, Arab anti-Semitism was generally for home consumption. After the oil crisis of the 1970s, the Arab states started disseminating anti-Semitic literature abroad. Indeed, some Arab and other Islamic states have become the greatest producers of anti-Semitic literature in the contemporary world.

> *Are they so ignorant all these evil men who swallow my people as though they were eating bread and never invoke the Lord.*
> Psalms 14:4

UNRWA SCHOOL HOUSES ARAFAT'S SCHOOL OF VIOLENCE:
A 1982 picture of Arafat and the Nazi swastika are among the wall decorations of a room in the UNRWA school in Siblin (South Lebanon) which was turned into a terrorist training center by the PLO that year. (Rahamin Israeli)

The following cartoon appeared in *El-Ahram* on December 21, 1986. Prime Minister Shamir is shown granting a decoration – with swastika – to an Israeli soldier who has killed a Palestinian Arab boy in the territories. Shamir says, "I would like to give the highest decoration . . ."

PART IV

THE ARAB RECORD OF BLOODSHED AND HOSTILITY AGAINST ISRAEL

CHAPTER TWELVE

THE WAR OF
INDEPENDENCE IN 1948

> *I may forgive the Arabs for killing our dear sons, but I will never forgive them for teaching our sons to kill.*
>
> GOLDA MEIR,
> Israeli Prime Minister
>
> *The sword shall not pass through your land. You shall pursue your enemies and they shall fall before your sword; five of you pursuing a hundred of them, one hundred pursuing ten thousand; and your enemies shall fall before your sword.*
>
> Leviticus 26:7-8

In order to understand the background of Israel's establishment in 1948, we have to go back thirty years. After the First World War, the Palestinian Arabs expressed their objection, in both words and actions, to the Jewish presence in Palestine. They demanded the nullification of the Balfour Declaration and the mandate. They called for an end to Jewish immigration to Palestine and the sale of land to the Jews. They called for the establishment of an Arab state in Palestine.

When the Arab demands were not met, the Palestinians moved into actions against the Jews and even against the British authorities in Palestine. Riots broke out in Palestine against the Jews in 1920, 1921, 1929, 1933, and 1936-39. The results of this blatant Palestinian Arab aggression was the death of thousands of Jews, Arabs, and British, severe damage to property, and heightened hatred between the sides involved.

> *Blessed be the Lord, my rock, who trains my hands for war and my fingers for battle.*
>
> Psalms 144:1-2

> *The Arabs had repeatedly insisted that they would resist partition by force.*
> TRYGVE LIE, Secretary General of the UN,
> *In the Cause of Peace*

Q: What happened to the Jews in Europe?

A: In Europe, six million Jews were slaughtered by the Nazis during World War II.

Q: What was the attitude of the Allies towards the Jewish refugees?

A: Nearly all the countries, including Great Britain, the United States, Canada, etc., refused to accept sizable numbers of Jewish refugees from Europe.

Q: What was the attitude of the Allies towards the Jews?

A: The Allies refused to bomb Auschwitz because it was "not an important military target."

Q: Who were the allies of the Arabs?

A: In the Arab countries, all leaders – from King Farouk to the "Free Officers" of Gamal A. Nasser, from Rashid Ali el Kilani in Iraq to Shuqry el Kuwatly in Syria – cooperated with the Axis. Jews were murdered in the streets of Baghdad and Cairo.

> *If not for the Lord who was with us, let Israel now say. If not for the Lord who was with us when men rose up against us, then they would have swallowed us up alive, when their anger was kindled against us, then the waters would have overwhelmed us, the stream would have gone over our soul.*
> Psalms 124:1-5
>
> ———————————————
>
> *The Germans know how to get rid of the Jews.*
> HAJ AMIN EL HUSSEINI,
> Berlin, November 1943

Q: What happened in Palestine in 1936-39?

A: Between the years 1936 and 1939, armed bands of the Mufti, the supreme clerical leader of the Muslims, killed hundreds of Jews and thousands of Arabs who sought a reconciliation with the Jews.

Q: Who cooperated with the Nazis?

A: The leaders of the Palestinian Arabs, who supported the Mufti, joined him in Iraq where they assisted in staging a pro-Nazi coup. Afterwards, they went to Germany and assisted with the "final solution." Among them were the Mufti himself, Emile Goury, Hasan Salame and Fawzi el Kaukjy.

Q: What was the main problem facing the Jews after the war?

A: After World War II, hundreds of thousands who survived the Holocaust waited in camps in Europe for permission to go to Palestine.

Q: What act of hostility was committed by the British in 1939?

A: In 1939, the British authorities in Palestine abandoned the Balfour Declaration and the League of Nations Mandate in order to appease the pro-Nazi Arabs.

Q: What did Great Britain decide at that time?

A: The British decided to end Jewish immigration to Palestine, to stop the sale of any land to Jews in Palestine, and to found an Arab state in the whole of Palestine within ten years. With this "White Paper," every promise to the Jews was betrayed.

Q: What was the direct result of the British White Paper of 1939?

A: The White Paper prevented the rescue of millions of Jews from Europe. Even the survivors from the Holocaust were not allowed to immigrate to Palestine, and if they tried and were caught, they were put in British detention camps in Cyprus and Mauritius.

Q: What was the Jewish reaction to British policy?

A: Jewish military underground groups began to fight the British. Life became unbearable for the British troops and Great Britain decided to return the mandate to the UN and let it decide the fate of Palestine.

Q: What was the United Nations' reaction to these developments?

A: The UN sent the Special Commission on Palestine (UNSCOP) there in 1947. The Commission recommended the partition of Palestine into a Jewish state in the areas predominantly Jewish and an Arab state in the areas predominantly Arab. It further proposed the internationalization of Jerusalem.

Q: When was the Partition Plan?

A: The Partition Plan was ratified on November 29, 1947, by the UN General Assembly with a two-thirds majority (33 "for" and 13 "against" – 6 Arab states included – and 10 abstentions). The United States and all the communist states voted "for." Great Britain abstained.

The representatives of the Jewish Agency told us yesterday . . .
that the Arabs had begun fighting. We did not deny this.
                                        JAMAL HUSSEINI,
                        "Arab Higher Committee" of Palestine,
                        in UN Security Council, April 16, 1948

Q: Who accepted the partition plan?

A: The Jews accepted the decision, although they were unhappy with some of the territorial details. For peace they were ready to compromise.

> *We shall spare no efforts to secure peace with our neighbors based on honor and security.*
>
> DAVID BEN-GURION,
> in the Knesset, March 1949

Q: Who rejected the partition plan?

A: All the Arab states and the "Arab Higher Committee" – the quasi-government of the Palestinian Arabs.

Q: What did the Arabs do to demonstrate their opposition?

A: The day after the November 29, 1947, Partition Resolution of the UN, irregular Arab armies, which were mainly recruited and trained in Syria, led by the Nazi collaborators Haj Amin al-Husseini, Fawzi el Kaukjy, and Abdul Kadar el-Husseini, began the war against the Jewish community in Palestine with the declared aim to liquidate it.

Q: When was the State of Israel established?

A: They failed in their attempt to liquidate the Jewish community and on May 14, 1948, the State of Israel was proclaimed in accordance with the 1947 resolution.

Q: Who invaded the fledgling State of Israel?

A: The regular armies of Egypt, Jordan, Lebanon, Syria, and Iraq.

Q: Was there any combined Arab declaration of intent?

A: Announcing the Arab invasion, Azzam Pasha, Secretary General of the Arab League, said on May 14, 1948: "This will be a war of extermination and a momentous massacre which will be spoken of like the Mongolian massacres and the Crusades."

Q: What was the result of the war?

A: The Arab armies lost after a year and a half of bitter fighting. When the fighting ended, Israel held some territories not allotted to her according to the Partition resolution, which the Arabs had annulled by making war. The Israelis suffered enormous casualties. The 650,000 Jews of 1948 Israel counted 6,000 dead – almost 1 percent of their population.

> *It is impossible for one who has studied at all the services of the Hebrew people to avoid the faith that they will one day be restored to their historic national home and there enter on a new and yet greater phase of their contribution to the advance of humanity.*
>
> WARREN G. HARDING,
> U.S. President, 1921-23

Q: What did Jordan do to the West Bank?

A: Transjordan conquered the West Bank and Eastern Jerusalem, annexed it and became Jordan. It was an illegal annexation. On May 12, 1950, the Arab League criticized Jordan for annexing a part of Palestine (West Bank). Only Iraq prevented the expulsion of Jordan from the Arab League.

Q: What did Egypt capture?

A: Egypt occupied the Gaza Strip and held it as a territory under military occupation. It was an illegal occupation, which lasted until the Six-Day War in 1967.

Q: What was the cause of the Arab refugee problem?

A: About 600,000 Palestinian Arabs fled, some because they were called to do so by their leaders, others because of fear.

> *The partition line proposed shall be nothing but a line of fire and blood.*
>
> JAMAL HUSSEINI, from the Palestinian
> Arab Committee, November 24, 1947

Q: What about Jewish refugees?

A: About 600,000 Jews fled from persecution and pogroms in the Arab countries and came to Israel.

Q: What did the belligerent sides do after the war?

A: In 1949, Israel signed Armistice Agreements with Egypt, Jordan, Lebanon, and Syria. Iraq refused to sign.

Q: Did the Arabs respect the Armistice Agreements?

A: No. The Arabs violated the agreements time and again.

> *This is not the first time that the Arab states, which organized the invasion of Palestine, have ignored a decision of the Security Council or of the General Assembly . . .*
>
> ANDREI GROMYKO, Soviet delegate to
> the United Nations, before the Security Council,
> May 29, 1948

Q: What happened in Deir Yasin?

A: Neither terrorism nor the indiscriminate killing of innocent helpless civilians – men, women and children – was ever the policy of the Israeli forces before or after the establishment of the State of Israel. Deir Yasin may be an exception. The Irgun, one of the Jewish forces, met with Arab resistance while operating in the settlement and killed Arab civilians. The Irgun action was condemned by most of the Jewish establishment in Palestine before 1948.

Q: What is the policy of the PLO in this respect?

A: The PLO, following the traditional policy of its predecessors the Palestinian Arabs, has made the killing of the innocent – Jews and non-Jews alike – a policy. Murder has become their means to their ends.

. . . the impetus given to the country's economic development by Jewish immigration and by the influx of Jewish capital conferred certain benefits on the Arab community. The government was able to expand its services, in the interest of the whole population, by means of revenue drawn in an increasing proportion from the Jewish taxpayer. And the Arab cultivator benefited from the expansion of the urban market for his produce.

British memorandum submitted
to the United Nations Special Committee
on Palestine in 1947

CHAPTER THIRTEEN

THE SINAI CAMPAIGN OF 1956

> *You may say in your heart, "These nations outnumber me; how shall I be able to dispossess them?" Do not be afraid of them . . .*
>
> Deuteronomy 7:17-18
>
> ---
>
> *During the six years during which this belligerency has operated in violation of the Armistice Agreement there have occurred 1,843 cases of armed robbery and theft, 1,339 cases of armed clashes with Egyptian armed forces, 435 cases of incursion from Egyptian controlled territory, 172 cases of sabotage perpetrated by Egyptian military units and Fedayeen in Israel. As a result of these actions of Egyptian hostility within Israel, 364 Israelis were wounded and 101 killed. In 1956 alone, as a result of this aspect of Egyptian aggression, 28 Israelis were killed and 127 wounded . . .*
>
> ABBA EBAN, Israel's ambassador
> to the United Nations Security Council,
> October 30, 1956

Since the Armistice Agreements of 1949, the Arabs did not cease their verbal attacks on Israel and the infiltration of individuals and groups into her territory in order to carry out terrorist actions. Life in Israel was hard. In the years 1955 and 1956, the Fedayeen (terrorists) raids from the Gaza Strip intensified. Many Israelis were either killed or wounded. It was unsafe to travel Israeli roads in the southern parts of the country.

> *. . . [no] paramilitary forces of either Party, including non-regular forces, shall commit any warlike or hostile act against the military or paramilitary forces of the other Party, or against civilians in territory under control of that Party.*
>
> Article III, Paragraph 2,
> Armistice Agreements, 1949

Q: What worsened the situation?

A: In 1954-55, Nasser, the Egyptian president, concluded agreements with the Soviet Union for the sale of a large amount of arms. Israel became heavily outnumbered in equipment and weapons.

Q: When was Israel actually alarmed?

A: In October 1956, a military alliance between Syria, Jordan, and Egypt was concluded, thus encircling Israel. Fedayeen attacks on Israel increased.

Q: Was there any other sign of deterioration?

A: Yes. In 1956, Iraqi troops moved into Jordan. (Israel had no armistice agreement with Iraq.)

> *There are many devices in a man's heart, but the counsel of the Lord, that shall stand.*
>
> Proverbs 19:21

Q: What else alarmed Israel?

A: The Suez Canal remained closed to Israeli shipping and foreign ships coming from or going to Israel. This is contrary to the Constantinople Convention of 1888 which demands free passage in the Suez Canal in times of peace and war for civilian and military vessels of any flag. The blockade of the canal is also contrary to the Security Council Resolution of 1951.

Q: What was the reaction of the United Nations to this violation?

A: On September 1, 1951, the Security Council ruled that Egypt could not remain in a state of belligerence and ordered Egypt to open the canal to Israeli shipping. Egypt refused.

> *God has gathered the Zionists together from the corners of the world so that the Arabs can kill them at one strike. This was impossible before, owing to their dispersion.*
>
> Egyptian daily *Al-Ahram*,
> September 6, 1956

Q: What about the Straits of Tiran?

A: The Straits of Tiran were blocked by Egypt in 1951 to Israeli ships and foreign ships sailing to or from Eilat. This was contrary to the age-old custom of international law, which became a written rule of international law in the Geneva Convention of 1958.

Q: What were Israel's goals in the Sinai Campaign?

A: The aims of the campaign were: (a) to destroy the war preparations and war capacity of Egypt, whose aim it was to "meet with the Syrian army on the ruins of the Zionist gangs," according to Egyptian President Nasser on December 18, 1955; (b) to strike at the Fedayeen bases in the Gaza Strip; and (c) to open the Straits of Tiran and, if possible, the Suez Canal for Israeli ships and other ships going to or from Israel.

> *I myself will fight against those who fight you.*
> Isaiah 49:25

Q: Did Israel cooperate with the colonial powers to achieve her goals?

A: Israel's motivation was not to oppose the nationalization of the Suez Canal by Egypt. This was the motivation of the British-French alliance. There may have been a coalition of interests among Israel, France, and Britain at that moment. However, Israel fought for her life and for nothing else. Someone who fights for his life accepts every aid.

Q: What was the result of the war?

A: Israel conquered Sinai in seven days.

> *They shall be destroyed and brought to nothing, those who made war on you . . . do not be afraid, Jacob . . . I will help you — it is the Lord who speaks.*
> Isaiah 41:11-13
>
> ---
>
> *Since the rebirth of the State of Israel, there has been an ironclad bond between that democracy and this one.*
> U.S. President RONALD REAGAN

Q: Who imposed upon Israel to withdraw?

A: In 1957, the Soviet Union and the United States imposed a settlement on Israel. Israel evacuated Sinai without getting either an Egyptian recognition, negotiations, or a peace treaty.

Q: What were the final arrangements?

A: The settlement included: (a) evacuation of Sinai by Israel; (b) UN troops on the Egyptian side of the border to prevent Fedayeen raids; (c) the Egyptian army's agreement not to reenter the Gaza Strip; and (d) the UN's and the major maritime powers' (including the United States, France, and Great Britain) guarantee of freedom of navigation through the Straits of Tiran and the Suez Canal.

Q: Did the Egyptians honor their commitments?

A: No. Contrary to the agreement, the Egyptian army reentered the Gaza Strip in 1957, and the Suez Canal was again closed to Israeli shipping.

> *I shall be enemy to your enemy; foe to your foe.*
>
> Exodus 23:21

Q: Why didn't the Sinai Campaign bear many fruits?

A: American and Soviet pressure forced Israel to withdraw from Sinai without Egyptian concessions for the sake of peace. The seeds of the Six-Day War of 1967 may be found in the results of the Sinai Campaign.

CHAPTER FOURTEEN

THE SIX-DAY WAR OF JUNE 1967

> *The borders of the State have become sanctified in the efforts of the settlers in the border village and by the streams of blood which they have had to shed in their defence. A people which has been attacked and which defended itself and emerged victorious has the sacred right of establishing for itself such a final political settlement as would permit it to liquidate the source of aggression . . . a people which has acquired its security with such heavy sacrifice will never agree to restore the old borders.*
>
> *Pravda*, September 25, 1964

T he Six-Day War is a prime example to prove the unstable nature of the Middle East. In just three weeks, dramatic changes occurred in the area: Israel was compelled, once again, to fight for her right to exist against the combined forces of Syria, Jordan, and Egypt.

Q: What was Egyptian President Nasser's excuse for sending forces into Sinai?

A: Nasser's pretext for troop concentration in Sinai, which started on May 15, 1967, was that Israel concentrated troops along the Syrian border, from which El-Fatah raided Israel.

Q: Was Nasser justified in his claims?

A: No. These allegations were refuted by UN observers on the spot. U-Thant reported that on the May 19, 1967.

Q: Did the Soviets help to refute Nasser's claims?

A: No. During the trial of General C. Badran (Egyptian Minister of Defense during the war) in 1968, it became clear that the Egyptians had checked the Russian reports and had discovered them to be false. Yet they decided to go to war against Israel. The Soviet Union played a key role by continually feeding Nasser with false information.

Q: What were the steps that cause deterioration of the situation?

A: On May 30, 1967, Hussein signed a pact with Egyptian President Nasser, whose radio broadcasts and agents had only hours earlier been inciting the Jordanian population to overthrow the Hashemite monarchy.

> *It goes without saying that this passage [through the Straits of Tiran] will remain free as in the past in conformity with international practice and with the recognized principle of international law.*
>
> Egypt to American Embassy
> in Cairo, January 28, 1950

Q: What added to the deterioration?
A: On May 16, 1967, Gamal A. Nasser demanded the withdrawal of the UN troops from Sinai. U Thant, the UN Secretary General, agreed. This was a direct breach of the 1957 arrangement in which it was agreed that the UN force could not be withdrawn arbitrarily. On May 22, Nasser declared the Straits of Tiran closed for Israeli ships. The act was contrary to international law (the 1958 Geneva Convention was signed by all nations; it included a special "Tiran clause") and to the agreement of 1957. According to international law, an act of blockade is an act of war.

> *We should not assume . . . Egypt will prevent Israeli shipping from using the Suez Canal or the Gulf of Aqaba. If, unhappily, Egypt does hereafter violate the Armistice Agreement or other international obligations, then this should be dealt with firmly by the family of nations.*
>
> U.S. President DWIGHT D. EISENHOWER,
> February 20, 1957

Yet, in May 1967, the international community stood by, helpless, as President Nasser forcibly closed the Straits of Tiran to Israeli shipping, thereby triggering the Six-Day War.

Q: Could Israel count on the promises of the big powers?
A: No. The guarantee of the maritime powers for freedom of passage in the Straits of Tiran was not effective.
Q: What did Arab leaders declare in those days?
A: Nasser, President Arif of Iraq, President El-Atasi of Syria, King Hussein of Jordan, and President Boumédienne of Algeria declared numerous times between May 15 and June 5, 1967, that Israel must

be destroyed. Ahmad Shukeiry, leader of the PLO, Ahmad Sa'id, chief propagandist of Radio Cairo, and others declared that the Jews of Israel would not survive.

Q: What was the conclusion of the situation?

A: Israel learned that, in times of trouble, she can count only on her military forces.

> *Our basic objective will be the destruction of Israel. The Arab people want to fight.*
>
> President GAMAL ABDEL NASSER,
> May 27, 1967
>
> _____
>
> *Kill the Jews wherever you find them. Kill them with your arms, with your hands, with your nails and teeth.*
>
> KING HUSSEIN,
> Amman Radio, June 8, 1967

Q: What did Israel do?

A: In order to survive, Israel made a preemptive strike on June 5, 1967. There were two main reasons for this action: (a) the smallness of its territory makes an offensive across the borders the only possible defense, and (b) the Israeli army is a people's army based on reserves. Israel cannot mobilize all its male population for too long without destroying its economy.

> *Soldiers of the fronts of Jordan, Syria, Gaza, and Khan Yunis – the holy march is on! Kill them and cleanse their blood off your weapons on the shores of Jaffa, Acco, and Haifa.*
>
> Damascus Radio, June 7, 1967

Q: What were the results of the war?

A: The results of the war were the occupation of Sinai, the Gaza Strip, the West Bank, and the Golan Heights. Israel then gained strategic borders. However, Israel's destruction remains the declared aim of the Arab states.

Q: What were other results of the war?

A: Although the continuous El Fatah raids against Israel were one of the causes of the war which brought disaster to the Arab states, ironically, one of the results of the war was the rapid growth of El Fatah. Another result of the war was a blow to Russian prestige, but also a growth of Russian involvement in the Middle East. On the other hand, a Nasserist victory would have been a victory for the Soviet patrons and this certainly would have meant the elimination of all governments not subservient to Russia in the Middle East.

> *Taking Sharm-el-Sheikh meant confrontation with Israel. Taking such action meant that we were ready to enter a general war with Israel.*
>
> GAMAL ABDEL NASSER,
> Arab Trade Union Congress, May 26, 1967

Q: When will the Arab countries attack Israel?

A: On the basis of past experience, Israel must calculate her military steps on the assumption that the enemy Arab states, if they detect any weakness on her part and feel they have a chance of defeating her, will not hesitate to attack in concert. Such was the situation in 1948 and in 1967.

Q: What was the American reaction to the closing of the Straits of Tiran?

A: The American position was expressed by the American President, Lyndon Johnson, on June 19, 1967: "If a single act of folly was more responsible for this explosion than any other it was the arbitrary and dangerous announced decision that the Straits of Tiran would be closed. The right of innocent maritime passage must be preserved for all nations."

Q: What were the real intentions of the Arabs in June 1967?

A: The Egyptian daily *Al-Achbar*, May 31, 1967, put it thusly: "Under terms of the military agreement signed with Jordan, Jordanian artillery, coordinated with the forces of Egypt and Syria, is in a position to cut Israel in two at Qalqilya, where Israeli territory between the Jordan armistice line and the Mediterranean Sea is only 12 kilometers wide . . . The military encirclement of Israel by Arab forces . . . bears out Ben Gurion's fear that Israel could yet find herself in the vise of a nutcracker."

> *The Jews of Palestine will have to leave . . . Any of the old Palestinian Jewish population who survive may stay but it is my impression that none of them will survive.*
>
> PLO leader AHMAD SHUKEIRY,
> June 1, 1967

Q: What was the meaning of the Egyptian blockade in the Straits of Tiran?

A: By international law, the blockade by naval forces is an act of war. The conclusion is very simple – the Six-Day War was the direct result of a war of aggression against the very existence of the State of Israel.

Israel was surrounded by enemies, who repeatedly and openly declared their wish to destroy her, and the international waters to and from her ports were blockaded. Israel had no choice but to fight back.

> *Our forces are now entirely ready not only to repulse the aggression, but to initiate the act of liberation itself, and to explode the Zionist presence in the Arab homeland . . . I . . . believe the time has come to enter into the battle of liberation.*
>
> HAFEZ AL-ASSAD,
> Defense Minister of Syria,
> May 20, 1967

THE ARAB SUMMIT: SEPTEMBER 1967

Israel withdrew its troops twice from Arab lands without getting recognition and peace. In 1949 Israel withdrew from southern Lebanon and northern Sinai, in 1957 from Sinai.

> *One can make a mistake for the third time, but no one is obliged to do so.*
>
> ABBA EBAN

Q: What did Israel do for the sake of peace immediately following the war?

A: Israel called upon the Arabs to negotiate peace. Israel then was willing to give up most of the land captured in June 1967.

Q: What was the Arab response?

A: The Arab leaders unanimously refused to accept the Israeli call for peace. At the end of August 1967, the Arab leaders met in Khartoum, Sudan. After three days of debate, the Arab leaders decided on September 1, 1967: "Kings and presidents have agreed to unified efforts at international and diplomatic levels to eliminate the consequences of aggression and to assure the withdrawal of the aggressor forces of Israel from Arab lands, but within the limits to which Arab states are committed: no peace with Israel, no negotiations with Israel, no recognition of Israel and the maintenance of the rights of Palestinian people in their nation."

Q: Why were the Israelis highly disappointed and even shocked by the Khartoum decision?

A: Many Israelis believed that after such a severe defeat, the Arabs might change their policy of hatred against Israel.

The most explicitly genocidal commands ever found in Arab military documents captured by Israel and made public are the following, which were instructions to the Jordanian army for the coming war with Israel, dated June 7, 1966, and found after the Six-Day War: "The intention of H.Q. Western Front is to carry out a raid on Motza Colony, to destroy it, and to kill all its inhabitants."

UN SECURITY COUNCIL RESOLUTION 242 OF NOVEMBER 1967

> *Historically, there have never been secure or recognized boundaries in the area. Neither the Armistice lines of 1949 nor the cease-fire lines of 1967 have answered that description . . . such boundaries have yet to be agreed upon. An agreement on that point is an absolute essential to a just and lasting peace . . .*
> ARTHUR GOLDBERG,
> U.S. ambassador to the United Nations,
> November 15, 1967

The main points of Security Council Resolution 242 are: (a) Israeli withdrawal from territories captured in the June 1967 war, to secure and recognized borders, (b) mutual acknowledgment of the sovereignty, territorial integrity, and political independence of every state in the area, and (c) settlement of the refugee problem.

Q: What is the Arab view of Israeli borders?
A: The Arabs believe that, according to Resolution 242, Israel should withdraw from all the territories captured in June 1967.
Q: What is Israel's view with regard to her borders?
A: Israel believes that Israeli withdrawal of forces to the pre-1967 war borders would pose mortal danger to her security. Israel claims that the vulnerable borders of June 4, 1967, which invited Arab aggression, cannot be secure borders.
Q: What does Resolution 242 say in this respect?
A: Security Council Resolution 242 does not say "all" or "the" territories before the term "withdrawal." Therefore, Israel is not required to withdraw from "all" or "the" territories. Israel should rightfully retain some territory for her security.
Q: What else does it say?

A: The resolution speaks about "inadmissability of the acquisition of territory by war." This applies also to Jordanian acquisition of the West Bank and Egyptian acquisition of the Gaza Strip and not only to territories occupied by Israel in 1967. Moreover, the resolution speaks about a just and lasting peace, not a temporary settlement. A lasting peace is a precondition for withdrawal. A lasting peace demands recognition, negotiations, peace treaties, etc. – all of which the Arabs, with the exception of Egypt, have rejected.

Lord Caradon, who was the British ambassador to the United Nations in 1967, together with the American ambassador, the late Professor Arthur Goldberg, wrote Resolution 242. Lord Caradon was very familiar with all the discussions concerning Resolution 242. He said, in the *Beirut Daily Star,* June 12, 1974: "It would have been wrong to demand that Israel return to its positions of June 4, 1967, because those positions were undesirable and artificial. After all, they were just the places where the soldiers of each side happened to be on the day the fighting stopped in 1948. They were just armistice lines. That's why we didn't demand that the Israelis return to them, and I think we were right not to . . ."

Q: What can be said about reference to the Palestinians in resolution 242?
A: Nothing at all. The Palestinians are not mentioned at all in this resolution – neither their national rights nor their refugee rights.
Q: How can that be?
A: The resolution speaks about ". . . a settlement of the refugee problem," meaning Jewish refugees (referring to the Jews who came from Arab lands to Israel as refugees) as well as the Palestinian refugees.

> *Either man will abolish war, or war will abolish man.*
> BERTRAND RUSSELL

Q: Who were the Jewish refugees?
A: About 800,000 Jews from Arab lands have emigrated to Israel since 1948. Most of these people had suffered torture, humiliation, and persecution. Their property was confiscated and their rights were denied by the Arabs. (For the full story, see the chapter about the Jewish refugees in this book.)

> *Israel, the Jewish people and the Hebrew culture and heritage have been an integral part of Middle Eastern history, from the dawn of civilization; they will continue to be so in the future. Alongside the twenty-one Arab states with their immense territories stretching from the Atlantic Ocean to the Persian Gulf, their vast manpower, natural resources, and oil, there is also ample room for a Jewish state in the region to which it historically and spiritually belongs.*
>
> YEHUDA BLUM, former Israeli
> ambassador to the United Nations

POINTS TO PONDER

✦ Do you know that the Jews accepted the November 29, 1947, Partition Resolution? If the Arabs had accepted it, the borders of Israel would have been those proposed by the UN.

✦ Do you know that the Arabs rejected that resolution by waging war? They cannot demand to return to the 1947 borders determined by a UN resolution which they themselves rejected.

✦ Do you know that in the 1949 Armistice Agreements, the Arab states insisted on a clause that the armistice lines are not final borders? The Arab states, by their precipitation of another war, denied those lines to be of any validity.

✦ Do you know that recognized and secure boundaries, as demanded in the November 22, 1967, Security Council Resolution, can be achieved by negotiations and a peace treaty?

✦ Do you know that until the Israeli-Egyptian peace treaty of 1979, Israel never had agreed-on, recognized, and secure boundaries? It had truce lines (1948-49), armistice lines (1949-67), and ceasefire lines. The Israeli lines "expanded" in 1948-49 and 1967 in wars imposed on Israel, in defensive wars. Israel conquered territory while repelling aggression.

✦ Do you know that "expansionism" is defined as war waged to enlarge a territory? Israel never did that. Israel fought all wars for its very existence. Expansionism is not proved by showing a map before and after a given war. With such logic, Poland would be considered expansionist in World War II and Nazi Germany would not. The conquest of Berlin is no proof that Nazi Germany was the victim of aggression.

What the Arabs thought about the Six-Day War is partially expressed in four cartoons. Below is a cartoon that appeared in Cairo's *Akhbar el-Yom* on June 3, 1967, and in Baghdad's *Al-Manar* on June 8. In both cases it was captioned "How to Use the Star of David." At page bottom is one that appeared in Beirut's *Al-Hayat* on May 31, 1967, entitled "The Armored Forces of the Arab Countries in Action." On the following page are a June 5th cartoon from Cairo's *Roz el-Yussef*, "Would You Like to Die by the Field Marshal's Scissors?", and one from Damascus' *Al-Jundi al Arabi*, June 6, "The Barricades in Tel Aviv."

١ ــ تعب تموت بمقص الشعر ؟

CHAPTER FIFTEEN

THE YOM KIPPUR WAR OF OCTOBER 1973

> *We have only one advantage over our enemies: our hatred of war and death. This small, blameless people, small as it is, surrounded as it is by enemies, has decided to live . . . We have known some very very bitter hours . . . We will not be destroyed.*
> GOLDA MEIR,
> at a Yom Kippur War press conference,
> Tel Aviv, October 13, 1973

> *The enemies that rise against you the Lord will conquer for your sake. They may come at you from one direction, but will flee before you in seven.*
> Deuteronomy 28:7

The Yom Kippur War broke out on October 6, 1973. For the Jews it was the holiest day of the Jewish year – the Day of Atonement. On this day, Jews the world over fast and pray.

Q: Who participated in the war?
A: In this war, Egypt and Syria launched simultaneous surprise attacks against Israel from their respective borders.
Q: Was Israel prepared for the war?
A: No. Israel was caught completely by surprise.
Q: What was the balance of power on the Golan Heights?
A: In the first days, 180 Israeli tanks fought on the Golan Heights against 1,400 Syrian tanks, massive quantities of sophisticated weapons, and masses of Syrian troops.

> *Our relationship with Israel is in our mutual self-interest, but a narrow calculation of interest is not the sole basis of the bond between our nations. At its heart is a moral obligation on our part to do whatever is necessary to defend and protect Israel.*
> U.S. President RONALD REAGAN,
> in a letter, May 13, 1988

Q: What was the balance of power along the Suez Canal?

A: The approximately five hundred Israeli troops stationed along the Suez Canal were attacked by about 80,000 Egyptian troops equipped with thousands of tanks, cannons, and a full arsenal of sophisticated weapons.

> *The chariots and the Army of Pharaoh he has hurled into the sea . . . He has covered himself in glory.*
> Exodus 15:4 and 15:22

Q: What were the Syrian gains?

A: In the first days of the war, the Syrians captured part of the Golan Heights territory. At the cost of heavy casualties, the Israeli forces succeeded in pushing back the Syrian forces. Israel captured all the territories temporarily lost at the outset and drove deep into Syrian territory.

Q: What happened on the Egyptian front?

A: The Egyptians, like the Syrians, took advantage of the element of surprise and managed to capture a strip of six to ten miles along the Suez Canal. Within ten days, on October 16, 1973, the Egyptian Third Army was encircled along the east side of the canal when Israeli forces crossed to the west side, cutting off their supplies.

> *The battle with Israel must be such that, after it, Israel will cease to exist.*
> President MUAMMAR QADDAFI of Libya,
> Algiers Radio, November 12, 1973

Q: Who aided the Arabs in this war of aggression?

A: The Soviet Union. The Russians supplied the Arabs with weaponry throughout the war.

Q: Who else helped the Arabs?

A: Nine Arab states: Jordan, Iraq, Saudi Arabia, Kuwait, Libya, Algeria, Tunisia, Sudan, and Morocco.

Q: What kind of assistance did these countries give Egypt and Syria?

A: They sent thousands of their own troops, along with huge quantities of weapons.

Q: To what extent did Lebanon assist in the war?

A: Lebanese troops did not participate in actual battles. However, Lebanon allowed the PLO terrorists to shell Israeli settlements from her southern border with Israel.

> *If the Lord had not been on our side when they attacked, they would have swallowed us alive and burned us to death in their rage. The torrent would have closed over us; the flood swept us away . . . but the Lord did not give us as prey to those teeth. We escaped like birds from the fowler's net. He tore the net and we escaped.*
>
> Psalms 124:2-7

Q: Whose intervention on behalf of the Egyptian army prevented disaster?

A: The United Nations Security Council. The UN, which did almost nothing to end the fighting in the beginning of the war when the Arabs seemed bound for victory, intervened once the Arabs – especially the Egyptians – were on the verge of catastrophe.

> *Our forces continue to pressure the enemy and will continue to strike at him until we recover the occupied territory and we will then continue until all the land is liberated.*
>
> HAFEZ AL-ASSAD,
> Damascus Radio, October 16, 1973

Q: When was the ceasefire?

A: On October 22, 1973, the UN Security Council passed Resolution 338 calling for an immediate ceasefire and negotiations between the warring parties, based on Resolution 242.

Q: Did the fighting stop?

A: No. In the light of this, the UN Security Council then adopted Resolution 339 on October 24, 1973 and the real ceasefire was put into effect on October 24, 1973. The Egyptians honored the ceasefire; the Syrians did not.

> *I shall panic ahead of you; I shall throw into confusion all the people you encounter. I shall make all your enemies turn and run from you. I shall send hornets in front of you.*
>
> Exodus 23:27-28

Q: What were the losses of the war?

A: 2,560 troops paid with their lives to defend the state of Israel. Thousands of Arab troops perished. The monetary damages to Israel amounted to billions of dollars and for the Arabs even more.

> *If I want to open the canal, I do not have to ask permission of the U.S. or Israel. But the problem is not that of the canal . . . There is the issue of Palestine, the issue of liberating the occupied lands.*
>
> Egyptian President ANWAR AL-SADAT,
> September 26, 1973

Q: Was there any controversy between Egypt and Syria during the war?

A: Yes. At the outset of the war, Syria's Assad asked Egypt's Sadat to accept a ceasefire. The Syrian forces had gained some territory on the Golan Heights and Assad wanted an immediate ceasefire to ensure that the newly captured territory would remain in Syrian hands. He wanted to secure the ceasefire before the Israelis would have the chance to push back the Syrian forcesin a counter-attack. Sadat refused.

Q: Was there another rift between Egypt and Syria during the war?

A: Yes. On October 19, 1973, when Egyptian President Sadat learned that his Third Army was encircled and faced destruction, he asked for a ceasefire. This time Assad refused. Sadat decided to end the fighting without Assad's consent and the Syrian President accused Sadat of treason.

Q: What heightened the tension between Syria and Egypt?

A: Egypt attended the Geneva Conference in December 1973, signed the first disengagement agreement in January 1974, and the second disengagement agreement in September 1975. Sadat visited Israel in November 1977, signed the Camp David Accords in September 1978, and ultimately signed a peace treaty with Israel in March 1979. All this was achieved without consulting the Syrians and contrary to their opinion.

> *There is some curse upon us, the Arabs. Whenever we achieve some unity, something happens to disunite us again.*
> the late Egyptian President ANWAR AL-SADAT

> *I must tell you quite frankly, and this is very unfortunate, that we are accustomed to this conflict among ourselves in the Arab world. It is not now or last year or so; it is since history. And we shall always be having these conflicts and difficulties until the end of the world.*
>
> ANWAR AL-SADAT,
> ABC interview, October 4, 1976

Q: How did Israel treat Syrian prisoners-of-war?

A: The representative of Amnesty International, Hugh Baker, wrote, in the *Jerusalem Post* on January 4, 1974, the following: "They are being treated well . . . and they seem to be getting the best medical treatment possible. The doctors are treating them as human beings."

Q: What the Syrian attitude towards Israeli prisoners-of-war?

A: Israeli prisoners-of-war were tortured, beaten, and 28 of them were murdered in cold blood after having already surrendered. All of this is in clear violation of the Geneva War Convention.

Q: What further attests to Syrian Barbarity?

A: After the war, for months Syria refused to submit a list of Israeli prisoners, not to mention allowing the International Red Cross visitation rights with them.

Q: How did Egypt treat Israeli prisoners-of-war?

A: The Egyptian treatment of Israeli prisoners-of-war was not better than that of the Syrians. Israeli troops were tortured, starved, and in some cases even murdered.

> *Ten drops of fanaticism were given to the world. Nine were given to Syria and one was divided throughout the world. The Syrians insisted in getting their portion from the tenth drop as well.*
>
> Israeli saying

The following cartoon appeared in the Egyptian daily *El-Mawkif El Arabi* in October 1987. It was captioned ''The October war will not be the last war.''

CHAPTER SIXTEEN

OPERATION "PEACE FOR GALILEE" OF 1982

On June 6, 1982, the Israeli cabinet defined the goals of the operation thus: (a) to instruct the Israel Defense Forces to place all the civilian population of Galilee beyond the range of the terrorists' fire from Lebanon, where they, their bases, and their headquarters are concentrated; (b) the name of the operation is "Peace for Galilee"; (c) during the operation the Syrian army will not be attacked unless it attacks our forces; and (d) Israel continues to aspire to the signing of a peace treaty with independent Lebanon, its territorial integrity preserved.

Operation "Peace for Galilee" started on June 6, 1982. The Israeli operation was not directed against the Lebanese government or her sovereignty. Since 1969, PLO terrorists had infiltrated Lebanon and succeeded in creating a kind of state within a state. After the expulsion of the PLO terrorists from Jordan in September 1970, known as "Black September," the Palestinians flocked to Lebanon. In 1976, the Syrian forces entered Lebanon in order to assist the Christians in their struggle against the PLO. Later on, the Syrians joined the Moslems of Lebanon in their fight against the Christians. To date, 60 percent of Lebanon is no longer under the control of the Lebanese government.

Q: What was the reason for Operation "Peace for Galilee"?
A: The PLO, with its cannon and Katyusha rocket shellings, made life in northern Israel unbearable.
Q: What was "the straw that broke the camel's back"?
A: On June 3, 1982, PLO terrorists shot and severely injured Israel's ambassador in London, Shlomo Argov.

> *A gang of terrorists broke into my house. There were about 10
> armed young men. They tied me and my two sons, subdued my
> wife and two daughters, and raped them in front of all of us.*
> an Arab from Nabatieh, southern Lebanon,
> *Ma'ariv,* Israeli daily,
> July 16, 1982

Q: For how long were the Israeli settlements under harassment?

A: For 12 years, the people of Israel – particularly in the northern towns
and villages (the Galilee) – were the target of hundreds of attacks
launched from PLO strongholds in southern Lebanon. The PLO never
sought out military objectives, but rather ambushed buses, killing and
wounding school children and vacationers, stormed apartment houses
and schools, and attacked towns and villages with artillery and rocket
fire.

Q: What did Israel do to protect her citizens during these years?

A: Israel made every effort to protect the lives of its citizens by trying
to curb the PLO threat through diplomatic exchanges and limited
military means, but with no success.

> *Any injury done to a man's honor must be avenged, or else he
> becomes permanently dishonored.*
> an Arab proverb

Q: Did the UN forces help end PLO terror against Israeli civilians?

A: No. Even the deployment of United Nations forces (UNIFIL) in
southern Lebanon proved mostly ineffective in deterring the PLO's
activities against Israel.

Q: What happened in March 1978?

A: An example of PLO-style "armed struggle" was the hijacking of a bus
travelling the Tel Aviv-Haifa coastal road in March 1978. The bus
carried vacationing families home from a day's outing. Thirty-five
people were killed and 75 were wounded by 11 Lebanon-based
terrorists. Subsequently, Israel launched "Operation Litani," which
put a temporary halt to PLO attacks from southern Lebanon.

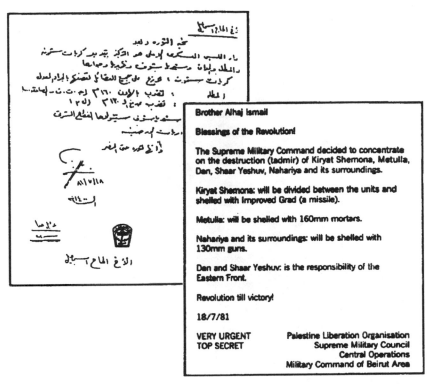

Brother Alhaj Ismail

Blessings of the Revolution!

The Supreme Military Command decided to concentrate on the destruction (tadmir) of Kiryat Shemona, Metulla, Dan, Shear Yeshuv, Nahariya and its surroundings.

Kiryat Shemona: will be divided between the units and shelled with Improved Grad (a missile).

Metulla: will be shelled with 160mm mortars.

Nahariya and its surroundings: will be shelled with 130mm guns.

Dan and Shaar Yeshuv: is the responsibility of the Eastern Front.

Revolution till victory!

18/7/81

VERY URGENT
TOP SECRET

Palestine Liberation Organisation
Supreme Military Council
Central Operations
Military Command of Beirut Area

Above: one of the numerous documents found in southern Lebanon dealing with operational matters. These orders of the PLO's Supreme Military Council are clear proof of the PLO's aggressive intentions towards Israel.

[The PLO] had an army, a police force, a crude judicial system, an educational and welfare system, a civil service and a foreign policy. Those who lived within its rough boundaries said they were too terrified then to describe it to outsiders. Now, for the first time, they are describing what it was like, telling of theft, intimidation and violence.

DAVID SHIPLER,
New York Times,
July 25, 1982

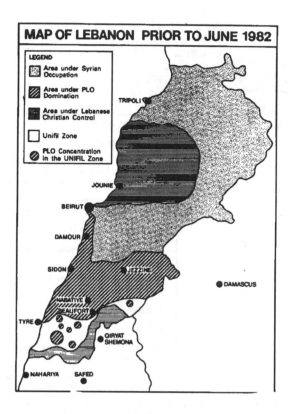

The following cartoon appeared in the Egyptian newspaper *Ruz El-Yussef* on January 26, 1987. It was captioned "Israel in Lebanon."

THE ISRAELI OPERATION AND INTERNATIONAL LAW

Salah Mari Khalil, 13, and Ahmed Burham, 12, were kidnapped by the PLO and taken from their village near Damascus, Syria, to a PLO training camp for children in Nabatiyeh, Lebanon. After training, they were assigned to active military duties while their parents were still unaware of their fate. Salah and Ahmed were manning a roadblock when the "Zionist forces" approached. PLO mentors had fled in the meantime. The Israeli soldiers disarmed the boys, gave them food and clothing, then sent them home to Damascus through the International Red Cross.

Q: Did Israel violate international law by entering Lebanon?
A: No. Paragraph 51 of the United Nations charter speaks about the right of states to take measures in order to defend themselves.
Q: Which states used this right in the past?
A: The United States exercised this right when Soviet missiles were found in Cuba. The British used this right in 1982 in the Falklands.

But politics here was much more than patronage and debate. The major tool of persuasion was the gun, according to those who lived through it.

DAVID SHIPLER,
New York Times,
July 25, 1982

Q: What is the meaning of this international law?
A: International law allows one state to infiltrate and even attack a second state if the latter was found to be making military preparations for an attack on the first. Any country has the right to remove an armed threat against her.

Where incursion of armed bands is a precursor to an armed attack or itself constitutes an attack, and the authorities in the territory from which the armed bands came are either unable or unwilling to control and restrain them, then armed intervention, having as its sole object the removal or destruction of their bases, would . . . be justifiable under Article 51 [of the UN Charter].

"Intervention in International Law:
A Study of Some Recent Cases,"
by Fawcett (103 Recueil des Cours, 1961, Vol. II)

THE VALUE OF PLO PROMISES

> *You can't imagine how distorted kids get around here [in Lebanon]. They have to prove themselves early, imitating their elders at violence and war.*
>
> LILLIAN TYANE, President,
> "Help Lebanon"
>
> ---
>
> *You see kids who tie dead rats behind their bicycles because they have seen grown-ups tie their prisoners behind their jeeps.*
>
> ELIAS T., social worker,
> *Jerusalem Post*,
> August 10, 1982

The PLO has proved time and again that its promises are one thing, keeping them is quite another.

Since the PLO infiltration into Lebanon, different attempts were made on the part of the Lebanese government to control or curb its activities and to find some ground of agreement with it. All the agreements and all the commitments of the PLO were not honored.

Q: What was the first agreement?

A: The first agreement was the "Cairo Agreement" in 1969. At that time, the PLO promised to refrain from shelling Israeli settlements from Lebanese territory, and that it would not operate bases on Lebanese soil. The PLO did not honor this agreement and in 1973, the Lebanese Army went into action in order to stop the PLO violation of Lebanese sovereignty.

Q: What was the second agreement?

A: The second agreement is known as the "Melkert Agreement" of 1973. The PLO pledged not to admit heavy weaponry into the refugee camps in Lebanon and to end terrorist activities against Israel from Lebanese territory. This agreement was not honored.

Q: What was the third agreement?

A: The third agreement was the agreement of Shtura in 1977. Once again the PLO agreed to honor Lebanese sovereignty and to end the use of refugee camps as terrorist training camps. The PLO agreed to hand over all the heavy weaponry in the camps to the Lebanese army. This agreement was not honored as well.

By the early 1980s, the PLO was virtually a state within a state, clearly crushing Lebanese sovereignty. The Lebanese Ambassador to the United Nations, Edouard Ghorra, addressing the UN General Assembly on October 14, 1976, stated: "The Palestinians increased the influx of arms into Lebanon . . . They transformed most of the refugee camps, if not all, into military bastions . . . Common-law criminals fleeing from Lebanese justice found shelter and protection in the camps . . . Those camps in fact became centers for the training of mercenaries sent and financed by some other Arab states . . . Palestinian elements belonging to various organizations resorted to kidnapping of Lebanese – and sometimes foreigner – holding them prisoners, questioning them, and sometimes killing them . . . They committed all sorts of crimes in Lebanon and also escaped Lebanese justice in the protection of the camps. They smuggled goods. They went so far as to demand 'protection' money . . . It is difficult to enumerate all the illegal activities committed by those Palestinian elements . . ."

An army which sets up machine guns in the center of an area occupied by civilians assumes a heavy responsibility with regard to this civilian population. A town from which guns are fired on troops elsewhere cannot claim to be an open town, immune to bombing.

M. GEORGES-PICOT,
representative of France to the UN,
speech to the Security Council,
June 2, 1958

THE RESULTS OF THE OPERATION

We found in South Lebanon ten times as many arms as we had expected.

MENACHEM BEGIN, then-Israeli Premier,
Jerusalem, June 1982

The PLO had enough weapons to equip an army of 100,000, or six times its estimated total strength. Some 150 heavy truckloads of this booty came each day for nearly two months to Israel and there was still more to come as new caches were found.

The Israeli forces destroyed the PLO bases in southern Lebanon from which the PLO terrorist shelled Israeli settlements. Huge quantities of military equipment were discovered and confiscated. Thousands of PLO terrorists were either killed, wounded, captured or fled. The Israeli forces reached as far as the Lebanese capital, Beirut.

Q: Why did the Israeli troops go to Beirut?

A: Israel's purpose was to uproot the Beirut-centered international terrorist network and thus end the ominous threat to the safety of people all over the world.

Q: What was Beirut for the PLO?

A: The Lebanese capital served as the headquarters of the PLO. It was from the PLO offices in Beirut that the PLO organized and planned all the terrorist actions against the world in general and Israel in particular. The PLO turned Beirut into the capital of organized terror.

Q: What made the PLO leave Beirut?

A: PLO forces in Beirut were beseiged by the Israeli army. They understood that they had no alternative but to leave Beirut and they did.

A: Where did these terrorists go?

A: The PLO prestige reached its lowest ebb. The PLO was forced to abandon its headquarters, lost its strongholds, and proved that it could not stand against the superiority of the Israeli forces. PLO terrorists were dispersed to eight Arab states.

> *For seven years our life was worth nothing, and the world did not know? We came back to like when you [the Israelis] came in and threw out the Muharibin [PLO terrorists].*
> Mayor of Burj Bahl, Lebanon, 1982

Q: What added to Arafat's troubles?

A: As a result of its defeat, the PLO split. Colonel Abu Musa, one of the PLO cammanders, blamed Arafat for the PLO failure and subsequent defeat. He established his own organization and claims that he, rather than the PLO, represents the Palestinian people. The Syrian government supported Abu Musa and his group.

Q: Why did Syria support Abu Musa?

A: The Syrians thought that Arafat was too independent and does not listen to their good advice. Moreover, the Syrians believed that Arafat was acting in Lebanon against the national interests of Syria.

> *No sovereign state can tolerate indefinitely the build-up along its borders of a military force dedicated to its destruction and implementing its objectives by periodic shellings and raids.*
> U.S. Secretary of State HENRY KISSINGER,
> defending the Israeli operation on June 16, 1982

THE SABRA AND SHATILA TRAGEDY

> *No nation is eager for peace more than the Israeli nation and no nation is more ready to sacrifice for survival.*
> CHAIM HERZOG, Israeli President
>
> ---
>
> *Pray for peace of Jerusalem. They shall prosper that love thee. Peace be within thy walls and prosperity within thy palaces.*
> Psalms 122:6

The tragedy of the Sabra and Shatila refugee camps occurred on September 16-17, 1982.

Q: What happened there?
A: On September 16, 1982, forces of the Maronite Christian Phalange entered the two camps situated in Lebanon. They massacred 460 Palestinian Arabs, as well as a number of others of different nationalities.
Q: How was it possible for the massacre to occur?
A: In the Arab world in general and in Lebanon in particular, the killing of the innocent is a way of life.
Q: Why did the Christians kill the Moslem Palestinians?
A: The Christians came to massacre the Moslem Palestinians because they blamed the Moslems for the assassination of their beloved, newly elected president, Bashir Gemayel, two days earlier.

> *In the name of all the Christians of the Middle East, and as Lebanese Christians, let us proclaim that if Lebanon is not to be a Christian national homeland, it will nonetheless remain a homeland for the Chrisitians . . . Yassir Arafat has transformed the church of Damur into a garage. We forgive him, and . . . we will rebuild it. Had we been in Egypt or Syria, perhaps we would*

> *not even have had the right to rebuild a destroyed church. Our desire is to remain in the Middle East so that our church bells may ring our our joys and sorrow whenever we wish. We do not want . . . to be transformed into citizens existing in the "dhimmitude."*
>
> Lebanon's President-elect, BASHIR GEMAYEL,
> September 14, 1982 (several hours
> before his assassination)

Q: Did Israel convince the Christians to massacre the Palestinians?
A: Absolutely not.
Q: Did Israel know that the Christians were intending to kill the Palestinians?
A: Absolutely not.
Q: How did the Israeli people react to the massacre?
A: There was an immediate and huge demonstration in Tel aviv calling upon the government fo investigate the sad event.
Q: In what respect was Israel at fault?
A: The Kahan Committee, which was established by the Israeli government to investigate the tragic incident, accused Ariel Sharon, then-Minister of Defense, and Rafael Eitan, Israel's Chief of Staff at that time, of negligence. The committee concluded that the two men were indirectly guilty in that they did not take all the necessary measures in order to prevent the events that occurred in the Sabra and Shatila camps. Both men lost their posts as a result.

> *[The Kahan Commission of Inquiry is a] great tribute to Israeli democracy that they could accept such a heavy responsibility by such hig-level people. It is true that there are very few governments in the world that one can imagine making such a public investigation of such a difficult and shameful episode.*
>
> U.S. Secretary of State HENRY KISSINGER

Q: What was the reaction in the Arab world?
A: The Arabs blamed Israel for the massacre, using this tragic case in order to make propaganda gains.

The following cartoon appeared in Egypt's *El-Shaab* on September 22, 1987. It was captioned "Anniversary of the massacres of Sabra and Shatila."

CHAPTER SEVENTEEN

THE *INTIFADA* – OLD/NEW
ARAB WAR AGAINST ISRAEL

> *Contrary to some doubts voiced in the press, Israel has not "lost its soul." Its soldiers are not sadists. They do not enjoy fighting stone-throwing adolescents. But confronted by them, what would a soldier do? Run away? Where?*
>
> ELIE WIESEL,
> *New York Times*, June 23, 1988

The Palestinian Arabs, in their struggle against Israel, have used different and various means and methods: armed struggle, terrorist operations, intensive propaganda, intimidation, boycott, etc. The Palestinian Arabs rioted against the Jewish national home in 1920, 1921, 1929, 1933, 1936-39, and 1947-48. Since Israel's establishment in 1948, the Arab armies have fought against Israel five times: in 1948, the War of Independence; 1956, the Sinai campaign; 1967, the Six-Day War; 1973, the Yom Kippur War; and 1982, the war in Lebanon. The Palestinian Arabs, like the other Arabs, lost all the wars.

Q: What is the proper term by which to define the most recent disturbances that started in December 1987?

A: The Israeli authorities refer to these as "disturbances," the Western media calls them the "uprising" and the Palestinian Arabs themselves call them the *Intifada* – meaning "shake-off" in Arabic.

Q: Who is behind the disturbances?

A: For the first time since 1947-48, the Palestinian Arabs in Judea, Samaria, and the Gaza Strip themselves have been leading the struggle. Supporters of the PLO have been active, along with Islamic fundamentalists, and people who have no clear political affiliation.

Q: What is the role of the Islamic elements?

A: Since the late 1970s, not only have the traditional fundamentalist groups in Judea, Samaria, and the Gaza Strip gathered strength, but new and radical fundamentalists have emerged. These elements have combined Islamic fundamentalism with Palestinian Arab nationalism, and are advocating a Jihad (holy war) to eradicate Israel and to replace it with an Islamic state.

Q: What is the philosophy of these Moslems?

A: Characterized by a high degree of organization and discipline, the radical Islamic fundamentalist groups are known collectively as "Islamic Jihad." The Gazan leader of the group, Sheikh Abd al-Aziz Awdah, stated in the *Financial Times* on November 1987 that Palestine was the most important homeland in the Moslem world.

Allah is the target, the prophet is its model, the Koran its constitution, Jihad [holy war] is the path and death for the sake of Allah is the loftiest of its wishes.

slogan of the Islamic Resistance Movement

I swear by the holder of Mohammed's soul that I would like to invade and be killed for the sake of Allah, then invade and be killed, and then invade again and be killed.

as related by *Al-Bukhari* and Moslem Article 15,
the Covenant of the Islamic Resistance Movement,
August 18, 1988

The great Islamic historian Ibn Khaldun (1332-1406) defined the Jihad as follows: "In the Muslim community the holy war is a religious duty because of the universalism of the [Muslim] mission and the obligation to convert everybody to Islam either by persuasion or by force."

The Ayatollah Khomeini wrote in 1969: "Holy War means the conquest of non-Muslim territories. It is possible that it may be declared after the formation of an Islamic government worthy of the name, under the direction of an Imam or at his command. It will then be incumbent upon every adult able-bodied man to volunteer for this war of conquest, whose final goal is the domination of Koranic law from one end of the earth to the other."

REASONS BEHIND THE *INTIFADA*

> *There is no solution for the Palestinian question except through Jihad. Proposals, international conferences are all a waste of time and vain endeavors.*
>
> from the Covenant
> of the Islamic Resistance Movement

The violent events that erupted on December 9, 1987, and have since continued at various degrees of intensity are due to a combination of factors, some spontaneous and some deliberate. There are various reasons, some known and others less known:

1. For over twenty-two years, Judea, Samaria, and the Gaza Strip have been under military administration. People would like to see a change.
2. The new generation (postwar 1967) refuses to accept the misery and hardships of life in the refugee camps as their way of life.
3. The religious motives play an important role. Fanatic Moslems believe that whoever falls in battle against non-Moslems never dies. On the contrary, he is alive and enjoys the glory of God.

> *And say not of those slain in God's way, they are dead; rather they are living but you are not aware.*
>
> The Koran 2:154

4. Palestinian nationalism is another factor. The success of the PLO in the world and the fact that the world has become aware of the Palestinian dilemma has boosted the national feelings and aspirations of the Palestinians in these territories. The PLO has become a symbol. The PLO speaks of a Palestinian state, so they want a Palestinian state.
5. Israel is a democracy based on human values and justice. This fact has been exploited by the Palestinian Arabs who express their opposition to Israel openly and without fear. Moreover, Israel's democratic values have been misjudged by the Palestinians as a weakness.
6. In November 1987, the Arab League Summit in Amman did not focus its agenda on the Palestinian issue. Instead, it concentrated on other inter-Arab issues. The Palestinian inhabitants of the territories viewed this as a sign of growing Arab apathy toward them and, as a result, their discontent and frustration grew.

7. The economic reason is another factor. The oil-rich Arab Persian Gulf states suffer from economic depression. As a result, thousands of Palestinian professionals employed in these countries found themselves jobless and returned to Judea, Samaria, and the Gaza Strip. Upon their return, they joined ranks with the thousands of other unemployed residents. Israel found herself unable to help these people due to her own economic recession in the years 1987, 1988, 1989, and 1990. Jordan could not supply them with jobs because of her very severe economic depression. There are over 20,000 unemployed Arab professionals in these territories and tens of thousands who may join the circle of unemployment in the future. The new generation of Palestinians is bitter economically, emotionally, and nationally.

8. The exchange of prisoners between Israel and the Jibril faction of the PLO in 1985. Israel agreed to release 1,100 dangerous terrorists in exchange for three Israeli soldiers. Moreover, Israel agreed that some of these terrorists could remain in the territories. Equipped with intensified feelings of radical Palestinian nationalism, many of these Palestinian prisoners became part of the leadership of the *Intifada.*

9. On November 25, 1987, an Arab terrorist from the Popular Front for the Liberation of Palestine – General Command succeeded in crossing the Lebanese border into Israel proper on a glider. He managed to enter an Israeli military camp and shot six Israeli soldiers before he was shot to death. The fact that a young Palestinian could shoot and kill six Israeli soldiers in their own camp boosted the pride of the Palestinians and served as an example to the young Palestinians.

10. After the stabbing deaths of several Israeli civilians, four Arabs died in a Gaza traffic collision involving an Israeli truck. Rumors spread that the accident was in reprisal for the terrorist murders.

Those arriving from the West Bank define the situation thus: We have not forgotten nor will we ever forget the type of rule which degraded our honor and trampled the human feelings within us, a rule which they built by their inquisition and the boots of their desert men. We have lived a long period under the humiliation of Arab nationalism, and it pains us to say that we had to wait for the Israel conquest in order to become aware of human relationships with citizens.

from an interview with Arab residents
of Judea and Samaria,
Al-Hawadith, Beirut, April 23, 1971

WHAT ARE THE GOALS OF
THE *INTIFADA*?

> *We must remember, however, that Israel has shown far more restraint toward violent demonstrations than any hostile neighboring state has ever shown toward peaceful demonstrations against government policy. Israel remains the only country in the entire Middle East in which Arabs can enjoy any measure of political freedom.*
>
> U.S. Senator DANIEL P. MOYNIHAN,
> in a letter to a constituent, May 3, 1988

The goals of the *Intifada* are the following: (a) to force Israel to withdraw from Judea, Samaria, and the Gaza Strip and to establish a Palestinian state in these territories; (b) to make life in Israel miserable by creating a feeling of unsafety throughout the country; (c) to frighten the Jewish settlers in Judea and Samaria and to force them to abandon their settlements; (d) to ensure that new immigrants, not to mention tourists, would not come to Israel; moreover, to make life so difficult that Israelis would be willing to leave and live abroad; (e) to make the world aware of the Palestinian struggle; (f) to inflict severe damage on the Israeli economy; (g) to strengthen the chances of political Israeli-Palestinian negotiations, according to one faction of the Palestinians; and (h) to cause a new round of war between Israel and the Arab states, according to another faction.

> *Whoever mobilizes a fighter for the sake of Allah is himself a fighter. Whosoever supports the relatives of a fighter he himself is a fighter.*
>
> related by *Al-Bukhari*,
> Moslem Abu Dawood, and *Al-Tarmadhi*

As reported by *Newsday*, December 21, 1988, PLO Chairman Yassir Arafat, speaking in Belgrade, Yugoslavia, said: "Our decision was and has been to continue the *Intifada* until the occupier is pushed from our territories, and until our people get a chance to enjoy their sovereignty under PLO leadership on their national soil."

HAS THE *INTIFADA* SUCCEEDED IN ACHIEVING ITS GOALS?

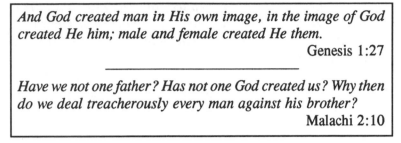

And God created man in His own image, in the image of God created He him; male and female created He them.

Genesis 1:27

Have we not one father? Has not one God created us? Why then do we deal treacherously every man against his brother?

Malachi 2:10

The *Intifada* has achieved some of its goals, yet has failed to achieve many others. It has succeeded with the following:

1. The *Intifada* brought the dilemma of the Palestinians to world public opinion, thereby exerting international pressure on Israel.
2. It bolstered the national feelings of the Palestinian Arabs.
3. It proved that the Palestinian Arabs could sacrifice for the sake of nationhood.
4. It strengthened the position of the PLO in the world.
5. It damaged Israel's image in the world.
6. It cost Israel hundreds of millions of dollars on military expenditure and caused some damage to the Israeli economy and morale.
7. It intensified the internal debate in Israel with regard to finding a solution to the Palestinian Arab dilemma.
8. It pressured Israel into initiating a new peace plan.

Of Ishmael, whom the Arabs claim to be their forefather, the Bible reads: *"And the angel of the Lord said to her, behold thou art with child and should bear a son and shalt call his name Ishmael because the Lord has heard thy affliction. And he will be a wild man, his hands will be against every man and every man's hand against him."*

Genesis 16:11-12

WHERE DID THE *INTIFADA* FAIL?

> *Our heroic sons of the Gaza Strip, oh proud sons of the (West) Bank, oh heroic sons of the Galilee, oh steadfast sons of the Negev... The fires of the revolution against the Zionist invaders will not fade out . . . until our land – all our land – has been liberated from these usurping invaders.*
>
> YASSIR ARAFAT,
> PLO Radio, Baghdad, December 10, 1987

The *Intifada* failed in the following:

1. The *Intifada* failed to force Israel to leave Judea, Samaria, and the Gaza Strip.
2. It did not cause Jewish settlers to abandon their settlements. On the contrary, in two years of the *Intifada* (1988-89) thousands of new Jewish settlers have made their homes in Judea and Samaria.
3. It did not compel Israel to negotiate with the PLO or to agree to the establishment of a Palestinian state.
4. It did not discourage or end Jewish immigration to Israel. On the contrary, more and more Jews have come to live in Israel.
5. It did not discourage tourism to Israel.

The *Intifada* caused the following adverse effects on the Palestinian Arabs:

1. The Palestinian Arabs lost hundreds of millions of dollars. About 600 lost their lives and thousands more have been injured. Many thousands were detained, arrested, or expelled.
2. The *Intifada* caused misery and unsafety among the Palestinian Arabs in these territories.
3. According to the Jordanian government, since the outbreak of the *Intifada* at the end of 1987, over 24,000 Palestinians have left Judea and Samaria and have gone to Jordan as a direct result of the hardships caused by the *Intifada*.

The failure of the *Intifada* to achieve most of its goals has kindled some new thinking among Palestinian leaders. One of those, who dared to express an opinion different from the PLO leadership by calling for an end to the *Intifada,* was the Christian mayor of Bethlehem, Elias Freij.

In reaction to Mr. Freij's suggestion, PLO chairman Yassir Arafat said the following in *Al-Qabas* (Kuwait) on January 1, 1989, and again on Radio Monte-Carlo the following day: "Any Palestinian leader who proposes an end to the *Intifada* exposes himself to the bullets of his own people and endangers his life. The PLO will know how to deal with him."

> *[The PLO is] opposed to a Zionist state . . . Zionism is a racist movement [and] we don't want a racist state in this area.*
>
> YASSIR ARAFAT,
> *Los Angeles Times,*
> December 19, 1988

> *Many visitors to Jerusalem – Archbishop Tutu, for one – are ready to slang Israel but remain strangely demure about Arab tyrannies. Perhaps it is because if you denounce Israel in Jerusalem, all you get is a pained look. Try denouncing the government in Syria or Iraq and you never get back, whether for business or for political tourism.*
>
> A. M. ROSENTHAL,
> *New York Times,*
> March 25,1990

WHAT GIVES THE *INTIFADA* MORE LIFE

> *True believers, if a wicked man come unto you with a tale, inquire strictly into the truth thereof; lest ye hurt people through ignorance, and afterwards repent of what ye have done.*
>
> The Koran,
> *The Inner Apartment,* Verse 6

Pro-PLO groups and extremist Islamic fundamentalists are working hard to ensure the continuation of the *Intifada.* In their efforts to obtain and maintain public support and participation in the disturbances, these radicals target their violence against their fellow Arabs as well whom they consider unsympathetic or uncooperative with their goals. Local merchants are pressured to close their businesses under threats of violence and vandalism, and workers are forcibly prevented from commuting to their jobs. Their vehicles are damaged, local public transportation is attacked, and buses have even been burnt. Arab has attacked Arab. By March 1990, more than 185 Arab residents had been murdered by Arabs and 150 were injured by extremists who accused them of having connections with Israel.

The nature of the unrest, however, has changed. The radical activists and inciters are generally no longer able to motivate large-scale riots. Activity now is concentrated on smaller confrontational groups and violence has assumed a more localized nature, directed against Israeli soldiers and civilians and other Arabs.

The following are catalysts to the disturbances:

1. The world media covers the events and brings the pictures to all the world. At times, it is the presence of the camera that creates the uprising. The Palestinians know that the world is now aware of the conflict and this adds fire to their motivation.
2. The fact that not only most Israeli Arabs, but some leftist Jewish groups in Israel and abroad support the Palestinians as well.
3. The fact that within the Israeli government there were sundry views with regard to a desired solution.
4. The wishful thinking on the part of the Palestinians that the super-powers may impose a solution upon Israel that would bring about a Palestinian state.
5. The fact that the PLO has gained far more momentum and prestige since the end of 1988. In December 1988 Arafat declared that the PLO accepts United Nations Security Resolution 242 and renounces terrorism.
6. The fact that tens of states the world over have already recognized the Palestinian state.

> *In our view Israel clearly has not only the right, but the obligation, to preserve or restore order in the occupied territories and to use appropriate levels of force to acomplish that end . . . [Israel] has made a significant effort (to use non-lethal equipment including tear gas, rubber bullets, and water cannons) and similiar items which will allow for a more measured response to situations that are not inherently or imminently life-threatening.*
>
> RICHARD SCHIFTER, Assistant Secretary of
> State for Human Rights and Humanitarian Affairs,
> March 28, 1988

WHAT WEAKENS THE *INTIFADA*

> *The IDF is conducting (in the territories) a harsh, brutal struggle that has been forced upon it. It is not easy, not easy at all. The IDF is allowed to, and it must, defend itself, impose order and detain suspects. It is entitled to use force for all these things; there is no other way. It is unpleasant, difficult, but that's the way it is . . .*
>
> Israeli Minister of Justice DAN MERIDOR,
> IDF Radio's evening newsreel,
> February 1, 1989

There are a number of factors that weaken the uprising: (a) the economic difficulties as a result of self-imposed curfews, strikes, demonstrations, arrests, and detentions; (b) there are no immediate concrete results to the uprising; (c) the reality that tens of thousands of Palestinians from these territories must find employment in order to earn a living; (d) the fact that there is violence of Palestinian Arabs against other Arabs; people are more concerned about their lives than about the uprising; (e) the fact that the PLO leadership is outside the area and the local leadership is too weak to fully control the events, not to mention to make policy decisions; (f) the Palestinians in these areas find themselves between the hammer and the nail; that is to say, between Israel and the PLO; (g) ideological differences have been increasingly felt between the pro-PLO activists and the Islamic fundamentalists, and within the various PLO factions themselves; and (h) opposing and contradictory orders to the Palestinians in the territories from various different factions.

> *Maybe he was trying to swim for it.*
>
> ABU ABBAS, mastermind
> of the *Achille Lauro* hijacking
> and murderer of Leon Klinghoffer,
> *New York Times*, November 14, 1988

IS THE *INTIFADA* A NEW PHENOMENON AMONG THE PALESTINIANS?

The *Intifada* is nothing more and nothing less than the opening of a new old front and the adoption of new tactics in the relentless war that the Arab world and Palestinian Arabs have been waging since 1948 to destroy the Jewish state. In its efforts to look for and find new ways and methods to fight against Israel, the PLO has never agreed to a truce, a ceasefire or a compromise.

Arab rioting against other people, other regimes, and even their own people in the Middle East is not a new phenomenon.

Q: Can an example be cited?
A: Yes. The Palestinian Arabs fought against the British government and the Jewish national home in Palestine during the Mandate period.

> *Yawaylak Ya Katel Alabriah.*
> *(Woe upon you, murderer of the innocent.)*
>   Islamic saying

Q: Did they fight against one another?
A: Yes. In the riots of 1936-39, approximately 500 Jews were killed by the Palestinian Arabs. In this same period, over 3,000 Palestinian Arabs were murdered by Palestinian Arabs.
Q: How many Palestinian Arabs have been killed by Palestinian Arabs in the *Intifada*?
A: In the *Intifada,* over 185 Arabs were murdered by Arabs in the years 1988-89. Most of these victims were innocent. They were killed by their fellow Arabs simply because someone had said they were collaborators with the Israeli authorities. Still others were murdered as a result of some personal conflict with the murderer.

> *Why did the Creator form all life from a single ancestor? they*
> *ask, and the reply is, "that the families of mankind shall not*
> *. . . lord one over the other . . . with the claim of being sprung*
> *from superior stock . . . that all men . . . may recognize their*
> *common kinship in the collective human family.*
>   Tosefta Sanhedrin 8:4

SECURITY MEASURES AND
THE LEGAL ASPECT

The uprising in Judea and Samaria could have been stopped within 48 hours had Israel used ruthless means to stop it. In any Arab state, such an uprising would have been dealt with harshly. However, Israel is a democracy based on the supremacy of the law. The Palestinian Arabs interpret Israeli democracy as a weakness and believe and react accordingly.

Q: Aren't Israeli security measures such as expulsions, administrative detentions, house demolitions, legal procedures, and prison conditions contrary to international law and the principles of human rights?

A: Those residents of the territories who are suspected of having committed security offenses are dealt with in accordance with international law and the humanitarian provisions of the 1949 Geneva Conventions.

Q: What does international law say about that?

A: Article 43 of the 1907 Hague regulations stipulates that the controlling authority ". . . shall take all the measures in his power to restore and ensure, as far as possible, public order and safety, while respecting, unless absolutely prevented, the laws in force in the country."

Q: What are the characteristics of Israeli policy?

A: The various security measures taken by Israel are in keeping with its international obligations. As the authority currently responsible for maintaining order and public safety in the administered areas, Israel constantly seeks to find the proper balance between security and humanitarian requirements.

Q: Can the Arab residents gain access to the Israeli courts?

A: Yes. The right of the residents of the administered territories to gain access to the Israeli legal system is unprecedented in international practice and such access serves as a unique safeguard of the rule of law.

> *The Jewish faith is predominately the faith of liberty.*
> U.S. President CALVIN COOLIDGE

Q: Is the legal system in these territories run according to democratic standards?

A: Absolutely. Trials pertaining to security offenses are heard before a military court and are held in accordance with the procedures and rules of evidence obtaining in the courts of common law in Western states. Convictions in such trials must be based on evidence, and cannot be based on a confession alone.

Q: What happens when there is not enough evidence to prove the defendant guilty?

A: Many defendants were released from custody following their arraignment as a result of insufficient evidence presented to the court against them.

Q: What are the living conditions in prison?

A: Proper food is supplied and meals are prepared by cooks chosen from among the inmates. Family visits are permitted, representatives of the International Red Cross are entitled to inspect all detention facilities, and do so regularly. Access has also been granted to journalists.

Q: What is "administrative detention"?

A: The decision to place certain residents of these territories under administrative detention is taken because of the danger they pose to the lives and safety of others, and because of their involvement in violence.

Q: Is this action legal?

A: Yes. Such detention is in full accordance with Article 78 of the Fourth Geneva Convention. Moreover, every prisoner has the right to appeal his detention up to and including the Supreme Court. In the event that such detention is found to have no sufficient basis, the prisoner must be released.

Q: What about expulsion?

A: Expulsion orders are rarely issued. They are carried out only in extreme cases where other measures have not succeeded in stopping hostile activity.

Q: Who are those who are expelled?

A: Those expelled are neither innocent activists nor peaceful demonstrators, but individuals prominent in instigating and perpetuating hostile, and at times even violent acts. Many of those expelled were leaders of local PLO factions and some even bear direct responsibility for acts of terror and murder committed under PLO orders.

Q: What can be said of others who were expelled?

A: Some were prominent in local extremist Islamic fundamentalist organizations, such as the Islamic Jihad. Also among those expelled were several tried and convicted terrorists who were later released from prison as a result of the 1985 prisoner exchange with the Jibril faction of the PLO. Though, as a condition of their release, these convicts committed themselves to refrain from all terrorist activities their pledges were subsequently disregarded.

Q: Can such individuals oppose the expulsion order through a legal appeal?

A: Yes. Each and every one of the individuals who received an expulsion order was given the opportunity to submit an appeal to Israel's Supreme Court.

> *And thou shalt proclaim liberty throughout the land, unto all the inhabitants thereof.*
> Leviticus 25:10

Q: What can be said about Israel's policy of house demolition?

A: The demolition of a structure is one of the security measures which, according to the Fourth Geneva Convention, is permitted under international law when demanded by imperative military considerations. Moreover, these demolitions are in accordance with the emergency regulations promulgated by the British Mandatory power maintained by Jordan and carried over in Israeli law.

Q: What is the purpose of such demolitions?

A: The purpose is to deter those who perpetrate criminal acts and disturb public order and who, by their very conduct, cause serious and fatal injuries to others.

> *We never intend to open fire at fleeing children. There has never been such a thing. No such intention exists . . .*
> Israeli Minister of Justice DAN MERIDOR,
> IDF Radio evening newsreel, February 1, 1989
>
> *The children of the* Intifada *are victims. They are victims of those who, seemingly lacking elementary human decency and basic parental protectiveness, use them as cannon fodder. Except for rare instances, the victims are not young bystanders hit by a stray rubber bullet or tear gas. They are not children at play assaulted in their backyards. They are children incited by their elementary school teachers to throw bricks and rocks at those described in their books as the "Zionist murderers and ravishers of their land . . ."*
> *Jerusalem Post* editorial,
> June 27, 1990

THE PLO ENCOURAGES
MURDER OF THE INNOCENT

> *The following is in relation to the PLO killing other Palestinians: The PLO is a murderer of women, children, pregnant women, teachers, nurses, etc. – systematic killing of the innocent . . . This is terror.*
>
> BENJAMIN NETANYAHU,
> Deputy Foreign Minister of Israel
> in the Knesset, March 21, 1990

On July 7, 1989, a Palestinian terrorist forcibly pulled an Israeli passenger bus off the road and down a ravine, causing the death of 15 innocent passengers.

From Tunis, the PLO issued a declaration accusing the radical leaders of Israel for the death of the 15 Israeli citizens in the incident. In its declaration, Ahmad Abd Alrahman, the PLO spokesman said: "Those who were killed are the victims of the Israeli leaders who lost any responsibility towards their nation and towards our nation."

Q: What was the reaction of the PLO News Agency?

A: The PLO News Agency, WAFA, declared that the heroic suicide action – a new kind, carried out by a young man – is one step before a general civil uprising and a people's revolution and that no one can foresee its results. For sure, no one can stop it.

Q: What was Mr. Sharif's reaction?

A: Bassam Abu Sharif, advisor to public relations in the PLO said: "Shamir and his government and the Israeli troops who kill children are terrorists." About the Arab murderer he said: "He protected his rights of opposition to the occupation. He is not a terrorist."

Q: Why was the former PLO leader, Ahmed Shukeiri, denounced?

A: Shukeiri said, before the 1967 war, that the Jews should be thrown into the sea. He was denounced not because the PLO considered the idea stupid. He was denounced for having made the declaration publicly. To have said this in advance was stupid.

> *A notorious rape concerns the Mukhtar of Anser, whose political statements made him unpopular with the PLO. One night they attacked his village and surrounded his house. They tied up the Mukhtar and his wife and forced them to watch as they raped their daughter, killed her, sliced off her breasts and left her mutilated body on their doorstep.*
>
> *Jerusalem Post,* July 23, 1982

PALESTINIANS KILLING PALESTINIANS

> *Do not kill unjustly.*
>
> The Koran 17:33
>
> ---
>
> *We ordered Palestinians to kill Palestinians . . .*
>
> YASSIR ARAFAT,
> in the Kuwaiti newspaper *Al-Qabas,*
> October 1989

One need not necessarily be a guilty Palestinian to be murdered in Judea and Samaria by another Palestinian sent to carry out the execution by PLO agents in these areas. It is enough to criticize the uprising, to speak out against Arafat, to refuse to pay protection money, or simply to carry on routine business with Israel. These "sins" may cause one's murder at the hands of Palestinians acting under PLO support, indoctrination, and encouragement.

> *A false witness shall not go unpunished, and he that utters lies shall perish.*
>
> Proverbs 19:9
>
> ---
>
> *Do not make false accusations.*
>
> The Koran 25:72

The PLO policy of terror and intimidation against Arabs, Jews, and other innocent people the world over is a clear sign to its supporters in Judea and Samaria to murder anyone who does not follow the PLO path.

> *135 Palestinian Arabs were murdered by Palestinian Arabs in the year 1989. 360 Palestinian Arabs were wounded by Palestinian Arabs.*
>
> Israeli News Agency ITIM

Q: What about other atrocities?

A: Israeli officials claim that 48 percent of the 1,403 beatings, stabbings and attacks on property by Arabs during the first half of 1989 were directed against Palestinians rather than Israeli targets. In the January 25, 1990, issue of the Egyptian newspaper *Al-Musawar,* Arafat gave explanations for the PLO terror against the innocent: "In the first stage, the decision to assassinate [Palestinian Arabs] must be accepted by the majority. In the higher stages, the decision must be accepted unanimously. Despite this we are telling you, the united leadership [namely, the leaders of the uprising], if you send the file before the execution, we would look at it . . . If it is hard, it is imperative to send the file after the execution."

Q: Were the victims of PLO terror collaborators?

A: No. The majority of the victims were innocent people and by no means collaborators with Israel.

Q: What is the PLO's purpose with these killings and intimidations?

A: The purpose is simple: to force all the Palestinians to accept the PLO as the sole representative of the Palestinians. The goal is to dissuade Palestinians in Judea, Samaria and the Gaza Strip from bypassing Arafat and dealing directly with Israel in terms of an interim settlement.

> *Evil men understand no justice, but those who seek the Lord understand all things.*
>
> Proverbs 28:5

Q: What are the other reasons for the killings?

A: Many of the slayings are Lebanese-style: they use the charge of collaboration to cover feuds and personal conflicts.

> *The PLO rules by the bullet, not the ballot.*
>
> MENACHEM BEGIN,
> former Israeli Prime Minister

Q: Is the killing of innocent Palestinians a new phenomenon?

A: No. On October 15, 1938, a correspondent of the *New York Times* reported: "Extremist Arab followers of the Mufti are rapidly achieving their aims by eliminating political opponents in Palestine who are inclined toward moderation. More than 90 percent of the total casualties in the past few days have been inflicted by Arab terrorists on Arabs."

According to a *Jerusalem Post* editorial, June 27, 1990: "The use of children in war is not new to this area. When the British had to deal with the three-year "intifada" of the 'thirties, they bitterly complained about Arab gunmen hiding behind women and children in the knowledge that their Western enemy would have scruples about shooting women and children. Israel troops in Lebanon encountered PLO fighters who used children as shields, and 12-year-olds who had been pressed into service as operators of anti-tank weapons. The *Intifada* strategy, struck in the same mold, was described by the Palestinian leader and journalist Daoud Kuttab in the 1988 spring issue of the *Journal of Palestinian Studies:* "The youngest category of children involved in demonstrations is the seven-to-ten age group. Most of the time these children may be seen rolling tires to the middle of the road, pouring gasoline on them, and then setting them afire . . . Since these children are under the legal age, their capture does not lead to a prison term. At worst, they may be slapped around a bit and then released . . . "

PART V

THE ISLAMIC ATTITUDE TOWARDS JEWS, CHRISTIANS, AND OTHER MINORITIES

CHAPTER EIGHTEEN

MOHAMMED AND THE JEWS

> *. . . and it is known to you that no nation stood against Israel more hostile than they (meaning the Moslems), that no nation did evil to perfection in order to weaken us and belittle us and degrade us like them.*
>
> Jewish philosopher MAIMONIDES,
> from a well-known letter to
> the suffering Yemenite Jews in 1172

When Islam was established in the seventh century CE, there was a very active Jewish community in Medina in the Arab Peninsula. The Jews of pre-Islamic Arabia were active advocates of their religion to the extent that several kings of Himyar, now Yemen, had converted to Judaism. Contemporary inscriptions described Dhu Nuwas As'ar, the last Jewish king of Himyar, as a believer in one deity whom the king called Rahman, the Merciful One, as God was called in Judaism and later in Islam.

The prophet of Islam, Mohammed, was highly impressed by the Jewish religion and especially the idea of one God – monotheism. The influence of Judaism is felt almost everywhere in the Islamic holy book, the Koran. Moreover, Jewish law deeply influenced Mohammed as well. He sought closeness to the Jews and begged them to recognize him as a prophet.

Q: How did Judaism influence Mohammed?
A: In the early days of Islam, Moslems prayed in the direction of the Jews' holy city, Jerusalem, and observed the most solemn Jewish holiday, Yom Kippur (the Day of Atonement).
Q: When did they change these common customs?

A: Only later, when Mohammed reluctantly concluded that the Jews would not embrace him as their prophet and convert to Islam, did he substitute Mecca for Jerusalem, and the fast of Ramadan for Yom Kippur.

Q: What were other Judaic influences on Mohammed?

A: Mohammed based Moslem dietary laws upon Judaism's laws of Kashrut: "You are forbidden carrion, blood, and the flesh of swine; also any flesh of animals sacrificed to idols" (Koran 5:3). The five daily prayers of Islam are likewise modeled on the thrice daily service of the Jews.

Q: How does Mohammed relate to Abraham, the father of monotheism?

A: Second in importance only to his adoption of the Jews' God was Mohammed's adoption of the Jews' founding father, Abraham, as Islam's founder. In *sura* 2, verse 125, Mohammed writes how Abraham and his son Ishmael converted the Kaaba (the holy rock of Arabian paganism) into the holy shrine of Islam.

Q: What did Mohammed want from the Jews of Arabia?

A: Believing himself to be the final and greatest prophet of basic monotheism, and having adopted so much of Jewish thought and practice, Mohammed appealed to the Jews of Arabia to recognize his role and to adopt Islam as the culmination of Judaism.

Q: Why did the Jews reject Mohammed?

A: The Jews rejected Mohammed's claims on the grounds that what was true in his messages was not new, and that what was new was not true. Islam may have served as a religious advance for Arabian pagans, but for the Jews it was merely another offshoot of Judaism.

Q: Did Mohammed ever read the Bible?

A: No. Mohammed was illiterate. Yet Moslems are proud that despite his illiteracy, their prophet could produce a unique book such as the Koran. Mohammed had heard stories from the Bible and tried to remember them, not all the time successfully.

Q: Is there an example?

A: Yes. Mohammed's references to the Bible were often erroneous. In *sura* 28:38 for instance, he has Pharaoh (from the Book of Exodus) ask Haman (from the Book of Esther) to erect the Tower of Babel (which appears at the beginning of the Book of Genesis).

Q: What were other deterrents to Jewish acceptance of Mohammed?

A: In 33:50, for example, Mohammed exempts himself from his own law limiting a man to four wives, and in 4:34 he instructs men to beat disobedient wives. Finally, Mohammed's suspension of many Torah Laws invalidated him in the eyes of the Jews.

Q: What made Mohammed even more furious with the Jews?

A: The Jews not only rejected his prophecy, but they publicly noted the errors in Mohammed's Biblical teachings and may have even ridiculed his claims to prophecy.

> *Oh brothers! Let us not regard this holy and sacrificial war as a war between the Arabs and Israel. Let us regard it as a war of Moslems together against Jews and their leaders. It is the responsibility of all the Islamic governments with their peoples, with all their forces, and potential, to aid and support Feyadeen (guerrillas) on the lines of fire.*
>
> AYATOLLAH KHOMEINI,
> *Confronting Israel*

MOHAMMED AGAINST THE JEWS

Ibn Khaldun (1332-1406), the great Arab historian, in *The Muqaddamah* (Introduction to History), defines the loss of collective consciousness of the children of Israel, their dispersion throughout the world, their alienation from the rest of humanity, and their living a life of disgrace and degradation. He even claims that the Jews were infected with such evil character traits as corruption and deceitful plotting.

As a result of their rejection of him, Mohammed turned against the Jews and their religion and he never forgave them. Mohammed's angry reactions to the Jews were recorded in the Koran, giving millions of Moslems throughout history divinely based antipathy to the Jews.

Q: What did Mohammed change?

A: First and most significantly, he changed Abraham from a Jew to a Moslem: "Abraham was neither Jew nor Christian. [He] surrendered himself to Allah. Surely the men who are nearest to Abraham are those who follow him, this Prophet . . ." (Koran 3:67-68).

> *Verily ye are stronger than they, by reason of the terror cast into their breasts from Allah. This, because they are not people of prudence.*
>
> The Koran,
> *The Emigration*, Verse 13

Q: What was his view about certain Jewish laws?

A: Mohammed said that the many Torah laws had been given to the Jews as punishment for their sins: "Because of their iniquity we forbade the Jews good things which were formerly allowed them" (Koran 4:160).

Q: What was his accusation against the Jews?

A: Mohammed charged the Jews with falsifying their Bible by deliberately omitting prophecies of his coming. For example, in the Koran (2:129) Mohammed has Abraham mouth a prophecy of his (Mohammed's) coming. Mohammed charged that the Jews "extinguish the light of Allah" (Koran 9:32) by having removed such prophecies from their Bible.

Q: How else does Mohammed accuse the Jews?

A: Mohammed asserted that Jews, like Christians, were not true monotheists, a charge he substantiated by claiming that the Jews believed the prophet Ezra to be the son of God. "And the Jews say: Ezra is the son of God. "And Allah fights against them. How perverse are they . . ." (Koran 9:30).

Q: What can be concluded?

A: These anti-Jewish fabrications, articulated by Mohammed as reactions to the Jews' rejection of him, have ever since been regarded by Moslems as God's word. As such, they have formed the basis of Moslem anti-Semitism until the present day. Though originally directed against specific Jews of a specific time, these statements often have been understood by succeeding generations as referring to all Jews at all times.

> *And humiliation and wretchedness were stamped upon them and they were visited with wrath from Allah. That was because they disbelieved in Allah's revelations and slew the prophets wrongfully. That was for their disobedience and transgression.*
>
> The Koran 2:61

By the Jews' remaining Jews they constituted a living refutation. Thus, under Islam, Jew-hatred was ultimately Judaism-hatred. Any Jew who converted to Islam was accepted as an equal. Important to note is the fact that Christians under Moslem rule fared little better. Moslems and their laws generally dealt harshly with both Christians and Jews.

> *The most splendid thing our prophet Mohammed, God's peace and blessing on him, did was to evict them [the Jews] from the entire Arabian peninsula . . . I pledge to you that we will celebrate on the next anniversary, God willing and in this place with God's help, not only the liberation of our land but also the defeat of the Israeli conceit and arrogance so that they must once again return to the condition decreed in our holy book: "humiliation and wretchedness were stamped upon them" . . . We will not renounce this.*
>
> Egyptian President ANWAR SADAT,
> April 25, 1972
>
> ---
>
> *Make war upon those who have been given the scripture [the Jews] . . . until they pay tribute being brought low.*
>
> The Koran, *sura* IX:29

The Moslem legal code, which prescribed the treatment of Jews and Christians, or Dhimmis – as they are both referred to in Islam – follows in the next pages.

CHAPTER NINETEEN

THE DHIMMI –
SECOND-CLASS CITIZENS

The removal of the Israeli occupation from our occupied land, Palestine, is the first and basic condition for just peace . . . The Islamic nation and just believers in any religion or creed will not accept the situation of the land of the Prophet's flight to heaven and the cradle of prophets and divine messages being captive of Zionist occupation.

Jordan's KING HUSSEIN,
speech at Islamic conference,
Amman Domestic Service, July 11, 1980

The famous claim of Arab propaganda is the following: Jews and Christians were treated fairly under the rule of Islam. They were protected and enjoyed civil and religious rights. The main reason for the Arab-Israeli conflict is Zionism. Zionism as a political and national movement is alien to the region. It destroyed the good Moslem-Jewish relations that have prevailed for generations and has caused the Arab-Israeli conflict.

Then were they [the Jews] smitten with abasement and poverty, and met with wrath from God. That was because they had misbelieved in God's signs and killed the prophets undeservedly; that was for that they were rebellious and had transgressed.

The Koran, 2:58

> *The resurrection of the dead will not come until the Muslims will war with the Jews and the Muslims will kill them; until the Jews will hide behind the rocks and trees, and then the trees and rocks will say "O Muslim, O Abdullah, here is a Jew behind me, come and kill him.*
>
> *Hadith* ,
> Egyptian publication of the 1930s and 1940s

THE DHIMMI: JEWS AND CHRISTIANS

> *Al Islam Yu'li Wala Yu'la.*
> *(Islam is always superior, never inferior.)*
>
> Islamic saying
>
> _____
>
> *A Jew will not be found alone with a Muslim without plotting to kill him.*
>
> AMR IBN BAHR AL-JAHIZ,
> Eighth Century,
> *Hadith*

The Dhimmis, as inferior scriptural communities, were required by law to pay a skull tax (the Jizya), in return for which they were allowed to practice their religions and to maintain their local institutions. However, all this was in the context of certain infirmities, besides the Jizya tax, imposed upon them by the Moslem majority. In Islam's view, these minorities were to be tolerated as a sign of their powerlessness under Islam. Islam would care for them in this way so long as they demonstrated their own inferiority by recognizing the legitimacy of Moslem rule over them. Any attempt on the part of the minorities to seek independence would be a violation of the contract.

> *"First the Saturday people [Jews], then the Sunday people [Christians]."* (Arab phrase heard in the Arab world prior to the 1967 war.) *The Saturday people have proved unexpectedly recalcitrant, and recent events in Lebanon indicate the priorities may have been reversed.*
>
> BERNARD LEWIS,
> *Commentary*, January 1976

Q: When did the Dhimmis come to the region?

A: Jews and Christians had been living throughout the Orient, Egypt, and North Africa for centuries before they were overrun in the seventh and subsequent centuries by successive waves of Bedouin invaders from Arabia who, under the banner of Islam, subjugated peoples and territories from India to Spain.

Q: What was the status of the Jews?

A: Their status was that of *Ahl Al-Dhimma* – protected peoples. In short, peoples tolerated in the Moslem lands: *Dar Al-Islam* (House of Islam).

Q: How did the Jews live in these regions?

A: Up to the last decades of the nineteenth century, and even into the twentieth, the Jews in most of North Africa (until European domination: i.e., Algeria – 1830, Tunisia – 1881, Egypt – 1882, Libya – 1911, Morocco – 1912), Yemen, and other Moslem lands of the Orient were still obliged to live in isolated groups amidst the general population.

> *Those who adhere to Zionism are destined to dispersion by the Deity (as it is said), and humiliation and wretchedness were stamped upon them and they were visited with wrath from God.*
> Rector of Al-Azhar,
> statement from the 4th Conference
> of the Academy of Islamic Research, 1968

Q: How did life compare for the Christians?

A: The indigenous Christian populations had fared no better. Throughout the Islamic lands they had, like the Jews, been reduced to the inferior status of Dhimmis and had been virtually eliminated from North Africa by the twelfth century during the Almohad persecutions.

Q: What was the attitude towards the Dhimmis?

A: For twelve hundred years, the Dhimmis were tolerated in Moslem lands on the terms laid down in the covenant of 'Umar, the refusal or infringement of which could incur the death penalty.

> *[The Jews are] monsters of mankind, a nation of beasts lacking the good qualities which are characteristic of humanity.*
> Egyptian textbook, 1966

Q: What is the contemporary attitude of Islam towards the Jews?

A: The Dhimmi status was referred to by an Egyptian, Abu Zahra, at an important conference of theologians (1968) held at the Islamic University of Al-Azhar in Cairo under the patronage of President

Nasser: "But we say to those who patronize the Jews that the latter are Dhimmis, people of obligation, who have betrayed the covenant in conformity with which they have been accorded protection . . ." President Sadat's declaration on the feast of Mohammed's birth (April 25, 1972) also relates to this basic Islamic Dhimmi concept ". . . They [the Jews] shall return and be as the Koran said of them: 'condemned to humilation and misery'. . . We shall send them back to their former status."

Q: What about the Arab attitude towards the Jews in the medieval era?

A: In a bitter anti-Jewish ode against Joseph Ibn Nagrella, the Jewish minister of the Moslem ruler of Grenada, Spain, Abu Ishaq, a well-known eleventh-century Arab jurist and poet wrote: ". . . Put them back where they belong and reduce them to the lowest of the low . . . turn your eyes to other [Moslem] countries and you will find the Jews there are outcast dogs . . . Do not consider it a breach of faith to kill them . . . They have violated our covenant with them so how can you be held guilty against the violators?"

Q: What was the result of such hatred?

A: Nagrella and an estimated five thousand Jews of Granada were subsequently slaughtered on December 30, 1066.

> *Secular nationalism throughout the Arab world has lost ground to a militant revival of Islamic orthodoxy, making all minorities tremble.*
>
> PATRICK SEALE,
> *The Observer*,
> October 2, 1977

Q: Is this the only case?

A: Throughout their history in Moslem lands, Jews have suffered time and again from pogroms and humiliation.

Q: Is there any testimony of modern historians to prove this?

A: Yes. Antoine Fattal, in his authoritative study on the legal status of non-Moslems in Moslem lands, has written: "The Dhimmi is a second-class citizen. If he is tolerated, it is for reasons of a spiritual nature, since there is always the hope that he might be converted." Likewise Louis Bardet, a Catholic theologian and a respected orientalist, one of the leaders of the contemporary "dialogue" between Islam and Christianity, has stressed: "The Dhimmi should always behave as an inferior; he should adopt a humble and contrite attitude. For example, on the payment of the Jizya, or poll tax, the Qadi on receiving the money, must make as if to give the Dhimmi a light slap in the face so as to remind him of his place. The Dhimmi should everywhere give way to the Muslim . . . If Islam did not invent the ghettos, it can be said that it was the first to institutionalize them.''

> *Our war against the Jews is an old battle which Mohammed began . . . It is our duty to fight the Jews in the name of Allah and in the name of our religion, and it is our duty to finish the war which Mohammed began.*
>
> ANWAR AL-SADAT,
> as Egyptian Minister of State, 1955

Lebanese Maronite bishops issued a resolution in April 1975 protesting '' . . . vigorously against the abuse of sacredness of churches and places of worship, desecration of Holy Places, firing at monasteries, hospitals, and ambulances . . . attacks on ecclesiastics . . . as well as monks and nuns.''

THE YELLOW BADGE: CHRISTIAN OR MOSLEM CREATION?

> *Thou wilt surely find that the strongest in enmity against those who believe the [Moslems] are the Jews and the idolators; and thou wilt find the nearest in love to those who believe [the Moslems] to be those who say, "We are Christians."*
>
> The Koran, 5:85

The historian Robert Brunschwig remarked: '' . . . Islam subjected the Dhimmis to special fiscal and vestimentary obligation.'' He noted that towards the end of the twelfth century, in the Almohad empire (North Africa and Spain), the Jews were compelled to wear a distinctive mark, besides ridiculous clothing. He wrote: ''Would it not be strange if it were the Almohad example which decided Christendom to adopt the same sort of measure? The Jews were first compelled to wear a distinctive badge in Christian lands at the beginning of the thirteenth century.''

Q: How did the Jewish philosopher Maimonides relate to the intolerant Almohad attitude towards the Jews?
A: In his well-known letter to the suffering Yemenite Jews in 1172 he wrote: '' . . . and it is known to you that no nation stood against Israel

more hostile than they [meaning the Moslems], that no nation did evil to perfection in order to weaken us and belittle us and degrade us like them."

Q: What about Jewish rights in the Golden Age?

A: Bernard Lewis, the much-respected historian and co-editor of *The Encyclopedia of Islam*, emphasized in a 1968 article: "The golden age of equal rights was a myth, and belief in it was a result, more than a cause, of Jewish sympathy for Islam. The myth was invented in nineteenth-century Europe as a reproach to Christians – and taken up by Muslims in our own time as a reproach to Jews."

A Romanian Jew, "Benjamin II," who traveled extensively (1846-51) during five years in the Orient and the Maghreb, drew a revealing comparison: "How happy I would be if [by my book of travels] I could interest them [the Jews of Europe] in the plight of their coreligionists who are the victims of oriental barbarism and fanaticism. Our strong and free brethren who have the good fortune to live under liberal regimes, where they are governed by wise laws and are treated humaneiy, will understand how deplorable and urgent is the abnormal situation – of their brethren in the Orient. Religion demands it, humanity requires it."

Job discrimination is at all levels. The Christians (between 10 and 15% of the population) are denied leadership positions. No Christian is a college dean, a police commissioner, a city manager, or a province governor. There are two Christian Egyptian ambassadors out of more than 120 ambassadors. Christian college students are exposed to harassment by Moslem students.

SHAWKY F. KARAS,
President of the American Coptic Association,
Christian Science Monitor, December 9, 1976

THE LAND TAX (KHARADJ) AND THE SKULL TAX (JIZYA)

> *Make war upon those who have been given scripture [the Jews]*
> *. . . until they pay the tribute having been brought low.*
> The Koran, 9:29

Q: What is the Kharadj?

A: The Kharadj is a tax levied on the lands left to the indigenous Dhimmis. This tax symbolized the Arabization of the land of the Dhimmis, meaning its addition to the patrimony of the Arab-Islamic community. In the early period of colonization, lands given in fief were exonerated from the Kharadj.

Q: What is the Jizya?

A: Each male Dhimmi, with the theoretical exceptions of the aged, invalids, and slaves, had to pay a poll-tax, the Jizya, which symbolized the subjection and humiliation of the Dhimmis.

Q: What is known of other taxation or ransoms paid by the Dhimmis?

A: The Dhimmis also were compelled to pay double the taxes of the Moslems. In addition, ransoms were frequently extorted from the local Jewish and Christian communities under threat of collective sanctions including torture and death.

Generally speaking, the traditional approach of the Moslem Arabs to the Jew has been ambivalent: ethnic kinship and cultural affinity, on the one hand, together with a belief in Arab political superiority and religious supremacy, on the other. Thus, the image of the Jew as an enemy of the Moslems evolved in the classical Moslem literature and particularly in modern Arab literature into a demonological stereotype of a Jew who is also the enemy of mankind.

HUMILIATION AND DISCRIMINATION AS A WAY OF LIFE

In order to demonstrate his lower status and to show his poverty and misery, the Dhimmi was forbidden to do certain things and at the same time was obliged to do others.

Q: What was forbidden the Jews?

A: The Dhimmi was forbidden the following on pain of death: (a) to carry or possess weapons, (b) to raise a hand against a Moslem, even against an aggressor unjustly determined to kill him, (c) to ally himself with the enemies of the Arabs, (d) to criticize Islam, the Prophet, or the Angels, (e) to convert to any religion other than Islam, and having converted to Islam, to revert to one's original religion, (f) to be linked by marriage to a Moslem woman, and (g) to hold a position giving him authority over a Moslem.

Q: What was the Dhimmi obliged to do?

A: The Dhimmi was obliged to: (a) live separated from Moslems, in special quarters of a town, the gates of which were closed every evening, or as in Yemen, outside the limits of towns inhabited by Moslems, (b) to have lower houses than those of Moslems, (c) to practice their religion secretly and in silence, (d) to bury their dead hastily, (e) to refrain from showing in public religious objects, such as crosses, banners or sacred texts, (f) to distinguish themselves from Moslems by their exterior aspect, and (g) to wear clothes distinguished not only by shape (length, style of sleeves, etc.) but by specific colors assigned to each group of Dhimmis as well.

> . . . *an explicit documentation of indictment, based upon clearcut evidence that the Jewish people permit the shedding of blood as a religious duty enjoined in the Talmud.*
>
> HABIB FARIS,
> *Talmudic Sacrifices*, 1840
> Egyptian Ministry of Education, 1862

The Dhimmis were forbidden to ride horses or camels since these animals were considered too noble for them. Donkeys were permitted, but they could only ride them outside town perimeters and they had to dismount on sight of a Moslem. In certain periods they were forced to wear distinctive badges in the public baths, and in certain regions were even forbidden to enter them at all.

The Dhimmis were obliged: (a) to make haste on the streets, always passing to the left (impure) side of a Moslem, who was advised to push them to the wall, (b) to walk humbly with lowered eyes, (c) to accept insults without replying, (d) to remain standing in a humble and respectful attitude in the presence of a Moslem, (e) to leave Moslems the best places, (f) never speak to Moslems except to reply.

Any litigation between a Dhimmi and a Moslem was brought before an Islamic tribunal where the Dhimmi's testimony was unacceptable.

Q: Were all these severe prohibitions and obligatory acts against the Jews fulfilled at all times and in all places?

A: No. If the Moslem ruler at a given time was liberal, he might decide to exempt the Jews from some or most of these regulations and prohibitions. If, on the other hand, the leader was fanatic, he would fulfill all these and would not hesitate to add even more.

On the Sabbath and all holidays the Jew is permitted to offer food to dogs, but he cannot offer anything to people of other faiths, because [in the Jews' opinion] dogs are better than such people.

And when the Ten Commandments say to the Jews, do not steal, do not commit adultery, do no not murder, it means do not do that to another Jew.

The Jewish religion claims that anyone who is not a Jew has no right to life. And should he live he has no right to acquire anything. And should he acquire something, then his property may be stolen by the Jews.

The Torah says to the Jew: "All that you trample under foot is yours. All that your eye sees belongs to you." The Jews, then, see that everything God has made is for them, even the life and blood of those who are not Jews.

HABIB FARIS,
Talmudic Sacrifices, 1840
Egyptian Ministry of Education 1862

NATIONAL INDEPENDENCE FOR ARABS, MISERY FOR JEWS AND CHRISTIANS

> *It is known that [the Jew] . . . is the most cursed of all God's creation, the most evil-natured, and the most deeply rooted in infidelity and accursedness . . . When they manage to be alone with a man, they bring him to destruction, they introduce, by trickery, a stupifying drug into his food, and then they kill him.*
> ABD AL-RAHIM AL-JAWBARI,
> thirteenth-century Syrian Arab writer

Q: When did the Jews gain equal rights in Arab countries?

A: It was only after the establishment of European protectorates in all of North Africa, Egypt, and the Orient (with the exception of Yemen, where the Jews had to wait till 1949-50, when they were airlifted to Israel in "Operation Magic Carpet").

Q: How long did the Jews enjoy equal rights?

A: Under European rule, Christians and Jews enjoyed physical security, and some even a certain affluence, which lasted for two or three generations.

Q: When did the Jews' situation worsen?

A: As each Arab country won its national independence, the situation of the minorities worsened, often becoming intolerable. More than one thousand Jews were killed in anti-Jewish rioting 1938-49: in Baghdad (1941/46/48); Tripoli (1945-48); Aden (1947); Aleppo (1945/47/48); Damascus (1938/45/49); Oudja, Djerade, Cairo (1948); etc. Similar tragedies occurred during the same period to many indigenous Christian groups throughout the Arab world.

> *The worst insult one Moroccan can make to another is to call him a Jew . . .*
> SAID GHALLAB, Moroccan Moslem,
> *Les Temps Modernes*, 1965

Q: What can be said about Arab opposition to Israel since her establishment in 1948?

A: The general Arab opposition to the existence of an independent sovereign State of Israel in its ancient homeland has its roots in traditional Islamic attitudes and Dhimmi concepts. The contemporary hostile Arab attitudes towards Jews and other minorities is not something unusual in the Arab world. What was unusual, for the

241

Dhimmis, was the relative calm of the preceding two or three generations during the period of European domination.

> *Humiliation was accepted by the Jew as part of life. He learnt to endure the slap in the face with which he was rewarded when he paid his tax, the blow administered as he walked down the street, the deliberate jostling, the insult. He was an outcast of inferior status.*
>
> ALBERT MEMMI,
> North African historian

Q: What about Moslem opposition to Christian Lebanese?

A: The root of the present Lebanese tragedy is religious. In 1860, the brutal massacre of several thousand Christians in Syria and Lebanon occurred soon after the passing of the Hatti-Humayun edict (1856), which granted equal rights with Moslems to Christians and Jews.

Q: Are the PLO's declarations about a democratic secular state another one of its propaganda bluffs?

A: Yes. One should bear in mind that this "politicidal" goal is fully supported by all Arab leaders, including Libya's Qaddafi, who is a fervent believer in the fundamental unchangeable truths of Islam and the Koran.

> *. . . The children of Ishmael deal more harshly with the people of Israel than the children of Esau.*
> RABBI BAHYA IBN PAQUDA,
> *Medieval Days*

JEWS AND CHRISTIANS: BROTHERS IN TROUBLE IN THE MIDDLE EAST

> *We have in the Lebanese experience a significant example that is close to the multi-religious state we are trying to achieve.*
> YASSIR ARAFAT,
> *The Economist*, April 12, 1975

> *Land of tolerance, human synthesis, fraternal and peaceful. This Lebanon, thus made by the grace of God and the merit of its people, is it not a symbol of what the world could be, delivered from the reign of violence and undertakings inspired by religious or racial exclusivism?*
> SULEIMAN FRANJIEH,
> former Lebanese President,
> at the UN, November, 1974

Both the former Lebanese president and the terrorist leader did not realize how quickly developments in Lebanon would prove that these beautiful declarations have no foundation.

Jews as well as Christians are Dhimmis and, therefore, should be treated accordingly. The case of Lebanon, where the Arab Christians have had to fight for their existence against Moslem aggression, is another proof of the Moslem attitude towards non-Moslems. Lebanon exposes the true face of the Arab world, showing that its claims of tolerance for people of different religions is a lie. According to Islam, Jews and Christians are equal to each other, but are, by no means, equal to Moslems.

> *The Libyan government proclaimed its "aim to avenge the past . . . The feeling of holy revenge runs in our veins." The Cathedral of the Sacred Heart in Tripoli was converted into the Gamal Abdel Nasser Mosque on November 26, 1979.*
> *Washington Post*, November 27, 1979

TRADITIONAL JEWISH HELP
TO CHRISTIANS

> *From the first week of December 1947, disorder in Palestine had begun to mount. The Arabs repeatedly had asserted that they would resist partition by force. They seemed to be determined to drive that point home by assaults upon the Jewish community in Palestine.*
> TRYGVE LIE, former UN Secretary General,
> *In the Cause of Peace*

The Jews as well as the Christians understood that in order to survive and to face Arab aggression against them, they would have to cooperate and help one another.

In 1947, the Maronite Archbishop of Beirut, Ignatius Moubarak, told the United Nations committee which came to study the Palestinian-Israeli dilemma: "Major reasons of a social humanitarian and religious nature require the creation of two homelands for minorities – a Christian home in Lebanon as there has always been, and a Jewish home in Palestine. The neighborly relations between these two nations will contribute to the maintenance of peace in the Near East which is so divided by rivalries and will lessen the persecution of minorities, who will always find refuge in these two countries . . . Lebanon demands freedom for the Jews in Palestine – as it desires its own freedom and independence."

Q: What was the reason behind Archbishop Moubarak's support for a Jewish state?

A: The words of Archbishop Moubarak expressed the fear and the concern of the Christians in Lebanon who knew how dire their fate would be if the Moslems achieved political control in the country.

Q: What encouraged the Christians?

A: The fact that Jews established their state in the region, despite Arab opposition, encouraged the Christians to feel that they were not alone in their fight against Moslem enmity. Some believed that Jews and Christians were like "brothers in trouble," capable of uniting their forces against Moslem opposition to their independence.

Q: How did the Jews view the Christian-Jewish cooperation?

A: In the early 1940s, Abraham Stern-Yair, the leader of the Lehi (Fighters for Israel's Freedom), wrote that the term "Hebrew nation" does not apply only to the tribe of Israel. It includes another important and large tribe – the Phoenicians (ancient Lebanese). These two groups are brethren in both language and culture. Stern-Yair wrote: ''. . . A turning point in Hebrew history was the coalition that was established between [King] Solomon and Hiram, king of Tyre [Lebanon today]. The goal of this coalition was to unite the two Jewish branches for a conquering campaign in the overseas countries. In order to demonstrate the importance of this alliance, both sides made mutual concessions. Solomon enlarged the territory of Tyre by giving them twenty Israeli cities and Hiram built the Israelis a fleet in Eilat . . .''

Q: What is known about the massacre of 1860?

A: In 1860, the Lebanese Druze attacked the Christian Maronites. Thousands of men, women and children were murdered. The Christians sent forth a desperate plea for help to the European powers in order to save them from complete annihilation.

[After] having lived intimately for several years amongst the Arabs, I know them to be amongst the most racist people on earth. This is particularly true of their attitude toward black people . . . Many Arab families, who can afford to, keep one or two black slaves to do their menial labor. Sometimes they own an entire family. I have seen such slaves with my own eyes.''

ELDRIDGE CLEAVER,
former Black Panther leader,
The Boston Herald American, January 1977

Q: Who came to the aid of the Christians?

A: Sir Moses Montefiore, the well-known British Jewish leader, astonished by the disaster that befell the Lebanese Christians, did his utmost to assist them. After receiving the tragic report about the 20,000 Christian dead, he approached the *Times* (London) in the middle of the night insisting that it publish the story about the plight of the Christians in order to awaken world public opinion to their misery. He then set up a fund to help the survivors of the pogroms and included money of his own in the fund.

There is a tradition in the whole [Arabian] peninsula of slavery, . . . To be a Kuwaiti is to be very privileged . . . But if you are a foreign worker, you stand to be exploited and live, by Kuwait standards, in very bad conditions.

ALAN CONWELL,
New York Times correspondent, 1987

245

Q: Who else helped?

A: Adolph Crémieux, a Jewish minister in the French government, joined Montefiore's efforts and later persuaded and encouraged his government to send its troops to Lebanon in order to rescue the remnant Christian population.

Q: How did the Christians express their thanks and appreciation for such help?

A: The Maronite Patriarch, Antoine Arida, who at that time was a child, was miraculously saved from death and later extolled Jewish assistance to the Christians during those dark days. He later appeared in synagogues throughout Beirut, praising the Jewish community not only for its help, but also for calling on the world to rescue the Christians. Arida also sent a telegram to the director of the Alliance Jewish school in Beirut, in which he wrote: "We will not forget the generous help of Alliance."

Q: Is there any other testimony concerning Arab hatred for Christians?

A: Yes. Britsh Arabist Gertrude Bell recounted how the Moslems, upon hearing of the Japanese victories over Russia, 1904-5, would shake their fists at the Christians, saying: "The Christians are suffering defeat. Now we too will shortly drive you out and seize your goods."

Q: What happened to the Christians in southern Lebanon?

A: Following the First World War, Syria was given to France by the League of Nations as a mandate territory. Arab nationalists subsequently called for a revolt against French rule, including its Christian supporters. As a result, Arab nomads brutally attacked the Christians of southern Lebanon as well as the Jewish community. Many fleeing Christians found shelter in Jewish settlements, especially in Metula (a town in Israel situated near the Lebanese border).

Q: What was the result of the Arab pressure against the Christians?

A: As a direct result of the pogroms and vehement hostility, a large number of Syrian and Lebanese Christians emigrated to America, establishing an Arab Christian diaspora (MAHGIAR).

FROM THE ATLANTIC OCEAN TO THE ARAB (PERSIAN) GULF

> *The Arab nations should sacrifice up to 10 million of their 50 million people, if necessary to wipe out Israel . . . Israel to the Arab world is like a cancer to the human body, and the only way of remedy is to uproot it, just like a cancer.*
>
> SAUD IBN ABDUL AZIZ,
> King of Saudi Arabia,
> Associated Press, January 9, 1954

Q: What is the slogan of Arab nationalism?

A: The slogan of Arab nationalism is "From the Atlantic Ocean to the Arab (Persian) Gulf."

Q: What is the meaning of this slogan?

A: All this area must be Moslem with no independent Christian or Jewish state in its midst. Any such state would exist in clear defiance of Islam and Arab nationalism.

Q: Yet Christian Arabs are still Arabs. Why weren't they accepted by the Arab nationalists?

A: Careful observation of Christian history in the Middle East in general and in Palestine in particular reveals that Christian Arabs, despite their great contributions to Arab nationalism, were always secretly or openly suspected by their Moslem compatriots.

Q: Did Christian Palestinian Arabs fight against the Jews in Palestine?

A: Yes. In Palestine, during the British Mandate period, Christian Arabs were in the forefront in the struggle against the establishment of a Jewish national home. They cooperated with the Moslems against the Jews, believing that by doing so, the Moslems would accept them as equals. In order to appease their Moslem bosses, the Christians did not hesitate to use anti-Semitic accusations against the Jews. Yet, from the outset, their efforts were doomed to failure. They were not accepted by the Moslems because of their permanent "sin": their Christianity.

Q: What about the Christians vis-à-vis the PLO?

A: Even today, among the Palestinian terrorists, the Christian section of the PLO – the Popular Front for the Liberation of Palestine, led by George Habash – is the most extreme. Yet Habash's ardent fanaticism is not a valid entrance ticket into the Moslem world. Sooner or later, he and his fellow Christians will realize that their problem is their Christianity.

There is a general Arab policy against the existence of any non-Arab nation in the Middle East. This is true with respect to the Kurds and Assyrians of Iraq, the Maronites of Lebanon, the Druze of Syria, the Copts of Egypt, the Berbers of Algeria, the non-Moslems of the Sudan and, of course, Israel.

> *The Arabs will not only demand the West Bank and the Gaza Strip, but all of the land conquered since 1948 . . . The slogan that the rights of the Palestinians be restored and Palestine liberated can have but one meaning – the elimination of Israel.*
> Radio Damascus, December 22, 1976

THE DHIMMI STATE OF ISRAEL

> *The goal of our struggle is the end of Israel, and there can be no compromise.*
> YASSIR ARAFAT,
> *Washington Post*, March 29, 1970

The State of Israel's establishment is totally unaccepted by the Moslems. Israel, they believe, inflicted injustice upon the Palestinian Arabs by taking their homes and their country. Moreover, the most serious problem is the fact that the Jews, who are Dhimmis, not only established their state in the midst of the Moslem world, but also defeated and even humiliated the Arab Moslem armies, time and again, within one generation. This course of event is contradictory to the spirit and laws of the Koran. The conclusion, according to the Moslems, is that Israel must disappear.

The Jihad "War of Ramadan," known to the world as the 1973 Yom Kippur War, was officially declared by the Moslem authorities in Egypt, Syria, and Saudi Arabia as Jihad (holy war), which the Moslem is commanded to wage against the infidels, the enemies of Islam. In a pamphlet specifically published by the Egyptian Ministry of War at that time, entitled "Our Faith Our Way to Victory," Chief of Staff Shazli, referring to a verse from the Koran, addressed himself to the troops in these words: "The Jews have overstepped their bounds in [acts of] injustice and conceit. Kill them wherever you find them. "

> *We cannot think of recognition (of Israel) because this would mean conceding a part of our lands. Our intermediate goal is the creation of an independent Palestinian state on all parts of our land that will be liberated. There have been similiar developments in the world. In Vietnam, for example, the Vietnamese decided on the creation of North Vietnam, and after ten years they liberated South Vietnam.*
>
> FAROUK KADDOUMI,
> head of the PLO's Political Department,
> Voice of Palestine, July 2, 1977

Q: Why do the Moslems refuse to accept the State of Israel in their midst?

A: The Moslem Arabs refuse to accept Israel as a reality in the region. The reason is simple: Israel has traumatized the Arab political consciousness. Why? Traditional Arab domination has produced feelings of superiority among the Arabs. These feelings were confirmed by the abasement of the Dhimmi. If, however, the Dhimmi can achieve equal rights, then the superior feels himself doubly inferior and unquestionably humiliated.

Q: What is the Arabs' reaction to this situation?

A: The less the Israeli image of a Jew fits into the Dhimmi stereotype – as a servile, cowardly, debased being – the more violent and bloodthirsty becomes the efforts of the ancient oppressor to force the victim back into his low status.

> *After we perform our duty in liberating the West Bank and Jerusalem, our national duty is to liberate all the Arab territories.*
>
> KING HUSSEIN of Jordan,
> Radio Amman, December 1, 1973

Q: What should be Israel's image?

A: Israel is regarded as the Dhimmi State. If such a state rebels against Arab domination, it must be condemned to destruction. Jews must return to their Dhimmi image and status.

Q: What is the background to Arab behavior towards the Jews?

A: In this sense, Arab treatment of Jewish minorities in its midst is rooted in the Islamic approach to Jews.

> *You are the generation that will reach the sea and hoist the flag of Palestine over Tel Aviv.*
>
> YASSIR ARAFAT,
> speech to guerrilla training camp ANSA,
> from Cairo, July 25, 1974

Q: What does Israel do to the Arab image?

A: The creation of the State of Israel is regarded in the Arab world as an unacceptable reversal of history. Furthermore, it is an intolerable insult to the might and "manhood" of the Arab world. This trauma produced the attempts to strangle the Jewish community under the Mandate, to crush the infant State of Israel, to the four Arab-Israeli wars that followed Israel's independence, to the maintenance of a permanent state of war in the periods between the actual wars, to the famous "three no's" of the Khartoum Conference, and to the Palestinian Covenant – which calls for Israel's demise.

> *Islam Taslam. (Convert to Islam, your life will be saved.)*
> Islamic saying
>
> ---
>
> *I declare a holy war, my Moslem brothers! Murder the Jews! Murder them all!*
>
> HAJ AMIN AL-HUSSEINI,
> Mufti of Jerusalem, 1948
>
> ---
>
> *All countries should wage war against the Zionists, who are there to destroy all human organizations and to destroy civilization and the work which good people are trying to do.*
> KING FAISAL of Saudi Arabia,
> from a speech in Uganda,
> *Beirut Daily Star*, November 17, 1972
>
> ---
>
> *. . . there is a minimal Palestinian national position. This minimum is the rejection of any recognition of the Zionist entity . . . our rejection of any settlement based on the continued existence of this foreign entity.*
> PFLP leader GEORGE HABASH,
> *Al-Bayrad*, Beirut, February 4, 1975

250

THE MEANING OF
ARAB DEFEAT BY ISRAEL

> *The right of self determination in the Arab nationalist sense*
> *means the total liberation and return of all the national*
> *historical rights of the Palestinian nation in its land . . . The*
> *right of the Palestinian nation to self-determination is expressed*
> *in the exposure and the destruction of the Zionist idea, and of*
> *Israel, which is the result of that idea.*
>
> SAMI EL-ATRI,
> Secretary, Palestinian Central Committee,
> *Al Kabas*, Kuwait, March 1978

Q: Why were the Arab defeats by Israel so painful to the Moslems?

A: The only previous experience the Arabs had had with the Jews, prior to the establishment of Israel, was with the Jewish communities in the Arab countries. Throughout history, the Jews in Arab lands held a definitely low status, to say the least. Islam regarded the Jews as under a kind of patronage or protection. To the Moslem, if the Jews could defeat the Arab world, then Arab society must be very sick indeed.

Q: What terms did the Arabs use to describe their defeats?

A: The term "disaster" was used for the defeat (Hazima) of 1948, the term "setback" (Naksa) was used to describe the defeat of 1967.

> *The existence of Israel is an error which must be rectified.*
> *This is our opportunity to wipe out the ignominy which has been*
> *with us since 1948. Our goal is clear – to wipe Israel off the face*
> *of the map.*
>
> Iraqi President ABDEL RAHMAN AREF,
> May 31, 1967

Q: Why did the Moslems find it very difficult to accept Israel's victory?

A: The real "disaster" was connected with the fact that Israel's victories marked the most humiliating experience for the Arab world – i.e., that six Arab states, with armies representing countries that had tens of millions of people, were unable to defeat Israel, this small splinter of European civilization.

Q: Who was to blame for the 1948 defeat? for the 1967 defeat?

A: The 1967 defeat was suffered mainly by the socialist countries. The Arab world could not rationalize it, as they did in 1948 by blaming

251

traditionalism and the reactionary nature of Arab societies. Morover, in 1948, the blame was placed upon the "corrupt monarchs."

Q: Who were the revolutionary officers?

A: Almost all the revolutions in Arab countries had been led by officers who had experienced the first Arab defeat by Israel. Almost all these governments were headed by officers who had fought in the Arab-Israeli war of 1948. Syria first, then Nasser's Egypt and later Iraq.

Q: What is the Arab attitude towards non-Arab nations in the Middle East?

A: There is a general Arab policy against the existence of any non-Arab nation in the Middle East. This is true with respect to the Kurds and the Assyrians of Iraq, the Maronite Christians of Lebanon, the Druze of Syria, the Copts of Egypt, the Berbers of Algeria, the non-Moslems of Sudan and, of course, the Jews in Israel.

> *The partitioning of Palestine in 1947 and the establishment of Israel are fundamentally null and void . . . the liberation of Palestine will destroy the Zionist and imperialist presence . . .*
> PLO National Convenant,
> Articles 18 and 22

Q: Should Israel offer the Palestinian Arabs a state, would that be enough to make peace?

A: Various schools of thought in Israel are arguing in terms of this two letter word, "if." The greatest "if" concerns the problem of the Palestinians. If they only achieve a state of their own, wouldn't they accommodate themselves to Israel? Would the Arab world be satisfied with that? As if Jordan was not, in effect, a Palestinian state until 1967, as if the Palestinians did not attempt then to liquidate Israel, as if the Arabs did not then define Palestinian self-determination in terms of the total destruction of Israel.

> *Do not believe that it is possible to regain Palestine and to return to Jerusalem by means of a political settlement. You will not return to Palestine or raise the flag of the revolution over Jerusalem other than by means of the rifle. We will not achieve political victory so long as we do not achieve military victory. You must strengthen the iron fist around the rifle which will lead to victory.*
> YASSIR ARAFAT,
> Voice of Palestine, Beirut, June 16, 1980

"OUR FAITH: OUR WAY TO VICTORY"

> *O heroic sons of the Gaza Strip, O proud sons of the [West]*
> *Bank, O heroic sons of the Galilee, O steadfast sons of the Negev*
> *. . . the fires of revolution against these Zionist invaders will not*
> *fade out . . . until our land – all our land – has been liberated*
> *from these usurping invaders.*
>
> YASSIR ARAFAT,
> PLO Radio, Baghdad, December 10, 1987

The booklet "Our Faith: Our Way to Victory" was published on June 30, 1973, just three months before the outbreak of the 1973 Yom Kippur War. It was intended to be read and reread by the Egyptian troops as a morale booster, a kind of Moslem version of the Quotations from Chairman Mao Tse-tung. Written for officers and rank and file alike, it warranted a mass issue of a million copies. Its small format (8 x 12 cm.) was designed to enable each recipient to carry it in his pocket.

The introduction is by the then Egyptian Chief of Staff, Lieutenant-General Sa'ad Shazli. He bids the soldiers to purge the shame and humiliation of the 1967 defeat and to restore their honor and pride. He stresses the value of religious belief as a morale-building factor. He attacks the problems of fear, panic and flight, impatience and intolerance of stress. Retreat, he threatens, is punishable in this world and the next. His treatment of the fear factor is psychologically more sophisticated than the main section of the booklet, which simply urges the soldier not to be afraid. He assures his men that fear is natural, that even the brave Moslem conquerors of the past were not fearless.

Regarding the Jewish enemy, Shazli instructs his men: "Kill them wherever you find them." This is an allusion to a verse in the Koran cited at times in Egyptian indoctrination pamphlets. He warns his troops that the Jews are a treacherous people, and may merely feign surrender so as to kill their captors. He orders: "Kill them, and let not compassion or mercy for them seize you."

The main theme of the booklet is the Holy War – Jihad. The Holy War of traditional Islam was the effort for Allah's sake to spread His word by the sword among non-believers. In the booklet, it is presented not only as that and as a struggle for the glory of the nation of Mohammed; it is also for the ideals of justice and truth and the noble causes of peace and security for mankind. Thus, the sting of religious fanaticism is somewhat removed, or at least disguised as a form of militant idealism. By this ideology of the Holy War, a conflict over territory is transformed, certainly in the mind of the believer, into a relentless religious war against the non-believer: in this case, the Jews.

> *. . . We are speaking of the normalization of the West Bank, and even if we have strayed and begun to say only "the West Bank" and we have seemingly forgotten Palestine, we must talk of Palestine and nothing less, for Palestine is our occupied homeland . . . It is our right that we should have a state, and not just on paper, because this state will be an independent Palestinian state and will function as a base from which to liberate Jaffa, Akko, and all of Palestine, after which we will take Palestine and turn it into a part of the greater Arab nation.*
>
> SALEH KHALEF (Abu Iyad),
> number two in the PLO leadership,
> *Al-Sacrah*, Kuwait, January 6, 1987

". . . the limits of conceit. The sons of Egypt, are therefore determined to set them back on their heels, killing and destroying, so as to wash away the shame of the 1967 defeat " and to restore their honor and pride. Kill them wherever you find them, and take heed that they do not deceive you, for they are a treacherous people. They may feign surrender in order to gain power over you, and kill you vilely. Kill them and let not compassion or mercy for them seize you!"

لقد جاوز اليهود حدودهم ظلما وعلما . ونحن ابناء
مصر قد عقدنا العزم على ان نردهم على اعقابهم وان
نجوس خلال مواقعهم قتلا وتدميرا كى نغسل عار
هزيمة ١٩٦٧ ونسترد كرامتنا وكبرياءنا . اقتلوهم حيث
تفتنوهم واحذروا ان يخدعوكم فهم قوم خادعون قد
يتظاهرون بالتسليم كى يتمكنوا منكم فيقتلوكم بخسة .

. اقتلوهم ولا تأخذكم بهم شفقة او رحمة فانهم لم ......

"Islam forbids fleeing from the ranks and considers it one of the grave sins. Allah says: 'O believers, when you encounter the unbelievers marching to battle; turn not your backs to them. Whoso turns his back that day to them, unless withdrawing to fight again or removing to join another host, he is laden with the burden of God's anger, and his refuge is Gehenna – an evil homecoming!' " (The Koran 8:15-16)

ونهى الاسلام عن الفرار من الصفوف وعده من
الكبائر قال تعالى :
(ياأيها الذين آمنوا إذا لقيتم الذين كفروا زحفا
فلا تولوهم الأدبار ومن يولهم يومئذ دبره إلا متحرفا
لقتال أو متحيزا إلى فئة فقد باء بغضب من الله ومأواه
جهنم وبئس المصير .) .

"And say not of those slain in God's way, 'They are dead'; rather they are living, but you are not aware." (The Koran 2:154)

إ ولا تقولوا لمن يقتل فى سبيل الله
أموات ، بل أحياء ، ولكن لا تشعرون)

"So let them fight in the way of God who sell the present life for the world to come; and whosoever fights in the way of God and is slain, or conquers, we shall bring him a mighty wage." (The Koran 4:74)

(فليقاتل فى سبيل الله الذين يشرون الحياة الدنيا
بالآخرة ومن يقاتل فى سبيل الله فيقتل أو يغلب
فسوف نؤتيه أجرا عظيما) .

"Cursed were the unbelievers of the Children of Israel by the tongue of David, and Jesus, Mary's son; that, for their rebelling and their transgression." (The Koran 5:78)

لعن الذين كفروا من بنى إسرائيل على لسان
داود وعيسى بن مريم ذلك بما عصوا و كانوا يعتدون .

254

"And He says: Thou wilt surely find the most hostile of men to the believers are the Jews and the idolators . . ." (The Koran 5:82)

لَتَجِدَنَّ أَشَدَّ النَّاسِ عَدَاوَةً لِلَّذِينَ آمَنُوا الْيَهُودَ اِ وَالَّذِينَ أَشْرَكُوا ه .

« قال تعالى :

"And he says, 'And we decreed for the Children of Israel in the Book: You shall do corruption in the earth twice, and you shall ascend exceeding high.' "

« وَقَضَيْنَا إِلَى بَنِي إِسْرَائِيلَ فِي الْكِتَابِ لَتُفْسِدُنَّ فِي الأَرْضِ مَرَّتَيْنِ وَلَتَعْلُنَّ عُلُوًّا كَبِيرًا .

The printing of the above booklet was completed on Saturday, 29 Jumada I 1393 A.H. (corresponding to June 30, 1973), by the Armed Forces Department of Printing Publication. Acknowledged was Major-General Ahmad Ali Muhammad Amir, Director of the Armed Forces Department of Printing and Publication.

CHAPTER TWENTY

THE HAMAS
ISLAMIC MOVEMENT

The Hamas movement in Judea, Samaria, the Gaza Strip, and East Jerusalem is a highly fanatic and violent movement. In August 1988, Hamas published the Covenant of the Islamic Opposition Movement, in which it elaborated its thoughts and methods on different subjects. In the covenant, it described itself as one of the sections of the Islamic Brotherhood in Palestine.

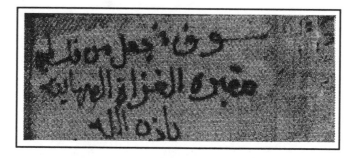

Above is a slogan of the Hamas Islamic Movement found on a wall of a school in Taybeh (within Israel) on June 4, 1967. Taybeh is known to have a strong group of Hamas followers. The slogan reads: "We will make Palestine a cemetery for the Zionist occupiers."

Q: What are the main concepts of Hamas?
A: The main ideological concepts of the movement are equal to the central trends of the Islamic Brotherhood. They include: (a) the liberation of all of Palestine and its return to the Moslems; (b) the resistance to the "Zionist enemy" and the Jihad – holy war – against the Jews as compulsory for every Moslem; and (c) complete opposition to any peace initiative, since this may cause Arab-Israeli compromise that would enable the Jews to keep a part of Palestine.

بـــم اللـــه الـــر حمـــن الـــر حـــيم

« كنتم خير أمة أخرجت للناس تأمرون بالمعروف وتنهون عن المنكر
وتؤمنون بالله ، ولو آمن أهل الكتاب لكان خيرا لهم منهم المؤمنون
وأكثرهم الفاسقون .
لن يضروكم إلا أذى وإن يقاتلوكم يولوكم الأدبار ثم لا ينصرون ،
ضربت عليهم الذلة أين ما ثقفوا إلا بحبل من الله وحبل من الناس وباءوا
بغضب من الله وضربت عليهم المسكنة ذلك بأنهم كانوا يكفرون بآيات الله
ويقتلون الأنبياء بغير حق ذلك بما عصوا وكانوا يعتدون ».
١٠٩ ـ ١١١ آل عمران

They are smitten with vileness wheresoever they are found;
unless they obtain security by entering into a treaty with Allah,
and a treaty with men; and they draw on themselves indignation
from Allah, and they are afflicted with poverty. This they suffer,
because they disbelieved the signs of Allah, and slew the
prophets unjustly; this, because they were rebellious, and
transgressed.

The Koran, *Al-Imran*, Verses 109-11
(expressing the Koran's view of the Jewish people
as quoted in the Covenant of the Islamic
Opposition Movement)

Q: When was Hamas declared illegal?

A: At the end of August 1989, the Hamas movement was declared illegal
by the Israeli military authorities. The meaning of this Israeli step is
simple. It is now illegal to be a member of Hamas, to help, it and to
be present at its gatherings.

Q: When was Hamas established?

A: Hamas was established at the outset of the uprising in December 1987.
The movement gained momentum during the uprising in Judea and
Samaria, but especially in the Gaza Strip. The leaflets of Hamas call
upon the Palestinians to initiate clashes with the soldiers and to cause
general disorder.

Q: Who is Hamas' leader?

A: The famous leader of this new movement is Ahmad Yasin, from the
Gaza Strip. He has been arrested and then freed a number of times.

> *If faith is lost, there is no security and there is no life for him who does not adhere to religion. He who accepts life without religion has taken annihilation as his companion for life.*
> MOHAMED IKBAL, Moslem poet,
> quoted in Article 6 of the
> Covenant of the Islamic Opposition Movement

Q: What was the guilt of Ahmad Yasin?

A: The supporters of the Islamic Brotherhood conducted a severe struggle against the PLO in the Gaza Strip prior to the uprising. A short time before the uprising, Ahmad Yasin, the Hamas leader and a member of the Islamic Brotherhood, called upon every Moslem to fight Israel. He advocated that the territories be transferred to the United Nations. He established Hamas and became its political chairman. He also established the Hamas military section known as *Al-Mujahudoon* (the fighters). Sheikh Salach Shahada of Beth Hanoon became the commander of this military arm. A special unit called "Majd" was set up with one task to do: punish and even murder collaborators.

Q: When did Israel discover that Hamas was involved in terrorist activities?

A: At the end of March 1988, Israel discovered that the Hamas organization was involved in terrorist activities. In the Gaza Strip, explosives, Molotov cocktails, and axes were found in some mosques. At that time, Yasin was arrested.

Q: What is the power of the PLO vis-à-vis the power of Hamas?

A: Observers believe that about 40 percent of the Palestinians in Judea and Samaria and another 80 to 90 percent in Gaza adhere to the fundamentalist umbrella organization, and no longer consider the PLO as their representative.

Q: What are the differences between the PLO and Hamas?

A: A deep ideological gap separates Hamas and the PLO. Hamas holds that a Palestinian state must be Islamic with a constitution based on the Koran. Some PLO factions advocate a secular state for Palestinians that might include factions that are Marxist and atheist. Hamas does not intend to challenge the PLO until the Palestinians are free of the Israelis, but its leaders express no doubt that an armed clash will ultimately come about between Hamas and the PLO.

> *And he says: Thou wilt surely find the most hostile of men to the believers [namely, the Moslems] are the Jews and the idolators.*
> The Koran 5:28

PART VI

THE ARAB SAVAGE KINSHIP

CHAPTER TWENTY-ONE

ARABS AGAINST ARABS

> *The people of Yemen and 'Asir are still savage; not one of them*
> *would trust his brother. They live in perpetual fear and anxiety*
> *. . . They are like wild beasts which fear everything and*
> *everybody that may come near them. As to the Yemen . . . all*
> *our people are armed, all fight, and all kill for the least thing.*
> *We are very jealous of our rights . . . If in this village two houses*
> *would suddenly engage in a fight, the entire population would*
> *split into two parties and join in the fight. War could break out*
> *in the village. When it subsides, and only then, would the people*
> *ask what the cause of the fighting was. They fight first, and then*
> *inquire as to the cause of the fight. This is our way of life in*
> *Yemen. We fight our own relatives. The brother would fight his*
> *own brother, the son his own father . . . .*
>
> AMEEN FARIS RIHANI,
> from *Muluk Al-Arab (Kings of the Arabs)*,
> 3rd edition, Beirut, 1953

The Arabs quite often in their propaganda campaign against Israel claim that the source of all the Arab troubles and conflicts in the Arab world is the existence of Israel. Israel's disappearance would, therefore, ease the Arab frictions and would subsequently cause more harmony and understanding among the Arabs.

The truth is that Israel's existence has nothing to do with Arab troubles and upheavals. The origin of the Arab disputes is to be found in the inherent sociopolitical instability of many Arab states and their endemic territorial, political, religious and ideological disputes. The Arab-Israel conflict, therefore, is not the source of these disputes; it is rather one of the more tragic, dangerous, and prolonged conflicts in the region.

Israel's former ambassador to the United Nations, Benjamin Netanyahu, correctly related this in the *Wall Street Journal* on April 5, 1983:

"To assume that this turbulence and endemic instability will disappear, or even subside, by theoretical resolution of the Arab-Israeli conflict is to expect the impossible. Even the disappearance of Israel would not make the slightest difference."

The history of the Arab world since 1948 is a story marked by murder, subversion, coup d'etats, persecutions, civil wars, hatred and bloodshed. Hundreds of thousands of Arabs were murdered by fellow Arabs. Many hundreds of leaders, presidents, kings, ministers, religious leaders and other dignitaries were assassinated. At different times, the Arab armies fought one another and caused tens of thousands of casualties.

> *King Hussein speaking about the tragedy of Lebanon: "It can now be seen that Arabs themselves, citizens of the same country, not only cannot coexist but collide day and night."*
> Jordan's KING HUSSEIN,
> interview with *Newsweek*
> editor Arnaud de Borchegrave

COUPS AND REVOLUTIONS

SYRIA
Q: How many successful coups d'etat occurred in Syria in this period?
A: Seven.
A: How many known unsuccessful coups d'etat were attempted from 1950 to 1988?
A: Eleven.

IRAQ
Q: How many successful coups d'etat occurred in Iraq in this period?
A: Four.
Q: How many known unsuccessful coups d'etat were attempted?
A: Nine.

> *If we look at a map of the Arab Homeland, we can hardly find two countries without conflicts . . . We can hardly find two countries which are not either in a state of war or on the road to war.*
> ABD ALHALIM KHADDAM,
> Syrian Foreign Minister in Oman,
> November 1980

EGYPT

Q: How many coups d'etat occurred in Egypt?
A: One.
Q: How many known unsuccessful coups d'etat were attempted?
A: Four.

JORDAN

Q: How many unsuccessful coups d'etat were attempted?
A: Eight.

[The Arabs] are a savage nation, fully accustomed to savagery and the things that cause it. Savagery has become their character and nature . . . it is their nature to plunder whatever other people possess . . . [they] are not concerned with laws, [not concerned] to deter people from misdeeds or to protect some against the others. They care only for the property that they might take away from people through looting and imposts . . . Under the rule of [the Arabs] the subjects live as in a state of anarchy, without law. Anarchy destroys mankind and ruins civilization . . . It is noteworthy how civilization always collapsed in places the Arabs took over and conquered, and how such settlements were depopulated and the [very] earth there turned into something that was no [longer] earth. The Yemen where [the Arabs] live is in ruins . . . The same applies to contemporary Syria . . .

IBN KHALDUN,
famous Arab historian (1332-1406),
The Muqaddamah (Introduction to History)

LARGE MASSACRES AND MASS MURDER

IRAQ

In successful and unsuccessful coups in 1958, 1959 and 1963, thousands of Iraqi people were murdered. In the Iraqi-Iranian War of 1980-1989, hundreds of thousands were either killed or wounded.

The Iraqi-Kurdish War caused the death of over 200,000 Kurds. In both wars, the Iraqi forces used poison gas.

SUDAN

An estimated 500,000 Sudanese were murdered in civil wars.

JORDAN

In the 1970 "Black September" massacre, over 7,000 Palestinians were massacred by the Jordanian army.

LEBANON

Between April 1974 and February 1990, over one hundred thousand people were either murdered or wounded in the Lebanese civil war.

SYRIA

In March 1982, a Moslem Brotherhood rebellion against the regime of President Hafez al-Assad in the city of Hama was crushed by the Syrian army. The result was the death of between 20 and 30 thousand Syrians. Many others were murdered at various times in cold blood by Syrian rulers.

SAUDI ARABIA

In July 1987, 500 Iranian pilgrims were killed in Mecca by the Saudi armed forces in fighting that erupted near the holy shrine in Mecca.

Numerous other incidents, in which tens of thousands lost their lives, occurred in the Arab world in this same period.

The PLO, which is a professional murderer of the innocent and an expert of indiscriminate killing follows this same road. Documents captured during the 1982 war attest to the PLO's intentions to hit Israeli civilian targets. One such document dated July 1981 read: "Blessings of the Revolution! The supreme Military Command decided to concentrate on the destruction of Kiryat Shmona, Metulla, Dan, Shaar Yeshuv, Nahariya and its surroundings. Kiryat Shmona will be divided between the units and shelled with improved Grad rockets. Metulla will be shelled with 160mm mortars. Nahariya and its surroundings will be shelled with 130mm guns."

> *It was not the first such execution in Nablus. Adli al-Thalji was clad in pajamas when his corpse was found dangling from a meat hook in the market. In Gaza, Jamil Mahmud Shehedeh, a resident of the teeming Jabaliya refugee camp, was stabbed to death and his arm hacked off at the shoulder. A message near his body said, "Death sentence carried out against a collaborator."*
>
> R. Z. CHESNOFF, DAOUD KUTTAB,
> D. MAKOVSKY,
> *U.S. News and World Report,* August 21, 1989

POLITICAL ASSASSINATION OF LEADERS

> *And the angel of the Lord said to her, Behold thou art with child and shalt bear a son and shalt call his name Yishmael (the biblical Arabs). And he will be a wild man, his hand will be against every man, and every man's hand against him . . ."*
> Genesis 16:11-12

The Arab world is one of the most assassination-prone subsystems in the world. It is no coincidence that the word "assassin" is of Arabic origin and is connected with the Shi'ite Ismaili sect in Syria in the eleventh century – a sect which made political progress by killing its opponents while under the influence of hashish.

IRAQ

King Faisal the second, Prince Abd Ilah, and Prime Minister Nuri Said in July 1958; President Kassem in 1963; President Aref in 1968; one foreign minister, one former minister, a former vice-president, two Jordanian ministers who happened to be visiting Iraq in 1958; several other ministers; three religious leaders, one ambassador; over 400 different-ranking Iraqi politicians. All these leaders have been murdered in Iraq since 1948.

**Arab journal
*Al-Usbuh Al-
Arub*, No.935,
August 1, 1977.
The captions, a
bit unclear,
read: "Middle
East war" and
"Middle East
peace."**

JORDAN

King Abdullah in July 1951, Prime Minister Almagalli and his entourage in August 1960, Prime Minister Wasfi Al-Tal in November 1971. In addition, there were several aborted attempts on the life of King Hussein.

LEBANON

Former Foreign Minister Riad Assulh in July 1951; former minister Naim Mughabghab in July 1959; former President Camille Chamoun was wounded in an attempt on his life in August 1968; Kamal Jumblat, political Druze leader, was murdered in March 1977, Tony Franjieh, son of a former president in June 1978; President-elect Bashir Gemayel in September 1982, and President René Muawwad in November 1989.

SYRIA

President Husni Zaim and Premier Mushin Barazi were executed in April 1950; the commander of the Air Force, Hassan Nasser, in July 1950; former President General Sami Hinawi in October 1950; former President Adib Shishakli was murdered in exile in September 1964; former Minister of Defense Muhammad Umran in March 1972; President Hafez al-Assad was wounded in July 1973 in an assassination attempt; as well as many other political and religious leaders.

SAUDI ARABIA
King Faisal in March 1975.

EGYPT
Prime Minister Nukrashi Pasha in December 1948, as well as Hasan al-Banna, leader of the Islamic Brotherhood. In the summer of 1967, Field Marshal Abd al-Hakim Amer committed suicide. He was the Minister of War during the Six-Day War. President Anwar Sadat was murdered on October 6, 1981.

Scene of Anwar al-Sadat's assassination, Cairo, October 6, 1981.

YEMEN
Imam Yahya and three of his sons were murdered in October 1963, President Ibrahim Al-Hamdi in October 1977. President Ahmad Al-Ghasmi was assassinated in June 1978, former minister Said Muhammed in February 1967, and Faisal Shaabi, former Prime Minister, in April 1967.

The troubles and upheavals in the Middle East have nothing to do with Israel. In *For Zion's Sake* (New York, 1987), Israel's former ambassador to the United Nations, Professor Yehuda Blum, put it thus: "The sources of instability in the Middle East fall, broadly speaking, into three categories: internal upheavals inside countries of the region; conflicts between states of the region; and subversion and aggression from countries outside the Middle East. To those three categories one should add another source of instability, of more recent vintage, namely the misuse of staggering oil wealth by certain countries in a manner which threatens the security and well-being of other countries both inside the region and beyond it."

MILITARY CONFRONTATIONS: ARAB VIS-A-VIS ARAB

> *Sabah Kanaan knew she was going to be murdered. The 32-year-old single mother had been accused of collaborating with Israeli intelligence and of promiscuity. A Palestinian ''shock committee'' broke into her home in the West Bank city of Nablus and held her prisoner for three nights while they brutally beat her. Taken to a hospital by neighbors, Kanaan denied all the whispered charges against her and told reporters ''they will never let me live.'' Two months after she was released, her bludgeoned body was found near the Nablui's onion market, axed and riddled with stab wounds.*
>
> R. Z. CHESNOFF, DAOUD KUTTAB,
> D. MAKOVSKY,
> *U.S. News and World Report,* August 21, 1989

Over the last 30 years, hundreds of thousands of Arabs were killed in battle against their fellow Arabs. Tens of times Arab states have fought against one another:

- Egypt fought against North Yemen.
  Egypt fought against Libya.
  Iraq fought against Kuwait.
- Algeria fought against Morocco.
  South Yemen fought against Saudi Arabia.
  South Yemen fought against North Yemen.
- South Yemen fought against Oman.
- Jordan fought against Syria.
  Syria fought against Iraq.
  Libya fought against Chad (non-Arab).
  Somalia fought against Ethiopia (non-Arab).
- Iraq fought against Iran (non-Arab).
- Libya fought against Sudan.
- Syria fought against Lebanon.
  Syria fought against Jordan.

Following the "Es Samu affair" some of my many Arab allies, instead of going after Israel, turned against me! Thereafter, I learned by way of the international press and "The Arab Voice," the Cairo radio and that of Damascus, that "before liberating Tel Aviv, we must liberate Amman [the Jordanian capital]." On May 21, 1967, the Syrians sent us a car which exploded on our border at Ramtha . . . Result: 14 Jordanians killed . . . The incident filled Jordan with unease. In such delicate circumstances, we no longer knew who was less trustworthy: Israel or our Arab Allies!

KING HUSSEIN, from his book entitled
My "War" with Israel

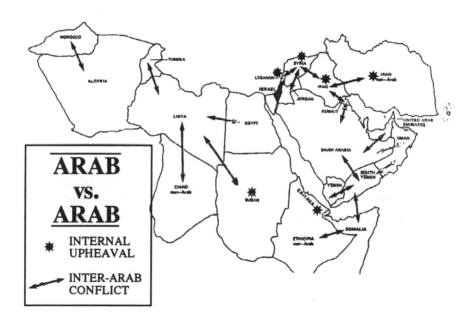

ARAB vs. ARAB

✴ INTERNAL UPHEAVAL

➤ INTER-ARAB CONFLICT

CHAPTER TWENTY-TWO

SADDAM HUSSEIN –
THE SLAUGHTERER FROM
BAGHDAD

Saddam Hussein is our national hero.
> MUHAMMED MILHEM,
> top aide to Yassir Arafat,
> Associated Press, Rome,
> August 23, 1990

IRAQI AGGRESSION AGAINST
KUWAIT: AUGUST 1990

On August 2, 1990, over one hundred thousand Iraqi troops invaded
Kuwait, capturing it in just a few hours. Iraqi President Hussein surprised
all the world and acted against all world norms of order. This case proves
again the cruel nature of the Iraqi dictator and his unexpected behavior.

Q: Who supported the Iraqi aggression against Kuwait?
A: PLO chairman, Yassir Arafat (see photo on the following page).
Q: What does Arafat think of Saddam Hussein?
A: Arafat's words speak for themselves: "We say to the brother and
   leader Saddam Hussein – go forward with God's blessing" (Iraqi
   News Agency, April 3, 1990). "We will enter Jerusalem victoriously
   and raise our flag on its walls . . . We will fight you [the Israelis] with
   stones, rifles and El-Abed [the Iraqi missile] . . ." (Associated Press,
   March 29, 1990).
Q: What has Saddam Hussein said to Arafat?
A: "You are not alone . . . We have always said that once the war [with
   Iran] is over, our efforts will be directed towards Palestine . . ."

(Iraqi News Agency, March 30, 1990). "In the name of Allah, we shall cause fire to devour half of Israel . . ." (Iraqi News Agency, April 2, 1990).

Iraqi television, August 6, 1990.

> *It is ironic that it is other Arabs who are the first to say that the character of the PLO has been exposed by its alliance with Saddam. There surely is no longer any excuse for wishful thinking. If the U.S. political culture doesn't understand the PLO now, we guess it never will.*
> *Wall Street Journal*, August 31, 1990

Q: Why would the Palestinians support Saddam Hussein?
A: Yassir Arafat and his colleagues have followed the road of radicalism. Saddam is most definitely radical, therefore, he enjoys the support of the PLO.

271

Q: Did Kuwait ever help the Palestinians?

A: Yes, and far more than Iraq ever did. Kuwait supported the PLO and West Bank Palestinians through grants from the Kuwaiti treasury, a Kuwait – administered tax on the 300,000 Palestinians in Kuwait and the private remittances from Palestinians in Kuwait to relatives on the West Bank and elsewhere.

Q: What was the result of the PLO's support of Iraq?

A: Kuwait's government-in-exile has, as a result, cut off its subsidies to the PLO. Meanwhile, Palestinians are being fired and expelled from sheikdoms up and down the Gulf since they are feared as a potential fifth column. In Judea and Samaria, where living standards have already been cut in half by the uprising, the loss of the Gulf's assistance will be devastating.

Q: Is the damage only financial?

A: No. The damage Arafat has done by backing Saddam Hussein goes beyond the financial. Arab newspapers have noted that the PLO chairman who opposes the seizing of land by force and the denial of self-determination in Judea, Samaria and Gaza seems to favor such action in the Gulf.

We wish to thank Saddam Hussein for bringing the Arab nation to such a technological level.

YASSIR ARAFAT,
Jordanian television,
April 25, 1990

It should be noted that Saddam Hussein is the only Arab leader referred to by Arafat as Al-Faris, which means "the Knight." He also referred to the Iraqi president as "the first and foremost" in the presence of all the Arab leaders at the Baghdad Summit in May 1990.

Q: How did the Palestinians express their support for Saddam Hussein?

A: A congratulatory telegram on his conquering Kuwait was sent to Saddam Hussein by the *Intifada* leadership. Moreover, leaflet No. 55 of the *Intifada* leadership expressed full solidarity with Iraq. Then, on September 26, 1990, the day on which the United Nations imposed an aerial blockade on Iraq, there was a general strike in support of Saddam Hussein in Judea, Samaria, and Gaza.

> *Saddam has paved the way for the confrontation with the Zionist entity which now threatens the Arab Nation more than ever before. Saddam's statement has become a true factor in the reinforcement of the uprising as well as a guarantee for its continuation, until the creation of an independent Palestinian state whose capital is Jerusalem.*
>
> ABU IYAD, Arafat deputy,
> Iraqi News Agency,
> April 23, 1990

Q: How does Iraq support the terrorist activities of the PLO?

A: Thousands of terrorists were stationed in Iraq, most of whom were members of Arafat's Fatah faction. Others were members of Abu Abbas' Popular Liberation Front. Also located in Baghdad are the headquarters of the "May 15th Organization," headed by Abu Ibrahim Salim, and the Popular Front for the Liberation of Palestine –Special Command, headed by Salim Abu Saalam. These two factions have close ties with Iraqi Intelligence and are involved in terrorist activities abroad.

Q: What else did Arafat do to express PLO support for Iraq?

A: The PLO, together with Iraq and Libya, were alone in opposing the August 10, 1990, decision of the emergency Arab summit. The summit adopted a multi-point resolution condemning the Iraqi invasion, supporting Kuwaiti sovereignty, condemning the Iraqi threats against Gulf states, and dispatching an Arab force to join Western forces in defense of Saudi Arabia.

On Wednesday, September 26, 1990, there was a general strike in Judea, Samaria, and Gaza. The Palestinian leadership declared the strike in support of Iraq and against the United States and all other nations that use sanctions against Iraq. The call for the strike appeared on a leaflet distributed by the above-mentioned leadership.

> *We will fight until the American ships sink in the waters of the Gulf.*
>
> MUHAMMED MILHEM,
> top Arafat aide,
> Associated Press, Rome,
> August 23, 1990

Q: What can be said of Iraqi financial support to the PLO?

A: Iraq sends financial aid to the PLO and to its various factions with which it maintains contacts. Following the recent Baghdad summit, in a gesture intended to prompt other Arab countries to follow suit; Iraq decided to contribute 25 million dollars to the PLO in support of the Intifada. This is in addition to the regular monthly payments Iraq has made to the PLO since the beginning of the uprising. Iraq has also decided to increase the transmission time of the PLO radio station broadcasting from Baghdad, from 3 to 6 hours a day (Azam Al-Achmad, PLO representative in Baghdad, French News Agency, June 3, 1990).

Q: Where does PLO leader Abu Abbas reside?

A: It is common knowledge that Abu Abbas holds an Iraqi passport. The first announcement, in which Abu Abbas' Palestine Liberation Front took responsibility for the abortive attack on Israel's coastline on May 30, 1990, was published by the organization's spokesman in Baghdad (Reuters, May 30, 1990). Moreover, following the *Achille Lauro* affair of 1985, and Abbas' release from detention in Italy, he was given asylum in Baghdad. Abu Abbas' headquarters in Iraq are located near Al-Ratba (Sunday *Times*, London, November 24, 1986). This was Abbas' destination after his release from Italy.

Q: How does Arafat help Saddam Hussein?

A: In reciprocation for Iraqi support, Arafat has affirmed his commitment to Saddam by supporting him in the Arab world, through public statements, encouraging him in his action and serving as his emissary on political missions.

Q: What demonstrates even more the close PLO-Iraqi relations?

A: The PLO has moved its main headquarters to Baghdad. Arafat has frequently met with Saddam and other key Iraqi officials in order to update them on his plans of action. Arafat was very active in improving Iraq-Iran relations as well.

Q: The PLO has allied itself with Iraq at a time when other Arab states, both moderate and rejectionist, are siding with the United States and the Western world against the Iraqi aggression.

> *May you purge these sanctified Moslem lands of contamination of the American armed forces and their helpers and save the holy cities of Mecca and Medina.*
>
> Sheik SAAD AL-DIN AL-ALAMI,
> Mufti of Jerusalem, in a message
> to Saddam Hussein, August 12, 1990

> *By seizing the desert sheikdom of Kuwait, Mr. Hussein betrayed and terrified his Arab brothers, destoyed the balance of power in the Persian Gulf, plunged the world's oil markets into chaos and challenged the assumption that the end of the cold war would bring peace to the world.*
> ELAINE SCIOLINO,
> *New York Times*,
> August 4, 1990

THE GULF CRISIS AND ISRAEL

> *The State of Israel is one of the outcomes of World War II and must disappear, just as the Berlin Wall and other results of that war are disappearing.*
> YASSIR ARAFAT and MUAMMAR QADDAFI,
> agreement quoted in Libyan News Agency
> official release, January 6, 1990

Q: Is Israel involved in the Gulf crisis?

A: Not at all. This crisis proves that the Arab-Israeli conflict has nothing to do with Arab upheavals. Arabs have been killing one another and would continue to do so in the future even if Israel were not in the Middle East.

Q: What did Israel do to minimize the Iraqi threat?

A: Israel bombed and destroyed the Iraqi nuclear reactor in May 1981. By doing so, Israel removed a horrific threat that hung over the lives of millions. One can imagine the feeling of the Saudis, the Americans, and all others near the Iraqi borders had the atomic option been in the hands of Iraq today.

Q: Was Israel at that time praised for her action?

A: Not at all. Israel was, in fact, condemned by the United Nations for violating Iraqi sovereignty. Even the United States condemned Israel at that time. Perhaps now these nations will understand in retrospect the great contribution Israel made to world safety by destroying the Iraqi nuclear reactor.

Q: Who supplied weapons to Saddam Hussein?

A: The Soviet Union, France, Germany, and others. For a price the

275

French and Germans supplied Saddam with massive destructive weapons.

Q: Did Israel warn these nations against supplying such weapons to Saddam Hussein?

A: Yes, Israel explained, time and again, that such weapons in the hands of such a dictator would endanger the safety of the world in general and the Middle East in particular. Israel's warnings fell on deaf ears.

Open fire on the American enemy everywhere. Quake the earth under the feet of the invaders and the collaborators.

ABU ABBAS,
leader of the Popular Liberation Front,
Wall Street Journal, August 31, 1990

Revolutionary groups in the Arab world . . . should consider Saddam's battle as their own deeds and words. They must fight and struggle with all means at their disposal alongside Iraq in support of the revolutionary stance it has taken.

PLO leader GEORGE HABASH,
Iraqi News Agency,
September 3, 1990

The following cartoon appeared in the Israeli daily *Ma'ariv* on October 1, 1990. It was captioned "The Iraqi nation is 'behind' Saddam Hussein."

Q: What role does Israel play in the Gulf crisis?

A: Throughout the crisis in the Persian Gulf, Israel has expressed time and again its complete support for the international effort to put an end to Iraq's aggression against Kuwait. Israel has cooperated with the United States in order to solve the crisis. Saddam Hussein tried to involve Israel in the crisis in order to break the international siege against Iraq. Israel has deliberately remained in the background and has not given Saddam Hussein any excuse to involve her.

There is no doubt that the Israeli presence in the area contributes to the stability of the region. The presence of a strong Israel prevents Iraqi expansion into Jordan – Israel's eastern neighbor. The Israeli-Egyptian peace treaty contributes to the stability of the entire Mediterranean basin.

While Palestinian workers were expelled from the Gulf states because of PLO support for Iraq, Israel has proved her strong humanity. Israel's policy was noted by the *Wall Street Journal* on August 31, 1990, when it wrote: "Typically for the Middle East, the country that has kept its borders the widest open to accept Palestinians fleeing Kuwait and Iraq was not Jordan, Syria or Lebanon, but Israel."

Egypt's semi-official daily, *Al-Achbar*, September 1, 1990, published this cartoon depicting a downtrodden Iraqi saying: "Woe is me, they're going to find a solution for hostages of all nationalities – except for us." The words on a slip of paper beneath the Iraqi may be translated: "The Iraqi Nation."

SADDAM HUSSEIN: THREATS BEFORE THE GULF CRISIS

> *You cannot imagine what having 50 fighting divisions can do to a man's psychology. Saddam is not kidding. For 10 years Hafez al-Assad in Syria has been talking about achieving strategic parity with Israel, but Saddam has done it with these chemical weapons.*
>
> YOUSSEF M. IBRAHAM,
> quoting the PLO leader,
> *New York Times,*
> June 17, 1990

Iraq is one of the most radical Arab states in the Middle East. Iraq, which participated in the 1948 war, has never signed a ceasefire agreement with Israel. Despite the fact that Iraq has no common border with Israel, she fought against Israel in 1948, 1967, and in the 1973 war – wars which were imposed upon the Jewish state since her establishment in 1948. Following the signing of the peace treaty between Israel and Egypt, the Arab leaders met in Baghdad, the Iraqi capital, in 1979 in order to oppose the agreement and to decide upon the appropriate punishment for Egypt for "betraying" the Arab cause by signing such a peace treaty.

> *In the name of Allah, we shall cause fire to devour half of Israel, should she try to do anything to Iraq . . . we have binary chemical weapons.*
>
> SADDAM HUSSEIN,
> at a military ceremony on April 1, 1990,
> Iraqi News Agency, April 2, 1990

Q: Who is Saddam Hussein?

A: The Iraqi president Saddam Hussein is famous for his cruelty and barbarity against his own people, not to mention against others. Long before his rise to power, he earned the reputation of being a malicious assassin.

Q: Can an example be cited?

A: Yes. In a single afternoon, in the summer of 1988, Hussein gassed to death thousands of Kurds, among them small children.

Q: What is the real threat posed by Iraq?

A: The real threat to Israel lies in a revival of the Eastern Front, which has recently caused more concern in view of Iraq's military cooperation with Jordan. The two countries formed a joint squadron and Iraqi planes have flown along Israel's border.

Q: What was Iraq's part in the 1948 war?

A: Iraq invaded Israel on the eve of its establishment in 1948; its armies crossed the Jordan at Naharayim, south of the Sea of Galilee, and, in cooperation with the Jordanian "Arab Legion," occupied Samaria. The Iraqi attempt to cut Israel in two at Netanya was defeated by the Israeli forces and Iraq subsequently withdrew its forces from the front lines.

Q: What was Iraq's part in the 1967 war?

A: In the 1967 Six-Day War, the Iraqi leaders threatened to destroy Israel. Iraq participated in the war; its jets bombed Israeli targets and its armor moved into Jordan.

The existence of Israel is an error which must be rectified. This is our opportunity to wipe out the ignominy which has been with us since 1948. Our goal is clear – to wipe Israel off the map.
ABD ALRAHMAN A'REF,
former President of Iraq,
May 31, 1967

Q: What was Iraq's part in the 1973 war?

A: In the 1973 Yom Kippur War, Iraqi armor fought alongside the Syrians against Israel on the Golan Heights.

That is why we said 'Absolutely No' to Baker, to America, when they tried to harm our rights, our representation.
YASSIR ARAFAT to Saddam Hussein
Al-Muharrir, April 19, 1990

Q: Did Iraq support Arab terror against Israel?

A: Yes. Iraq has consistently supported Arab terror against Israel indirectly, via the PLO or Abul Abbas of the 1985 *Achille Lauro* ship hijacking and the abortive operation on Israel's coastline on May 30, 1990, and directly through the "Arab Liberation Front," which specialized in attacking children's quarters in Israeli kibbutzim.

Q: Did the Iraq-Iran war change Iraq's strong hostility against Israel?

A: No. The Iraqi president answered this question in his own words. According to the Gulf News Agency, on February 18, 1988, while the Iraq-Iran war was still in progress, Saddam Hussein said the following: "Iraq believes in the liberation of Palestine, not as a slogan, or for domestic consumption, but as an aim to be concretely attained."

We can cross other countries to strike at Israel . . . we have a joint Arab defense pact, making all Arab lands one . . . our planes and missiles will reach Israel . . . indeed we have sited our missile launch pads facing West, not East.
SADDAM HUSSEIN,
speaking to the Union of Arab Workers,
Iraqi News Agency, April 18, 1990

Q: What are Iraq's intentions towards Israel?

A: The commander of the Iraqi Air Force, Sa'ab Hassan, put it thus: "We can preempt an enemy strike even before it happens . . . we are preparing against Israel" (*Hurras-al Wattan*, military magazine, Baghdad, April 22, 1990).

Q: What does Iraq think about Israel?

A: Speaking at the "Solidarity with Iraq" Convention in Baghdad on May 8, 1990, the Iraqi president, Hussein, said: "As for [tension with] Israel, I am asked how can we calm things down? Why should we, though, before we get all that we demand, and in full? We demand the rights of the Palestinians. The enemy has turned the West against Iraq. If we let matters subside without fully carrying out our counter-offensive; it means they will have beaten us . . . we have no choice except to stand up for Arab rights, Arab honor and be ready for all the sacrifices, glorious sacrifices that Allah has ordained for us."

We will hit back fiercely . . . even if the remotest point in Mauritania or Hafez Assad's Syria is attacked, we will strike back and repel Israel.

SADDAM HUSSEIN,
quoted in the *Jerusalem Post*,
June 22, 1990

Q: What are the chances for a political option?

A: The Iraqi Foreign Minister, Tareq Aziz, told a visiting PLO delegation the following: "War with Israel is inevitable. The Palestinian masses of the *Intifada*, who constitute the largest fighting force in the occupied country, must be well prepared for battle" (*Al-Muharrir*, May 8, 1990). The Deputy Prime Minister of Iraq, Taha Yasin Ramadan, said: "We are sure that should Israel be involved (in war) this will mean the end of her existence on the soil of Palestine. I have not the slightest doubt" (*Al-Sharq Al-Awsat*, Paris, May 18, 1990).

Q: Would Iraq chance fighting Israel alone?

A: Speaking to senior Ba'ath party members, Tareq Aziz, Iraqi Foreign Minister, said: "Iraq expects the Egyptian army to join the battle on her side, two weeks after the outbreak of war, despite the limitations of Camp David" (*Al-Muharrir*, May 8, 1990). The Iraqi Information Minister, Latif Nasif Jasem, said: "Any new war with Israel will be a long one, and all the Arabs will take part" (Iraqi News Agency, May 10, 1990). Saddam Hussein, talking to Arafat, and quoted in *Al-Muharrir*, on April 19, 1990, said the following: "Iraq, today, is more powerful than Israel in weapons and equipment. We have to make Israelis fear us. As for Syria and Jordan; those who don't want to fight [against Israel] should let us cross their territory if we need space in which to maneuver our divisions towards Israel."

> *From now on we must escalate our demands . . . I am still loyal to the three "No's" of Khartoum [1967] – no peace, no recognition, no negotiation . . . We must help the Intifada with planes and missiles, that can hit the enemy and defeat him, [perhaps] even without [needing] a land battle or a clash at sea. We have not reduced the size of our army, but are developing it steadily.*
> SADDAM HUSSEIN to Arafat,
> *Al-Muharrir*, April 19, 1990

Q: What are Iraq's expectations from the forthcoming war against Israel?

A: "Iraq means what she says, Israel and the West must understand that war, when it comes, will bring victory to the Arabs" (Iraqi Information Minister Latif Nasif Jasem, *Al-Thawrah*, Baghdad, May 10, 1990).

In the Israeli daily *Ma'ariv* on September 9, 1990, the following cartoon appeared. In it Saddam Hussein, carving up, as it were, the Kuwaiti "chicken," says: "Because of the blockade, Iraqi babies are starving to death."

◆ Do you know that in 1973 the Iraqi forces amounted to three divisions out of six or seven which were present at the outset of the war against Israel?

◆ Do you know that Iraqi forces fought via Jordan when it was directly involved in the 1967 war?

◆ Do you know that in 1990 Iraq totals over 50 divisions (military manpower of 1,000,000 active and 850,000 reserves) and 6,000 tanks?

◆ Do you know that the Iraqi airforce has about 300 or more sophisticated attack aircrafts from Iraq's total arsenal of over 500?

◆ Do you know that these aircrafts include Soviet-made Sukhoi 24 bombers, which are not even supplied to the Warsaw Pact member countries?

✦ Do you know that in the event of war, Iraqi forces would fight against Israel backed by several groups of advanced surface-to-surface missiles, which would probably be launched from the area of the Jordanian border from the Iraqi base known as "H3"?

✦ Do you know that these missiles are scud missiles, whose range has been extended by the Iraqis to 400 and 560 miles – 650 and 900 km respectively?

✦ Do you know that Iraq and Egypt have been developing the "Condor 2" with the help of Argentina? This is an Arab advanced surface-to-surface missile with an even longer range, perhaps more than 1000 miles – 1600 km.

✦ Do you know that Iraq is also developing chemical warheads for its missiles?

✦ Do you know that Iraq and Syria have both taken the view that chemical weapons are meant as a response to Israel's perceived nuclear capability?

✦ Do you know that the time needed to transfer large numbers of Iraqi forces to Israel's border is less than 24 hours?

✦ Do you know that there is no guarantee that Israel's airforce would be able to prevent or significantly disrupt the movement of these forces to battle, just as it was unable to in 1973?

Q: What is the Iraqi view of Russian immigrants to Israel?

A: According to Iraq's Deputy Foreign Minister, Nzir Hamdoon, as quoted in *Mail on Sunday* in London on May 13, 1990: "The flood of Soviet immigrants to Israel could lead to war."

If Israel attacks Iraq or any other Arab country, Iraq will use all her weapons against Israel.

SADDAM HUSSEIN,
to the Islamic Conference in Baghdad,
Radio Baghdad, June 17, 1990

Q: What was Iraq's position at the Arab summit conference in Baghdad, May 28-30, 1990?

A: Iraq, together with Libya and the PLO, were the leading powers behind the radical resolutions at the conference.

Q: How did Libya and the PLO express their intentions towards Israel?

A: On May 30, 1990, the last day of the Arab summit, a gang of sixteen Abu Abbas PLO terrorists conducted an aborted operation against Israeli civilians along Israel's coastline. Upon his capture, the deputy commander of the operation confessed that Abu Abbas was behind the action and that the terrorists were trained in Libya for their criminal mission against innocent civilians. Abu Abbas is a member of the PLO executive and a close friend of Arafat.

Q: What kind of war does Iraq intend to wage against Israel?

A: Saddam Hussein's words explicitly express the answer to this question. Speaking to Arafat and quoted in *Al-Muharrir* on April 19, 1990, he said: "Iraq is familiar with every inch of Palestine, every [Israeli] airfield, base, factory and research facility. We have been able to photograph all the targets we need, deep inside Israel. We started to do this when the war with Iran ended. Israel knows, and we know she knows. The age of lightning battles is over: Should war break out, we will not cease fire, even if it lasts for a century. But we Arabs know it will not last for years, at most, a couple of months."

Q: What is the Iraqi attitude towards America?

A: In the same interview in *Al Muharrir* on April 19, the Iraqi president said: "Should there be an American attack against us, the results will be no different. With the help of Allah we shall rid this region of American influence. After the [U.S.] senators were here, I received a letter to say that the U.S.A. regarded Iraqi missiles as a threat to her interests. No more, no less! Our missiles cannot reach Washington. But if they could, we would hit there as necessary. However, we can still strike at Washington in other ways, at other U.S. targets in the world." Hussein continued: "There are Israeli military and civilian targets, as well as British and U.S. naval targets, all within our range, These will be obliterated if Iraq, or her leadership, come under attack. My own death will not prevent our response, but will hasten it, whether it be against Israel, or foreign warships, in the Gulf or elsewhere,"

The West and the Soviet Union helped create this man of evil dreams. They simply refused to believe he would turn against them, not after they had supplied him with weapons and loans and all.

A. M. ROSENTHAL,
New York Times, September 8, 1990

LESSONS FROM THE GULF CRISIS

> *But an Iraqi withdrawal that is not accomplished by the destruction of Saddam Hussein's war machine will leave the western world in grave danger. The rejoicing would in time turn to despair, the triumph to defeat. Indeed, the Administration's admitted best-case scenario – the restoration of the status quo ante – would be devastating for stability and security in the gulf.*
>
> *Consider the ramifications of a voluntary Iraqi withdrawal. Iraq's massive military machine would remain intact. Having demonstrated the capability to overwhelm and plunder Kuwait and hold the U.S. and its allies at bay, the Iraqi army would go home to regroup for its next adventure. Having struck a dagger in the heart of Kuwait, it would now strike fear in the heart of all within its reach.*
>
> RICHARD PERLE,
> former Assistant Secretary of Defense,
> Reagan Administration,
> *New York Times*, September 23, 1990

No matter what will be the results of the Persian Gulf crisis, the world must know the lessons of such a crisis:

1. The Arab-Israeli conflict is not the heart of the problem in the Middle East. Iraq and other radical Arab states, such as Syria and Libya, together with the PLO and Islamic fundamentalists are playing a destabilizing role in the Middle East. They are, in fact, the heart of the troubles in the region.
2. The Iraqi president, Saddam Hussein, has proved beyond a doubt that he is a cruel man with wild ambitions. In order to achieve his dreams, he would not mind crushing an Arab sister-state, Kuwait, murdering his opponents, and even using non-conventional weapons to torture and murder thousands of innocent people.
3. Israel's warning about the dangers posed by Iraq was not seriously accepted by the world. Time and time again, Israel warned the Western world, which supplied Iraq with huge quantities of sophisticated weapons, of the danger of such an arsenal to the world in general and to Israel in particular. The Persian Gulf crisis proved that Saddam Hussein's threats must be evaluated at face value.

4. Without the world's active cooperation, there would have been no Iraqi threat today. The belt of war industries around Baghdad and the military research and development plant near Mosul were built and equipped by European companies. European scientists play an active role. American money is being handed to Saddam. All these encouraged Iraq's megalomania.

5. Baghdad has been officially and openly supplied by 22 different countries from both the Eastern and Western bloc. According to a Simon Wiesenthal Center report released in October 1990, 207 companies have supplied Iraq with chemical weapons and other means of mass destruction over the past decade. The report names these companies and specifies the type of military supplies and expertise they furnished to Iraq. Singled out is the Federal Republic of Germany leading the list with no less than 86 firms supplying Saddam Hussein. Other major suppliers have been the U.S.S.R., communist China, France and Brazil. Other suppliers include Italy, Poland and Egypt. The Osirak nuclear reactor, which was hit by Israel in May 1981, was supplied by the French government. It was named Osirak after the then-premier of France.

6. Iraq's various threats against Israel should be given full consideration. Israel is not Kuwait and not Saudi Arabia. Israel does not need American troops to defend her against Arab or Iraqi aggression. Israel asks only for the weapons by which to defend herself.

7. The world trend – to end the cold war and to find more compromise and understanding between East and West – has not reached the Arab world yet.

8. Both the Iraqi threats against Israel and the Iraqi occupation of Kuwait prove that the advancement of an Israel-Palestinian settlement cannot be separated from the advancement of peace between Israel and the Arab states. The Israeli peace initiative of May 1989 addressed these two main issues: a comprehensive peace between Israel and the Arab states and a settlement of the Palestinian problem.

9. PLO chairman Yassir Arafat, by supporting the aggression of Saddam Hussein against Kuwait, proved once again that the PLO has never contributed to peace prospects in the Middle East. On the contrary, the PLO is an obstacle to peace between Israel and the Palestinians.

10. The Israel Defense Forces are the sole permanent military power in the area that can successfully combat the Iraqi army, either defensively or offensively as required. This fact, well known to the Iraqi leader, is a powerful deterrent to further Iraqi aggression.

11. Israel has issued repeated public and private warnings that she will take military measures if any Iraqi troops enter Jordan. Israel has, in fact, guaranteed the territorial integrity of Jordan against Iraqi aggression. The continuance of Jordan as a buffer state between Iraq and Israel is essential for the maintenance of stability in the region.

12. Israel is not only the sole democracy in the area, but is the only stable American ally in the region as well. Israel can, in the future, serve as a base for American forces. These forces could deter any aggression that may arise to endanger the flow of Middle Eastern oil to the free world. The Persian gulf crisis has reaffirmed Israel's vital strategic importance to the United States.

13. Even in her present low-profile state, Israeli cooperation has been extremely valuable. Israeli military intelligence has focused on Iraq much more carefully over the years than has the U.S. intelligence community. Israel, therefore, has been able to provide Washington with detailed tactical intelligence on the growing Iraqi threat. Although not publicized, this is currently the most important aspect of strategic cooperation between Israel and the United States.

14. The present crisis in the gulf proved that the Israeli bombing of the Iraqi nuclear reactor in May 1981 was the proper action at the proper time to protect the safety of the world at large.

15. The crisis raised a new question as to the reliability of so-called "Arab moderates" such as Jordan and the PLO – after Arafat's declaration in December 1988 in Geneva that he recognized Israel. The PLO and Jordan have supported Iraq.

16. The Iraqi atttempt to link its occupation of Kuwait with Israel's relinquishing of Judea and Samaria has nothing to do with reality. Saddam Hussein did not attack Kuwait in order to solve the problem of the Palestinians.

17. Israel captured Judea and Samaria from Jordan, the Gaza Strip from Egypt, and the Golan Heights from Syria as a result of a combined Arab attack against her in June 1967. Kuwait did not attack Iraq.

18. Israel accepted Security Council Resolution 242. Iraq has rejected all the Security Council resolutions calling for unconditional withdrawal from Kuwait.

19. The capture of the bulk of the Kuwaiti arsenal by the Iraqi invaders emphasizes the heavy risk entailed in providing sophisticated U.S. weapons to the weak Arab oil-producing states.

Here is one of the leaflets published on August 25, 1990, by the PLO leadership. The leaflet condemns the United States, Israel, and the reactionary Arab states that support America.

The leaflet ends with a promise to liberate all of Palestine and a wish for long life for Saddam Hussein.

بيان الى جماهير شعبنا المناضل

ياجماهير شعبنا البطل . ايها الرفاق بان شعبنا العربي العراقي ومقدساتنا تتعرض لهجمة عدوانية من الامبريالية والصليبية والصهيونية والانظمة الرجعية . ان شعبنا في العراق يتعرض للمجاعة والموت من هؤلاء الاعداء الذين احتلوا مقدساتنا .

لوكانت هذه الجيوش الضخمة والاساطيل الحربية والحصار العسكري والاقتصادي عندما اخذ العدو الصهيوني فلسطين والجولان ولبنان ؟

ياجماهير شعبنا المسلم به انها حملة صليبية هدفها احتلال الوطن العربي والسيطرة على البترول وعلى ثروات امتنا العربية بمساعدة الانظمة الخائنة ؛

ايها الرفاق: ندعوكم لما يلي به

١ـ الثورة على الحكام الخونة والاطاحة بهم .

٢ـ ضرب المصالح الامبريالية والصهيونية في جميع انحاء العالم .

٣ـ اعلان حالة الحرب والسماح للمتطوعين بالسفر الى العراق .

٤ـ نطالب النظام السوري بوضع الخلافات جانبا والوقوف الى جانب اخواتنا في العراق وفتح الحدود امام جيشه لتأدية واجباته نحو العدو .

٥ـ ندعو الاتحاد السوفياتي الى تحمل مسؤولياتهم وعمل ما يلزم لمنع الامبريالية من ضرب العراق .

ايها الشعب العربي البطل به

اننا نناشدكم بالوقوف الى جانب العراق ومساعدته ، ماذا تنتظرون ؟

اننا من فلسطين الحبيبة نتوجه بالتحية والتقدير الى الشعب العراقي والاخ صدام حسـ بطل الامة العربية... نشد على ايديكم والله معنا ؛

اننا نرى في عيونكم تحرير فلسطين كلها ، وانها لثورة حتى التحرير والنصر.....

عاشت فلسطين حرة عربية

عاشت منظمة التحرير الفلسطينية

المجد والخلود لشهدائنا الابرار

الخزي والعار للعملاء والخونة

عاش البطل صدام حسين

والله معنا والنصر قريب

جبهة النضال الشعبي الفلسطيني

ـــ دولة فلسطين ـــ

التاريخ :ـ ٢٥ / ٨ / ١٩٩٠م

PART VII

ABOUT JEWISH REFUGEES, ARAB REFUGEES, JEWISH HOSTAGES – AND ABSURDITY

CHAPTER TWENTY-THREE

PALESTINIAN ARAB REFUGEES – POLITICAL WEAPON IN CRUEL ARAB HANDS

> *The Arab armies entered Palestine to protect the Palestinians from the Zionist tyranny but, instead, they abandoned them, forced them to emigrate and to leave their homeland, imposed upon them a political and ideological blockade and threw them into prisons similiar to the ghettos in which the Jews used to live in Eastern Europe.*
>
> ABU MAZEN,
> member PLO Executive Committee,
> *Falastin el-Thawra,* official journal of the PLO,
> Beirut, March 1976

> *The Arab League announced its plan for "the occupation of Palestine by the armies of the League's member states and the forcible prevention of the establishment of the Jewish State.*
>
> *New York Times,*
> November 30, 1947
> (the day after the UN Partition plan)

Few problems on the international political scene have been debated as often and as fruitlessly as that of the Arab refugees. For the past four decades, the basically humanitarian problem of homeless, uprooted people has been thrust aside by considerations of political interests and national pride. Fear and deliberate deceit have also played their roles.

"Refugeeism" is no new phenomenon in human history. In the last generation millions of people have been uprooted unwillingly from their homes and cast into the role of refugees. In the post-World War II period, many millions of refugees have been produced by territorial partition and redivision. The establishment of the States of India and Pakistan resulted in 14 million refugees; 400,000 Karelians were absorbed by Finland; more than 3 million Sudeten Germans, who fled Czechoslovakia, have been absorbed; West Germany has conferred citizenship on 9 million refugees from the other side of the Wall; Turkey, Greece, Korea and Austria have all absorbed large influxes.

Only in the case of the Palestinian Arab refugees has no progress of any consequence been achieved, despite the relatively small number involved.

Q: Who rejected the United Nations Partition Plan of November 29, 1947?

A: In 1948, the Arabs rejected the UN General Assembly's resolution to establish a Jewish state alongside an Arab state in Palestine.

Q: How did the Arabs express their opposition?

A: The regular armies of five Arab states invaded Israel with the intention of eradicating it.

Q: What did the Arab armies call upon the Palestinian Arabs to do?

A: The belligerent Arab states called upon the Palestinian Arabs to temporarily leave the country in order to make way for the invading armies.

Q: How many Arabs left Palestine?

A: As a result of this call, approximately 600,000 Arabs left. The subsequent failure of Arab war plans created a refugee problem.

Q: Did all the Palestinians leave at that time?

A: No. Many did not leave and those who remained and their descendents now constitute some three-quarters of a million Arab citizens of Israel.

Q: How many refugees fled as a result of the 1967 war?

A: Following the Six-Day War in 1967, another war which Israel had to fight for its survival, the number of new refugees varied from some 125,000 (Israeli estimate) to 250,000 (United Nations Relief and Works Agency – UNRWA – estimate).

> . . . *armed Arab bands from neighboring Arab states have infiltrated into the territory of Palestine and together with local Arab forces are defeating the purpose of the Partition by acts of violence.*
>
> UN Palestine Commission,
> report to Security Council, April 10, 1948

> *15 May 1948 arrived . . . on that very day the Mufti of Jerusalem appealed to the Arabs of Palestine to leave the country, because the Arab armies were about to enter and fight in their stead . . .*
>
> AKHBAR EL-YOM,
> Cairo, October 12, 1963

Q: How many Palestinians were allowed to return?

A: Of those who left in 1948, 50,000 Arab refugees had returned by the early 1950s under a family reunion policy. Of those who left in 1967, a further 72,900 have also been permitted to return. Altogether a total of 122,000 refugees have been reunited with their families since 1950.

Q: How many refugees were rehoused by Israel?

A: Some 70,000 refugees (10,000 families) were rehoused voluntarily through an Israeli program. Since 1970, nine residential projects were built in the Gaza District.

> *The fact that there are these refugees is the direct consequence of the act of the Arab States in opposing partition and the Jewish State.*
>
> EMILE GHOURY,
> Secretary Palestine Arab Higher Committee,
> *Beirut Telegraph,*
> September 6, 1948

PALESTINIAN REFUGEES (IN NUMBERS)

Israel is the only country that has tried to do something for the people in the camps. In 1971 and again in 1981, Israel unilaterally built permanent housing for Arab refugees in Gaza in which 70,000 former inhabitants of camps now live. Yet every November the UN passes a resolution calling upon Israel to return these people to camps.

Q: How many Arab refugees are in refugee camps today?

A: According to the annual report of UNRWA in 1988, the number of Palestinian camp residents throughout the Middle East is 792,832.

Q: Where are the refugees located?

A: There are Palestinian refugees in Lebanon, Syria, Jordan and the areas of Judea, Samaria and the Gaza Strip.

> *As the time for the British withdrawal drew nearer, the zeal of the Arab league was redoubled. Meetings and conferences took place almost daily and burning calls and appeals were issued. Brotherly advice was given to the Arabs of Palestine, urging them to leave their land, homes and property and to stay temporarily in neighboring, brotherly States lest the guns of the invading Arab armies mow them down.*
>
> *Al-Hoda*, daily of the
> U.S. Lebanese immigrant community,
> June 8, 1951

Q: Why is it difficult to know the exact number of all the Palestinian refugees?

A: One of the main reasons for discrepancies is that many of the Palestinians who registered with UNRWA in 1948 as refugees left the camps long ago, radically improved their living conditions, and even received citizenship of another country, thus remaining refugees in name only.

Q: What is the official number of Palestinian refugees for 1988 according to UNRWA?

A: The 1988 UNRWA report gives a figure of 2,268,595 registered Palestinian refugees. The UNRWA figures do not, however, reflect the actual number of refugees.

Q: What is the percentage of Palestinians living in refugee camps?

A: According to UNRWA figures, only about 35 percent of registered refugees live in refugee camps, which is 792,832.

Q: What can be said of the other refugees?

A: Some refugee camps, built on the outskirts of cities, have over the years developed and become indistinguishable from other sections of the cities.

Q: Are the estimated number of Palestinian refugees accurate?

A: UNRWA itself noted in its publication that its statistics were based on figures of registration with the Agency and do not necessarily reflect the true population figures.

Q: How can discrepancies in the estimations be accounted for?

A: Discrepancies in the estimations are due to such factors as unreported births and deaths as well as false or duplicate registration.

> *We have never concealed the fact that we began the fighting*
> *[in 1948].*
>
> JAMAL HUSSEINI, in charge of
> Palestine Arab Higher Committee,
> April 23, 1948

PALESTINIAN REFUGEES IN ARAB STATES

As we mentioned before, we should distinguish between real refugees, who live in refugee camps, and registered refugees, who are, in reality, not refugees. The number of registered refugees totals almost two times the number of real refugees.

Q: How many Arab refugees are in Jordan?
A: According to UNRWA figures for 1988, there are an estimated 870,000 registered refugees in Jordan.
Q: Are the Palestinian refugees Jordanian citizens?
A: According to Jordanian law, all Palestinian refugees have the right to become citizens of Jordan. Indeed, virtually all Palestinian refugees there have become Jordanian citizens and have integrated into the political and economic life of the country.
Q: What can be said of the Palestinians in the Gulf States?
A: Many of the Palestinians in the Gulf States (in Kuwait they constitute 40 percent of the work force) are Jordanian citizens.

> *We shall smash the country with our guns, and destroy and*
> *obliterate every place the Jews will seek shelter in. The Arabs*
> *should conduct their wives and children to safer areas till the*
> *fighting has died down.*
>
> Iraq's prime minister, quoted in
> *The Secret Behind the Disaster*
> by Niwar Al Hawari, commander paramilitary
> Arab Youth Organization in Palestine, 1948

Q: How many Palestinian refugees are in Lebanon?
A: In the UNRWA statistics for 1988, there are approximately 288,000. registered refugees in Lebanon. Many of the Palestinians in Lebanon arrived after King Hussein's destruction of the PLO's terror base in Jordan in 1970.

> *The Arab States, which had encouraged the Palestine Arabs to leave their homes temporarily in order to be out of the way of the Arab invasion armies, have failed to keep their promises to help these refugees . . .*
>
> *Falastin,* Jordanian daily,
> February 19, 1949

Q: Did Lebanon allow the Palestinian refugees to become Lebanese citizens?

A: No. The Lebanese government has opposed dismantling the camps and denies the refugees citizenship. Many nevertheless, have been integrated into the Lebanese economy.

> *The Arabs announced their intention " . . . to conduct a war of extermination and momentous massacre which will be spoken of like the Mongolian massacres and the Crusades. "*
>
> ASSAM PASHA,
> Secretary General of the Arab League,
> May 14, 1948

Q: How many Palestinian refugees are in Syria?

A: According to the UNRWA report of 1988, there are approximately 265,000 registered refugees in Syria. As a matter of policy, Syria has avoided integrating Palestinians into the country's social and economic structure.

Q: How much financial support has UNRWA spent on the Palestinian refugees?

A: Palestinian refugees have been left largely to the responsibility of UNRWA. This agency has spent more than 2.5 billion dollars (1985 figures) since 1950 on the financial support of the camps.

Q: What was the contribution of the Arab States to UNRWA?

A: The Arab states have contributed less than six percent of this sum.

Q: What was the income from oil of Kuwait and Saudi Arabia in the years 1967-85?

A: During the years 1967-85, the combined oil revenues of Kuwait and Saudi Arabia alone were 830 billion dollars.

Q: What was the contribution of these two oil-rich countries to UNRWA in this period?

A: Their contribution to UNRWA in this period was only 84 million dollars – approximately 0.01 percent of the above-mentioned income.

Q: How much has Israel contributed to UNRWA since 1950?

A: Since 1950, Israel, despite its limited resources, contributed 12 million dollars in services. That amounts to 2 million dollars more than Jordan's contribution and more than three times Syria's contribution.

Q: How much has the U.S. contributed since 1950?

A: About 1,500 million dollars.

Q: What has Israel done about resettling the Palestinian refugees of the Gaza Strip?

A: Since 1970, Israel has built nine residential projects in the Gaza District, housing some 70,000 Palestinian refugees. The new neighborhoods were built on state land within municipal areas near the camps. Moreover, in each neighborhood, public buildings – schools, health clinics, shopping centers, and mosques – were built.

Q: Who helped Israel in these humanitarian gestures?

A: No one. It is ironic that since 1971 the United Nations General Assembly has annually adopted resolutions opposing Israel's resettlement of Palestinian refugees.

The Arab governments told us: "Get out so that we can get in!" So we got out, but they did not get in.

Ad-Difaa, Jordanian daily,
September 6, 1954

The leaders of the Arab states, when they cry about the poor fate of the Palestinians, remind me of the child who killed his father and then cried for pity because he is an orphan.

an Arab in a refugee camp

REFUGEES IN THE WORLD

In recent history, other conflicts have also created refugees. The difference is that the Arab world decided to perpetuate the Palestinian refugee problem as an instrument in, and a symbol of, their conflict with Israel.

> *We, the refugees, who have brothers and friends among the Arabs of Israel, have the right to address the members of the Arab League Council and declare: "We left our land on the strength of false promises by crooked leaders in the Arab States. They promised us that our absence would not last more than two weeks, a kind of promenade, at the end of which we would return.*
>
> *Falastin*, Jordanian daily,
> May 30, 1955

Q: What can be said about other refugee problems in the world?

A: In Europe, the postwar movements of population were enormous. Official West German statistics show that by September 1950, almost three million Sudeten Germans had been expelled from Czechoslovakia. Of these, 2,068,000 had settled in West Germany and 916,000 in East Germany.

Q: What happened in Germany proper?

A: More than three and a half million East Germans fled to the West. Six and three-quarter million Germans left their homes in the provinces annexed by Poland.

Q: What can be said about the refugee problem in the Indian subcontinent?

A: After the partition of the Indian subcontinent, conservative estimates speak of seven million Hindus moving from Pakistan to India and seven million Moslems in the reverse direction. Altogether 14 million.

Q: What happened in North Vietnam?

A: When Vietnam was partitioned in 1956, 800,000 North Vietnamese fled to South Vietnam.

Q: What happened in Korea?

A: More than one million refugees from North Korea settled in South Korea after 1952.

Q: Do all the refugees in the world receive world attention?

A: No. Other refugee problems exist which have received little or short-lived attention in the world. For example, Cambodian refugees, Vietnamese boat people, and the Kurds.

Q: What are some of the most recent waves of refugee movement?

A: More than 170,000 ethnic Turks have fled Bulgaria since May 1989 in a forced exodus touched off by an official drive to obliterate Turkish and Moslem influences. The Bulgarian government refers to them as "tourists." Tens of thousands of Germans, settled for centuries in Eastern Europe, have begun to trek west to the Federal Republic as controls over emigration ease.

The conclusion is clear. In conflicts between neighboring societies, refugee problems emerge. For example:

✦ There were 14 million refugees between India and Pakistan when those countries became independent.

✦ There were 6 1/4 million German refugees from the areas annexed to Poland at the end of World War II, and 3 million German refugees from Czechoslovakia.

✦ 800,000 North Vietnamese fled to South Vietnam.

✦ More than one million refugees from North Korea settled in South Korea after 1952.

✦ Altogether, since World War II, more than 40 million persons have become refugees all over the world.

Nowhere in the world has a refugee problem, created by a conflict, been solved by the return of the refugees to their original place of residence. Nowhere in the world – except among the Arabs – has a society refused to absorb refugees of its own culture.

The perpetuation of the refugee problem by the Arab Governments exploits the refugees as an instrument for keeping the Israeli-Arab conflict alive.

ISRAEL'S HUMANE APPROACH
TO REFUGEES

> *Every effort is being made by the Jews to persuade the Arab*
> *population to stay and carry on with their normal lives . . .*
> British police report to Jerusalem
> headquarters, April 26, 1948

Q: Has Israel been aware of the problem of the Palestinian refugees?

A: Most definitely. Israel has been sensitive, over the years, to the Palestinian refugee problem, and has raised several practical ideas for solving the problem.

Q: What are the ideas Israel has come up with in order to solve the problem?

A: Prime Minister Shamir's call for an international conference on refugees is one idea. As recently as February 13, 1989, in an interview on Israel television, the Director General of the prime minister's office, Mr. Ben-Aharon, talked about the prime minister's proposal for an international fund of some 2 billion dollars to begin constructing housing for Arab refugees.

Q: What else has been suggested?

A: Another proposal is the full integration of Palestinian refugees in the Arab countries where they live.

Q: What about the Palestinian refugees in the territories?

A: Israel has suggested solving the refugee problem in the territories through peace negotiations. The Camp David Accords provide for negotiations with the participation of local Palestinian representatives, to determine the final status of the territories. Furthermore, the Camp David Accords specifically state that Israel, Egypt and other interested parties will work together ". . . to establish agreed procedures for a prompt, just, and permanent implementation of the resolution of the refugee problem."

> *During subsequent days the Jewish authorities, who were now*
> *in complete control of Haifa . . . urged all Arabs to remain in*
> *Haifa and guaranteed them protection and security . . . It was*
> *clearly intimated that those Arabs who remained in Haifa and*
> *accepted Jewish protection would be regarded as renegades [by*
> *the Arab Higher Executive].*
> eye-witness account,
> *The Economist,* London,
> October 2, 1948

Q: What are the Arabs' intentions?

A: The Arabs' intentions are clear. "It is obvious that the return of one million Arabs to Palestine will make them the majority of Israel's inhabitants. Then they will be able to impose their will on the Jews and expel them from Palestine" (official Cairo Radio broadcast, September 1, 1960).

> *Israel has turned the Jewish immigrants, and especially those coming from underdeveloped countries, from primitive illiterates to active citizens, farmers and soldiers, whereas we, in the year of disaster 1948, have turned the Palestinian people – which was fairly developed by the standards of the Arab world – into refugees having to fight for crumbs from the table of UNRWA . . . Hundreds of thousands of Palestinians are living in many Arab countries without rights, without even an identity card or passport . . . Whereas Israel left nothing undone to attract Jewish immigrants and thereby strengthen its existence from a demographic, cultural, social and military point of view, and even tries to fashion, as in a melting pot, a new people [of these immigrants], the Arabs allowed the human, social and cultural existence of the Palestinians to disintegrate . . .*
>
> Journalist AHMAD BAHA AL-DIN,
> *Al-Anwar*, Beirut,
> December 8, 1973

PALESTINIAN REFUGEES VIS-A-VIS OTHER REFUGEES

> *No nation, regardless of past rights and wrongs, could contemplate taking in a fifth column of such a size. And fifth column it would be – people nurtured for 10 years [now twenty-two] in hatred of Israel and totally dedicated to its destruction. The readmission of the refugees would be equivalent to the admission to the U.S. of nearly 71,000,000 sworn enemies of the nation.*
>
> *New York Times*,
> May 14, 1967

Do you know that, since 1945, West Germany has resettled over ten million refugees from Poland, Czechoslovakia, and East Germany?
Do you know that India and Pakistan resettled over 14 million refugees after their partition in 1947?
Do you know that from 1961 to 1962, France resettled 1.4 million refugees, many Moslem and Asian, from Algeria and Indochina?
Do you know that since 1948, the Arab world has failed to resettle some 600,000 of their brethren – Palestinian refugees who share the same language, religion, and culture?
Do you know that over the same period, Israel resettled 800,000 dispossessed Jewish refugees expelled from Arab countries and offered to resettle 100,000 Palestinian refugees if their Arab neighbors followed suit? The Arabs refused.
Do you know that all but one of these Arab nations deny Palestinians citizenship? Most, like Saudi Arabia, import workers from as far away as South Korea rather than hire more Palestinians to fill their labor shortages.
✦ Do you know that from 1950 through 1979, Algeria, Bahrain, Egypt, Iraq, Oman, Syria and Yemen combined gave less aid to the Palestinian refugees through UNRWA than Israel?
✦ Do you know that there is a Moslem country where Palestinian refugees are welcome? Where they have automatic citizenship? Where Palestinians make up two-thirds of the population, hold three-quarters of the government posts, and control 70 percent of the businesses?
Do you know that the name of this country is Jordan? It is a Palestinian country and occupies 77 percent of the original Palestine Mandate.

How could the Arabs in the United Nations force the world community to spend so many thousands of hours debating the Arab-Israeli conflict? The answer to this question is reflected in the following story:
Two Israeli diplomats once met and discussed the huge power of Arab propaganda in the United Nations. One diplomat said that if the Arabs were to propose in the United Nations that the world is square and not round, they would probably get the two-thirds majority necessary for approval. The other diplomat said that with the Arabs having so much power, even the Ten Commandments would be rejected today in the United Nations only because of their Jewish origin.

WILL THE PALESTINIANS
BE REFUGEES FOREVER?

> *We shall be most insistent in perpetuating the Palestine problem as a life question . . . The Palestine war continues by dint of the refugees only. Their existence leaves the problem open.*
> ABDULLAH NAWASS, member of
> Jordanian Parliament, June 6, 1952

On August 1, 1982, the Government of Israel appointed a ministerial commission to deal with the refugee problem in the Middle East. The commission was charged with the task of formulating principles, methods and means of solving the Middle East refugee problem by resettling the refugees in their places of residence.

The commission was composed of the following members: Minister Mordechai Ben-Porat, Chairman; Deputy Prime Minister and Minister of Housing and Construction David Levy; Minister of Defense Moshe Arens; Foreign Minister Yitzhak Shamir; Minister of Justice Moshe Nissim; Minister of Economics and Inter-Ministerial Coordination Yaacov Meridor; Minister of Science and Development Yuval Ne'eman.

The recommendations of the commission have been approved by the government. Its report and findings are summarized here.

The war launched by the Arab states against Israel in 1948 created two groups of refugees: Jewish refugees who fled to Israel and elsewhere from Arab lands and Arab refugees who fled from Israel to other parts of Palestine and elsewhere. The two groups are roughly the same size, and their cases are clearly interrelated.

Ever since 1948, the Arab states have done all in their power to perpetuate the Arab refugee problem using it as the spearhead of their ongoing campaign against Israel.

Instead of helping their refugees integrate, as speedily as possible, in the life of the nation, as Israel did, they isolated them and denied all responsibility for their welfare and rehabilitation, placing this on the shoulders of the UN and others. Proposals aimed at helping these people become normal and productive members of society have been strenuously resisted by the Arab governments.

Israel's consistent policy concerning the refugee problem has been to do what it could to help in the rehabilitation and integration of the refugees – Jewish and Arab – within the area of its control, while offering to participate in a discussion of the problem as a whole within the framework of peace negotiations.

In seeking an overall solution to the problem today, Israel is using a three-pronged approach: (a) emphasis on the interrelation of the Jewish and Arab aspects of the problem and the Arab states' responsibility for the creation of this problem; (b) the rights and just claims for compensation of Jews from Arab lands; and (c) rehabilitation of Arab refugees living today in the Land of Israel, under Israel administration, while demanding that the Arab states do the same for the refugees who are within their domain.

Assistance to the refugees on the international level is administered through the UN Relief and Works Agency (UNRWA); largely because of official Arab opposition to rehabilitation projects, its main effort has been devoted to relief. The brunt of the financial burden, in the refugee assistance program, has been borne by the United States, which contributes about 55 percent of UNRWA's annual budget. Between 1950 and 1983, the Arab states together contributed a total of 136.7 million (7%) to UNRWA's budget, while the United States alone gave $1,067.4 (45%). Israel's total contribution to date comes to $11.2 million: This is more than the sum contributed by any Arab country except Saudi Arabia ($59.8 million), Libya ($17.9 million) and Kuwait ($16.3 million).

The rehabilitation program, to be implemented in two stages over a five-year period, is based on the following steps:

1. Establishment of new housing quarters for the camp population, and, as an interim measure, improvement of living conditions in the existing quarters: 5 percent of the camp population in Year 1, 10 percent in Year 2, 25 percent in Year 3, and 30 percent each in Years 4 and 5.
2. Each refugee camp is to be either appended to a nearby municipality or granted municipal status of its own.
3. Allotment of land and financial assistance for a "Build Your Own Home" program according to a Master Plan to be drawn up for this purpose (a new Master Plan will be drawn up for the Gaza district, while in Judea-Samaria use can be made of the existing plan, which, however, will have to be revised and extended).
4. Unification of health and welfare services in Judea and Samaria, and gradual integration of UNRWA's educational facilities in the national school network.
5. All these steps to be taken in full coordination with UNRWA.

The program will cost an estimated $1.5 billion – not including the cost of the lands to be allotted for this purpose and the operational costs of the various projects, which cannot as yet be realistically assessed. Financing is expected to be provided from various international sources.

THE PLO ADMITS THAT THE ARAB ARMIES CAUSED THE PALESTINIAN REFUGEE PROBLEM*

The Arab armies entered Palestine to protect the Palestinians from the Zionist tyranny but, instead, they abandoned them, forced them to emigrate and to leave their homeland, imposed upon them a political and ideological blockade and threw them into prisons similar to the ghettos in which the Jews used to live in Eastern Europe, as if we were condemned to change places with them: they moved out of their ghettos and we occupied similar ones. The Arab States succeeded in scattering the Palestinian people and in destroying their unity. They did not recognise them as a unified people until the States of the world did so, and this is regrettable. For seventeen years the Arab radio stations broadcasted their intention of throwing the Jews into the sea and of returning the refugees to their homes. They did not throw the Jews into the sea, nor did they return the refugees to their homes, until the October War presented itself as the only glitter of victory in the gloomy Arab-Israeli struggle. (The preceding may be seen below, in Arabic.)

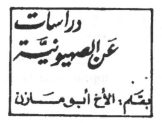

الصحيفة المركزية لمنظمة
التحرير الفلسطينية

مـــاذا عــمــلـــنـا.. ومَـاذا يجب أن نعـــمَـل

لقد دخلت الجيوش العربية لتحمي شعب فلسطين من طغيان الصهيونية؛ فهجرته واخرجته من بلاده لتفرض عليه فيما بعد حصارا سياسيا وفكريـــا وتلقي به في السجون هي اشبه بالغيتوات التي كان يعيش فيهـا اليهود في شرق اوروبا ، وكأنه مقدر لنا ان نتبادل المواقع ، هم ينتقلون من الغيتوات لنحتل نحن مثيلاتها . ونجحت الدول العربية في تمزيق الشعب الفلسطينـي وتدمير وحدته ، ولم تعترف به شعبا موحدا ألا بعد ان اعترفت دول العالم به وهذا شيء بآسف للأنسان له .

وبقيت ابواق اذاعاتها طيلة سبعة عشر عاما تدوي بالقاء اليهود في البحر واعادة اللاجئين الى ديارهم ، فلا هي ألقت اليهود بالبحر ولا ارجعت اللاجئين الى ديارهم ، الى ان كانت حرب تشرين وهي بصيص النصر الوحد في تاريـــخ الصراع العربي الاسرائيلي المظلم .

*Excerpt from an article by Abu Mazen, member of the PLO Executive Committee, entitled "What We Have Learned and What We Should Do," published in *Falastin el-Thawra*, official journal of the PLO, Beirut, March 1976.

WHY THE ARABS LEFT PALESTINE IN 1948

In 1973, the memoirs of Haled al-Azm, who served as Prime Minister of Syria in 1948 and 1949, were published in Beirut. They included the following: "We have brought destruction upon a million Arab refugees, by calling upon them and pleading with them to leave their land, their homes, their work and their business, and we have caused them to be barren and unemployed though each one of them had been working and qualified in a trade from which he could make a living. In addition, we accustomed them to begging for hand-outs and to suffice with what little the UN organisation would allocate them." (The Arabic is given below.)

اهذه هي السياسة الحكيمة المستقرة؟ اهذا هو الانسجام في الخطة؟ لقد قضينا على مليون لاجىء عربي ، وذلك بدعوتهم والالحاح عليهم بترك ارضهم ودورهم وعملـــــم وصنعتهم . نجعلناهم مشردين عاطلين من العمل ، بعد ان كان لكل واحد منهم عمل ومهنة يكسب منها عيشه ، كما عودناهم على الاستجداء والاكتفاء بالقليل الذي توزعه عليهم منظمة الامم المتحـــــدة

JEWS CALL UPON THE PALESTINIAN ARABS TO STAY

The following is what appeared on an Arabic-Hebrew poster of the Haifa (Jewish) Workers' Council, April 28, 1948, appealing to Arabs to remain in their homes and jobs:

APPEAL BY THE HAIFA WORKERS' COUNCIL TO THE ARAB RESIDENTS OF HAIFA, TO THE WORKERS AND OFFICIALS

For years we lived together in our city, Haifa, in security and in mutual understanding and brotherhood. Thanks to this, our city flourished and developed for the good of both Jewish and Arab residents, and thus did Haifa serve as an example to the other cities in Palestine. Hostile elements have been unable to reconcile themselves to this situation and it has been these elements which have induced conflicts and undermined the relations between you and us. But the hand of justice has overcome them. Our city has been cleared of these elements who fled for their lives. Thus, once again does order and security prevail in the city and the way has been opened for the restoration of cooperation and fraternity between the Jewish and Arab workers.

At this juncture we believe it necessary to state in the frankest terms: We are peace-loving people! There is no cause for the fear which others try to instill in you. There is no hatred in our hearts nor evil in our intentions towards peace-loving residents who, like us, are bent upon work and creative effort.

Do not fear! Do not destroy your homes with your own hands; do not block off your sources of livelihood and do not bring upon yourself tragedy by unnecessary evacuation and self- imposed burdens. By moving out you will be overtaken by poverty and humiliation. But in this city, yours and ours, Haifa, the gates are open for work, for life, and for peace, for you and your families.

UPRIGHT AND PEACE-LOVING WORKERS:

The Haifa Workers Council and the Histadrut advise you for your own good to remain in the city and to return to your normal work.

WORKERS: OUR JOINT CITY, HAIFA, CALLS UPON YOU TO JOIN IN ITS UPBUILDING, ITS ADVANCEMENT, ITS DEVELOPMENT. DO NOT BETRAY YOUR CITY AND DO NOT BETRAY YOURSELVES. FOLLOW YOUR TRUE INTERESTS AND FOLLOW THE GOOD AND UPRIGHT PATH.

Federation of Jewish Labor in Palestine
THE HAIFA WORKERS' COUNCIL

نداء من مجلس عمال حيفا

الى سكان حيفا العرب.

الى العمال والمواطنين.

لقد مرت على حيفا فترة طويلة من الزمن ، عشنا وعشتم فيها تحت ظلال الطمأنين والإخوه والتعاون والتفاهم ، فازدهر هذا البلد المشترك وازدهرت حالة سكانه يوماً وراءً . حتى أصبح نموذجاً لباقى البلدان .

وهل حين غرة انقلبت الحال وتغيرت وبتنا وبتكم فجأة بعيدة عنا . نظراً لأمر نجهل بها ونقف طرفاً من عواقبها الوخيمه .

اما اليوم والحمد فه فقد طهرت المدينة من عراصيل العدو ، وزر المغامرون غير من ان نظام به السلامة . وارتفع جانب الاستقرار . نبات هذا البلد يرجوا الامن وتعمه الطمأنين . وانفتح به المجال .

قائمة لتقارب بين السكان والعاملون بين العمال والمحصول على قوتى الحلال .

ان الخوف التى غرسها العاملون فى صدور ولا اساس لأن من قبضه انتا قوم نحب السلم ولا نضمر الشر للاملين السالمين الذين يأخذو مثلنا على السبيل الشريف والسعى الشريف . فلا تخافوا . لا تخربوا بيوتكم بأيديكم . لا تقطعوا الرزائكم بأنفسكم . ولا تجلبوا على انفسكم متفقف الرحيل وعذاب الجلاء .

اعطروا انكم اذا رحلتم فلا يطوركم سوى الفقر والذله والاستقرار . اما هنا فى حيفا البلد الباب لاملكم مفتوح للعمل وللسلام ولاملكم عمل هيرتحكم وامواتكم وراحة بالكم واطفالكم .

يا ايها السكان المسالمين

ان على عمل حيفا فرع المسعودت فى هذا البلد ينصحكم بالبقا . وبجموع الرجوع الى اعمالكم الاعتيادية . انا مستعدون لمساعدتكم على اعانة الأمور الى عازيها المحله . وتسهيل المحصول على حاجيات المعيشه . وفتح ابواب العمل يرجوعكم . وادخال الطمأنين فى قلوبكم .

فيا ايها السكان ان بلد المشترك حيفا يدعوكم الى التعاون متا على تسهيره وترقيته . وازدهاره وتقدمه . فلا تخونوه ولا تخونوا انفسكم . كونوا على حمية من امركم وسيدروا الى سبيل المجد والسداد فذلك خير لكم .

اللجنة الدائمة لعمال اليهود (المسعودت)
مجلس عمال حيفا
حيفا ٢٨-٤-٤٨

> *I can recollect no precedent in history for such irresponsible action on the part of those in power. The Arab governments were largely responsible for the ruin of the Palestinian Arabs.*
> Sir JOHN BAGOT GLUBB, British
> Commander of the Arab Legion

ABOUT REFUGEES AND THE ABSURDITY OF THE SITUATION

The Arab refugee problem has become a heavy burden on the world community. The Arab states, with their income of many hundreds of billions of dollars from oil exports over the last years and with 60 percent of the known oil reserves in the world, refused to take care of their brethren – the Palestinian refugees. These oil-rich Arabs want the world to pay for the refugees' welfare.

Since 1948, the Palestinian refugee problem became an annual subject of debate in the United Nations and in different international forums. The world has heard or read or seen tens of thousands of articles, programs, debates and speeches concerning the "poor Palestinians." One gets the impression that this is the most difficult dilemma facing the world in the last generation, while in reality the Arab refugee problem is neither the largest (and is in fact one of the smallest) nor the most difficult. Moreover, nothing is heard about the other tens of millions of people who are or were refugees in the last generation. Among these refugees are over 800,000 Jews who came to Israel from the Arab states.

This is perhaps the greatest absurdity of the Middle East dispute.

CHAPTER TWENTY-FOUR

THE SAD STORY OF JEWS
FROM ARAB LANDS

> *Recognition of the inherent dignity and of the equal and inalienable rights of all members of the human family is the foundation of freedom, justice, and peace in the world.*
> Universal Declaration of Human Rights

In 1945 there were more then 870,000 Jews living in the Arab world. Many of their communities dated back 2,500 years. Throughout 1947 and 1948 these Jews were subjected to continual pressure and persecution. There were anti-Jewish riots in Aden (where 82 Jews were killed), in Egypt (where 150 Jews were killed), in Syria (where Jewish emigration was forbidden and in Iraq (where Zionism was made a capital crime). 650,000 Jews of the Arab world were thus driven to seek refuge in the new State of Israel. Arriving in Israel destitute, they were absorbed into the society, and became an integral part of the state. A further 150,000 found refuge in Europe and the Americas.

The transfer of populations on a massive scale, as a result of war has been a constant feature of twentieth century history. In almost every case, those uprooted from one land were absorbed into the life and society of their new home. The movement of more than 650,000 Jewish refugees from the Arab lands to Israel and of a similar number of Palestinian Arabs to Gaza, the West Bank, Jordan, Syria and Lebanon, was typical of such movements, although actually on a smaller scale than most of them. However, whereas the uprooted Jews strove to become an integral part of Israeli life, the Palestinian Arabs remained, often as a deliberate act of policy by their host countries, isolated, neglected, and aggrieved.

> *For seventeen years the Arab radio stations broadcasted their intention of throwing the Jews into the sea and of returning the refugees to their homes. They did not throw the Jews into the sea, nor did they return the refugees to their homes . . .*
>
> PLO leader ABU MAZEN,
> *Falastin el-Thawra*,
> PLO journal, Beirut, March 1976

Q: Is this, in fact, an exchange of populations?
A: Yes.

> *The Arab armies entered Palestine to protect the Palestinians from the Zionist tyranny but, instead, they abandoned them, forced them to emigrate and to leave their homeland, imposed upon them a political and ideological blockade and threw them into prisons similar to the ghettos in which the Jews used to live in Eastern Europe, as if we were condemned to change places with them. The Arab States succeeded in scattering the Palestinian people and in destroying their unity.*
>
> ABU MAZEN,
> *Falastin el-Thawra*,
> Beirut, March 1976

Q: Why is it that the world speaks only of Palestinian Arab refugees?
A: The reason is simple – the Arabs are experts in propaganda, the Jews are not.
Q: Which population was expelled and which was not?
A: Unlike Jews in Arab countries, Palestinian Arabs were neither expelled nor forced to leave. The majority left Israel of their own free will – as has many times been ascertained by Arab sources among other – having been instigated by their leaders to take flight in order to clear the way for the Arab armies which invaded the newborn State of Israel in 1948.
Q: What happened to the Arabs who did not flee Israel in 1948?
A: The 160,000 Palestinian Arabs who did not heed their leaders' call and remained in Israel were granted full citizenship. They and their descendants number in 1990 over 800,00 within the 1967 borders.
Q: What does Security Council Resolution 242 of November 22, 1967, say about the refugee problem?
A: The resolution reads: ". . . a just solution to the refugee problem."

Q: Does that mean only Arab refugees?

A: No. The resolution did not say "Arab" or "Jewish" in reference to refugees; therefore, it applies to both.

Q: Is this a new interpretation of the resolution?

A: No. According to Lord Caradon, British ambassador to the United Nations after the war of 1967 and one of the writers of Resolution 242, it refers to "Jewish" as well as to "Arab" refugees.

Q: Who else supports this interpretation?

A: The late Professor Arthur Goldberg, American ambassador to the United Nations in 1967. (Both Lord Caradon and Prof. Goldberg reiterated this interpretation to Resolution 242 personally to the author of this book, Dr. Yitschak Ben Gad.)

UN SECURITY COUNCIL RESOLUTION 242: RIGHTS FOR BOTH JEWS AND ARABS

> *Moslem Islamic Governments should treat them [Jews in Arab states] as aggressive combatants. Similarly, the Islamic people, individually and collectively, should boycott them and treat them as deadly enemies.*
>
> World Islamic Congress,
> Amman, Jordan,
> September 22, 1967

> *Then Mordechai commanded to answer Esther. . . For if thou dost at all remain silent at this time then shall relief and deliverance arise to the Jews from elsewhere.*
>
> Esther 4:13-14

Q: Which are the Arab countries in which Jews have lived or are still living today?

A: Morocco, Tunisia, Algeria, Egypt, Libya, Yemen, Lebanon, Iraq, and Syria.

Q: When did Jews come to the Arab lands?

A: There has been an uninterrupted presence of Jewish communities in the Middle East since the Assyrian and Babylonian exiles in the eighth and sixth centuries BCE – 1,000 years before the Arab invasion of the Land of Israel, and more than 2,500 years before the birth of the modern Arab states.

Q: How many Jews from Arab lands immigrated to Israel after its establishment?
A: Over 650,000 Jews.
Q: How many Palestinian Arabs left Israel for Arab lands in 1948?
A: Approximately 600,000 Palestinian Arabs.
Q: How many Jews left Arab lands following the establishment of Israel?
A: Approximately 800,000. 650,000 resettled in Israel and 150,000 are scattered all over the world, some still bearing no citizenship.

> *This organization was established in 1975. Its purpose is to enlighten the world about the suffering of Jews from Arab lands, to fight for the rights of these Jews and to insist that no final settlement be achieved without consideration of the rights of Jews from Arab lands. Mordechai Ben-Porat, former Israeli minister, was for many years WOJAC's chairman. WOJAC has held several international conferences in New York, London, Paris, etc. Tusia Cohen is the present chairman.*
> WOJAC, World Organization
> of Jews from Arab Countries

Q: Why did the Jews leave the Arab states?
A: In most cases, the Jews left the Arab states because life had become intolerable for them in the Arab countries. As a result, they were compelled to flee their countries of origin. In some cases, they immigrated to Israel out of longing for the land.
Q: Did the Jews leave behind in the Arab lands any property or real estate?
A: Jewish property remaining in their Arab countries of origin is estimated to be many billions of dollars.
Q: Is this Jewish property more or less than that of the Palestinian refugees who left Israel before and after 1948?
A: The Jewish property left in the Arab states is more than five times the value of the Arab refugees' property in Israel.
Q: What does the Jewish property include?
A: Homes, factories, institutions, synagogues, shops, land, money, jewelry, etc.
Q: Is the Jewish people's rights to their property mentioned in any document?
A: Yes. The Working Paper agreed upon between Israel and the United States on October 5, 1977, states: "The solution of the problem of the Arab refugees and the Jewish refugees will be in accordance with terms to be agreed upon . . ."

Q: Does the Camp David Accord mention the rights of Jews from Arab lands?

A: In the Framework Agreement for Peace signed at Camp David on September 17, 1978, it was stated that "a Claim Committee may be established for the mutual settlement of all financial claims."

Q: Where else are Jewish refugee rights mentioned?

A: Former American President Jimmy Carter announced in a press conference on October 27, 1977: "Well, the Palestinians have rights. Obviously, there are Jewish refugees also . . . They have the same rights as others do . . ."

I do not know any more miserable, hapless, and pitiful individual on God's earth than the Jahudi [Jew] in those countries.
ARMIN VAMBERY, Hungarian traveler who recorded plight of Jews in Arab lands, early 1900s

---

Q: Did the Jews from Arab lands come to Israel as refugees?

A: The answer to this question can be found in the following description by Raphael Patai in *East and West:* "One of the main immigrants' reception camps was that of Rosh Ha'ayin, in which, at the height of its occupancy in 1950, there were some 15,000 Yemenite Jewish immigrants. They were all lodged in tents, fifteen of them in each tent. The few buildings in the camp were used to house the hospital and the clinics, the babies' homes, the kitchen and dining room, and the school. When the immigrants arrived, many of them were very weak. Mortality was high, and as many as 20 deaths occurred daily."

While it would not be difficult to catalog a significant quota of Jewish subjects who rose to a high rank in Islamic lands in places of power, in financial influence and in impressive and recognized intellectual achievements . . . it would be just as easy to cite a long inventory of persecutions, arbitrary confiscations, attempts at forcible conversion and pogroms.
G. E. VON GRUNEBAUM,
"Eastern Jewry Under Islam – Reflections on Medieval Anti-Judaism," *Viator,* Vol. 2 (1971)

HOW JEWS WERE DRIVEN OUT OF THEIR HOMES AND THEIR PROPERTY CONFISCATED

> *When Israel was established, on 14 May 1948, it had an estimated population of 650,000 Jews. Today the number is three million, of which half a million came to Israel during the last twenty-seven years from eight Arab states, all currently members of the Arab League . . . This is hardly the place to describe how the Jews of the Arab states were driven out of the countries in which they lived for hundreds of years, then how they were shamefully deported to Israel after their property had been confiscated or taken over at the lowest possible price . . . It is plain that Israel will air this issue in the course of any serious negotiations that might be undertaken one day in regard to the rights of the Palestinians.*
>
> PLO leader SABRI JRAYYIS,
> *Al-Nahar*, Beirut, May 15, 1975

Treatment of Jews by Arab and Moslem governments and the conditions that have influenced Jewish departure have varied from country to country: active persecution, like the hanging of Jews and tortures inflicted in Iraq, the jailing of Jews in Egypt after the various Arab-Israeli wars, Syrian policies forbidding emigration and allowing torture of those caught seeking to depart or the families of those who succeeded, mob riots and murder as occurred in Libya, psychological pressures and discomfort and fear as Arab populations in Tunisia and Morocco expressed their support of the Arab and Palestinian cause even where the governments actively sought to protect the Jews.

> *It is not Zionism that caused Arab anti-Semitism, but the other way around . . . Israel is a rejoinder to the oppression suffered by Jews the world over including our own oppression as Arab Jews . . .*
>
> ALBERT MEMMI,
> Tunisian-born Jewish writer and historian

Q: How is Jewish property to be claimed?
A: Israel must handle all claims when she sits to negotiate a comprehensive peace treaty with the Arabs.

Q: Did the Jews in Israel get more land than they deserved?

A: The Jews, who constituted in 1948 1.5 percent of the total population of the Arab lands in which they had been living, evacuated approximately 100,000 square kilometers. That amounts to five times the territory of Israel prior to the Six-Day War of 1967.

Q: Can one specific example be cited?

A: Yes. The Jews in Libya in 1948 numbered approximately 38,000 from the general Arab population of about 2,000,000. In territory, Libya is about 680,000 square miles. If the Libyan Jews alone would receive their portion in their country of origin, they would be entitled to an area of land much more than all of Israel today with Judea, Samaria, and the Gaza Strip.

Q: What is the percentage of Jews from Arab lands of the total Jewish population?

A: About one and a half million out of the 3,500,000 constituting Israel's Jewish population today have come from Arab countries, while the Arabs who left Israel constitute less than 2 percent of the total Arab population in the area.

Q: What happened to the Jews from Arab lands who came to Israel as refugees?

A: Despite the tremendous difficulties, especially in the early years of Israel's independence, the Jewish refugees from Arab lands were economically and socially absorbed and given a secure haven in the State of Israel.

Q: How do the Arab refugees live?

A: The Arab refugees were deliberately herded into refugee camps, devoid of minimal conditions for decent life, so that they might become a political and propaganda tool in the hands of the Arab governments in their fruitless fight against the very existence of the State of Israel.

On January 27, 1969, nine Jews were hanged by the neck in the central square of Baghdad, Iraq. The only fault of these Jews was their being Jews. The Iraqi authorities called upon the Iraqi masses to celebrate the hangings. Hundreds of thousands came to see the hanging bodies. They shouted and chanted, "Death to Israel," "Death to the traitors." The then-President of Iraq, Hassan al-Bakar, dismissed the world protests by calling the protestors "the barking dogs." This was not the end of Iraqi barbarity. Between 1970 and 1972, more Jews were hanged, terrorizing the small, helpless Iraqi Jewish community. Jews were forced to collect funds for the PLO and to serve as hosts for Palestinian refugees.

> *Allah loveth those who act justly.*
>
> The Koran, *Tried*, Verse 8

Q: Have the Jewish refugees received international support?

A: Jewish refugees received no financial support whatsoever from the international community. Their absorption was financed solely by the Israel government and by their Jewish brethren in Israel and abroad.

Q: Why are Jews from Arab lands considered forgotten refugees?

A: Because Israel refused to use them as a propaganda weapon against the Arabs. Every effort was made to settle the Jews from Arab countries in the State of Israel.

> *But the more they afflicted them, the more they multiplied and grew.*
>
> Exodus 1:12
> (about the nature of the Jewish people)

SABRI JRAYYIS – PLO LEADER: ARABS CAUSED THE EXPULSION OF THE JEWS FROM ARAB COUNTRIES

Following are excerpts from an article in Arabic by Sabri Jrayyis, a well-known Palestinian Arab researcher at the Institute for Palestinian Studies in Beirut, published in *Al-Nahar,* Beirut, May 15, 1975:

"It is not true that foreign States, especially Czarist Russia, Nazi Germany, Britain and the United States, were the only agents behind the conditions that led to the creation of Israel. The Arabs also took part in the process; sad to say, they were very active in it. When Israel was established, on 14 May 1948, it had an estimated population of 650,000 Jews. Today the number is three million, of which half a million came to Israel during the last twenty-seven years from eight Arab states, all currently members of the Arab League and representing every type of regime that exists in the Arab world: monarchic, revolutionary, socialist and progressive. This is hardly the place to describe how the Jews of the Arab states were driven out of the countries in which they lived for hundreds of years, then how they were shamefully deported to Israel after their property had been confiscated or taken over at the lowest possible price.

". . . It is plain that Israel will air this issue in the course of any serious negotiations that might be undertaken one day in regard to the rights of the Palestinians.

". . . Israel's claims are these: It may perhaps be the case that we Israelis were the cause of the expulsion of some Palestinians, whose number is estimated at 700,000, from their homes during the 1948 War, and afterwards took over their properties. Against this, since 1948, you Arabs have caused the expulsion of just as many Jews from the Arab States, most of whom settled in Israel after their properties had been taken over in one way or another. Actually, therefore, what happened was only a kind of "population and property exchange," and each party must bear the consequences. Israel is absorbing the Jews of the Arab States; the Arab States, for their part, must settle the Palestinians in their own midst and solve their problems.

"There is no doubt that, at the first serious discussion of the Palestinian problem in an international forum, Israel will put these claims forward."

JEWS VERSUS ARABS: TWELVE FACTS

The world has heard time and again about the Palestinian issue, yet the world has not heard about the plight of the Jews from Arab countries. Here are twelve facts that must be brought to the attention of the world:

1. Most of the property of the Jews from Arab countries was confiscated.
2. Their citizenship was revoked.
3. Barbaric pogroms were carried out against the peaceful Jewish communities with the tacit consent of the local Arab authorities.
4. Many Jewish communities were expelled en masse or were compelled to flee in order to save their lives.
5. The Jews left behind them substantial personal and communal property.
6. They left behind their rightful share in the natural resources of their native Arab lands.
7. The number of Jews from Arab lands is more than the number of Palestinians who left Israel in 1948.
8. Israel accepted and settled the Jews from Arab countries without the financial assistance of the United Nations. The very wealthy Arab states asked other states to support their refugees – the Palestinian Arabs.
9. The Arab states refused to settle the Arab refugees, Instead, they turned them into a political propaganda weapon against the State of Israel.
10. Considering the total number of the world's refugees, the problem of the Palestinian refugees is neither the largest nor the most difficult to solve.
11. 1½ out of 3½ million Jewish citizens in Israel today originated from the Arab countries. This million and a half comprise 43 percent of the total population of Israel while the Palestinians who left Israel and their offspring constitute less than 2 percent of the total Arab population in the area.
12. The Jews in Syria, Yemen, and Iraq have become political hostages at the hands of their cruel leaders. These Jews are not free to demonstrate as the Palestinians do in Judea and Samaria.

Oriental Jews came to realize that there was no future for them in Arab countries, either as individuals or as part of a Jewish community. Under the new nationalist regimes they found themselves robbed of legal status, stripped of whatever rights they had possessed, and potential future victims of Arab political extremists.

> *Since the rise of Israel, it has invested great efforts into integrating immigrants from all over the world. These efforts have been particularly successful as regards the new generations, born and raised in Israel. Continuing the external pressure impels them to greater unity. And so, whether they like it or not the Palestinians will be forced to share the consequences, whether or not they directly contributed to their creation.*
>
> PLO leader SABRI JRAYYIS,
> *Al-Nahar*, Beirut, May 15, 1975

JEWS MURDERED AND HUMILIATED IN ARAB LANDS IN THE TWENTIETH CENTURY (1907-76)

> *We always get what may have been the mistake of Deir Yassin thrown in our faces. Good heavens! We have suffered a hundred, a thousand Deir Yassins! and not only in Russia, in Germany or in Poland, but actually in Arab lands with the world never caring.*
>
> ALBERT MEMMI,
> Tunisian-Jewish Freedom Fighter

> *Ever since the days of the Abbasids it has been part of the Charter of Omar that, to put it briefly, the Jew is at best protected like a dog that is part of the chattels. But let him raise his head or behave like a human being, and he must be beaten . . . to remind him of his condition.*
>
> ALBERT MEMMI,
> Tunisian-Jewish Freedom Fighter

> *Of all the non-Moslems, the Jews were the safest targets.*
>
> a European observer

MOROCCO

1907: The great massacre of Jews in Casablanca, including rape, the burning down of homes, businesses, etc.

1912: Any Jew leaving the Jewish quarter in Morocco was required to remove his shoes, as if it was sacrilege for them to touch Moroccan soil.

1912: The great massacre of Jews in Fez.

1948: The massacre of Jews in Oudja. 5 were killed and 30 were seriously injured. Shops and homes were sacked. The city of Djerada's Jewish population suffered 39 dead and 30 wounded.

ALGERIA

1934: The great massacre of Jews in Constantine.

EGYPT

1945: The mobs in Cairo burned down a synagogue, a hospital, and numerous homes and shops in the Jewish quarter.

1948: The great massacre in Cairo. The Jewish quarter was shaken by an explosion, killing 34 and wounding 80. Big pogroms followed, killing or wounding hundreds of Jews. From then on, bomb explosions occurred in July, September, October, and November, leaving at least 38 more dead, 137 injured, and much Jewish property destroyed.

ADEN

1946: The local authorities officially declared that Jews were not entitled to live like human beings.

1947: The great massacre of the Jewish quarter. 82 were killed, 76 were wounded, and two-thirds of the Jewish shops (about 110 in all) were looted and burned. The community was in shock and their means of livelihood were destroyed in just a few days.

IRAQ

1941: Between the second and third day of June, 600 Jews were killed, 1,000 were seriously wounded, 600 shops were looted, women were raped and 1,000 houses were burned. This occurred in Baghdad.

1948: 300 Jews were arrested in May 1948, when Zionism was made a capital offense.

LIBYA

1945: Within two days, hundreds of Jews were either murdered or wounded in Tripoli, Zanzour, Zaouia, Zelitin, and elsewhere.

1948: Riots broke out against the Jews. Jews were either killed or wounded.
1967: In reaction to the Israeli victory in the Six Day War, Jews were murdered in the streets and many expelled.

SYRIA
1947: The Jewish quarter in Aleppo was set ablaze in December 1947. The mobs butchered an unknown number of Jews, burned 19 synagogues and destroyed 150 Jewish homes.
1948: Bombs were found in numerous locations in the Jewish quarter of Damascus.

Q: Why were the Jews so readily attackable?
A: "They are considered to be Europeans and as such any barefoot Mohammedan is glad to shoot at them. They are not supported by a powerful empire and attacks on them do not create diplomatic incidents. Moreover, they are 'infidels' which make them particularly attractive victims of the more fanatical Mohammedans. They are Jews, which satisfies those who are more specifically anti-Semitic." These are the words of Professor Albert Memmi, a Jewish historian born in Tunisia.

In 1948, with the proclamation of the State of Israel and the Arab armies' invasion of the new state, the following measures were taken against Jews in several Arab countries. On May 14 and 15, 1948, Egypt, Iraq, and Syria arrested Jews and interrogated and beat them. On May 30, 1948, Egyptian authorities began the sequestration of Jewish property and forced Jews in Cairo and Alexandria to contribute 40,000 and 60,000 lira sterling respectively to the Arab war fund. This was followed by other Arab countries. In Damascus and Baghdad, Jews were compelled to give 40,000 lire sterling and 500,000 dinars, respectively. Furthermore, several Arab countries restricted the movement of Jews.

As the Arab countries of North Africa began to receive their independence, the Jews – who had suffered in the often bloody struggles which preceded it – began to be squeezed out of the economy, replaced, and boycotted by the Moslems. Rabbinical tribunals and community councils were dissolved in the name of "national unity" (Iraq, 1958; Syria, December 1949; Egypt, 1960; Tunisia, July 1958; Libya, 1958); ancient synagogues, cemeteries, and Jewish quarters were destroyed for urban renewal (Tunisia, 1958).

The Six-Day War marked another turning point in the deteriorating situation of the Jews in Arab lands. The war itself set off anti-Jewish riots in Tunisia, Algeria, Libya (where they were especially bloody) and Aden. These and the growing hatred for the Jews in Morocco caused many to flee to Israel, Europe, and the Americas. In Egypt there were mass arrests of Jews. Some were released directly from jail to the airport, given 30 minutes to bid farewell to their families, made to sign a renunciation of all property and of their citizenship and expelled, taking only their personal belongings along. In Syria and in Iraq, the war also meant mass arrests, torture, growing insecurity, and virulent governmental anti-Jewish campaigns. Moslem religious leaders also gave legitimization to the extermination of Jews in Arab countries in the name of Islam. At the World Islamic Congress in Amman, on September 22, 1967, it was resolved: "Jews in Arab Countries: The Congress is certain that the Jewish communities living in Islamic countries do not appreciate the Moslems' good treatment and protection over the centuries . . .The Congress declares that the Jews residing in Arab countries who contact the Zionist circles or the State of Israel do not deserve the protection and care which Islam provides for the free non-Moslem subjects living in Islamic countries. Moslem Islamic Governments should treat them as aggressive combatants. Similarly, the Islamic peoples, individually and collectively, should boycott them and treat them as deadly enemies."

The theme of Jews as a fifth column was picked up by governments and media after the Six-Day War and used to legitimatize the dismissals, persecutions, arrests, and executions of the Jews remaining in Arab lands. Since 1967, even more stringent restrictions have been in force, especially in Syria and Iraq.

In Iraq, the Jewish community was also economically paralyzed, unable to withdraw more than a small sum each month, under constant surveillance – politically, physically, and mentally crippled. An Iraqi Jew (who later escaped) wrote in his diary in February 1970: "Ulcer, heart attacks, and breakdowns are increasingly prevalent among the Jews. The dehumanization of the Jewish personality resulting from continuous humiliation and torment . . . have dragged us down to the lowest level of our physical and mental faculties, and deprived us of the power to recover."

Jews were never allowed to live in Saudi Arabia or Jordan. Jordanian law reads that any man can be a Jordanian subject *unless* he is Jewish (Paragraph 3).

ESTIMATED JEWISH POPULATION
IN ARAB COUNTRIES,
1948 AND 1976

	1948	1976
Morocco	265,000	17,000
Algeria	40,000	500
Tunisia	105,000	2,000
Libya	38,000	0
Egypt	75,000	100
Iraq	35,000	400
Syria	30,000	4,350
Lebanon	5,000	500
Yemen	55,000	1,000
Aden	8,000	0
Total	856,000	24,850

Q: When did the situation of the Jews deteriorate?

A: The declaration of the State of Israel in 1948 as an independent Jewish state in the Middle East served as an additional pretext for the intensification and legitimization of anti-Jewish measures in Arab lands.

Q: Did the leaders of the Arab states want the Jews to emigrate?

A: Yes. Several Arab countries have in some instances indirectly encouraged this trend by closing an eye to the clandestine Zionist activities and operations in their countries.

Q: What happened after the partition resolution?

A: With the United Nations resolution on the partition of Palestine, Arab riots broke out against numerous Jewish communities throughout the Arab world. Conforming to Arab anti-Jewish practices in the past, Jewish shops, homes, and synagogues were burned and looted; hundreds of Jews were murdered in the streets, thousands were imprisoned in the following months as criminals and suspects.

Q: What was the economic condition of the Jews?

A: Jews, who at one time were influential in commerce, suddenly lost their holdings; bank accounts belonging to Jews were frozen, and property valued at millions of dollars was gradually confiscated. As in previous centuries, Jews were further removed from government agencies and their admission to public office was severely restricted. Jews lost their means of survival; they became hostages in their own countries of origin. Consequently, they could no longer remain there.

> *From the time my friends and I were twelve years old, long before [the Holocaust in Europe], we conspired, amid an Arab world that always been hostile, for the construction of a Jewish state.*
>
> ALBERT MEMMI,
> Tunisian-born Jewish writer and political theorist

UPDATE: THE REMAINING JEWS IN MOSLEM ARAB COUNTRIES

> *The prophet Mohammed advises his believers to beware of the Jews: "O true believers, contract not an intimate friendship with any besides yourselves: they will not fail to corrupt you. They wish for that which may cause you to perish: their hatred hath already appeared from out of their mouths; but what their breasts conceal is yet more inveterate. We have already shown you signs of their ill will towards you, if ye understand."*
>
> Covenant of the Islamic Movement
> (The Koran, *Family of Imran*, Verse 118)

An estimated 65,000 Jews remain in Arab and Islamic lands including Iran and Turkey today, although their number was over 1,000,000 just one generation ago. About seventy-five percent of this wide-ranging community made its way to Israel between 1947 and 1961. They have been absorbed by Israel and are full and equal citizens of the Jewish state.

The following are estimations of the Jews under Islam and Arab rule today (1990):

EGYPT
There are 220 Jews living in Egypt today.

ETHIOPIA
10,000 Jews remain, longing to reach Israel.

MOROCCO
7,000 Jews remain, free to travel and trade as they please. The government takes special care to ensure their freedom.

TUNISIA
3,500 Jews live in perpetual worry. The most recent manifestation of hatred was on Succoth of 1987 when a guard at a synagogue opened fire on the worshippers, killing several Jews and wounding others.

IRAN
About 25,000 Jews are forbidden to leave. A recent liberalization has permitted some to leave Iran in the course of their business transactions.

TURKEY
Some 12,000 Jews live a normal and full communal life with full religious and political equality.

SYRIA
About 4,500 Jews continue to live in Damascus, Aleppo, and Kamishly. Emigration is forbidden and any Jew who is allowed to leave on business must leave his family behind as hostage, as well as a deposit of $3,000 to $5,000. Hundreds of unmarried young women have almost no hope of finding Jewish husbands in Syria, yet are not allowed to leave.

LEBANON
170 Jews are free to leave but have not yet exercised that option. There have been recent incidents of kidnapping and murder.

YEMEN
About 1,200 Jews live in Yemen, though various limitations are in place.

IRAQ
About 300 Jews remain out of 135,000. The last Jew to leave was allowed to do so in 1983. This community has suffered horrible persecutions.

LIBYA
There are no Jews left in Libya today. The story of the Libyan Jews is one of persecution, harassment, and even execution. Hundreds of Jews were murdered by Arabs and most of the Jewish people's property in this country has been confiscated.

> *As to those who have not borne arms against you on account of religion, nor turned you out of your dwellings, Allah forbiddeth you not to deal kindly with them, and to behave justly towards them; for Allah loveth those who act justly.*
>
> The Koran, Tried, verse 8

ABOUT JEWISH REFUGEES, PALESTINIAN REFUGEES, AND ARAB HYPOCRISY

This was a refugee camp in Israel. The refugees were Jews – who had to flee their homelands in the Arab world where they had lived since long before the birth of Islam. They were in Iraq, Syria, and Libya thousands of years before these countries even had their names.

They built a life and culture in the shadow of Islam's traditional intolerance of minorities – Christians, Jews, or otherwise. When they fled, they left behind land five times the size of the State of Israel. Yet nobody waited for compensation. Israel, her people, and brethren abroad saw to it that every refugee was rehabilitated. Not a single trace of the camps remains today.

Have the Arabs looked after their brothers? Why are the Arab refugees, who numbered 600,000 in 1948 (about the same number of Jewish refugees from Arab lands), still herded in refugee camps, when the population density in the Arab countries is among the lowest in the world.

Why have the oil-rich Arab states contributed only 3.5 percent of the 2.5 billion dollars spent by the United Nations on Arab refugees? One month's oil revenues of Saudi Arabia could solve the entire problem.

> *Who hath gathered wealth [of this world] and arranged it. He thinketh that his wealth will render him immortal. Nay, but verily he will be flung to the Consuming One . . . It is the fire of Allah kindled.*
>
> The Koran, sura CIV: 2-4, 6
>
> ---
>
> *We must protest if we are to survive. Protest is the only realistic form of civil defense.*
>
> E. P. Thompson

THE JEWISH REFUGEES IN THE *MA'ABARAH* (TRANSIT CAMP)

Tents such as these marked the living conditions of thousands of Jews from Arab countries during the early years of statehood. This *ma'abarah* (transit camp) was photographed in February 1951, near Haifa.

The *ma'abarah* (transit camp, similiar to the Arab refugee camps) was the most common form of temporary settlement. Thousands of people were often crammed into a small space where shelter consisted of tin huts, tents, shacks made of cardboard or whatever materials were at hand. Often the great influx of immigrants arriving in Israel at the time made it impossible for the authorities to provide the necessary housing facilities. As a result, the immigrants had no choice but to construct their own shelters from whatever they could find. Families of seven, eight and even ten children were forced to huddle together, under cramped conditions and with little to eat. Disease and illness were thus common in those early years of distress.

An immigrant from Egypt building his home in Ashdod, May 1950.

ARAB THREATS TO KICK OUT
THE JEWS FROM ARAB COUNTRIES

> *The Jewish communities lived in the shadow of history, under arbitrary rule and the fear of all-powerful monarchs whose decisions could not be rescinded or even questioned . . . But the Jews were at the mercy not only of the monarch but also of the man in the street. My grandfather still wore the obligatory and discriminatory Jewish garb, and in his time every Jew might expect to be hit on the head by any Moslem whom he happened to pass.*
>
> *I have lived through the alarms of the ghetto; the rapidly barred doors and windows, my father running home after hastily shutting his shop, because of rumors of an impending pogrom. My parents stocked food in expectation of a siege, which did not always materialize, but this gives the measure of our anguish, our permanent insecurity.*
>
> ALBERT MEMMI, Tunisian-born Jewish
> writer and historian,
> *Juifs et Arabes,* Paris (1974)

Arabs have done their utmost to force their opinion upon other nations. They called upon the United Nations to reject the partition of Palestine. When the UN accepted the Partition Plan of November 29, 1947, the Arabs increased their attacks on the Jews in Palestine. Moreover, the Arabs threatened that the Jews in the Arabs countries might suffer if the UN Partition Plan was carried out. On November 24, 1947, the Egyptian ambassador to the UN, Dr. Muhammed Hussein Heykal Basha, told the General Assembly: "The lives of a million Jews in Moslem countries will be jeopardized by the establishment of the Jewish State."

When the Iraqi Foreign Minister, Muhammad Fadhil Bey al-Jamali, told the UN Committee on Palestine in 1947 that the fate of the Jews in Moslem countries was dependent on developments in Palestine, he was only stating what was already accepted in practice.

On November 25, 1947, Dr. Hussein Heykal told the *New York Times:* "The United States, which has not been able altogether to suppress outbursts of racial passion in the form of lynching, will appreciate that with the best will in the world the Near Eastern governments might not be able to control the infuriated Moslems."

The Syrian delegate, Faris al-Khuri, was more direct, warning that "unless the Palestine problem is settled, we shall have difficulty in protecting and safeguarding the Jews in the Arab world" (*New York Times,* February 19, 1947). These threats were not empty ones. On one hand, with the Arab press "fulminating against the perfidy of Zionism," and on the other, Arab politicians mobilizing the masses to the point of hysteria, the situation was beyond control.

Professor Yacov Miron from the Ministry of Justice in Jerusalem, wrote in Arabic an open letter to "Alhamas" and the "Jihad Islami": "The words of Haykal Basha were not the position of Egypt alone, but the position of most, if not all, the Arab states, member states in the United Nations, and the Arab League."

Another sign that serves to strengthen the belief that the Arabs may have thought about or had in mind the expulsion of Jews from Arab lands can be found in an article found in the Syrian paper *Al-Kifah* of March 28, 1949. According to this paper, "If Israel rejects the return of the Arab refugees to their home in Palestine [which had become Israel], then the Arab nations should expel the Jews from their midst."

The then prime minister of Iraq, Nuri Sai'id, on his visit to the Jordanian capital, Amman, offered to send a caravan of trucks loaded with Jews from Iraq to the Jordanian-Israeli border. The plan was to then force the Jews to cross the border into Israel. Nuri Sai'id spoke about this plan at six different times to different officials, including the British and United Nations officials, and once to an American official at the American Embassy in Baghdad. Nuri Sai'id offered that the 100,000 Jews of Iraq leave for Israel in exchange for the Palestinians that left Palestine.

In reality, most Jews in Arab lands left their countries of origin after establishment of the State of Israel. In most cases, the Arab states did not have to expel the Jews forcibly. The Jews left and went to Israel as a direct result of fear and the atmosphere of unsafety in the Arab states or out of their longing for the Land of Zion: the newly established State of Israel.

Dry Bones

Two of the nine Jews hanged in Liberation Square, Baghdad, on January 28, 1969, to the delight of cheering crowds.

KNESSET RESOLUTION CONCERNING JEWS FROM ARAB COUNTRIES FROM 10/26/87

1. The Knesset sends greetings to the Third International Conference of the World Organization of Jews from Arab Countries, convening in Washington today.
2. After hundreds - perhaps thousands - of years of Jewish life marked by significant cultural and economic contributions to their surroundings, the establishment of the State of Israel served to bolster both the yearning for Zion among the Jews of the Arab countries and also the manifestations of hostility and violence towards them. The Knesset hails the instances of human courage that characterized the *aliya* to Israel of Jews from Arab and Islamic lands. The Knesset also notes the liberal attitude of Morocco towards its Jews.
3. Most of the Jews from Arab countries came to Israel penniless, leaving behind in those countries a rich cultural heritage and much personal property. Even at this late date, with their integration in the life of the state an accomplished fact, the Knesset determines that they must receive compensation from the Arab states for their property of which they were forcibly deprived, or which was confiscated, frozen, or nationalized, and for the persecution they were made to suffer; and that the Arab states must return to the Jewish communities the cultural and religious objects and artifacts of which they have been deprived.
4. Israel, for its part, has made it known that, within the framework of a peace settlement, it will be prepared to compensate the Arabs who left Israel. In the talks concerning this compensation, the rights of the Jews who were compelled to leave the Arab states and abandon their property will be taken into account.
5. The Knesset expresses its deep concern for the fate of the Jews remaining in Arab and Islamic lands, and calls upon the Government, the countries of the world and world public opinion to continue to act to safeguard their rights and their freedom.

"Dry Bones" cartoon, *Jerusalem Post*.

PART VIII

ISRAEL AND THE ARABS – VARIOUS QUESTIONS AND ANSWERS

CHAPTER TWENTY-FIVE

ARAB PROPAGANDA SLOGANS AND ISRAELI CREATIVE SLOGANS

> *Four shall not enter paradise: the scoffer, the liar, the hypocrite, and the slanderer.*
>
> The Talmud

The Arab war of propaganda against Israel has never ended. In this war, the Arabs have never agreed to a truce or a ceasefire. This is in direct accordance with the philosophy of the notorious Hitler who believed that the bigger the lie, the better the chance of its being believed. When it comes to propaganda, the sons of biblical Ishmael (the Arabs) are far superior to the sons of biblical Yisrael (the Jews).

> *The existence of Israel is a fact. However, we as the Arab nation struggle against that fact in arms and words until it is eradicated from the map of Arab reality.*
>
> *Al-Jezirah,* Saudi paper,
> July 22, 1981

ARAB PROPAGANDA SLOGANS

Slogan 1: "The national rights of the Palestinians"

This slogan is accepted everywhere in the world. Yet many people are unaware that the fulfillment of this slogan would mean an end to Israel's very existence. The national rights of the Palestinians were fulfilled and should be further fulfilled in Jordan.

Slogan 2: "Territories for peace"

Peace has nothing to do with territories. The Arabs attacked Israel in 1948 when Israel agreed to the ridiculous borders determined by the Partition Plan of November 1947. Moreover, the Arabs threatened Israel in 1967 when Israel was not present in Sinai, Judea, or Samaria.

Slogan 3: "Jews are not a 'nation' " (from the PLO Covenant)

The Jews were a nation thousands of years before the founding of Islam. To say that the Jews do not constitute a nation is tantamount to saying that the world is square instead of round. The Jews are a very ancient nation and contributed the Holy Bible to the world.

Slogan 4: "The poor Palestinians in refugee camps"

In its National Covenant, the PLO claims that the Palestinian Arabs are an integral part of the Arab nation. In 1978 alone, the Arab oil states had an income of 100 billion dollars from oil. The Arab states, whose combined territory is double the size of the United States, could readily solve the problem of the Palestinians with just a small part of the 100 billion dollars. They could build homes for and accommodate the Palestinians. This would be of mutual benefit to the Palestinians and Arab states alike.

> *I can recollect no precedent in history on the part of those in power. The Arab governments were largely responsible for the ruin of the Palestinian Arabs.*
>
> Sir JOHN BAGOT GLUBB,
> British commander of the
> Arab Legion

Slogan 5: "Zionism is racism"

World history proves that the Jews suffered from racism for a long period. Judaism and racism do not go together. By its very nature, democratic Israel is not racist. What can be said about the Arab states in this respect? Saudi Arabia does not permit Jews to enter her territory. Jordan forbids the sale of land to Jews. Syria and Yemen persecute their Jewish minority. The Jews suffer only because they are Jews, Therefore, who is racist?

Slogan 6: "A Palestinian state on the West Bank and in the Gaza Strip"

The PLO cleverly hides the fact that its purpose is not a Palestinian state on the West Bank, but rather Israel's destruction. The Arabs successfully hide the fact that a Palestinian state already exists and its name is Jordan. The Middle East needs peace, not a second Palestinian state.

> *Behold, he who keeps Israel shall neither slumber nor sleep.*
> Psalms 121:4

Slogan 7: "PLO moderates"

The difference between PLO "moderates" and PLO radicals is in tactics, not in the final goal. The "moderates" believe that since Israel is so very strong, the Arabs would be wise to follow the policy of stages: a small Palestinian state at the outset that would be ultimately expanded in the future to include all of Palestine including Israel. PLO radicals believe only in the military option.

Slogan 8: "A democratic Palestinian state in which all can live in peace – Jew and Arab alike"

The Arabs do not believe in democracy. Twenty out of 21 Arab states are not democracies in the Western sense of the term. Lebanon is close to a democracy, yet even in that country the Christians are threatened by the Moslems. To claim that the PLO would establish a democracy under "democrat Arafat" is to claim the impossible. Arafat believes in the bullet rather than the ballot.

> *After a long debate about that question [the "democratic state" slogan] the need was expressed to balance the propaganda slogans and the strategic aim . . . so that there will be no misunderstanding and no comparison between the waves of Jewish-European immigration to Palestine and the original sons of the country.*
> from the 6th Convention
> of the Palestinian National Council
>
> *. . . the slogan of a democratic state is intended only to counter the argument that we aspire to throw the Jews into the sea.*
> SHAFIK AL-HAOOT (PLO), 1970
>
> (*Both* were reported in the Lebanese paper, *Al-Muharrer*, September 9, 1969.)

Slogan 9: "Arab tolerance"

The Arabs are far from tolerant with one another, therefore, how can they claim to be tolerant towards others? The story of the minorities in the Arab and Moslem states has been a story marked by persecutions, torture, pogroms, and even executions. No, the Arabs are not tolerant in the least.

Slogan 10: "The Israeli threat"
Interestingly enough, the Arabs who time and again have threatened and attacked Israel since her inception claim that they are threatened by Israel. The Arabs, who were behind all the provocations and aggression against Israel and who caused all the bloody wars in the area, are the ones to speak about the Israeli threat.

> *Must a state wait until it is too late before it may defend itself? Must it permit another state the advantages of military build-up, surprise attack, and total offense, against which there may be no defense? It would be unreasonable to expect any state to permit this – particularly when given the possibility that a surprise nuclear blow might bring about total destruction, or at least total subjugation, unless the attack were forestalled.*
>
> MORTON KAPLAN and
> NICHOLAS DE B. KATZENBACH,
> *The Political Foundations of International Law*
>
> *No state can be expected to await an initial attack which, in the present state of armaments, may well destroy the state's capacity for further resistance and so jeopardize its very existence.*
>
> DEREK BOWETT,
> *Self-Defence in International Law*

ISRAELI CREATIVE SLOGANS

> *There is, of course, no difference whatsoever between anti-Semitism and the denial of Israel's statehood. Classical anti-Semitism denies the equal rights of Jews as citizens within society. Anti-Zionism denies the equal rights of the Jewish people to its lawful sovereignty within the community of nations. The common principle in the two cases is discrimination.*
>
> ABBA EBAN,
> *New York Times*

Slogan 1: " Arab anti-Semitism"

The Arabs cannot tolerate, not to mention give equal rights to, non-Moslems. Jews and Christians have been persecuted and even executed by the Moslems simply because they were not Moslems. The opposition to Israel in the Arab world is deep-rooted in Arab theological and national philosophy. Arab hatred against the Jews has become clear anti-Semitism.

Slogan 2: "21 Arab states versus one Jewish state"

The Arab states, which in territory are double the size of the United States and larger than Europe by one-third, seek to capture Israel as well – Israel, which is about the size of New Jersey, one of the smallest states in America.

Slogan 3: "Jordan is Palestine"

In Palestine there are two nations – one is very ancient (the Jewish people) and the other is a very new nation (the Palestinian Arabs). The Palestinian Arabs already have a state which constitutes three-quarters of mandatory Palestine. This state is Jordan. This Palestinian state has no Jews.

The other state constitutes a mere one-quarter of mandatory Palestine. This state is Israel. One-third of this state is populated by Arabs, two-thirds by Jews. To sum up, there are two states for the two different nations. There is no need or justification to establish a second Arab state in west Palestine.

> *Eretz Israel for the Jewish people and Palestine for the Arab people are not one and the same thing. Our land is only a small district in the tremendous area of territory populated by Arabs...But for the entire Jewish nation this is the one and only country with which its fate and future as a nation are linked.*
> DAVID BEN-GURION,
> Israel's first premier, in *Return to Zion*,
> Jerusalem, 1974

Slogan 4: "Jewish refugees"

Over 650,000 Jews from Arab lands came to Israel immediately after her establishment. Most of these people were uprooted from the Arab states. In most cases, their property was confiscated and they suffered harsh persecutions at the hands of the Arabs in their countries of origin. It is unfair to speak about the rights of the Arab refugees while at the same time failing to speak of the rights of the Jewish refugees.

Slogan 5: "Israel's secure borders"

Israel, which has consistently suffered from Arab aggression since her establishment, has the legal and moral right to have secure and recognized borders. The Jordan River is a natural border on the east for Israel. Moreover, it includes the historical Eretz Yisrael – the Jewish homeland.

> *. . . armed struggle is the only way to liberate Palestine.*
> PLO Covenant, Article 9
>
> *Liberation [of Palestine constitutes] a national duty.*
> PLO Covenant, Article 15
>
> *The Arab Palestinian people . . . reject all solutions which are substitutes for the total liberation of Palestine . . .*
> PLO Covenant, Article 21

Slogan 6: "Zionism made Palestine green and flourish"

Zionism, the national movement of the Jewish people, has turned a once barren Palestine green and blooming. The Israeli pioneers came to Palestine when it was neglected swampland and desert. They achieved the almost impossible and turned the desert green. As a result, the Palestinian Arabs have benefited as well from the successes of the Jewish pioneers.

Slogan 7: "Israel is the sole democracy in the region"

The world should recall that the only democracy in the region is Israel. The Arab regimes are harsh and authoritarian. The Palestinian Arabs in Judea and Samaria exploit the democracy in Israel in order to inflict damage upon her. Some incorrectly interpret Israeli democracy as a weakness.

> *There is no way to peace, peace is the way.*
> A. J. MUSTE

Slogan 8: "Western pressure on Israel is futile"

Israel is the country being threatened by her neighbors. Since it is Israel's security and future at stake, Israel is the only country which has the moral right to decide what is beneficial or detrimental to her. Foreign countries should not exert any pressure on Israel.

In 1957, after the Sinai Campaign, the Soviet Union and the U.S.A. imposed a settlement on Israel. Israel withdrew from Sinai without any Egyptian concessions for the sake of peace. The seeds of the Six-Day War may be found in the results of the Sinai campaign.

Slogan 9: "Islam vis-à-vis western democracies"

The power of Islam is growing and Islamic fanaticism is spreading. The spirit of democracy and the values of the western world are alien to Islam. Israel, as a non-Moslem democracy, suffers from Islamic fanaticism. Many of the activities of the Palestinian terrorists are perpetrated by Moslem fanatics in the territories.

Slogan: 10: "The PLO is not a national movement"

A national movement seeks to kick out foreign, colonial powers from its land. The F.L.N. in Algeria removed the French from Algeria as the Mau Mau removed the British from Kenya. However, the PLO seeks to kick out the Israelis from Israel. The PLO has made the murder of the innocent – Jews and Arabs alike – a policy. Neither by its goals nor by its actions can the PLO be considered a national movement. The PLO is, by definition, a terrorist movement.

> *If President Reagan thinks that we will stop attacks against Israeli military targets, then I tell him to stop the dialogue now. Neither military attacks nor our heroic* Intifada *will stop. We will carry on our struggle until the Palestinian flag is hoisted over Jerusalem.*
>
> SALEH KHALEF (Abu Iyad), deputy to Arafat in Fatah PLO faction, *New York Times,* December 19, 1988

The following cartoon appeared in the Egyptian daily *Sawt-El Arab* on page 1, September 6, 1987. It was headlined "Eight Years to Gulf War." (Note that the inverted "V" is the number 8 in Arabic.)

CHAPTER TWENTY-SIX

ISRAEL AND THE ARABS – VARIOUS DISCUSSIONS AND COMMENTS

> *If we look at a map of the Arab Homeland, we can hardly find two countries without conflicts which have either already erupted or are about to explode. We can hardly find two countries which are not either in a state of war or on the road to war.*
>
> assessment of the Arab world by
> Syrian Foreign Minister ABD AL-HALIM KHADDAM
> in Oman, November 1980

IS ISRAEL THE SOURCE OF INSTABILITY IN THE MIDDLE EAST?

Q: Is Israel the source of instability in the Middle East?

A: In the Middle East, there is tension between the rich and the poor, between secularists and traditionalists, between pro-Western and anti-Western. There was war between Egypt and Libya, between Morocco and Algeria, between Iraq and Iran, between Syria and the PLO, between the PLO and Jordan, between Egypt and Northern Yemen, etc., etc. All these wars had nothing whatsoever to do with Israel.

Q: How does the Arab-lsraeli conflict fit into this picture?

A: Israel does not intervene in the conflicts between the Arab states. Israel wishes for a reduction in the tensions between the Arab countries. Tranquility on the Arab side may cause the Arabs to adopt a more realistic policy towards Israel.

Q: Isn't Israel, which controls Southern Lebanon, behind the civil war in Lebanon?

A: Israel has nothing to do with the civil war in Lebanon. The ethnic war in Lebanon is between Christians and Moslems, between the Christians and the Palestinians, between the Christians and the Druze, etc. Civil warfare in Lebanon started long before the Israeli presence in Southern Lebanon.

> *But the growing double standard routine of attacking the Israeli democracy and remaining mute about the Arab tyrannies is presenting Israel as the great human rights violator in the Middle East. That game costs her friends and support. It is no small matter.*
>
> *Perhaps Mr. Carter and other decent travelers should consider that the next time they tour the Middle East. If they feel unable to tell the truth everywhere, maybe they should stay home. Truth cannot guarantee success in a search for peace. but lies can guarantee failure. When it comes to decade after decade of murder and torture, silence is a lie.*
>
> A. M. ROSENTHAL,
> *New York Times,*
> March 25, 1990

PEACE WITH EGYPT

> *Peace, peace to those afar and near . . . There is no peace, says my Lord, for the wicked.*
>
> Isaiah 57:19, 21

Q: What are the ingredients that made peace with Egypt possible?

A: Peace came about primarily because Egypt decided that it was now to its advantage to make peace. Its interest stemmed from military reasons, since Egypt had failed to defeat Israel in the Yom Kippur War of 1973, despite the element of surprise; from internal reasons, because of the country's overwhelming poverty and the realization that the Egyptian people gained little by continuing a struggle in which it had lost many of its sons; and from strategic reasons, because Egypt recognized the Soviet threat to the region as the real threat to its security.

Q: What is Israel's position towards peace?

A: Since her establishment, Israel has called for peace and her policy has not changed. Egypt was the one to change policy by relinquishing the military option.

Q: What lesson is to be learned from this?

A: The lesson is very clear: Israel must be very patient on the one hand and strong militarily on the other hand in order to prevent Arab aggression against her.

> *Patience is bitter, but it helps.*
>
> Arab saying

Q: Is the Camp David agreement a viable solution?

A: Yes. The Camp David agreement is a viable solution by the very fact that it is beneficial to all the sides involved. It offers the Palestinians autonomy, enabling them to run their own affairs. On the other hand, it offers Israel the security she needs in order to survive.

Q: What are the Egyptian benefits from the peace treaty?

A: Egypt is enjoying daily benefits from the peace treaty and the Camp David Accords: The Suez Canal is opened, tourists – including Israelis – are once again flocking to Egypt, the Abu Rodeis oil field in Sinai was returned to Egypt, American assistance to Egypt amounts to over two billion dollars annually. All these benefits are a direct result of the tranquil border between Israel and Egypt.

Q: Didn't Egypt forfeit Arab economic assistance because of the peace treaty?

A: Yes. Rich Arab countries decided to cease their economic assistance to Egypt as a result of the Egyptian-Israeli peace treaty. However, the benefits to Egypt from the Camp David Accords are much greater than her losses.

Q: What happened in 1988-89 with regards to Egyptian relations with the Arab world?

A: Egypt, which was immediately excommunicated by the Arabs after signing the peace treaty with Israel, has returned to the Arab world. More and more Arabs understand today that Sadat's initiative was the proper step for the Arabs. Most Arab states have since renewed their diplomatic relations with Egypt. Egypt has returned to the Arab League and even the Libyan leader, Qaddafi, came to see President Mubarak in October 1989.

Q: What is the Syrian policy towards Egypt?

A: The Syrians conducted a bitter propaganda war against Egypt after Sadat's visit to Jerusalem in November 1977. Yet even the Syrians had to follow the other Arabs seeking closeness to Egypt. In 1989, the

Syrians renewed their diplomatic relations with Egypt and on May 2, 1990, President Mubarak of Egypt visited Assad in Syria.

THE PLO IS NOT A PARTNER

> *An independent Palestinian state . . . will function as a base from which to liberate Jaffa, Akko and all of Palestine, after which we will take Palestine and turn it into part of the greater Arab nation.*
>
> SALEH KHALEF (Abu Iyad),
> January 1987

When asked whether a Palestinian state would mean the cessation of hostilities against Israel, Farouk Kaddoumi said that a Palestinian state "doesn't mean that we are giving up the rest of our rights . . . There are two [initial] phases to our return. The first phase to the 1967 lines, and the second to the 1948 lines . . . The third stage is the democratic state of Palestine."

Q: Why won't Israel negotiate with the PLO?
A: The answer is simple: Israel will not negotiate with the PLO because the PLO is a terrorist organization which seeks Israel's destruction.
Q: Hasn't the PLO changed?
A: No. The PLO changed only its tactics. The PLO has two faces – one for the outside world and the West and the other for "home consumption." For the outside world, the PLO pretends to be moderate and in search of a political solution. In reality, the PLO seeks Israel's destruction.
Q: Isn't it true that the United States, Israel's ally, is negotiating with the PLO?
A: Yes and Israel regrets the American-PLO dialogue. Israel believes that such a dialogue will not contribute to the chances for peace in this troubled area. On the contrary, such a dialogue will place an obstacle on the road to peace.

> *A time must come in which the Jewish nation shall be exalted,*
> *as has been promised, above all the nations and it shall reign*
> *by its saints, its prophets and apostles. For otherwise, I am bold*
> *to say that all the prophecies made to this people were delusive.*
> PIERRE JURIEU, Christian writer,
> *L'Accomplissement de prophétie*
> (Holland), 1686

Q: Why shouldn't the United States negotiate with the PLO?

A: The United States is bound by a 1975 agreement with Israel, which was reconfirmed in 1979, at the time of the signing of the Egyptian-Israeli peace treaty, not to talk to the PLO until the PLO recognizes Israel and accepts UN Resolution 242. Israel believes that the PLO has not yet met these demands.

> *We shall fight together, as one Moslem nation, under one flag.*
> YASSIR ARAFAT in Teheran,
> "Voice of Fatah," Beirut,
> February 19, 1979

Q: Did the PLO support Iran in the Iraqi-Iranian war?

A: Yes. The PLO has been the single most consistent supporter of the Khomeini forces. It was true throughout the 1970s when Khomeini and many of the revolutionaries were in exile and in opposition; it was true throughout the hostage crisis, Indeed, no other external entity has so fully identified itself with the Khomeini revolution as the PLO.

Q: Are there any facts to prove this?

A: According to *Time* magazine, in the past few years, more than 3,000 Iranian rebels were trained in guerilla tactics and sabotage by the PLO before and after the revolution. In February 1979, Yassir Arafat received a glorious welcome in Teheran as the first foreign "dignitary" to be received by the new Khomeini regime. PLO support for Khomeini rested on agreements of ideology, strategy, and tactics. The PLO saw Khomeini as the means to achieve its three central aims: the subversion of American interests, the undermining of moderate states in the Middle East, and the destruction of Israel.

> *Terrorist gangs love to present themselves as lone, brave bands, but many of them are linked to one another and sometimes join up for action. They all get funding from Iran, Syria, Libya and other Middle Eastern powers.*
>
> *The West believes – presumed would be a better word – that the collapse of the Communist system put the Soviet Union out of its business of supporting terrorism. If so, Moscow should open its secret files and provide information about names, addresses, sponsors and methods of operation of the terrorists it has trained.*
>
> A. M. ROSENTHAL,
> *New York Times,*
> March 25, 1990

Q: What can be said of relations between the PLO and the Soviet Union?

A: The PLO is known to be a strong supporter of the Soviet Union. Like Castro of Cuba, Arafat has served as the Kremlin's ally and ardent supporter. He has also journeyed to other capitals of the Soviet bloc's Warsaw Pact nations to confer with communist leaders.

Q: Does the PLO condemn the Russian invasion of Afghanistan?

A: The following quotations supply the answer to this question: From PLO leader Farouk Kaddoumi in Sofia, on January 8, 1980, came: "Russia rendered selfless assistance to the government of Kabul. All the U.S. is interested in is to exploit the natural resources of Iran and Afghanistan and to try to create military bases in the Middle East." From Arafat advisor Bassam Abu Sharif came: "Western hypocrisy is underlined by the fact that the U.S. and its Western friends were bitterly opposed to the Islamic forces in Afghanistan." And from PLO leader Yasser Abed Rabbo we have: "Russian involvement in Afghanistan is an important asset to all revolutionary forces which oppose the expansion of the American presence in the Middle East."

Q: Why isn't the right to self-determination an absolute right of all people?

A: In 1978, Freedom House, a public affairs organization which makes comparative surveys of freedom in societies throughout the world, found more than 100 peoples which did not have self-determination. Indeed, if these peoples were to achieve self-determination, many nation-states around the globe would dissolve. It is clear, therefore, that self-determination must be weighed against other factors. In the case of the Palestinians, there are two key factors to be considered:

(a) the threat of Palestinian self-determination to the State of Israel; and, (b) the ability of the Palestinians to achieve national and cultural expression through the largely Palestinian state of Jordan and through the process of autonomy negotiated at Camp David. The Camp David accords seek to do just that, by providing Palestinians on the West Bank with an opportunity to control their day-to-day lives without threatening Israel's security.

Q: Isn't the Palestinian problem the heart of the conflict?

A: The heart of the conflict is not the Palestinian dilemma, but the right of Israel to exist. Israel's right to exist has been denied by the Arab world since her infancy. Arab propaganda has blown the Palestinian problem out of proportion, making it seem to be the greatest problem facing the world today. In reality, the picture is completely different.

Q: Will the Camp David Accords solve this problem?

A: Yes, if (a) the Palestinian Arabs come and negotiate; (b) the PLO ends its threat to those Palestinians willing to negotiate with Israel; (c) the Arabs and other countries stop supporting the PLO; and (d) the United States, Israel, and Egypt continue to be committed to the Camp David Accords signed jointly by all three.

When we talk about armed struggle, the legitimacy of which is recognized by the United Nations, we are talking about all the occupied areas of Palestine . . . It is our right to wage war against an enemy who occupies our land, whether as a result of the conquest of 1967 or of the conquest of 1948.

PLO spokesman FAROUK KADDOUMI,
November 1985

ISRAEL'S SECURITY: THE MAIN ISSUE

> *The real issue in the Middle East had to do with the Arab refusal to recognize that Israel has a right to exist as a nation. To give up the buffer zones Israel took in the Six-Day War could be to put a cannon on her front walk aimed at her front door by those who have said she must be destroyed.*
>
> U.S. President RONALD REAGAN, 1977

Q: Why is Israel's special concern for her security?

A: Israel suffered time and again from Arab aggression. Despite this, Israel is willing to take a calculated risk for the sake of peace. For the sake of a treaty with Egypt, Israel gave up the entire Sinai desert which had been the site of five wars and a buffer zone between Egypt and Israel. At a time of acute energy shortages, Israel, in the interest of peace, gave up the oil fields which could have made the country self-sufficient. For peace, Israel gave up three of the most sophisticated airbases in the world. With this unique example of risk-taking, one has an obligation to listen to Israelis when they say that some risks are too great to take.

Q: Why won't Israel trust the big powers to guarantee her security?

A: Outside guarantees have been viewed as too risky and uncertain a basis for peace. Surely, in the narrow West Bank region, security must depend on Israel's own ability to prevent an incursion by foreign forces. The alternatives to Israel's ability to defend itself are for its survival to be conditional on Arab good will, on the effectiveness of international guarantees, or on the readiness of American soldiers to fight for Israel. All three alternatives are actually no alternatives.

> *Beware of him who gives thee advice according to his own interests.*
>
> The Talmud

Q: Can you supply one example?

A: Yes, in May 1967, when Nasser of Egypt closed the Straits of Tiran illegally, Israel appealed to the major Western powers that had promised to keep the Red Sea straits opened. Israel's request for help was diplomatically rejected. Israel had no alternative but to fight in order to remove the naval blockade around her.

Q: What can be said about Israel's withdrawing from Judea and Samaria and leaving the areas demilitarized?

A: Demilitarization is not an answer to Israel's security problems. Israel cannot count on it. Demilitarization may work in huge areas like the Sinai desert; however, it will not work in the small, over-populated areas of Judea and Samaria,

Q: Why wouldn't the United Nations guarantee Israel's security?

A: International guarantees cannot be relied upon because of the basically hostile attitude toward Israel of many members of the international community. To ask Israel to place its security in the hands of the United Nations, which regularly passes anti-Israel resolutions – including the outrageous view that Zionism is racism – is asking too much of any nation.

Q: Doesn't the United Nations' record prove that the world organization is very effective?

A: In Israel's case, it was not. One need only recall the events of 1967. UN forces were situated in the Sinai for the purpose of preventing hostilities between Egypt and Israel. Egyptian President Nasser suddenly demanded the immediate withdrawal of the UN forces. The UN acceded to Nasser's demands and Egyptian troops soon massed on Israel's borders and war became inevitable.

> *In every generation the enemies plan to kill us, yet the Almighty God saves us from them.*
>
> The Passover Haggadah

Q: Why wouldn't Israel trust United States' guarantees?

A: As a replacement for Israeli self-defense, American guarantees would only lead to an intolerable situation for both parties. Israel never wanted any foreign troops to fight on its behalf, and America is not eager to send its own soldiers to fight in a Middle Eastern war.

Q: Why couldn't Israel agree to return to the borders it had prior to the Six-Day War in 1967?

A: Israel cannot afford to return to its pre-1967 borders, particularly in the West Bank and the Golan Heights. A return to these borders would expose Israel to unacceptable risks. The heavily populated Israeli coastal region would be only nine to fifteen miles in width. What nation would place itself in such jeopardy?

Q: Isn't it true that in an era of sophisticated missiles, territory to ensure security loses its importance?

A: Wrong: With the use of missiles, one country may cause damage to another. However, countries cannot be captured by missiles but by soldiers and here lies the great importance of territory.

Q: Then what is the conclusion?

A: The conclusion is that Israel can depend only upon her forces and must maintain secure borders. International guarantees and demilitarization are not effective.

Q: What can be said about PLO terror against Israel?

A: The PLO was expelled by Israel from Judea and Samaria in the 1967 war, by Jordan from Jordan in 1970 ("Black September"), and from Lebanon by Israel in 1981-83. Today, the PLO almost does not operate from Israel's borders, PLO operations against Israel may be renewed if a PLO-dominated Palestinian state were to be established in Judea and Samaria.

> *They are going upcountry tomorrow. They have simple orders; kill Jews. We don't care whether the dead are civilians or soldiers just so long as they are Jews.*
>
> El-Fatah leader to
> B. Jordan, British journalist,
> *Daily Mail,* January 1, 1969

Q: Why would such a state be dangerous to Israel?

A: A PLO-dominated Palestinian state would pose a danger to Israel because in reality, the PLO has not changed its fanatic policy against Israel. Moreover, this state would maintain close relations with Libya, Iraq, Syria, and all the other radical states in the Arab world.

In October 1989, all the Arab states, with the exception of Egypt, supported the Arab proposal to kick out Israel from the United Nations. The proposal was rejected 95 to 35.

> *And I will bring back the captivity of my people Israel, and they shall build the wasted cities, and dwell therein; and they shall plant vineyards, and drink their wine; and they shall lay out gardens, and eat their fruit. And I will plant them upon their own soil, and they shall not be pulled up any more out of their land which I have given unto them, saith the Lord thy God.*
>
> Amos 9: 14-15

353

The following cartoon appeared in the Egyptian daily *El-Shaab* on November 18, 1986. It was entitled "The Gulf War."

PART IX

*SYRIA – FANATICISM AS
A POLICY, DREAMS
AND RIVALRIES*

PART IX

CHAPTER TWENTY-SEVEN

SYRIA – FANATICISM AS
A POLICY AGAINST ISRAEL

Despite the emergence of Iraq as the most radical Arab state, Syria is still the leader of the Arab "rejection front." She was behind all the most radical Arab resolutions against Israel. Syria claims that the military option is the only viable way in which to solve the conflict with Israel. She is continually making all the necessary preparations to achieve a military strategic balance with Israel. Syria's sacred goal is to put an end to Israel's existence in the Middle East. Syrian rejectionism has found different expressions on numerous occasions.

> *Let them be confounded and turned back, all who hate Zion.*
>
> Psalms 129:5
>
> ---
>
> *Blessed are the peacemakers, for they shall be called the children of god.*
>
> JESUS CHRIST,
> in Matthew 5:9

Q: How does Syria regard Israel's right to exist?

A: According to Syrian Information Minister Ahmad Iskandar, in *Ar-Ral Al-Am*, on December 18, 1982: "Syria is still the only Arab state that adheres to the resolutions of the Khartoum Conference of 1967, which decreed: NO PEACE, NO RECOGNITION and NO NEGOTIATIONS WITH ISRAEL. Syria will always adhere to these "resolutions."

Q: What are its views about UN Resolution 242?

A: According to Syrian Foreign Minister Abd al-Halim Khaddam, on Radio Damascus, July 7, 1980: "The Zionist entity is only temporary . . . UN Security Council Resolution 242 has to be rejected."

> *Begin in Cairo today. Do something, Egypt. Poison the Nile water that Begin will drink. Keep the grave of Abd Al-Nasser from Begin's sight . . .*
>
> Radio Damascus, April 2, 1979

Q: What about the Camp David Accords?

A: According to Syrian Information Minister Iskandar in *Al Akhbar* (Jordan), November 5, 1978: "We want a firm stand against the Camp David agreements . . . We want joint Arab action against the agreements . . . We reject the Camp David agreements."

Q: What was Syria's attitude towards the Israeli-Lebanese agreement of 1983?

A: At the beginning of 1983, Lebanon and Israel reached an agreement which terminated the state of war and established good neighborly relations between the two countries. The Syrians rejected and opposed this agreement. Radio Damascus on June 3, 1983, expressed President Assad's position: "Assad stated that Syria will spare no efforts to frustrate the agreement . . . The agreement, therefore, will fail . . ."

SYRIA: A STATE OF TERROR

In the words of American Secretary of State Alexander M. Haig, Jr. (1981-82), cited in the *New York Times,* August 15, 1989: "The terrorist states – Libya, Syria, Iran, and others – offer protection to terrorist organizations which in turn advance the interests of those states. Would Hizballah's terrorists be so confident in their actions if their bases did not lie in the perimeter of aggressive occupation of Lebanon? Would Hizballah be able to operate at all without the support of Iran and Syria?

> *Their throat is an open grave. Let them fall by their own counsels.*
>
> Psalms: 5: 9-10

Almost every significant terrorist group operating in the Middle East or western Europe has connections with Syria, as do some groups from other regions as well. These connections are made either through the provision of training facilities or through cooperation with Libya and Iran. The Syrian government, which controls most of Lebanon, exploits

its freedom in that country to sponsor a variety of terrorist organizations using training facilities in the Beka'a Valley. These include a large number of Palestinian groups.

Furthermore, Syria has set up a solid organizational infrastructure for its terror activities in the major capitals of Europe. This network is under the authority of the Syrian embassies, enabling terrorists to pass as diplomats and to use the diplomatic corps for the transfer of arms.

Q: What kind of cooperation exists between Syria, Libya, and Iran?
A: In three successive conferences in 1986 – in Tripoli on February 4, in Teheran on April 13, and in Damascus on August 23 – Libya, Syria, and Iran agreed to a division of labor. Syria would sponsor Jibril, Habash, Hawatmeh and the Musa factions of the PLO; Libya would assume joint responsibility for Abu Nidal with Syria, and Iran would oversee the fundamentalist groups such as the Hizballah, the Islamic Jihad and the radical wing of Amal.
Q: What were the results of such cooperation?
A: The results were soon to follow : the bombing of a club in West Berlin, the aborted attempt to bomb the El Al Airline offices in London, a similar attempt in Madrid, the bombing of City Hall in downtown Paris, etc.

> *We must establish the reign of reason and justice, and not violence, which is fit only for beasts.*
>
> EMERIC CRUCE

Q: Which terrorist groups operate from Lebanon with the assistance of Syria?
A: The Syrian government, which controls most of Lebanon, exploits its freedom in that country to sponsor a variety of terrorist organizations using training facilities in the Beka'a Valley. These include a large number of Palestinian groups, the Armenian Secret Army for the Liberation of Armenia (ASALA), the Popular Front for the Liberation of Oman, the Democratic Front for the Liberation of Somalia, and the Eritrean Liberation Front.
Q: Is there any proof that Syria is actually training terrorists?
A: Yes. At his trial in Rome, the Pope's assailant, Mehmet Ali Agca, testified that he and other members of the Grey Wolves, an extremist Turkish gang, were trained in Latakia, Syria, and taught by Bulgarian and Czech experts.

> *My son, don't walk in the way with them, restrain thy foot from their path. For their feet run to evil and they make haste to shed blood.*
>
> Proverbs 1: 15-16

Q: What about Iranian terrorists?

A: Most Iranian-backed fundamentalist Moslem terrorists, whose attacks take place anywhere between Copenhagen and Kuwait, work out of Lebanon.

Q: What about Syrian terror against other Arabs?

A: The resort to terror and assassination is an integral element of Assad's conduct in his relations with Arab states. To cite only one example: When the Palestinian National Council (PNC) managed to hold its meeting in Amman, Jordan, in November 1984, despite Syrian opposition and the strenuous efforts that it made to prevent the PNC from meeting there, or anywhere else, Syria launched an assassination campaign against Jordanian diplomats abroad. Syria also arranged for the murder of Fahad Kawasmeh, a prominent Palestinian member of the PNC, in his residence in the very heart of Amman.

Q: What about European terrorists?

A: A number of European terrorists, including members of the Baader-Meinhof gang and the Red Brigades, have spent time in Syrian-controlled Lebanese camps. Agca said that he trained alongside gangs from France, Italy, Germany, and Spain.

Q: Does Syria enjoy the cooperation of other states in support of terrorists?

A: Yes. To extend his reach, Assad often coordinates with Libya, Iran, or both. The two countries have a license to make mischief in Lebanon and both sponsor organizations in collaboration with Damascus.

> *Deliver me, Oh Lord from the evil man, preserve me from the violent men who devise mischiefs in their heart, continually they stir up war. They have sharpened their tongues like a serpent, a spider's venom is under their lips.*
>
> Psalms 140:2-5

Q: What is Israel's attitude towards the United States, according to the Syrians?

A: Deputy Prime Minister and Foreign Minister of Syria, Abd al-Halim Khaddam explains: "There is a deep and organic link between the U.S. and Israel. We have no illusion about this. The link is not due to the 'Zionist lobby' in the U.S. but to the fact that it is the only friend of the U.S. in the area and because it presents a major base for protecting U.S. interests."

Q: Has Syria adopted a Cold War-style of hostility towards the United States?

A: Yes. According to Damascus, the United States pursues a "general strategy of world imperialism" in a "colonialist" effort to control economic resources. Its goal in the Middle East is to set up military bases for two reasons: to "tighten" control over the oil regions and to threaten the Soviet Union.

THE FUTILE ATTEMPT TO BOMB AN EL AL PLANE IN FLIGHT

The affair of Nezar Hindawi – the Jordanian convicted and sentenced to 45 years in prison for a bombing attempt upon an El Al plane at Heathrow Airport, London – is a clear-cut case study of Syria's pervasive and systematic use of terrorism as an instrument of state policy. The Hindawi case was in the spring of 1986.

The following information is based largely upon evidence from Hindawi's London trial.

Q: Was Syrian Intelligence involved?

A: British security and police officials say that ranking officials of the Syrian Intelligence organized and financed the plot and recruited and trained Hindawi.

Q: Did Hindawi have connections with other terrorist organizations?

A: According to intelligence sources cited by the *Chicago Tribune,* Hindawi was a senior agent in Europe of one of those organizations – the Abu Nidal gang.

Q: Was the Syrian ambassador in London involved?

A: Syria's ambassador in London, Loutof Allah Haydar, was found to have played a key role in the affair. Several months before the crime he helped secure for Hindawi the sponsorship of Syrian intelligence. British security surveillance verified the ambassador's complicity. Hindawi maintained direct personal and telephone contact with the ambassador.

Q: Who is Muhammed Al Kholi?

A: Brigadier General Muhammed Al-Kholi is the Syrian Air Force

Intelligence chief and close confidant of Syrian President Hafez al-Assad. He is one of the pillars of international terrorism with close ties to terrorist groups in Iran, Libya, Lebanon, and elsewhere in the Middle East and Europe. Hindawi provided Al-Kholi's telephone number in Damascus to his British interrogators.

Q: Who obtained Hindawi's visa for entrance to England?

A: Requests for a visa for him to enter England were made by the Syrian Foreign Ministry in Damascus.

Q: Who equipped Hindawi with the explosives he intended to use?

A: Scotland Yard detectives reported that the explosives and other parts were smuggled in from Damascus and that the sopisticated three-pound luggage bomb was assembled at the Syrian Embassy in London by Syrian Air force intelligence agents using the Syrian Arab Airline as a courier.

Q: What did Hindawi do when the bomb was discovered?

A: Once discovered, Hindawi fled to the Syrian Embassy. He met there with the ambassador who then arranged for a Syrian diplomat to shelter him in a safe-house run by Syrian intelligence. Apparently, the Syrian plan was to smuggle him out of the country disguised as a Syrian Arab Airline crew member.

Q: Why did Hindawi flee from the Syrian Embassy?

A: Fearing for his life at the hands of Syrian security forces, Hindawi fled again. A brother of his led London police to him.

Q: Is there any other proof of the Hindawi connection to the Syrian authorities?

A: Yes. British security intercepted a letter Hindawi smuggled out of jail two weeks after his arrest in which he proposed to Syrian officials that British hostages be taken in Lebanon and then arrangements made to exchange the hostages for his freedom.

Q: Have the Syrians supported other terrorist actions in Europe?

A: According to West German police, another Hindawi brother, Ahmed Hazi, confessed that he bombed the building of the German-Arab Friendship Society in West Berlin in the spring of 1985. He did so after his brother, Nezar, had planned and cleared the operation with Damascus and instructed him to go ahead, and after the explosives were supplied by the Syrian Embassy in East Germany.

> *. . . the U.S., if it can summon the will, to issue a warning that any attacks by terrorists will meet with retaliation against their bases and supply lines in any country harboring them.*
> *That might convince the Middle Eastern countries involved that backing terrorism is no longer cost-free. It is the only way to break the net-work connecting the terrorist gangs, Middle Eastern Governments, and the objectives of the P.L.O.*
>   A. M. ROSENTHAL,
>   *New York Times,*
>   March 25, 1990

Q: Does Syria have terrorist bases?

A: Yes. Syria maintains terrorist bases both on Syrian soil and in Syrian-occupied Lebanon for the terrorist bands of Abu Nidal, Abu Musa, and the Jibril-Hawatmeh-Habash terrorist coalition.

Q: Has Syria conducted terrorist acts in Europe alone?

A: Evidence from independent diplomatic and intelligence sources conclusively shows that Syria has also been responsible for terrorist acts against Jordanians, Palestinian Arabs, and Lebanese targets.

> *. . . All those who raged against you shall be destroyed and perish. You will search for your enemies but you will not find them . . .*
>   Isaiah 41: 8-10

Q: What did America think of the Hindawi case?

A: Deputy Secretary of State John C. Whitehead acknowledged that the United States ". . . has no reason to doubt Syrian responsibility for an attempt to bomb the El Al plane."

Q: What do the Syrians say about the crime?

A: The Syrians deny any involvement. They claim total innocence.

MASS MURDER AND HANGING: SYRIAN DEMOCRACY IN ACTION

> *Whoever says no to President Assad is likely to find himself a head shorter.*
>
>   MUSTAFA TLAS, Syrian Defense Minister,
>   in an interview in the West German magazine
>   *Der Spiegel,* as reported in the *New York Times,*
>   September 12, 1984
>
> ----
>
> *Amnesty International report cites six cases of alleged mass political killings said to have been carried out by the security forces between March 1980 and February 1982. They include the reported killing on 27 June 1980 of between 600 and 1,000 inmates of Palmyra Prison.*
>
>   Amnesty International briefing,
>   London, November 1983

Since coming to power in 1970, President Assad's regime has accumulated a long record of gross violations of human rights. During recent years, more severe measures have been taken as a result of an increase in opposition activities. A report by the International Commission of Jurists in Geneva spoke of detentions without trial and torture to extract information. Families of those held are generally not informed of arrests and they find real difficulty in tracing the whereabouts of their relatives. At times, if the suspected person cannot be found, members of his family are imprisoned instead.

Here is one example of mass murder – one day in which 550 people were massacred:

Akram Ali Bishani and Issa Ibrahim Fayyad were two members of the terrorist gang of five which was sent to Jordan from Syria to assassinate the prime minister of Jordan. The terrorists were arrested and the following are excerpts from their confessions regarding mass killing committed in the Palmyra Prison.

CONFESSIONS OF AKRAM ALI BISHANI

Q: What are the operations which you were entrusted with during your service at the Defense Battalions (Saraya Al-Difa's, a special brigade of the Syrian army)?

364

A: I was entrusted with two operations.

Q: What was the first operation?

A: The operation of Palmyra Prison on June 26, 1980 . . . we were awakened at 3 a.m. and told that there was a meeting in full battledress with weapons . . . we were met by Brigadier Mouieen Nassif, chief of the brigade. He addressed us: ". . . today you will be attacking [the Moslem Brothers'] largest center, which is the Palmyra Prison". . . . We mounted the planes led by the commander of the 138th brigade, Brigadier Suliman Mustafa, an Alawite . . . we reached there at about 6:30 a.m. of the same day . . . in the prison we were divided into six smaller groups or more; e.g., my group was of about eleven persons . . . My group was led by Captain Munir Darwish. They opened a dormitory door, wherein there were about 60 to 70 persons . . . Then somebody called me and asked for ammunition. When I enquired why, he said, "There is one who has not died yet and we want to machine-gun him." The total of those whom I machine-gunned was about 15 persons; the total of those killed in the prison of the Moslem Brothers was about 550 persons . . .

In its report from 1983, Amnesty International stated: "Syrian security forces have practiced systematic violations of human rights including torture and political killing and have been operating with impunity under the country's emergency laws. There is overwhelming evidence that thousands of Syrians not involved in violence have been harassed and wrongfully detained without chance of appeal and in some cases have been tortured, others are reported to have 'disappeared' or to have been the victims of extrajudicial killings carried out by security forces."

Radio Damascus reported: "Before dawn on September 26, 1976, three PLO terrorists, captured after they attacked the Semiramis Hotel in Damascus, were hanged in a public square of that city where their bodies remained suspended for hours. The terrorists admitted under interrogation that they belonged to the Al-Fatah wing of the PLO."

Q: What was Assad's reaction to this brutality?

A: Commenting on the attack President Assad declared: "We condemn this act of terror, committed by a gang of traitors and criminals. We refuse to bargain with them."

Q: What does Syria think of the PLO?

A: Referring to those who sent the terrorists to Damascus, the Syrian president added: "The only thing these PLO leaders wanted was to attack Syria, despite its sacrifices on behalf of the Palestinians."

> *Seven months now since 259 people were blown apart in Pan Am flight 103, Ahmed Jibril, believed by Western intelligence to have carried out the operation, still lives in Damascus, supplied by the Syrians and under their orders.*
> *New York Times*, July 20, 1989

THE MASSACRE OF TWENTY-EIGHT ISRAELI PRISONERS-OF-WAR

> *Evil shall come from the north on all the inhabitants of earth.*
> Jeremiah 1:14

During the Yom Kippur War of 1973, twenty-eight Israeli troops were captured by the Syrian forces. They were prisoners-of-war; yet despite that, they were murdered in cold blood by the Syrian troops, thus violating one of the main paragraphs of the Geneva Conference.

Q: Did the Syrian authorities attempt to cover up this sad story?
A: No, on the contrary, they boasted about it.
Q: How?
A: The Syrian minister of defense awarded the state's highest medal for the cold-blooded murder of Israel P.O.W.s and for eating human flesh.
Q: Was the event publicized in Syria?
A: The following is a copy from the minutes of the session as published in the Syrian *Official Gazette* of July 11, 1974, with an English translation:

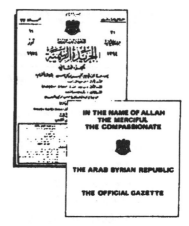

"There is the outstanding case of a recruit from Aleppo who killed 28 Jewish soldiers all by himself, slaughtering them like sheep. All of his comrades-in-arms witnessed this. He butchered three of them with an axe and decapitated them. In other words, instead of using a gun to kill them, he took a hatchet to chop their heads off. He struggled face to face with one of them and throwing down his axe managed to break his neck and devour his flesh in front of his comrades.

"This is a special case. Need I single it out to award him the Medal of the Republic? I will grant this medal to any soldier who succeeds in killing 28 Jews, and I will cover him with appreciation and honor for his bravery."

General Mustafa Tlas, Minister of Defense,
12th Session of Parliament, December 1, 1973

Q: Where is Mustafa Tlas today?
A: He is still Syria's minister of defense today.
Q: Was this sad story adequately covered by the world media?
A: No. The story is hardly known.
Q: Did the United Nations discuss or condemn this murder?
A: Not at all.

THE KILLING OF 20,000 MOSLEMS
IN HAMA

> *Assad: a lion in Lebanon yet a rabbit in the Golan Heights.*
> Palestinian saying
>
> *(Assad in Arabic means lion.)*
>
> ---
>
> *I went to Hama ten weeks afterward, when the city was reopened to foreigners. I have seen many scenes of destruction in the Middle East, but never anything like Hama. Whole neighborhoods had been plowed up "like cornfields and bulldozed as flat as parking lots. Seeing a stoop-shouldered old man with a checkered headdress shuffling along a stretch of rubble the size of four football fields, I asked him where all the houses were. "You are standing on them," he said. And where, I asked, were all the people who used to live there? "You are probably standing on them, too," he answered, shuffling away.*
> THOMAS FRIEDMAN,
> *New York Times Magazine,*
> October 7, 1984

The Hama massacre occurred in February 1982, and was the bloodiest massacre committed by Assad's regime. The victims were members of the Moslem Brotherhood which opposed the Alawite regime of President Assad.

Q: How serious was the massacre?
A: According to the study carried out by Amnesty International: "When law and order was restored, estimates of the dead on all sides ranged from 10,000 to 20,000.
Q: What did the Syrian regime do to cover up its crime?
A: At the time of the massacre, the Syrian regime of President Hafez al-Assad had hermetically sealed off the entire city to the outside world, as heavy artillery and aerial bombing pounded away at positions held by his bitter opponents – the Moslem Brotherhood.
Q: How many Syrian troops were involved in the massacre?
A: According to the Amnesty International study, some 6,000 to 8,000 soldiers including units from the 21st mechanized brigade of the 3rd armored division were reportedly dispatched to the city.
Q: What did the Syrian troops do to the city?
A: The study says that ". . . old parts of the city were bombarded from

the air and shelled in order to facilitate the entry of troops and tanks along the narrow roads . . .''

Q: What did the State Department's human rights report of 1983 say about the massacre?

A: "Evidence on the number of people killed is scanty because the government restricted access to the city for some time, and has attempted to stifle information on events there. Nevertheless, there have been press accounts that several thousand persons were killed.''

Q: What did the *Washington Post* write about the massacre?

A: The *Washington Post* reported a few weeks after the massacre that as many as 20,000 orphans may have been created during the ordeal.

Q: What did the Moslem Brotherhood sources say?

A: Moslem Brotherhood sources say that as many as 30,000 people may have been killed.

Freedom means the supremacy of human rights everywhere.
FRANKLIN D. ROOSEVELT

Q: What do the Syrians say about the massacre?

A: The Syrian governor of the area insisted that only 1,200 were killed on both sides.

Q: What happened on February 19, 1982?

A: Amnesty International has heard that there was, among other things, a collective execution of 70 people outside the municipal hospital on February 19, 1982; the Hadra quarter residents were executed by Syrian troops that same day.

Q: What were some of the means used to crush the resistance?

A: Cyanide gas containers were alleged to have been brought into the city, connected by rubber pipes to the entrances of buildings believed to house insurgents, and turned on, killing all the buildings' inhabitants. Amnesty International reported that people were assembled at the military airfield, at the sports stadium and at the military barracks, and left out in the open for days without food or shelter.

Q: What are the conclusions of the National Security Agency (NSA), which took before and after photographs of the massacre and devastation in Hama?

A: The "before" picture showed an ancient Arab town complete with small streets and alleys, a large marketplace and a large number of mosques. The "after" picture clearly showed that virtually all had been leveled during the massacre, including the numerous mosques. The reason was clear – the Moslem Brotherhood had based themselves in the mosques. By destroying them, the Syrian government believed it could deal a complete blow to the Moslem Brotherhood.

Q: Why was there no coverage of these atrocities in the American media?

A: American television networks neglected to cover the massacre for one simple reason. The Syrian government did not permit any camera crews into the area. It is very hard indeed to make the nightly news programs in the United States without some good, vivid footage to back up a story.

Q: Did the Arab League condemn the murder of thousands of Arabs and the demolishing of numerous mosques?

A: Not at all.

Q: Was there even a meeting of the United Nations Security Council to discuss the tragedy?

A: Not at all.

Q: What are the consequences of the Hama massacre?

A: If Syrian President Assad could slaughter so many of his own people, Moslems and Arabs, one can only imagine what he would do to the Jews, should they ever fall into his hands.

> *Political liberty can exist only when there is peace. Social reform can take place only when there is peace.*
> U.S. President WOODROW WILSON

In October 1983, Syrian television showed sixteen-year-old-girls, trainees in the Syrian Ba'ath party militia, fondling live snakes as President Assad and other Syrian leaders looked on approvingly. The girls suddenly bit the snakes with their teeth, repeatedly tore off flesh and spat it out as blood ran down their chins. After this, militiamen strangled puppies and drank their blood.

SYRIAN TERROR: VARIOUS TIMES, PLACES, AND METHODS

> *It is not only in internal affairs that the Syrian government has elevated extremist violence to an instrument of state. During 1980 and 1981, Syrian agents went on the offensive in Beirut, shooting and killing several Lebanese and western journalists in order to discourage reporters from writing negatively about Syria. As a member of the press corps at the time, I can testify that the campaign had its intended effect. Although unflattering stories about Syria still go out, there wasn't a journalist in Beirut who didn't think twice, or even three times, about writing ill of the Syrian regime.*
>
> THOMAS FRIEDMAN,
> *New York Times Magazine,*
> October 7, 1984
>
> *Say the opposite and people will know you.*
>
> Arab proverb

The Syrian regime has made it a policy to murder political opponents and to destroy their homes and offices. Opposition to the Syrian regime is considered treason and deserves death. This policy has been conducted inside as well as outside Syria.

Q: What happened to the pro-Iraqi weekly *Alwatan Al-Arabi* in Paris?

A: On April 22, 1982, Syrian agents planted a bomb in the building housing the editorial offices shortly after it had published an interview with a Moslem Brotherhood leader.

Q: Why was France chosen as the venue of Syrian terror?

A: Paris was chosen partly because some leaders of the Syrian opposition are now residing there and partly because of differences between Syria and France regarding the Middle East in general and Lebanon in particular.

Q: What was the reaction of France?

A: The French government recalled its ambassador to Syria for consultations.

Q: What are the aims of Syria's terror operation?

A: Syria has three main aims: (a) Israeli targets, (b) elements of Syrian opposition, and (c) various Arab elements connected with the Syrian opposition.

Q: Who fulfills the Syrian terror against Israel?

A: In their terror operations against Israel, Syria uses the organizations under her control: As-Saiqa and the "Eagles of the Revolution." In the past, it also employed the services of Abu Nidal's group.

Q: What about Syrian terror against opposition elements in Syria?

A: The greater the internal problems of the Alawite regime in Syria, the more it intensifies its campaign of terror against its opponents. In the past years, special "liquidation squads" have been stationed in various places.

Q: What about Syrian terror against Arab elements?

A: Syria's terror campaign against various Arab countries, particularly Iraq and Jordan, is related in part to the aid they supply, according to Syria, to the Syrian opposition. An additional factor in its vendetta against Iraq is the traditional ideological rivalry between their respective Ba'ath regimes.

Q: What are the Syrian targets in Lebanon?

A: Syria considers Lebanon to be an integral part of Syria, Therefore, Syria operates against various elements which it believes are interfering with Syrian interests in Lebanon.

Q: Is the Lebanese media free to criticize Syria?

A: One particular group that is targeted – Arab and western journalists who report on Lebanon and Syria in ways which do not suit Syria – has been subjected to a campaign of intimidation and terror.

Q: What happened to Salim Al-Luzi?

A: Mr. Al-Luzi, the editor of *Al-Hawadeth*, was murdered in March 1980. His hands had been burned by acid to symbolize the fate awaiting anyone who dares to write critically about Syria.

Q: Who else was murdered?

A: On March 16, 1977, the Lebanese leftist leader Kamil Jumblat was murdered. Perhaps this is the main reason why Walid, Kamil's son, is pro-Syrian. He does not want to suffer the same fate as his father.

Q: What happened to the Lebanese president-elect, Bashir Gemayel?

A: Mr. Gemayel was murdered because his views concerning Lebanon differed from those of Syria.

Q: What is the reason behind the Syrian hatred towards Premier Michel Aoun?

A: Mr. Aoun's "mistake" was to ask the Syrian troops to leave Lebanon and to let the Lebanese run their own affairs.

Q: What about Syrian support of hijackers?

A: In March 1981, a Pakistani airplane was hijacked to Syria. In its role as mediator, between Pakistan and the hijackers, Syria conducted the negotiations in a manner indicating its bias in favor of the hijackers.

In the end of the incident, Syria granted political asylum to the hijackers, refusing to hand them over to Pakistan.

The following is a partial list of terrorist activities over the last few years which Syria is known to have perpetrated or in which she has played an operational role:

◆ October 4, 1976: A Syrian intelligence agent seized on the Iraqi border admitted that he had been sent to carry out attacks against Iraqi government institutions and to murder Syrian exiles in Iraq.

◆ March 26, 1979: An explosive device was thrown at the Israeli Embassy in Ankara. The "Eagles of the Revolution" claimed responsibility.

◆ March 27, 1979: Two attacks in Paris, one against a Jewish restaurant, the other against a store owned by Jews.

◆ April 2, 1979: RPG missiles – Soviet antitank weapons – were fired at the American Embassy in Beirut. The "Eagles of the Revolution" claimed responsibility.

◆ April 7, 1979: A time bomb was discovered at a French cinema where a Jewish culture week was being held. As-Saiqa claimed responsibility.

◆ July 21, 1980: Salah a-Din Al-Bitar, a founder of the Ba'ath party who had been exiled from Syria, was murdered in Paris. It appears that this was the start of activity against Syrian opposition figures abroad.

◆ January 31, 1981: The Syrians dispatched a terrorist cell to assassinate the prime minister of Jordan, Mudar Badran.

◆ March 17, 1981: At Aachen, West Germany, the wife of Issam Al-Atar, a Moslem Brotherhood leader, was killed. The action was apparently aimed at Atar himself, but he was not at home.

◆ May 1, 1981: Heinz Nittel, chairman of the Austria-Israel Friendship Association and a member of the Vienna City Council was murdered in Vienna by the Abu Nidal group, operating under Syrian aegis.

◆ August 29, 1981: Two terrorists attacked a synagogue in Vienna with machine guns and grenades, killing two people and wounding 19 others. The Abu Nidal group claimed responsibility.

◆ January 4, 1982: The Turkish security authorities announced that the terrorists who in 1979 and 1980 blew up the Iraqi oil pipeline which passes through Turkey had been sent by Syria.

◆ January 11, 1982: An attack on a supermarket in Amman was carried out by personnel from the Syrian Embassy; as a result, the Syrian Third Secretary was expelled.

◆ March 26, 1982: Three Syrians were expelled from West Germany after being arrested there in late February with arms in their possession.

◆ April 24, 1982: An explosive device was detonated next to the offices of a French news agency in Beirut.

Friendship is the only cement that will ever hold the world together.

U.S. President WOODROW WILSON

A West German magazine said today that it had interviewed and photographed a Nazi war criminal in Syria, where he has reportedly been living in exile for three decades. Editors at the Munich-based weekly Bunte *said that two of its reporters spoke at length in Damascus this month with the war criminal, Alois Brunner, a 73-year-old former SS officer who is held responsible for sending more than 120,000 Austrian, German, French, Slovak, and Greek Jews to Nazi death camps.*

JAMES M. MARKHAM,
New York Times,
October 29, 1985

SYRIA: "AMERICA IS THE ENEMY"

A lot of people are happy when [the U.S.] is touched by catastrophe from God. That's because of your stupid policies.

PLO leader AHMED JIBRIL,
speaking with *U.S. News* at Jibril's
headquarters in Damascus, May 22, 1989

Syria considers the Americans to be the devil of the Middle East and the Israelis their agents in the area. Since Israel is an enemy, whoever supports Israel is an enemy as well. Syria, therefore, should do everything possible in order to damage American interests in the area, including killing American citizens and cooperating with the United States' greatest rivals – the communist countries.

Q: How can the relationship between Syria and the U.S.S.R. be defined?
A: As a Syrian newspaper commentary noted in 1980, the Treaty of Friendship and Cooperation, which has anchored the two govern-

ments' recent relationship has created a "strategic alliance between the two great forces of socialism and national liberation." So close are Syrian-Soviet ties that other commentaries call them "a bright point in the regions' sky" and "an example to be an example in relations among countries."

Q: How did Syria identify with the Soviet goals?

A: Syrian leaders have consistently identified with what were Soviet goals. Syria is one of very few states that freely chose to vote at the United Nations in favor of Soviet troops in Afghanistan: More generally, it has concurred with the U.S.S.R. on every significant issue facing the General Assembly in recent years. By contrast, Syria has termed NATO maneuvers in the Mediterranean "provocative" and has seen them as preparations for "war and aggression."

Q: What are the American goals in the Middle East, according to Syria?

A: The United States is seen by Syria to have its own goals in the Middle East – "imperialist hegemony over the Arab homeland" – and support of Israel is regarded not as a cause but as a consequence.

Be not envious of evil men, nor desire to be with them. For their hearts study destruction and their lips talk of mischief.
Proverbs 24:2

The way of the wicked is like darkness, they know not at what they stumble.
Proverbs 4:19

Q: How does Syria view Israel?

A: Israel, indeed, has no real autonomy; the United States can order Israel to do its bidding. Syria's prime minister says that "Israel is a U.S. base," Assad calls it an American "tool," and the newspaper, *Tishrin* terms it the "big stick" of the United States. Israel's "expansionism" serves to soften up the Arabs, to discourage them, and render them ready to capitulate to American wishes.

A report on state-sponsored terrorism prepared for the Senate Subcommittee on Security and Terrorism states: "According to intelligence analysts, the two trucks used in the October 23, 1983, bombing of the U.S. Marine headquarters in Beirut were rigged by Syrian professionals stationed in the Beka'a Valley (Lebanon) and even driven into Beirut along a route guarded by Syrian militias."

White House sources report that American intelligence intercepted the names and ranks of the Syrian officers directly involved in preparing the blow. 241 U.S. Marines died in the incident.

Q: What is the meaning of American-Israeli relations?

A: A Syrian daily concludes, "that the Zionist entity implements aggressive and expansionist action in the region only after total agreement with the U.S. administration." In Syrian parlance, Zionism is but a symptom of imperialism, and they are "two sides of one coin"; if the American influence in the Middle East could be eliminated, the Israeli challenge would be greatly reduced, if not ended.

Q: In light of all this, who, according to Syria, is the source of evil?

A: After the 1982 conflict in Lebanon, the Syrian prime minister stressed that "the war was not merely between Syria and Israel, but between Syria and those behind Israel." The U.S., not Israel, is the "essence of evil." Assad has been quoted as saying that "the United States is the primary enemy."

Q: Did Syria hit American targets in Lebanon?

A: Yes. Top American officials have reached complete agreement that Syria had a major role in the October 1983 bombing of the U.S. Marine barracks in Beirut. Former Secretary of Defense Caspar Weinberger accused the Syrian government of "sponsorship and knowledge and authority" for this crime and Former Secretary of State George Shultz said that "Syria must bear a share of responsibility." President Reagan stated that Syria "facilitates and supplies instruments for terrorist attacks on the people of Lebanon."

Q: Who are the other enemies of Syria?

A: In Syrian opinion, Israel is by no means the only American lackey in the Middle East. The revolt by the Moslem Brotherhood in 1980 was blamed on American agents as well: "The weapons are Israeli, the ammunition from Sadat, the training is Jordanian, and the moral support is from other parties well known for their loyalty to imperialism."

Q: What was Syria's reaction to the murder of Egypt's President Sadat?

A: When Anwar Al-Sadat was killed, Syrian radio broadcast a speech celebrating the event and calling for the death of other Arab "traitors," including King Hussein of Jordan and Saddam Hussein of Iraq.

Q: In light of this, what is the best choice for the Arabs?

A: According to Syria, the Arabs face the following choice: either "submit to a hostile United States or choose a strategic alliance with the friendly Soviet Union."

Q: Has Syria actually threatened the United States?

A: Syrian rulers from time to time explicitly threaten the United States, as when the prime minister asserted in 1980, "If I were able to strike at Washington, I would do so." A 1982 newspaper editorial called on the Arabs to "strike at every type of U.S. interest, to behead the snake." These threats are not idle. There have been repeated attacks against American soldiers and diplomats, perhaps the most spectacular being the Katyusha artillery rocket barrage in May 1983 on Secretary Shultz as he spent the night in the U.S. Ambassador's residence in Beirut.

> *The one who digs a pit shall fall into it.*
>
> Proverbs 26:27

The following cartoon appeared in Egypt's *Sawt El-Arab* on September 13, 1987. It bore the title "Eight Years to the Gulf War." (Note that the inverted "V" is 8 in Arabic.)

● حرب الخليج تدخل عامها الثامن ●

THE MILITARY OPTION
IS THE ONLY OPTION

> *My soul has long dwelt with haters of peace, I am a man of peace, but when I speak, they are for war.*
>
> Psalms 120:6-7

Q: What was Syria's attitude towards the Camp David Accords, the Reagan Plan and the Israeli-Lebanese agreement of May 1983?

A: Syria led the opposition to Egypt's peace treaty with Israel in 1979 and worked against Jordanian acceptance of the 1982 Reagan Plan. It forced the Lebanese government to abrogate the May 1983 agreement with Israel as well.

Q: What is the strategic parity?

A: Assad defines his goal as "strategic parity" with Israel, so that Syria can take on Israel in a one-to-one confrontation. Toward this end, he has increased the regular Syrian army from fewer than 300,000 troops in mid-1982 to 500,000 today and the number of divisions from six to nine.

Q: What is Syria's superiority over Jordan?

A: Former American Secretary of State Shultz noted in congressional testimony: "Syria holds major quantitative advantages over Jordan in personnel (5 to 1), tanks (4 to 1), armored personnel carriers (2.5 to 1), artillery (4 to 1), and combat aircraft (5 to 1)." Assad uses this strength to intimidate the Jordanian government.

Q: Is there a real Syrian threat to Jordan?

A: Syrian troops are deployed along the Jordanian border in times of crisis and sometimes sent into action. In December 1980, Syrian jets attacked locations in central Jordan with impunity. At other times, Assad provided aid to anti-government elements within Jordan, for example encouraging a group of officers in July 1985 to stage a coup d'etat.

Q: Has there been any Syrian threat to King Hussein of Jordan personally?

A: In the past, Syrian planes almost shot down King Hussein's personal plane when it flew over Syrian territory.

Q: What degree of Syrian control is there in Lebanon?

A: Assad has succeeded in extending Syria's hold to most of the territory of Lebanon. This process began in the early 1970s and received a boost with the outbreak of Lebanon's civil war in 1975. In June 1976, Syrian forces entered Lebanon, establishing control over most of the country. Damascus is at present attempting to bring the remaining portions of Lebanon under its dominion.

> *Peace is the highest good to which even the lovers of the world turn all their efforts.*
>
> ERASMUS

Q: What about Syrian-Turkish relations?

A: With respect to Syria's northern neighbor, Turkey, Damascus makes trouble in a number of small ways. It encourages agitation in Hatay, a province of Turkey that borders on Syria and is shown on official Syrian maps as part of Syria.

Q: What other claims does Syria have over Turkey?

A: Syria disputes Turkey's right to control its river waters. As noted earlier, Damascus supports the terrorist Grey Wolves and ASALA, an organization that guns down Turkish diplomats around the world.

Q: Does Syria support the causes of the Soviet bloc?

A: Syria supports all the causes of the Soviet bloc. Here are two small examples. A high ranking North Korean official brought a message from Kim Il-Sung thanking Syria for its "constant support for the Korean people's just struggle to reunite their homeland." An August 1985 cable from Assad to Fidel Castro on the 20th anniversary of diplomatic relations between Syria and Cuba praised the two countries' friendship as beneficial "for the two peoples in their joint struggle against world imperialism and its allies."

Q: What about Syria's relation with other communist countries?

A: Until the recent changes in Eastern Europe, visits, delegations and agreements were by no means restricted to the U.S.S.R. To take a single month as an example, during October 1983 one cooperative agreement was signed by Syria with Bulgaria, Hungary, East Germany, and Poland, and two with Rumania. Five delegations were exchanged.

Q: Who supports the communist parties in the Middle East?

A: In the Middle East, communist parties such as those of Saudi Arabia and Iraq are closely aligned with Damascus. Nearly all Middle East countries ban and persecute the communist party, but in Syria the party is an element in the ruling coalition.

Q: Were Russia and Syria in agreement on most issues?

A: Yes. Both felt betrayed by Sadat of Egypt, both condemned the U.S. sponsored "peace process," both sought to destroy the pro-western orientation of Lebanon. The differences that do exist – over Iraq before the invasion of Kuwait or over Yassir Arafat, for example – are considerable, but they are well within the bounds of what allies can tolerate.

CHAPTER TWENTY-EIGHT

THE GOLAN HEIGHTS

> *The Syrian masses and the whole nation declare, no recognition, no peace and no negotiations with Israel.*
> Radio Damascus, November 17, 1981

SYRIA'S STRONG HOSTILITY TOWARDS ISRAEL

Israeli troops captured the Golan Heights during the 1967 Six-Day War after bitter fighting. For years, Israeli settlements had suffered from Syrian shelling, which caused many casualties and heavy damages. Israel knew that the only way to release her settlements from the Syrian threat was to capture the Golan Heights.

Syria's loss of the Golan Heights occurred when Hafez al-Assad, Syria's president, served as minister of defense. As a result, Assad believes that since he was the one to lose the Golan Heights, he has the moral obligation to recapture it from the Israelis. Many of Assad's rivals and enemies frequently mock him with this expression: *"Assad fi Lubnan waarnab fi al Giulan"* Rhyming in Arabic this expression means: "You, Assad [Assad means lion in Arabic], are a lion in Lebanon, yet a rabbit on the Golan."

> *Blow, o wind of the Jihad [holy war], uproot the children of Zion in the storm and destroy them.*
> Radio Damascus, May 22, 1981

Q: What marked Syria's control of the Golan Heights for 19 years?
A: From 1948 to 1967, the Golan Heights were exploited by Syria to disrupt civilian life in northeastern Israel by shelling the villages of the Hula Valley and sniping at fishermen on the Sea of Galilee.

Q: Who called for peace during this period?

A: Throughout these 19 years, Israel repeatedly called upon the Syrian leadership, as on the other neighboring Arab states, to turn the fragile armistice signed in 1949 into a permanent peace settlement. All of these calls were either flatly rejected or ignored altogether.

Q: What exactly was Syria's reaction to the Israeli calls for peace?

A The Syrian attacks on the Israeli farms and villages continued unabated. The situation reached a point, in June 1967, where Israel was left with no choice but to strike back. Under withering Syrian fire, the Israeli troops scaled the 3,000-foot escarpment of the Golan on June 9, 1967, and engaged the entrenched Syrian forces atop the Heights. After two days of intensive battles, the Golan was in Israeli hands.

Q: What did Israel do after the war?

A: Israel immediately sent signals to all the Arab states that it would be prepared to make substantial withdrawals on all fronts, within the framework of peace negotiations.

Q: What was the reaction of the Arab states?

A: The unanimous Arab answer, given at the notorious Khartoum Summit on September 1, 1967, was the same as before: "No peace with Israel, no recognition of Israel, no negotiations with Israel." This line was to be reiterated by Syrian leaders, with great vigor and persistence, in the years that followed: In October 1973, Syria joined Egypt in a massive surprise attack on Israel – an attack which was beaten back after heavy initial casualties. In November 1977, Egypt announced its readiness to negotiate peace with Israel. The direct talks that ensued led to the conclusion of the Camp David agreements of September 1978 and to the signing of the Israel-Egypt peace treaty of March 1979. Syria rejected the peace treaty.

Q: What was Syria's reaction then?

A: Syria not only refrained from joining the peace process, but placed itself at the forefront of an all-out Arab campaign designed to stymie that process.

There is no rule of international law which requires a lawful military occupant, in this situation, to wait forever before putting the control and government of the territory on a permanent basis. Many international lawyers have wondered, indeed, at the long-suffering patience which led Israel to wait as long as she did before establishing that permanent basis.

JULIUS STONE,
California Hastings College of Law

Q: What was Israel's reaction to Syria's hostility?

A: On December 14, 1981, the Knesset applied the law, jurisdiction, and administration of Israel to the Golan Heights – a move that, by normal criteria of international behavior, was long overdue.

Q: Was the Knesset law proper?

A: Absolutely. Modern history is full of examples of nations altering their borders as a result of victory in war, not to mention wars which they did not initiate. Usually, such changes are ratified in the peace treaties that normally follow these wars.

Q: Does Syria have rights on the Golan?

A: Syria's abnormal behavior over the years – its inveterate belligerence and its longstanding politicidal designs against Israel – bestows no right upon it to maintain a permanent stranglehold on the possibility of normal life in an area that is vital to Israel's security.

> *Before 1967 the Syrian gunners were up on the plateau; their guns could deal death up to a range of 20 miles. No fishing was then possible on the Sea of Galilee, farmers had armour-plating on their tractors and children slept in shelters at night.*
> JOHN BULLOCH, Middle East correspondent,
> *Daily Telegraph*
> June 1, 1973

Q: The Israeli Golan Heights Law, passed on December 14, 1981, extends Israeli civilian law and administration to the residents of the Golan. This is instead of the military rule that had been in effect on the Golan since 1967. Is this in line with Security Council Resolution 242?

A: Security Council Resolution 242 stressed the need for "secure and recognized boundaries." The former armistice demarcation lines between Israel and Syria were in no sense boundaries, and they certainly were neither secure nor recognized. Ambassador Arthur Goldberg, on November 15, 1967, told the Security Council: "Historically there have never been secure or recognized boundaries in the area. Neither the armistice lines of 1949 nor the cease-fire lines of 1967 have answered that description . . . Now such boundaries have yet to be agreed upon."

THE GOLAN HEIGHTS: DATA AND HISTORY

The Golan was the biblical home of the tribe of Menasseh. During the Hellenistic period, the Maccabeans protected the numerous Jewish towns and villages in the Golan from marauders. In the revolt against the Romans, Josephus commanded the defense of northern Israel from the town of Gamla on the Golan.

The history of Jewish habitation on the Golan Heights continued through Byzantine times, until the end of the eleventh century. Jewish farming attempts resumed there in the 1880s and continued for some 40 years. In 1967, the Jewish presence on the plateau was re-established, with the founding of a network of farming villages, many on the sites of ancient Jewish towns.

> . . . to speak of co-existence with Israel would be tantamount to granting Israel legitimacy. And talk of withdrawal to the 1967 lines would be tantamount to recognizing Israel's right to four-fifths of Palestine.
>
> Syrian Foreign Minister ABD AL-HALIM KHADDAM, Arab League Summit at Fez, November 1981
>
> ---
>
> The people of Syria are Allah's lash in His land. He wreaks His vengeance through them against whomsoever He wishes among His slaves. It is unthinkable that those who are double faced among them should prosper over the faithful. They will certainly die out of grief and desperation.
>
> The Islamic holy Hadith

Q: What was the percentage of the Golan Heights of Syria?
A: The Golan Heights is only 0.5 percent of Syria's 71,498 square miles.

> A few months before the 1967 war, I was visiting Galilee, and at regular intervals the Russian-built forts on the Golan Heights used to lob shells into the villages, often claiming civilian casualties. Any future pattern for a settlement must clearly put a stop to that kind of offensive action.
>
> Sir ALEC DOUGLAS-HOME, former prime minister of England, *Daily Mail*, April 22, 1974

Q: What is the size of the Golan Heights?
A: The Golan is a small plateau 45 miles long, less than 16 miles wide and totaling only about 450 square miles. The strategic importance of the Golan Heights is out of all proportion to their size.
Q: What is its altitude?
A: Ranging in altitude from nearly 2,000 to about 3,000 feet above sea level, the Golan overlooks and controls the Sea of Galilee and the Hula Valley.

> *Palestine precedes the Golan.*
> Syrian President HAFEZ AL-ASSAD,
> April 11, 1981

Q: Who resides on the Golan?
A: The population of the region consists of Druze living in four villages, some Alawites in one village, and Jews living in one town and villages. The main source of income of Golan residents is agriculture. There is also some light industry.
Q: Is the Golan an integral part of Syria?
A: Most of the Golan was originally included in the territory of British mandatory Palestine after World War I. However, as a part of a division of colonial spheres of influence in San Remo in 1923, the British transferred it to France, which then had the mandate over Syria.
Q: What was the Golan considered prior to the 1967 war?
A: Prior to the 1967 war, Syria regarded the area as strictly a military zone and had gravely neglected civilian needs. Most homes had no running water or electricity. School attendance was sporadic at best. 70 percent of the workers were unskilled. Wages were low, welfare services non-existent, and agriculture primitive.

> *Syria will speak to Israel in the language of iron and fire.*
> Radio Damascus, December 22, 1980

Q: What has happened on the Golan since 1967?
A: Do you know that:
(1) Since June 1967, Israel has either connected the Golan villages to its electricity grid or equipped them with modern generators, and has piped in running water?
(2) Education is now free and compulsory till the end of the ninth grade. New schools have been built, with books and supplies provided free of charge?

(3) Israeli social welfare and national insurance benefits – including medical insurance, three-month paid maternity leave and old age pensions – have been extended to the region?

(4) Agriculture and construction have flourished, health care improved and living standards in general have risen dramatically?

(5) Religious freedom has replaced the Syrian restrictions on gatherings at Druze shrines and the Druze are now free to conduct their own religious and personal affairs?

On May 31, 1974, Israel and Syria signed a Disengagement Agreement. Israel agreed to evacuate part of the Golan Heights and security arrangements were put into effect. At that time, Syria confirmed that ". . . this agreement . . . is a step towards a just and durable peace on the basis of Security Council Resolution 338 dated October 22, 1973." In reality, Syria was reluctant to continue the peace process. After repeated declarations by high-ranking Syrian officials that Syria would never make peace with Israel, the Israeli Parliament passed the Golan Heights Law on December 14, 1981, extending Israeli law and administration to the residents of the Heights.

Israel is a foreign growth in the Arab nation and the entire region.

Syrian President HAFEZ AL-ASSAD,
Radio Damascus, January 14, 1981

Our nation chose the road of conflict with the Zionist enemy and we shall continue on this road whatever be the difficulties or sacrifices.

MUSTAFA TLASS,
Syrian Defense Minister,
Radio Damascus, October 20, 1981

THE GOLAN HEIGHTS: STRATEGIC IMPORTANCE

✦ Do you know that Syria has always been the most intransigent of Israel's enemies? As far back as 1947, the Syrian army attacked Jewish farming villages in the Hula Valley. In May 1948, Syria was among the Arab countries that invaded the newly established state and Syrian guns on the Golan wrought havoc on the agricultural communities below.

Do you know that after the war of 1948, Syria was the last of the four countries bordering Israel to sign an armistice? Soon after, it flagrantly violated that agreement when the Syrian army took Al-Hama, in the demilitarized zone, in 1951, as well as by its continued attacks on Israeli civilian life in the valley. Moreover, Syria insisted that ceasefire lines are not permanent borders.

Do you know that between 1948 and 1967, frequent Syrian artillery shelling from the Golan Heights made life in Israel's Hula Valley villages virtually unbearable? A full generation of children grew up in shelters, under the shadow of the Syrian guns.

Do you know that beginning in 1964, Syria tried to cut off Israel's principal source of water by attempting to divert the headwaters of the Jordan River, which flow into the Sea of Galilee?

> *With joy shall ye draw water . . .*
>
> Isaiah 12:3

Do you know that Syria was also one of the main sponsors of the PLO terrorist organization, to which it provided political backing, financial support, military equipment, training facilities, and logistics support? Do you know that Syria has even established its own terrorist faction within the PLO, As-Saika, which is under the direct control of the Syrian army?

Do you know that Syria was the last Arab state to accept Resolution 242?

Do you know that in June 1980, the Syrian government gave its unqualified support to the Damascus conference of the PLO's Fatah faction, which called for an armed struggle aimed at "the liquidation of the Zionist entity, economically, politically, militarily, culturally, and ideologically"?

> *On behalf of all the Arab delegations . . . we now confirm, as we have stated in the past, our non-recognition of the State of Israel . . . That denial of recognition to that state should be reaffirmed time and time again . . .*
> GEORGE TOMEH, Syrian representative
> to the United Nations General Assembly,
> July 17, 1967

Q: What was the Golan Heights before 1967?

A: Prior to the June 1967 War, the Golan Heights was one of the most massively fortified regions in the world. The terrain was covered by extensive minefields and by three solid lines of heavily armed concrete bunkers connected by trenches. The ascent from the Israeli side was steep and difficult, and anyone attempting it was exposed to heavy Syrian fire from the mountain tops.

Q: When was the Golan captured?

A: On June 9, 1967, Israel launched the counter-attack that finally put an end to the Syrian menace atop the Heights.

Q: What were Syria's true intentions?

A: Among the Syrian Army documents captured there were maps detailing an operational plan for the conquest of northern Israel, up to Haifa. Clear evidence was also found that Soviet military advisers had been stationed in forward positions on the Heights.

> *. . . even if the PLO recognizes Israel, Syria will not be able to recognize it.*
> Syrian President HAFEZ AL-ASSAD,
> *Al-Ra'i Al-'amm,* Kuwait, December 13, 1981

Q: What was the size of Syrian military power in 1973?

A: By the outbreak of the 1973 Yom Kippur War, Syria had increased its tank inventory nearly eightfold, to 2,000; its air force numbered almost 400 combat aircraft; it had 5 armored and mechanized divisions, 34 surface-to-air missile batteries and 1,200 artillery pieces.

Q: What was the meaning of Israeli presence on the Golan ?

A: It was only Israeli control of the Heights, at the outset of that surprise invasion of 1973, which prevented the Syrians from penetrating deep into Israeli territory and wreaking untold havoc and casualties on Israel's civilian population.

> *The map that the Arabs are presenting to Israel includes not only Jerusalem, Nablus, Gaza, Sinai, and the Golan – but, first and foremost, Tel Aviv, Haifa, Jaffa, and Nazareth. In other words, the Arabs are not merely demanding to get back the West Bank and the Gaza Strip, as Palestinian soil; rather, they are demanding their rights throughout their occupied land since 1948. The slogan "the restoration of the Palestinian people's rights" has found a more favorable reception, at the international level and in world public opinion, than the slogan "the liberation of Palestine" – meaning the liquidation of Israel. It must be noted, however, that these two slogans mean one and the same thing.*
>
> Radio Damascus, government-controlled
> broadcasting station, December 22, 1976

Q: Why is Israel unable to give up the Golan Heights?
A: The fact that some of Israel's main water sources, such as the Banyas River, originate on the Golan Heights is a crucial geophysical factor.

ISRAEL MOVES TOWARDS PEACE, SYRIA MOVES TOWARDS WAR

> *My soul has long dwelt with haters of peace. Whenever I speak about peace, they prepare for war.*
>
> Psalms 120:6.7

At the end of the Yom Kippur War, Israeli and Egyptian negotiators sat together in a tent at Kilometer 101 on the road to Cairo and worked out a disengagement agreement, signed on January 18, 1974. In spite of the general ceasefire that was in effect, Syria began shelling Israeli army positions and villages on the Golan Heights. More than one thousand violations of the ceasefire were recorded, before a disengagement agreement was finally worked out between Israel and Syria in May 1974.

Under that accord, the IDF, a mere 25 miles from Damascus, withdrew not only from all the territory it had taken in its Yom Kippur War counter-attack, but also, as a good-will gesture, pulled back from the Golan town of Kuneitra and the dominating hills surrounding it, to allow the Syrians to repopulate it. Israel also agreed to withdraw from the strategically important Rafid Junction.

Q: What was Syria's response to this Israeli gesture?
A: Syria responded by refusing to attend the Geneva Peace conference, where the disengagement agreement was to be signed on May 31, 1974. Instead it authorized the Egyptian delegation to sign for it.

We are not concerned merely with the Golan or the West Bank. There is a matter of basic principle connected with the presence of the Zionist entity in the Arab homeland . The problem must be viewed as part of the overall struggle with the Zionist foe. And the Arab nation will retrieve every inch of territory in and outside Palestine.

Syrian Foreign Minister KHADDAM,
Al-Raya, Qatar, September 13, 1980

Let the Arab nation strike at and purify its ranks of them [Israeli agents] when the national consciousness will reign amongst the Arabs . . . then Israel's Torah and existence will come to an end.

Al-Thawra, official Syrian newspaper,
May 10, 1980

Q: What happened in Kuneitra?
A: The Syrians, in violation of their own demand and commitment prevented the return of Kuneitra's population and turned the town into an anti-Israel propaganda monument, to which it has been bringing foreign diplomats and journalists to tour its war-torn ruins.
Q: What has Syria done since 1973?
A: Damascus has been engaged in a massive program to upgrade its armed forces, both qualitatively and quantitatively.
Q: Is Syrian hostility directed against Israel alone?
A: No. The ideological underpinnings of the ruling Ba'ath party call for a "Greater Syria" including Jordan, Lebanon, and "Palestine." The Syrians invaded Jordan in 1970 and threatened to do so again in 1980. They also invaded Lebanon in 1976 and now control most of that country.
Q: What was Syria's reaction to Sadat's peace initiative?
A: Since 1977, when Egypt set out to negotiate peace with Israel, Syria has been one of the leading and most outspoken members of the Arab "rejection front," again and again reiterating its total opposition to all Israeli peace overtures.

Q: What was Syria's reaction to the Camp David Accords?

A: Since the signing of the Camp David Accords between Israel and Egypt, Syria has expanded and reorganized its armed forces, to provide them with a more offensive orientation. This aggressive posture is expressed in the enhanced mobility and firepower of its armored and mechanized forces; improved logistics capability; and an increase in the number of surface-to-air missiles, commando units, helicopter gunships, and surface-to-surface missiles.

Q: What is the Syrian goal?

A: Syria's goal is to reach a military strategic balance with Israel in order to have a chance at victory in the next war that Syria may decide to initiate.

Where is Numayri, the Falasha merchant, who sold his people and nation for money and acted as a broker to smuggle Falasha Jews to Palestine? Where is Al-Sadat, who sold Egypt and its decision-making? He signed the document of submission and submissively and obediently handed it over to the Zionist diehards so they could make Egypt a Zionist protectorate. There is no Numayri now because the Sudanese people toppled him and are pursuing him. There is no al-Sadat now because he could not stand in the face of the Egyptian people. Al-Sadat wanted, in signing the document of submission in Camp David, to humiliate this people but failed. Al-Sadat faced his harsh judgement, but the Egyptian masses will continue their struggle to wipe out the effects of the capitulation deal.

Syrian President HAFEZ AL-ASSAD,
inaugurating the newly elected
People's Assembly, February 27, 1986, Damascus

All Arab resources should be channeled against the Zionist enemy.

Syrian Foreign Minister
ABD AL-HALIM KHADDAM,
Radio Damascus, January 13, 1981

THE GOLAN: PAST AND PRESENT

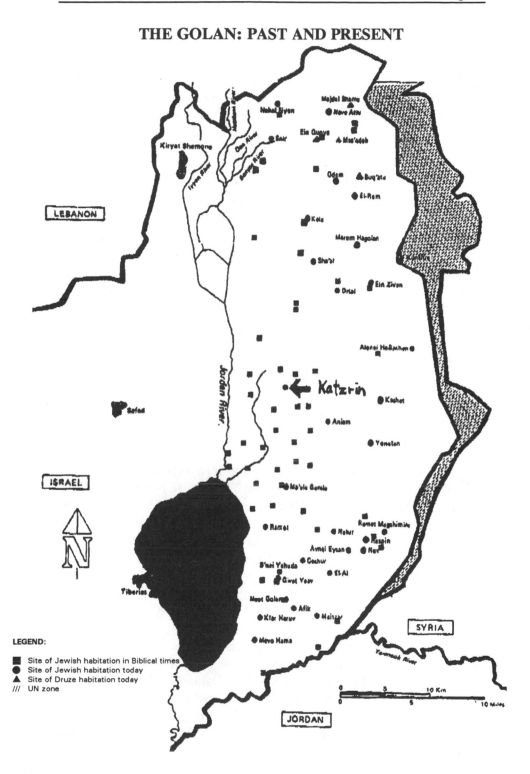

LEGEND:

■ Site of Jewish habitation in Biblical times
● Site of Jewish habitation today
▲ Site of Druze habitation today
/// UN zone

CHAPTER TWENTY-NINE

THE CONCEPT OF A "GREATER SYRIA"

> *It is common knowledge that Palestine is nothing but southern Syria.*
>
> AHMED SHUKAIRY,
> then-Saudi Arabian delegate
> to the UN, founder of the PLO,
> May 31, 1956, to the Security Council
>
> ---
>
> *Palestine is a basic part of Southern Syria.*
> Syrian President HAFEZ AL-ASSAD,
> *New York Times* March 9, 1974

The concept of "Greater Syria" (in Arabic: *Syryya Alkubrah*) is very popular among Syrian nationalists. The goal is that Syria will include Jordan, Israel, and Lebanon of today. Syria never had an ambassador in Lebanon and never permitted the Lebanese to have an ambassador in Damascus for this very reason – Syria believes that Lebanon is an integral part of Syria. The strong Syrian involvement in the Palestinian dilemma derives from the Syrian belief that Palestine on both banks of the Jordan River (namely, Israel and Jordan today) is also an integral part of Syria.

Q: What is Syrian President Assad's dream?
A: If Assad could dominate not only Lebanon but Israel and Jordan as well, he would not only restore to Damascus the glory of the Umayyad era (661-750 CE), but he would find himself at the summit of the Arab world, a position held in the past by Egypt's Gamal Abdel Nasser for a certain period of his life. This possibility should not be underestimated.

Q: What is the root of the name "Syria"?

A: The name is Hellenistic and was used by the Arab Moslem conquerors of the Middle East for a brief period in the early seventh century.

Q: Are there any other names?

A: Yes. The name Balad El-Sham, or Dar El-Sham, was used by the Arab Caliphs of the House of Umayya (661-750 CE).

Q: What were the borders of Balad El-Sham?

A: The Taurus Mountains (northern Syria), Hedjaz (now part of Saudi Arabia), the Gulf of Aqaba, and the Sinai peninsula in the south, the land of the Euphrates and the Tigris (roughly modern – day Iraq) in the east, and the land to the Mediterranean (modern-day Syria) in the west.

Q: What can be said about the French name, "La Syrie intégrale"?

A: According to one view developed mainly by local Christians and French writers, "Greater Syria" was defined as a geographic non-Arab entity that should be set up as a French protectorate.

Q: What do the Syrian leaders think today?

A: Syrian President Hafez al-Assad stated on March 8, 1974: "Palestine is not merely part of the Arab homeland, but is the main part of Southern Syria."

Q: Are there any other Syrian declarations?

A: Yes. In Damascus on May 24, 1978, a close advisor to Assad declared: "The citizenry of Syria regards Palestine as southern Syria and the Palestine citizenry regards Syria as northern Palestine . . . "

Q: What do the Palestinians think about "Greater Syria"?

A: The Palestinian representatives after the First World War spoke about Palestine as part of "Greater Syria." They used the term, "Surya Al Gianubia" – Southern Syria.

Q: Are there any historical facts with regards to the concept of a greater Syria?

A: From 1831 to 1840, Syria and Palestine were briefly under the rule of Ibrahim Pasha of Egypt. This experience contributed to the development of the "Greater Syria" concept.

Historically, Syria and Lebanon are one country.
Radio Damascus, July 20, 1976

CHAPTER THIRTY

THE FERTILE CRESCENT (SYRIA) VIS-A-VIS THE NILE (EGYPT)

> *He knows to give some, to get some . . . He is a master chess player.*
>
> a Western diplomat's description
> of Syrian President Assad
>
> ---
>
> *He is very patient, very astute, very persistent . . . He gives himself the time to think and he moves cautiously. But he is very determined. He knows how to block other initiatives, by force if necessary, and draws strength from that.*
>
> an Arab diplomat, about Hafez al-Assad
> *New York Times,*
> July 23, 1989

Q: What are the issues that may cause Assad discomfort?

A: The possibility of an Israeli-Palestinian dialogue that would exclude Syria and its demand for the return of the Golan Heights.

Q: What is Syria's thesis concerning strategic balance?

A: Assad believes that Israel's force can only be met by force. Therefore, Syria must reach a strategic balance with Israel. Namely, Syria's military power must be enough to challenge Israel. This goal has not been attained.

Q: What are the difficulties facing Syria and preventing her from achieving a strategic balance with Israel?

A: The Soviet Union, Syria's arms supplier, has urged President Assad to end his dispute with Arafat and told him it would not supply the necessary offensive weaponry in order to achieve strategic parity with Israel.

Q: What is another difficulty facing Syria?

A: Egypt has re-emerged as the focus of a moderate Arab consensus that excludes Syria.

Q: What are the roots of the controversy between Egypt and Syria?

A: There is the traditional rivalry between the Fertile Crescent (Syria) and the Nile (Egypt). Both countries, one in the north and the other in the south, seek the leadership of the Arab world.

Q: What sharpened the controversy?

A: The fact that the late President Sadat of Egypt accepted the ceasefire in October 1973 without the consent of Syria, which fought with Egypt against Israel in the Yom Kippur War, sharpened the controversy between the two countries.

Q: What other issues heightened the tension between the two countries?

A: Egypt's Sadat signed the first and second interim agreements in 1974 and 1975 respectively and finally signed a formal peace treaty with Israel, once again without consulting Syria and despite her bitter opposition.

Q: What are Syria's difficulties in Lebanon?

A: The inability of Syria to bring Lebanon under her control.

Q: How could the Syrian regime last so long (since 1970)?

A: The answer lies partly in the fact that this is a repressive regime. The State Department and Amnesty International reports draw a picture of arbitrary arrests, torture and political executions (*New York Times,* July 23, 1989).

Q: What can be said about Assad?

A: As a member of Syria's once denigrated Alawite minority, which comprises roughly twelve percent of the total population, Syrian President Assad has surrounded himself with loyalists from the same sect as an offshoot of the Shi'ite Islam.

Q: What is Syria's attitude towards the internal strife in Lebanon?

A: Syria is interested in preventing any single group from achieving dominance in Lebanon which would be beyond Syrian control.

Q: Why is Syria against Arafat?

A: President Assad believes that Arafat is "too independent." The PLO chairman does not listen to Syria's advice and, therefore, Arafat is an obstacle to Syria.

Q: How does Syria aid anti-Arafat groups?

A: The Syrian leader continues to arm many factions ready to pursue his opposition to the PLO chairman, Yassir Arafat.

Q: What is Assad's problem today?

A: Despite the Syrian opposition, the PLO in general, and Arafat in particular, have gained power and prestige due to the Palestinian uprising in Judea and Samaria.

> *Sometimes the wind blows in the direction the ships do not want to go.*
>
> Palestinian saying

Q: When was the real involvement of Syria in Lebanon?

A: Since 1976, Syria has kept up to 40,000 troops in Lebanon with the goal of preventing the country from falling under the influence of any other Arab country or Israel.

Q: Who is backing the anti-Syrian forces in Lebanon?

A: The greatest supporter is Iraq. Iraq wants revenge against Syria for supporting Iran's Khomeini and his eight-year war against Iraq.

Q: What is Syria's problem in Lebanon today (1990)?

A: Syria, even with her 40,000 troops, cannot impose full control over Lebanon.

Q: Why is Syria seeking the leadership of the Arab world?

A: Syria is recognized as the birthplace of other broad concepts. The ideology of pan-Arab nationalism developed in Syria, as did much of the anti-Zionist theory. Arab socialism was the product of the Syrian Ba'ath Party. Syria is the country with the glorious past of the Umayyads' Dynasty.

CHAPTER THIRTY-ONE

IS SYRIA MOVING TOWARDS
A REALISTIC POLICY
VIS-A-VIS ISRAEL?

Syria, whose record of execution, torture, imprisonment of its own citizens, and in peacetime, could and does fill volumes but still has not been told in full?

Syria? You mean he [relating to Mr. Jimmy Carter's visit to Syria in March 1990] had just come from Syria, which year after year has been host, trainer and paymaster to one of the most murderous gangs of terrorists on earth – the Popular Front for the Liberation of Palestine, General Command? The gang every anti-terrorist specialist believes bombed Pan Am 103 out of the sky and 270 people out of their lives?

A. M. ROSENTHAL,
New York Times,
March 25, 1990

Various and different analysts, visitors, and political leaders return to their home countries with optimistic news from their recent visits to Damascus, their subsequent meetings with the Syrian President, Hafez al-Assad. In March 1990, former American president Jimmy Carter said in Tel Aviv after his visit to Syria that the Syrian leader is willing to seek a political solution to the conflict with Israel.

Q: Has Syria changed its policy towards Egypt?

A: Yes. Syria, which only twelve years ago bitterly opposed Sadat's peace initiative and subsequently cut off her diplomatic relations with Egypt, has since renewed her diplomatic relations with Egypt in 1990.

Q: Why did Syria oppose the Camp David Agreements?

A: President Assad's war against the Camp David Accords was a matter of principle and practice. It was to him an ideological anathema and an obstacle to Syria's efforts to regain the Golan Heights its way. (See the Chapter about the Fertile Crescent.)

Q: Is there any other reason?

A: Yes. Egypt, which was excommunicated by the Arab states after signing the Camp David Agreement in 1979, has returned to the Arab League and the Arab world over the years. Arab states have renewed their diplomatic relations with Egypt and the Syrian president found himself in splendid isolation in the Arab world in the last few years.

Q: What was Egyptian President Mubarak's policy following the death of Sadat?

A: Mubarak, who served under Sadat as his vice-president, has followed Sadat's policy. After Sadat's assassination, Mubarak has maintained the essence of Sadat's policy while at the same time removing some of the acrimony and much of his personal stamp. Mubarak succeeded in achieving Egypt's readmittance into the Arab world without abrogating its peace treaty with Israel. This kept him in conflict with Assad, who persisted in his own war against the Camp David Agreements and all that they represented.

Q: What happened in the 1980s?

A: By the end of the 1980s, it became apparent that Mubarak was winning. More and more Arab states renewed their relations with Egypt culminating in May 1989, when Egypt was formally invited to renew its participation in Arab summits and the Arab League. Powerless to stem the tide, Assad has joined the other Arab states by initiating its own rapprochement with Egypt.

Q: What are other problems facing Assad that might have caused his turnabout?

A: Assad's decision to change his policy towards Egypt reflects a sense of weakness and isolation. Syria has been troubled by domestic problems and economic crises, the burden of Lebanon, Iraqi hostility, and differences with Turkey over water.

Q: Why did Iraq resent Syria?

A: The answer is simple: Syria supported Iran rather than Iraq in the bitter war against each other which lasted about eight years.

Q: Why did Syria oppose Arafat and the PLO?

A: Syria acted against the PLO as a result of the Syrian belief that Arafat was conducting policy contradictory to the interests of Syria in Lebanon.

Q: Has Soviet policy undergone any changes in the Middle East?

A: To a certain degree the answer is in the affirmative. Moscow continues to provide sophisticated weapon systems to Syria, but has pursued policies that Syria resents, such as improvement of relations with Israel, support of the PLO, and support of the idea of an Israeli-Palestinian settlement.

Q: What is the Soviet view of the Syrian-Israeli dispute?

A: Whereas the Soviets view the supply of weapon systems to Syria as necessary for preserving the essence of the patron-client relationship, they also realize that a potential Syrian-Israeli war could jeopardize their new foreign policy.

Q: What is the Russian attitude towards the Syrian doctrine of strategic parity?

A: The Russian ambassador in Damascus said in November of 1989 that the Soviet Union took exception to the Syrian doctrine of strategic parity with Israel.

Q: What are the signs of the changes in Syrian policy?

A: By renewing diplomatic relations with Egypt, Syria unwillingly accepted de facto the Camp David Agreements and got close to the Egyptian president.

Q: What were the main obstacles to some political settlement between Israel and Syria?

A: Syria is still the leader of the Arab "rejection front" and is known for her fanaticism against Israel. For 23 years, formidable obstacles have militated against a Syrian-Israeli settlement. They are the Golan Heights issue, Syria's insistence on linking the issue to the Palestinian question, Moscow's support for Syria and its search for a formal role in the settlement process. Most, if not all these difficulties remain today.

Q: Despite the Syrian difficulties, might Syria after all follow the road to peace?

A: Knowing the radical Syrians, one finds it almost impossible to be optimistic. Syrian policy is based on a very strong conviction that Israel should not exist in the area. Such strong convictions cannot disappear easily. However, Israel should be alert to more changes if and when they occur at some future time.

PART X

ABOUT LEBANON, JORDAN, SAUDI ARABIA – AND ISRAEL'S SECURITY

CHAPTER THIRTY-TWO

FOURTEEN YEARS OF CHAOS IN LEBANON – 1975-89

In the Lebanese war dictionary, we read the following words: "... out of a population of three million inhabitants, more than 100,000 [have been] killed, more than 300,000 wounded and almost half of the population uprooted from its homes ..." The were spoken by Bashir Gamayel in an ABC-TV interview on July 19, 1982, describing the results of PLO terror. Gemayel, President-elect of Lebanon, was assassinated shortly after.

Appearing before the United Nations on November 13, 1974, Yassir Arafat told the UN Assembly that the PLO will establish in Palestine a secular democratic state and that in this state Jews, Moslems and Christians would live in peace and harmony. A few months after this bombastic declaration, in April 1975, the PLO forces joined the Moslem factions in Lebanon in their war against the Christian factions. PLO intervention in Lebanon ruined the sovereignty of Lebanon, caused the death and injury or emigration of hundreds of thousands of Lebanese, and literally wrought havoc in Lebanon. This is the meaning of "democracy" Arafat style:

✦ April 1975: The beginning of the Lebanese civil war. War erupted when a group of Palestinians attacked a group of Christians. In retaliation, the Christian Phalangists attacked Moslem passengers on a bus.
✦ May 1975: Prime Minister Rashid Al Sulch resigned and Rashid Karame, pro-Syrian, took office.
✦ September 1975: An Arab reconciliation committee was established. The committee failed.
✦ October 1975: The pro-Syrian president, Suleiman Franjieh, could not put an end to the civil strife in Lebanon.

◆ January 1976: The PLO intervened in favor of the Moslems and against the Christians.

◆ May-June 1976: Syria sent 40,000 troops into Lebanon. They supported the Christians. The Christians conducted mass murder in the Palestinian refugee camp of Tal Al Za'tar. The beginning of Israeli-Christian contacts. Syria was unhappy about this development.

◆ March 1977: Syrian intelligence murdered the Druze leader, Kamal Jumblat. Other Lebanese leaders were executed. The area of southern Lebanon became an area of battle between the Palestinians and the Israelis.

July 1977: An agreement was signed in the town of Shtura in the Lebanese Valley. The agreement limited the quantities of weapons in the hands of the various militias, asked for the return of the Palestinians to certain areas, putting the Lebanese army as a buffer zone between the Palestinians and the Christians.

March 1978: Battles in Beirut and southern Lebanon as a result of Palestinian terrorist action against an Israeli bus on the coastal road. Israel infiltrated southern Lebanon in an operation later termed "Operation Litani."

◆ June 1978: Israeli withdrawal from southern Lebanon. The establishment of a security belt in southern Lebanon. Major Saad Haddad was appointed commander of the southern Lebanon army.

◆ April 1979: Saad Haddad declared that the territories under his command are "The Lebanese Free State."

July 1980: After a bitter fight, Bashir Gemayel united the divided Christian Lebanese militias, captured the city of Zahla in the valley and irritated the Syrians.

April 1981: Bitter fights between the Christians and the Syrians in Beirut. The Palestinians and Syrians seized Zahla. The Syrians claimed that Zahla, an eastern town between Beirut and southern Lebanon, is needed in order to protect their forces against Israeli aggression.

June 1981: As a result of the mediation of the American diplomat, Philip Habib, the Syrians ended their siege of Zahla. The Lebanese army took the positions of the Christian militias.

June 1982: Israel started the operation "Peace for Galilee."

August 1982: Bashir Gemayel was elected president of Lebanon.

September 1982: Bashir Gemayel was assassinated in an explosion planned and carried out by the Syrian intelligence. The Palestinian terrorists were forced to leave Beirut. Israeli forces enter Beirut. Palestinians are massacred in Sabra and Shatila by the Christians. Amin Gemayel was elected president in place of his brother, who had been murdered the month before. The beginning of the Lebanese, pro-Iranian, religious party Hizballah.

✦ May 1983: Under the mediation of the United States, Lebanon and Israel signed a peace treaty on May 17, 1983.

✦ September 1983: The war between the Druze and the Christians in the Shuf area.

✦ March 1984: As a result of Major Saad Haddad's death, General Antoine Lahad took power and command of the southern Lebanese army.

✦ March 1984: Lebanese president, Amin Gemayel, under severe Syrian pressure, canceled the Israeli-Lebanese peace treaty of May 17, 1983.

✦ June 1987: An abortive attempt on the life of premier Rashid Karame.

✦ August 1988: Unsuccessful attempts to elect a president in Lebanon instead of Amin Gemayel.

✦ September 1988: Iraq's intervention. Iraq supplies weapons to the Christians.

✦ October 1988: General Michel Aoun is declared prime minister of Lebanon. Syria declares that the only legal prime minister is Salim Al Chus.

✦ February 1989: General Aoun defeated the forces of Samir Ja'ja', commander of the Phalangia and recruited them into his own forces.

✦ March 1989: Michel Aoun declared an independent war against the Syrian occupiers.

✦ March-August 1989: Bitter fighting between the Christians on one hand and the Syrians and their supporters on the other hand. Thousands were killed or wounded, hundreds of thousands fled from Beirut.

✦ August 1989: The UN Security Council called upon all the sides involved to cease fire. The battles continued. Syria suffers from isolation.

✦ September 23, 1989: All the warring forces agreed to a ceasefire. The residents of Beirut returned to their homes. Beirut International Airport is reopened and the Moslems and Christians agreed to convene the parliament in order to elect a president.

✦ October 1989: The members of the Lebanese parliament met in Taif, Saudi Arabia, and came to an agreement about the distribution of power among the different warring groups in Lebanon and to elect a new president. After a few days of negotiations, they came out with the following recommendations: The presidency will remain in Christian hands, yet the authority of the president would be limited. The Moslem prime minister would be in charge of fulfilling Lebanese policy and would appoint his own cabinet ministers. The cabinet would be in charge of the governmental authorities, including the army. There would be a new parliament with 108 instead of the 89 members of today. Half of the members are to be Christian and half Moslem. The agreement speaks about putting an end to the ethnic structure of Lebanese politics. General Aoun, the Christian prime minister of Lebanon, rejected the proposals because they failed to mention the removal of the Syrians from Lebanon.

◆ November 1989: A new president was elected – René Awwad. A few short weeks after his election, he was assassinated. In this same month, a new president was elected – Elias Ramlawi.

CHAPTER THIRTY-THREE

JORDAN – HISTORICAL SPOTLIGHTS, 1920-89

> *The Jordanian Kingdom must become the Palestinian former Republic.*
>
> AHMAD SHUKEIRY,
> former PLO chairman,
> November 1966
>
> ---
>
> *The struggle of the national Jordanian front will continue until we establish a democratic regime element in Jordan.*
>
> YASSIR ARAFAT,
> *Le Monde,* January 7, 1975

1920: The Syrian Congress crowned Feisal, Hussein's great uncle (brother to his grandfather, Abdullah) in Syria and Abdullah in Iraq. Both brothers were born in Mecca. Both cooperated with the British in kicking out the Ottoman Turks from Hejaz (Saudi Arabia of today) during the First World War. The Hashemite efforts to help the British are known as the Arab Revolt.

1921: Feisal was kicked out of Syria by the French (Syria was under the French Mandate). Great Britain appointed Feisal King of Iraq, when in reality Abdullah was meant to be the King of Iraq. The British, in order to compensate Abdullah, appointed him the ruler of Transjordan for a six-month period with an option to become king. Transjordan was meant to be a part of the Jewish national home and had been previously promised to the Jewish people.

1922: Abdullah became the Emir of Transjordan, the east side of Palestine. Transjordan remained under the British mandate just like the west side.

1946: Abdullah was declared the King of Transjordan. He intended to call his kingdom "Palestine," yet under British pressure he avoided that.

> *Jordan is ours, Palestine is ours and we will build our national identity on all this area after it will be released from the Zionist presence and the presence of reactionist traitor [Hussein].*
> YASSIR ARAFAT,
> *Washington Post,* December 11, 1974

1948: Jordan participated in a war of aggression against the newly established State of Israel. Jordan captured Judea and Samaria and East Jerusalem. These areas were meant to be a second Palestinian Arab state, according to the UN Partition Plan of November 29, 1947.

1950: Jordan annexed Judea and Samaria and granted the Palestinians Jordanian citizenship.

1951: Abdullah was murdered by a Palestinian in Jerusalem. The Palestinian considered Abdullah a foreign element in Palestine.

1953: Talal, Abdullah's son, was declared insane and his son, Hussein, was declared King of Jordan.

1955: Hussein distributed land to the Bedouin tribes that had come to Jordan from Mecca with his grandfather, Abdullah. Hussein trusted them and based the security of his kingdom upon them.

April 25, 1957: After several aborted attempts on his life, and after a consistently long period of unrest in Jordan, Hussein declared a military regime. His cousin, Feisal – the second king of Iraq – sent Iraqi troops to Jordan to assist Hussein.

February 14, 1958: Both cousins, Hussein and Feisal the Second, the grandsons of the two brothers Abdullah and Feisal, respectively, established the United Kingdom of Jordan and Iraq. The purpose was to strengthen the hold of the Hashemites in both countries.

July 14, 1958: A coup d'etat erupted in Iraq, and Feisal, along with other members of the royal family, was murdered. This marked the end of the Iraqi Kingdom. The new ruler of Iraq was General Abd Alkarim Kasim.

February 4, 1960: Hussein promulgated a law granting each Palestinian the chance of obtaining Jordanian citizenship. This law was similar to the Israeli "law of return."

May 30, 1967: Hussein signed a military pact with Egypt's President Nasser in Cairo.

June 5, 1967: Hussein joined the war and as a result, in just three days, he lost Judea, Samaria, and East Jerusalem.

September 1970: The Palestinians declared northern Jordan a liberated territory after they took control of the cities of Irbid, Ramta, Giarsh, Zarka, and Salt.

> *The revolution must spread among the masses and the majority of our masses are in Jordan.*
> PLO leader FAROUK KADDOUMI,
> *Shuon Filastinya,* May 1977

"Black September" 1970: The Bedouin elements of the Jordanian army went into action against the Palestinians. Thousands were either killed, wounded, or arrested. Israel warned Syria against intervention. The Israeli and American pressure in support of Hussein prevented his defeat and prevented Palestinian control of Jordan,

November 28, 1971: Wasti Tall, prime minister of Jordan and the one who ordered the slaughter of the Palestinians in September 1970, was murdered in Cairo.

October 1974: The Arab leaders' summit in Rabat declared that the PLO is the "sole legitimate representative of the Palestinian people Hussein publicly accepted the resolution, while at the same time did everything possible to prove that he represented the Palestinians and not the PLO.

> *Don't forget this point ... There is no Palestinian nation. There is only Syria. You are an integral part of the Syrian nation. Palestine is an integral part of Syria.*
> Syrian President HAFEZ AL-ASSAD,
> April 1976

November 1987: As a result of the uprising in Judea and Samaria, Hussein changed direction. He declared that he is a main supporter of the Palestinian people's cause for self-determination on the West Bank. Hussein was concerned that the uprising may spread to his kingdom, where the Palestinians would want to establish their state.

1988: "Hussein – go back to Hijaz [Saudi Arabia today]." This slogan was chanted in Amman (the Jordanian capital) and in the refugee camps during the riots and demonstrations in the kingdom. The uprising attempts continue in Jordan today, yet very little is known through the world media. Hussein of Mecca cannot allow an uprising in Jordan.

The fifth point of the ten-point program of the Palestine National Council, held in Cairo on June 8, 1974, makes it clear that the West Bank and Gaza Strip would be used by the PLO as a base of attack of Jordan and Israel. It reads: ''To struggle with Jordanian national forces for the establishment of a Jordanian-Palestinian national front whose aim is the establishment of a national democratic government in Jordan – a government that will cohere with the Palestinian entity to be established as a result of the struggle.''

CHAPTER THIRTY-FOUR

THE RICH SAUDIS –
NOT MODERATE

> *Who hath gathered wealth [of this world] and arranged it. He thinketh that his wealth will render him immortal. Nay, but verily he will be flung to the Consuming One . . . It is the fire of Allah kindled.*
>
> The Koran, *Sura* CIV: 2-4, 6

> *The Arab nations should sacrifice up to 10 million of their 50 million people, if necessary to wipe out Israel . . . Israel to the Arab world is like a cancer to the human body and the only way of remedy is to uproot it, just like a cancer.*
>
> FAHD IBN ABDUL AZIZ,
> King of Saudi Arabia,
> Associated Press, January 9, 1954

ome observers may think that Saudi Arabia has the image of being a moderate, responsible Arab state. In reality, this assumption is totally wrong. Saudi Arabia is one of the radical Arab states and her policy over the last decades proves this.

> *The truth is that anything praised by the Jews is despised, and anything that is abused by the Jews and their organizations is precious.*
>
> PRINCE SULTAN, Saudi Defense Minister
> Riyadh television,
> October 19, 1985

Q: Did Saudi Arabia support a peace initiative with Israel in the past?
A: Saudi Arabia has systematically thwarted, not supported, authentic peace initiatives to negotiate and resolve the Arab-Israeli conflict. It

has taken no initiatives itself, nor has it contributed any substantial assistance to any progress towards that goal.

Q: What about the "Fahd Plan" and the "Fez Plan"?

A: The so-called Saudi peace plans – the "Fahd Plan" and the "Fez Plan" – are no more than Arab dictates designed to create a Palestinian Arab state and leave Israel in an extremely vulnerable position. None of these plans makes any mention of recognizing Israel, of negotiating with Israel, of a settlement with Israel, and of a peace treaty with Israel. This notable absence has enabled even the most extremist elements, such as the PLO, to voice support.

Q: Does Saudi Arabia tend to recognize Israel's right to exist?

A: No. Saudi Arabia continues to maintain a state of war with Israel and refuses to recognize Israel's right to exist. Furthermore, Saudi Arabia perpetuates an international economic warfare intended to strangle Israel through the Arab League boycott. The Saudi press and mass media are replete with expressions of profound hate and enmity towards Israel, calling for its demise.

Q: What is the official Saudi approach towards Israel?

A: Official Saudi representatives and periodicals often resort to blatant anti-Semitism, openly attacking the Jewish people and Judaism. *The Protocols of the Elders of Zion,* the infamous anti-Semitic fabrication of Czarist Russia, has been frequently quoted and distributed by the Saudi regime.

Q: Are Jews allowed to live in Saudi Arabia?

A: Not at all. Jews were never permitted to live in Jordan or Saudi Arabia.

> *He who trusts in his riches shall fall.*
>
> Proverbs 11:28

Q: What was the Saudi reaction to the Camp David Accords?

A: Saudi Arabia rejected the Camp David Accords which were negotiated between Egypt and Israel with the active involvement of the United States.

Q: In what way did the Saudis express their opposition?

A: Saudi Arabia persisted in its diplomatic, financial, economic, political and cultural boycott of Egypt because of the peace treaty between Egypt and Israel. Thus, Riyadh overtly opposed the cornerstone of American Middle East policy, which is its staunch support of both Camp David and the Egyptian-Israeli peace treaty.

Q: What was the Saudi reaction to the Lebanese-Israeli peace accord on May 17, 1983?

A: Once again, Saudi Arabia's failure to support peace in the area was reflected in its refusal to back the peace accord between Lebanon and Israel of May 17, 1983, an accord sponsored by American Secretary of State George Shultz.

> *. . . Efforts must be exerted to urge Moslems to Jihad [holy war] with all their potentials for regaining Palestine to Islam and for liberating Al-Aqsa Mosque from the Zionist usurpers . . . The world has become beset with heresy and degeneration with the soldiers of Satan mushrooming and trying to fight against Islam . . . fake principles invented to mislead Moslem societies . . . such terms as Nationalism, Democracy, Liberty. These are outwardly sweet words, but in essence they imply the meanest form of corruption, delusion and waywardness . . .*
> Saudi KING FAHD,
> *Al-Thadamun Al-Islami,*
> reported by Associated Press, July 15, 1986

Q: How do the Saudis view PLO terror against Israel?

A: The answer can be found in the Saudi News Agency on July 11, 1986. Reporting the Saudi press' praise for armed Fedayeen attacks against Israel, it noted that " . . . the continuation of acts such as these is the only and most effective way of forcing the Zionist entity to reassess its calculations, which are based on the results of Arab feuds and the absence of Palestinian armed activity."

Q: Does Saudi Arabia encourage international terror?

A: Indirectly, the answer is in the affirmative. Saudi Arabia is the financial supporter of Syria. Syria is not only the leader of the Arab rejectionist front refusing peace with Israel, but it is also the main supporter, along with Iran and Libya, of world terrorism. Through the terrorist gangs which it controls or supports – in Beirut, in Lebanon's Beka'a Valley, in training camps and launching sites on Syrian territory, and in terrorist offices in Damascus itself – it is Riyadh's political and financial support that makes it possible for Syria to play this central role of protector of terrorists who have murdered hundreds of Americans, torn Lebanon apart, and continue to target Israel.

> *[I] urge the Muslims to launch Jihad and to use all their capabilities to restore Muslim Palestine and the holy Al-Aqsa mosque from the Zionist usurpers and aggressors. The Muslims must be united in the confrontation of the Jews and those who support them.*
>
> Saudi KING FAHD,
> quoted by Saudi Press Agency, July 15, 1986

Q: Is there further proof of Saudi support of international terror?

A: Yes. In April 1985, the United States attacked Libya because of Libya's international terror activity. Saudi Arabia's criticism of the American strike against Libya and its expression of solidarity with Libya, clearly reflected its position on terrorism.

Q: What can be concluded?

A: In conclusion, in all these ways, Saudi Arabia not only has not contributed to the Middle East peace process, but it has adopted a wide range of policies that only heighten regional tensions, incite hostility and violence towards Israel, and harm American and Western interests. It has contributed substantially not to peace, but to its absence.

> *All countries should wage war against the Zionists, who are there to destroy all human organizations and to destroy civilization and the work which good people are trying to do.*
>
> Saudi KING FEISAL,
> *Beirut Daily Star,* November 17, 1972
>
> ---
>
> *For riches are not forever and does the crown endure to all generations?*
>
> Proverbs 27:24

◆ Do you know that Saudi Arabia is the only country in the world which has a verse from a holy book (The Koran) decorating its flag?

◆ Do you know that in Saudi Arabia people who have committed a crime can be punished by having their hands or heads cut off?

> *The Saudis beheaded 16 Arabs from Kuwait. The victims were found guilty in a Saudi court and sentenced to death. All the executions were carried out in public in the Holy city of Mecca.*
>
> Saudi Radio,
> September 21, 1989

414

◆ Do you know that people in Saudi Arabia who are found guilty are sentenced to hundreds of lashes in a humiliating manner?

◆ Do you know that Saudi Arabia contributes annually hundreds of millions of dollars to Syria and tens of millions of dollars to the PLO?

◆ Do you know that Saudi funding to Syria and PLO has enabled them over the years to purchase millions of dollars worth of Soviet arms? It has also enabled Syria to pay for the presence of 5,000 Soviet military and technical advisors on Syrian soil.

We are determined to wage a Jihad by all the means at our disposal in order to liberate our occupied territories . . . We assert our determination to confront aggression and pressures by all means and to make preparations for a Jihad for the liberation of the occupied Palestinian and Arab territories

Mecca Declaration of the Islamic
Conference, "Riyadh Domestic Service,"
January 29, 1981

◆ Do you know that during the years 1967-85 the income from oil of Saudi Arabia and Kuwait was 830 billion dollars? Yet their contribution to their brethren, the Palestinian Arab refugees, was only 84 million dollars.

◆ Do you know that the contribution of the United States to UNRWA since 1950 is over 1,500 million dollars?

◆ Do you know that Saudi Arabia refuses to utter the word "Israel" in a normal way? No credence can be given to Israel's recognition because Saudi Arabia has insisted time and again that no such recognition is implied.

◆ Do you know that Saudi Arabia has for years prevented Egypt's full return to the Arab world as long as Egypt adheres to the peace treaty with Israeli?

There will be strains in the Middle East until the State of Israel is removed.

Saudi KING FEISAL,
Financial Times, February 27, 1969

The escalation of Fedayeen [terrorist] activity in the occupied nation is the only means not only to liberate the land but also to strike at the enemy.

Al-Yom, Saudi daily,
quoted by Radio Riyadh, October 7, 1985

What we in the West mistakenly identify as Arab moderates and extremists actually represent two equally legitimate and ancient Moslem approaches to uncompromising conflict with infidels. The more popularly known is the path of Jihad, or holy war, the way of direct armed assault. However, Moslem law also offers the way of Hudaybiyah, named after the treaty concluded by the Prophet Muhammed himself with his Meccan foes at a moment of insufficient strength for outright victory. Though calling for a ten-year truce, he proceeded to break it twice – first, by infiltrating Mecca and then by conquering the weakened city.

. . . members of the governing board of the Riyadh Christian Fellowship were suddenly picked up and taken to the Ministry of Interior for lengthy interrogation . . . the government's major complaint was that the Christians had a governing board and a bank account for the congregation . . . New rules were issued – no governing board, no bank account, and no large meetings . . . sources confirmed that the Christians promptly met all the conditions . . . all members of the board were again rounded up and interrogated. They were ordered out of the country within 24 hours.

MICHAEL COLLINS,
The Christian Science Monitor,
August 8, 1983

The existence of Israel is a fact. However, we as the Arab nation struggle against that fact in arms and words until it is eradicated from the map of Arab reality.

Al-Jezirah, Saudi Arabia,
July 22, 1981

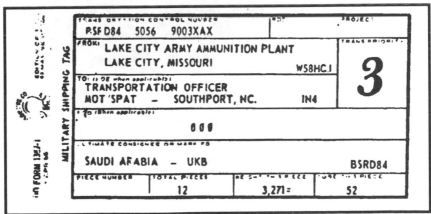

Shipping tag of United States ammunition sold to Saudi Arabia, and found in Lebanon, June 1982.

Following are two pictures from a series of six, by photographer Kaj Lauridsen, that appeared in the London *Daily Mirror* on February 6, 1981. The story, a two-page spread, was entitled "Desert Justice" and subtitled "Fathers Lifted Their Sons for a Better View." Quoting the newspaper, "The victim of the [public] execution was alleged to have murdered his bride-to-be and her father after they tried to call off the wedding . . ."

(Copyright Blue C Press Copenhagen)

CHAPTER THIRTY-FIVE

SECURE BORDERS AND
ISRAEL'S EXISTENCE

> *I swear to God, we will let our fire eat half of Israel if it tries to wage anything against us.*
> Iraqi President SADDAM HUSSEIN,
> Iraqi television, April 2, 1990

The only reason for all the bitter wars fought between Israel and her neighbors in the last generation is the blind Arab refusal to accept Israel as a reality in the Middle East. The conflict was neither about refugees nor Arab territories. The Arabs rejected the United Nations Partition Plan of 1947, by which Israel was meant to be tiny and with very ridiculous borders. Moreover, the Arabs conducted various wars again and again when Israel did not have Judea, Samaria, and the Gaza Strip and before the Arab refugee problem became a reality.

Furthermore, it was the ludicrous, dangerous cease-fire lines of 1948 that were the main reason behind the Arab aggression prior to the Six-Day War of 1967.

Referring to Saddam Hussein's April 2, 1990, televised speech cited above, Abd Alhamid Alsayeh, PLO National Council chairman, praised the Iraqi president the following day and said that the power of Saddam Hussein would assure the liberation of Palestine.

Q: What does the term "secure borders" mean?
A: Secure borders can be defined as those which, by their nature, reduce the danger and threat of war.
Q: What encouraged the Arabs in the past to initiate warfare against Israel?
A: Since her establishment, Israel has not had secure borders and this fact has bolstered the Arab hopes to destroy Israel.
Q: Is there any value to secure borders in this era of sophisticated weaponry?

419

A: There are those who claim that the sophisticated weaponry of modern warfare negates the value of defensible borders with strategic depth. In reality, the opposite is true. Precisely because of dramatic developments in conventional weaponry, the significance of territorial barriers and strategic depth has increased.

Q: Why?

A: With all the heavy damage that bombs and warheads can inflict, they alone cannot be decisive in war, so long as the other side is resolved to fight back. Security Council Resolution 242 of November 22, 1967, set forth the goal of ". . . a just and lasting peace in which every state in the area can live in security . . . the right to live in peace within secure and recognized boundaries free from the threats or acts of force."

Q: Can an example be cited?

A: Yes. Recent history demonstrates this clearly. The German "blitz" did not knock England out of World War II, nor did the heavy Allied air bombardments bring Germany to its knees. This happened only when the last bunker in Berlin fell. More recently, massive American air bombardments could not decide the outcome of the war in Vietnam.

Whoever is bitten by a snake suspects even the rope.
Arab saying

Q: What makes Israel even more vulnerable?

A: Since the quantitative factor contributes heavily to a nation's military power, Israel must compensate for her numerical inferiority in order to ensure her survival. Until the Yom Kippur War of October 1973, this was achieved by the use of qualitatively superior forces and the application of Israel's first-strike capability whenever the neighboring Arab armies began mounting a major military move against Israel, as happened in October 1956 and May-June 1967.

Q: What saved Israel from a disaster in 1973?

A: In the 1973 war, when Egypt and Syria launched their most massive attack ever, it was mainly Israel's defensible borders which saved her from disaster. The fact that the Sinai desert and the Golan Heights were in Israel's hands when hostilities commenced, enabled the Israel Defense Forces to fall back, recover from the initial loss of manpower, bring up reinforcements, re-group, and launch a successful counter-offensive.

> *I have personally followed and supported Israel's heroic struggle for survival ever since the founding of the State of Israel 34 years ago. In the pre-1967 borders Israel was barely 10 miles wide at its narrowest point. The bulk of Israel's population lived within artillery range of hostile Arab guns. I am not about to ask Israel to live that way again.*
>
> former U.S. President RONALD REAGAN,
> *Washington Post*, September 2, 1982

> *Hitler proclaimed what he intended to do – wipe out the Jews and then rule the world. But until the day he started the war against the world – even after – the world said he could not mean it, impossible.*
>
> *A half-century later, a new statement of intent to kill – this one from Saddam Hussein, dictator of Iraq. He rules absolutely and commands one of the largest armed forces – air, ground, and missile – in the world. He wants to wipe out the Jews of Israel and rule the Middle East. He has made that as clear as* Mein Kampf. *Nations in other parts of the world already toady to him and his power. What will they do then?*
>
> *Dictator Hussein told the world that he would annihilate "half of Israel" with missile-delivered chemical weapons if Israel "tries to do anything" against Iraq, now only a few years from the nuclear bomb.*
>
> A. M. ROSENTHAL,
> *New York Times*, April 5, 1990

INTERNATIONAL GUARANTEES AS A COMPONENT OF PEACE

> *History is not encouraging either as regards guarantees in general, or guarantees to Israel in particular . . . For example, in March 1957, [the Government of France] undertook to stand by us in the event of a new blockade of the Tiran Straits or at least to suppport us in our right to defend ourselves. France declared this not only in speeches, but in an exchange of notes on the highest governmental level. In 1967, I went to see President de Gaulle and said, "France is not showing any understanding of our right of self-defense. What has changed between 1957 and 1967?" I shall never forget his reply. "You are asking, Monsieur, what has changed? The date has changed! Then is not now." He then uttered the motto that I have never forgotten: "Guarantees are not absolute." The weight of a guarantee is a function of time.*
>
> ABBA EBAN, then-Israeli Foreign Minister,
> cited in *The Meaning of Secure Borders*,
> Tel Aviv University, March 2, 1978

Q: What about third-party guarantees?

A: Israel has had very bad experiences with guarantees. Third-party guarantees (United Nations or Big Power) are no substitute for defensible borders. The lessons of history, as they affected, for instance, Czechoslovakia in 1938, Israel's own bitter experience with UN and Big Power guarantees, the shifts in international relations and the possibility of contradictory analyses of intelligence data rule out guarantees as a reliable guard against aggression.

Q: Can an example be cited?

A: Yes. In May 1950, the United States, Great Britain, and France issued the Tripartite Declaration pledging to control the qualitative and quantitative flow of armaments to the Middle East so as to prevent any future imbalance in the region. The Declaration in no way tempered Arab aggressive designs against Israel. From 1949 to 1956 Israel suffered countless incursions and acts of sabotage from across the Armistice lines. In September 1955, Czechoslovakia and Egypt concluded a massive arms deal. This deal was a major cause of the 1956 Sinai War.

> *False friends are like migratory birds – they fly away in cold weather.*
>
> The Talmud

✦ Do you know that in the past, promises of demilitarization always turned out to be empty ones? Hitler was not impeded by the demilitarization of the Rhineland, because he knew that no one would go to war over the movement of German troops on German soil. Likewise, the United States sold Patton tanks to Jordan in the 1960s on the condition that they not be deployed in Judea and Samaria, yet they appeared in the hills around Jerusalem a week before the Six-Day War of 1967.

> *Do not put your trust in men in power or in any mortal man – he cannot save. He yields his breath and goes back to the earth he came from, and on that day all his schemes perish.*
>
> Psalms 146:3-4

✦ Do you know that the Straits of Tiran were blocked by Egypt in 1951 to Israeli ships and foreign ships sailing to or from Eilat? This was contrary to the age-old custom of international law, which became a written rule of international law in the Geneva Convention of 1958.

✦ Do you know that on May 16, 1967, Gamal A. Nasser of Egypt demanded the withdrawal of the United Nations troops from Sinai? U Thant, then-Secretary General of the United Nations, agreed. This was a direct breach of the 1957 arrangement in which it was agreed that the UN force cannot be withdrawn arbitrarily.

✦ Do you know that on May 22, 1967, Nasser declared the Straits of Tiran closed for Israeli ships? The act was contrary to international law (the 1958 Geneva Convention was signed by all nations; it included a special "Tiran clause") and to the agreement of 1957. According to international law, an act of blockade is an act of war.

✦ Do you know that in the 1950s Egypt blockaded the Suez Canal to Israeli ships contrary to the Constantinople Convention of 1888 and the Security Council resolution of the UN from 1951?

> *Even the most loyal friends would always be foreigners, and in the last analysis, could be expected to act in accordance with their own changing interests and concerns.*
>
> the late YIGAL ALLON,
> former deputy prime minister of Israel,
> *The Case of Defensible Borders*

ISRAEL'S MAIN REASONS FOR SEEKING SECURE BORDERS

> *Every one of us wants the retrieval of Jaffa and, indeed, every last inch of Palestinian soil. The Zionists took Palestine inch by inch, and we must retrieve it inch by inch. We believe that Palestine, from the river to the sea, is our country.*
>
> PLO leader ABU IYAD,
> Radio Amman, November 26, 1984

1. Israel's insistence on defensible borders stems from the asymmetry between her and the Arab states in terms of size, intentions, and expected fate.
2. Israel's right to defensible borders cannot be realized within the 1949-67 Armistice lines: (a) Israel has neither the manpower nor the economic capability to man these lines and maintain a constant state of alert; (b) strategic depth is a decisive factor in modern warfare; and (c) Israel cannot live behind such "borders" without preemptive strikes becoming the only means of assuring her survival.
3. Israel's right to defensible borders is understood, and recognized in principle, by a concerned international community.
4. Guarantees, however well-intentioned, are no substitute for defensible borders.

> *I know that our people will attain an independent Palestinian state which will signify the beginning of the liberation of the entire homeland. It will be the initial – not the final – stage of liberation, which will not end at the borders of that state. The Palestinian state . . . will constitute the beginning of the end for Israel. An olive branch is worthless without the backing of a rifle.*
>
> PLO leader ABU IYAD,
> *Al-Kabas*, November 11, 1984

5. Even a peace settlement must be based on defensible borders. Indefensible borders would create a standing invitation to hostile neighbors to launch such an attack at an appropriate moment and would be a constant cause of friction and instability in the region.
6. A definition of the term "defensible borders" as it applies to Israel: Defensible borders are such borders as will provide Israel with sufficient strategic depth and topographical conditions to ensure that

her small standing army will be able to withstand and contain any future assault by invading armies until the country's citizen reserves can be mobilized.

> *There is an important difference between damage and conquest. Israel's security problem is not only the threat of damage but the danger of conquest by Arab forces. Conquest would mean the death of the state and no doubt of large numbers of our people. Missiles, rockets and artillery can inflict damage, but not conquer. To seize territory one needs ground forces . . .*
>
> BENJAMIN NETANYAHU,
> former Israeli ambassador to the UN,
> *Washington Post,* January 8, 1983

7. Morally, Israel, which was attacked again and again from non-defensible borders, has the right to demand secure borders.
8. Modern world history proves that the Israeli demand for such borders is not an exception.

> *Let us assume for just a moment that, at Geneva, the PLO will achieve the right to create a Palestinian national entity on the West Bank and in the Gaza Strip. Israel knows full well that such a mini-state would not have a written constitution and would, therefore, not consider itself committed to any international boundaries. What this means is that the first article of the unwritten Palestinian constitution will be a call for a struggle to return the Palestinian territories on which Israel rests . . . Rosh Hanikra . . . Beit Shean . . . Haifa and Jaffa on the coastal plain – that is, all of Palestine, from Galilee to the Negev, and from the Jordan to the Mediterranean.*
>
> Radio Damascus commentary,
> February 15, 1977

POPULATION FIGURES

Year	Region	Population
1967	West Bank	586,000
1967	Gaza Strip	381,000
1988	West Bank	875,000
1988	Gaza Strip	570,000

✦ Do you know that half of Israel's population is within 20 kilometers of the Samarian hills, including Tel Aviv, Hadera, Herzliya, Netanya, Petah Tikva, Ramat Gan, Rehovot, Lod, and Jerusalem?

✦ Do you know that even if a "Prime Minister Arafat" could leave Israel alone, others would find it hard to resist using his new state as a base from which to fire Katyusha rockets? Let us not forget that the Galilee suffered nightly rocket attacks when the PLO had its own state in southern Lebanon.

✦ Do you know that Tunisia, Egypt, Syria, and Lebanon have all suffered terrible internal strife caused by the minions of fundamentalist Islam?

✦ Do you know that a Bir Zeit University poll conducted in 1989 indicated that 59 percent of the Arabs in Judea and Samaria would prefer an Islamic Republic to any other form of government? Even if Israel could trust Arafat to keep the peace, can Israel trust the Islamic fundamentalists who would be looking to depose him?

✦ Do you know that 2,500 Israeli soldiers lost their lives in 1973 due to what has gone down in history as "an intelligence blunder"? If the Yom Kippur attack had been launched from Samaria, tens of thousands of Israelis would have perished. Is it impossible that Israel might "blunder" again?

✦ Do you know that the assurance of sufficient water for a growing and industrialized Israel has for decades been a major worry of Israeli leaders? Judea and Samaria boast 40 percent of Israel's available fresh water resources. Water is life. According to Reuven Pedantsur, writing in the April 25, 1989, issue of the Israeli daily *Ha'aretz,* it therefore makes no sense to place it in the hands of those whose intentions towards Israel might not always be the kindest.

Q: Were the ceasefire lines of 1948 a permanent border?
A: Not at all. A major stipulation of the 1949 Armistice Agreements was that the Armistice lines would soon be replaced by negotiated boundaries. This did not happen. Instead, the Arab states flagrantly violated Israel's sovereignty and territory, claiming that the Armistice lines were not legally binding.

> *The [Armistice] Agreement did not pass judgment on rights, political, military or otherwise. Thus I know of no territory, I know of no boundary; I know of a situation frozen by an Armistice Agreement.*
>
> M. H. EL-FARRA, then-Jordanian
> ambassador to the United Nations,
> May 31, 1967

Q: Why can't Israel return to the 1949-67 Armistice lines?

A: Israel cannot return to the 1949-67 Armistice lines whose very nature invited aggression. These lines failed to provide Israel with the essential minimum of strategic depth. Within these lines, a single military strike would have been sufficient to dissect Israel at more than one point and to sever essential lines of communication.

Q: What are the intentions of the PLO and other Arabs towards Israel?

A: The PLO's Farouk Kaddoumi supplied the answer in an interview in *Newsweek,* on March 14, 1977. He said: "We have to be flexible, in order to establish peace in this part of the world, so we have to accept, in this stage, that we have this [Palestinian] State on only part of our territory. But this doesn't mean that we are going to give up the rest of our rights. There are two (initial) phases to our return. The first phase to the 1967 lines, and the second to the 1948 lines . . . the third stage is the democratic stage of Palestine. So we are fighting for these three stages."

Q: What were Israel's problems before the 1967 war?

A: Prior to 1967, Israel had neither the manpower nor the economic resources to maintain a standing army of the dimensions required to man the indefensible lines that existed before the Six-Day War. These lines lacked both strategic depth and suitable topography. Had Israel still been within her pre-1967 lines when the massive Arab assault of October 1973 took place, she would have had neither the time nor the space to recover and Israel and her people might well have been destroyed in a matter of days.

> *Artillery, missiles, and bombers . . . can wreak havoc on a large scale, but they alone cannot subdue a courageous people fighting for its survival and independence. Until one side's territory is occupied and the resistance of its people and army broken by land forces, no decisive result can be achieved.*
>
> the late YIGAL ALLON,
> former deputy prime minister of Israel,
> *The Making of Israel's Army,* 1971

Q: What is Israel's most crucial dilemma?

A: The facts are clear. Israel's very existence is at stake. Perhaps countries thousands of miles away, unfamiliar with the dangers posed by protracted conflict and hostile neighbors, can turn a blind eye to these harsh facts. Israel cannot. Other nations enjoy considerable security and strategic depth. Israel does not. Other nations have not been subjected to the consequences of four wars of aggression initiated by hostile neighbors in just three decades. Israel has. Other nations do not know what it is like to be encircled by countries that consider themselves to be in a state of war and which are arming for yet another war of annihilation. Israel does.

CHAPTER THIRTY-SIX

ABOUT NINE PROPOSALS
FOR A SOLUTION

> *The Arab leaders will fight for the Palestinians until the last Palestinian.*
>
> cynical Palestinian saying

Since 1967, Israelis as well as others have been searching for a solution to the Palestinian dilemma. The Israeli people would like to see a solution that would solve the Palestinian problem and at the same time would not endanger the security of Israel. The following are the nine major proposals that have been voiced in Israel since 1967:

1. The "Jordanization" of the Palestinian Arabs in Judea, Samaria, and the Gaza Strip – namely, to enable all the Palestinian Arabs to have Jordanian citizenship and as such, the right to vote for the Jordanian parliament.
2. The "Palestinianization" of Jordan – namely, that Jordan be declared a Palestinian state, since Jordan is Palestine and Palestine is, in fact, Jordan.
3. A Federation or Confederation between Jordan and the areas of Judea, Samaria, and Gaza.
4. Territorial compromise.
5. The transfer of Palestinian Arabs to Jordan by purchasing their property in Judea, Samaria, and the Gaza Strip and then asking them to willingly leave for Jordan or any other Arab country.
6. A Palestinian state in Judea, Samaria, and the Gaza Strip.
7. The annexation of Judea, Samaria, and Gaza by Israel.
8. To maintain the status quo that has existed since 1967.
9. The autonomy plan.

The only proposal that enjoys the support of the United States, most Israelis, and the Israeli government, and which was accepted by the Egyptians in the Camp David Accords, is the autonomy plan. Moreover, with regards to autonomy, Egypt and Israel made very significant progress in their negotiations. In reaction Arafat said:

> *"We have to admit that the talks between Burg (Israel's representative) and Mustafa Khalil (Egypt's representative) resulted in Khalil's agreement, according to Sadat's instructions, to the autonomy plan. So they reached some almost final agreements except for Jerusalem, state land and natural resources...."*
>
> from PLO documents ofNovember 13, 1979 – a talk between Andrei Gromyko andArafat in Moscow

> *Go through Zion, walk around her, counting her towers, admiring her walls, reviewing her palaces. Then tell the next generation that God is here....for ever and ever.*
>
> Psalms 48:12-14

CHAPTER THIRTY-SEVEN

ABOUT ARAB BOOKS, ARTICLES, CARTOONS, COEXISTENCE – AND ANTI-SEMITISM

Peace between nations is not only a peace agreement between governments; it is not only the signing of a document declaring that the two states are at peace with one another. Real peace is the opening of borders between nations giving people on both sides the chance to meet and to know one another. It is based on diplomatic, economic, commercial, and cultural ties between nations. It must be based on creating the proper atmosphere between nations. The media in these countries should serve the interests of peace by writing objectively about the other side.

Unfortunately, the media in the Arab world today is a main source of anti-Semitism and fosters hatred towards the Jews, Judaism, and the State of Israel. Such animosity not only does not promote the chance for peace, but creates the atmosphere of war. Among the Arab countries spreading this hatred is Egypt. The Egyptian media clearly violates the content and spirit of the Camp David Accords.

THE EGYPTIAN MEDIA AND TEXTBOOKS

Israel commits terrible crimes against the Arab nation by using new weapons such as AIDS and the distribution of germs that hit human animals.

Dr. BASHIR ALSHAFIN,
quoted in *Al-Waft* (Egypt), December 19, 1989,
from his ALWAFD Party convention lecture

431

One should expect Egypt, which signed a peace treaty with Israel and declared that the political solution is the only option to solve the Arab-Israeli conflict, to do its best to strengthen the atmosphere of peace, to guide at least the government-owned national newspapers to create such an atmosphere. In reality, the Egyptians, just like the other hostile Arab media in the Arab world, spread lies and hatred against Israel and the Jewish people in their books, newspapers, media commentaries, etc.

Here is an example. The cartoon depicts Israel establishing settlements over dead Arabs, and appeared in Egypt's *Al-Giumhuriah* on May 16, 1990:

Q: What is the view of the Holocaust?
A: In the words of Wajih Abu Zikri, in his *El-Maktab El-Masri El-Hadith*, Cairo, 1987, and published in Egypt's *Al-Ahram*: "The story, repeated by the Jews, about six million murdered by the Nazis, is only a fairy tale . . . Hitler established the ovens only to burn the corpses of those who died from the plague in order to prevent its spread . . ."
Q: What price should Israel pay in order to live in peace with the Arabs?
A: According to Ahmad Yahya, commenting on Wajih Abu Zikri's book: "The question is whether Israel can pay the price of peace with its new neighbors? The answer is yes. On one condition – that Israel will decide voluntarily to stop existing . . ."
Q: Does the PLO conduct terrorism?
A: Abu Zikri describes how he decided to study Jewish terrorism following his meeting with Arafat in Tunis in May 1986. Arafat denied to him that the PLO ever carried out any terrorist action.

Mustafah Amin wrote about Russian Jewish immigration to Israel. He was quoted in Egypt's *Al-Achbar,* on April 2, 1990: "The immigration of half a million Soviet Jews to Israel is not the last disaster that befell the Arab nation. This is the beginning of the disasters. The half a million will be followed by three more million Soviet Jews. This is in fact a new hostile country that will be established near our border and another sword in our neck."

Q: How is *The Protocols of the Elders of Zion* regarded?

A: *The Protocols of the Elders of Zion* is a notorious fabrication by the enemies of the Jewish people in which the Jewish people are accused of conspiring against the entire world. This anti-Semitic book was condemned and then forgotten. The Egyptians still deal with it today. Abu Zikri wrote: *"The Protocols of the Elders of Zion* are part of Jewish heritage, which dictate their conduct." He then quoted a Jewish dentist from Mahalla in Egypt who told him that the *Protocols* are kept in every Jewish synagogue and that the rabbis know them by heart, explaining some of the text to the people on Saturdays without explicitly referring to the book. "The *Protocols* are a call for the destruction of the world and for Jewish rule everywhere using every possible means," he continued, and: "Hatred and violence are dominant characteristics of the Jewish personality, because of the 'sacred' teachings of the rabbis."

> *The world must curse the Jews, and curse the day on which they came on earth . . . The Jews prepare for humanity every form of torture . . .*
>
> ANIS MANSUR,
> Wound in the Heart of Israel

Q: Who is Anis Mansur?

A: Anis Mansur is the ex-editor-in-chief of the Egyptian weekly *October,* and was a close confidant of the late Anwar al-Sadat. Although he is known for his support of the peace process and has visited Israel a number of times, Mansur never neglected to pour some anti-Semitic undertones into his book. (The above quote is from the second edition of Mansur's book *Wound in the Heart of Israel,* Zahra'a Publishers, Cairo, 1986.)

433

The following cartoon, from the Egyptian newspaper *Al-Masa*, on May 5, 1990, depicted Israel's Prime Minister Shamir as the murderer of peace.

● مبارك : تصريحات شامير تدل أن السلام
ليس هدفاً أمام عينيه

Egyptian President Mubarak: "Shamir's declarations prove that peace is not the goal in front of his eyes."

من قال إن -
السلام ليس
أمام عيني

"Who said peace is not in front of my eyes?"

Q: What is the character of the Jewish people, according to Mansur?

A: The following quotation from Mansur's book answers this question: "The world must curse the Jews, and curse the day on which they came on earth . . . The Jews prepare for humanity every form of torture . . . They sell to people the lust for money and offer them sex instead of morals and values . . . They spread anarchist, communist and deviationist schools of thought to destroy the society in which they wish to live. They stab hands and hearts . . ."

Q: How does Mansur regard American Jewry?

A: "During America's War of Independence, the Jews supported both parties 'to make profit in any case,'" he says. "The Jews totally control New York." And: "Jews have taken over all the media in the U.S. after realizing that the American people care only for those who speak loudly."

> *Israel has no future or past and her existence is temporary.*
> *Alahali*, Egypt,
> December 13, 1989

Q: What is the main point of Israeli education?

A: According to Mansur: "The essence of Israeli education is to reach consensus over one question: whom to kill – ourselves or somebody else . . ."

In this cartoon from the Egyptian paper, *Ruz Al-Yusuf,* **August 1989, Israeli Prime Minister Shamir is depicted wearing the notorious Nazi uniform with the swastika and Star of David.**

In *El-Ahram,* **December 21, 1986, Prime Minister Shamir is seen awarding the highest decoration to an Israeli soldier for supposedly killing a Palestinian child. Note that the military decoration has a swastika.**

■ السكوت العربي على جرائم إسرائيل ■

In Saudi Arabia's *Al-Nadwa* on May 22, 1990, the frightening silence of the civilized world to Israeli crimes against young, helpless Palestinians is depicted. Note the Jew is characterized in the age-old anti-Semitic fashion, with a big nose.

ISLAM, ISRAEL, AND THE JEWS

> *Islam commits us to Jihad [holy war] and if we do not conduct Jihad we will be humiliated because of God's wrath . . .*
> *Al-Haqiqah* (The Truth), Egypt,
> June 1, 1990

In two chapters in this book – about Mohammed and the Jews and about the Dhimmi – we dealt with the Islamic attitude towards the Jews. Jews, by Islam, may be tolerated, yet they can, by no means, be equal to Moslems. Today, Moslems throughout the Arab world are using Islam in order to defame the Jewish people. In a book entitled *The Moslem Brothers and the Peace with Israel*, the well-known Egyptian writer Hasnein Krum wrote: "Israel is a lethal germ inserted in a Moslem Land to destroy and to multiply and finish off everything. There is no cure to this menace but to uproot Israel completely from this region . . ." (The book was published by Naderco Co., Cairo, in 1985.)

436

> *Woe to he who calls evil good and good evil.*
>
> Isaiah 5:20

Below, Israeli Prime Minister Shamir is depicted as a vulture over Arab bodies. This appeared in the Lebanese paper *Al-Muharrir* on June 5, 1990.

In Bahrain's *Achbar Al-Chaleege*, May 24, 1990, Shamir is shown to be world champion of murder.

437

In *Al-Qabas International*, June 4, 1990, Israel is depicted as the weapon in the hand of the United States shooting at the Arabs.

In part of the Arab literature, Jews are described as more than the enemies of Islam, the Arab people, and the Palestinians. Jews are accused of harboring hatred for other people. Arab writer Muhammed Abd el-Aziz Mansur has said: "A Jew has to curse the Christians three times every day" and "Jews consider dogs as better than Gentiles" and "Only Jews, the chosen people, deserve life. The rest of the nations are donkeys." He also wrote: "Jews are encouraged to rape non-Jewish women" and "Jews are permitted to steal from non-Jews." The book also includes a collection of anti-Semitic quotations from the Koran.

> *The Imperialists in Palestine say by God we will take your land and kill you . . . They attack us on behalf of Judaism . . . The Palestine dilemma is a religious dilemma since its eruption and will continue to be so. The Jews are sly . . . The Prophet Mohammed succeeded in punishing them . . . our enemies want to destroy us and destroy the Koran and they are planning the way step by step.*
> Islamic leader MUHAMMED ALGIAZALI,
> quoted in Egypt's *Al-Giumhuriah*,
> December 19, 1989

The caption of the above cartoon reads: "Be patient, say 'hello' to him and afterwards, wash your hands." It appeared in *Al-Ittihad* of Abu Dhabi (a Gulf Arab state) on May 23, 1990, and shows America supporting murderous Israel.

PALESTINIAN BOOKS AND THE IMAGE OF A JEW

Kha'ula Abu Bakr of Acre, Israel, recently wrote a study on contemporary Palestinian children's literature as her M.A. thesis at Haifa University. Her study received extensive attention in the press since several of the stories she analyzed were published in the Hebrew quarterly *Hetz,* and she was reported to have been questioned by the police about the Palestinian texts that formed the basis for her study.

Q: According to this study, what is the image of Israel?
A: Israel, as reflected in the stories Abu Bakr analyzed, was shown to be: a robber, a savage soldier, a rapist, a crafty cruel liar who blows up houses, closes schools, burns babies and breaks the bones of children, and a vicious beast.
Q: What is the most alarming point in this study?
A: There is no doubt that this literature teaches bitter hatred of Israelis, according to Professor Adir Cohen, who supervised the preparation of the thesis. Abu Bakr said that, first and foremost, it reflects a bitter reality of hatred and legitimizes the *Intifada.*

> *Israel deals with the organs of dead Palestinian bodies and plants them in the bodies of sick Jews.*
>
> *Al-Achbar*, Egypt,
> October 3, 1989

Q: Is this hatred the result of the *Intifada* or the Six-Day War of 1967?

A: Neither is correct. Arab children were taught to hate Zionists well before the War of Independence in 1948 – when the massive homelessness began – or the Six-Day War, when Israel occupied Judea, Samaria, and the Gaza Strip. All this occurred many years prior to the *Intifada*.

In the Saudi paper *Al-Madina*, June 4, 1990, Israel is depicted as the terrorist state destroying with a hammer what the peaceful Arabs are building.

This cartoon was published in the Saudi paper *Al-Sharq Al-Awsat* on May 19, 1990. It depicts Israeli Prime Minister Shamir as sitting in control of the world while watching Israeli soldiers cold-bloodedy murdering innocent Arabs.

Mr. Judas Salam, deputy chairman of the "Nation Party" of Egypt was quoted in the Egyptian paper *Al-Ummah* on February 2, 1990, praising the Palestinian uprising. He said: ". . . the enemy that stole the land of Palestine since 1948 continues to hold the land . . . It is a duty upon the Arab states that border Israel to open their borders and equip the Fidayyin [Arab fighters] with weapons and all the other modern means of fighting and this in order to defeat the Israeli army and people and cause them serious casualties."

Q: What is the conclusion?
A: The conclusion is very sad. As long as this conflict continues, it will serve to strengthen hatred of Arabs against Israel and the Jewish people. Israel's various calls for peace and the Israeli peace initiative were rejected by the Arab states, except Egypt. Israel is continually "advised" to negotiate with the PLO – the very organization which seeks her destruction.

This cartoon was published in the Jordanian paper *Al-Dustur* on June 4, 1990. The American administration is shown tipping the United Nations vote against the Arabs in favor of Israel.

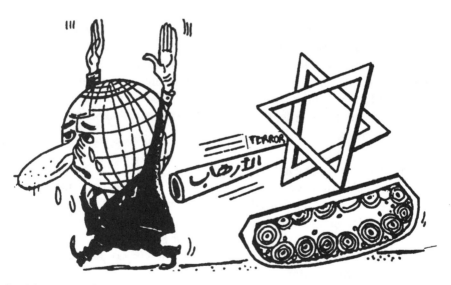

In this cartoon from the Saudi paper *Al-Madina* of May 15, 1990, Israel is the terrorist country shooting at the world.

The Jordanian poet Muhammed A-Daher wrote the following piece of poetry, "Begin," in his book entitled *Sing for the Sake of Palestine*:

> He stole the moon.
> He uprooted the trees.
> He killed the birds,
> Do you know who? Begin.
>
> He painted the walls with human blood captured in
> Lebanon.
> Do you know who? Begin.
>
> He is a thief, a dictator.
> He killed the children.
> Do you know who? Begin.
>
> Get up immediately
> like an earthquake
> kill immediately.
> Do you know who? Begin.

The element of "return" is mentioned quite often in Palestinian literature. There are various and different stories about the Homeland, which is described as a house which a Palestinian cannot live without. Once again, A-Daher expresses this sentiment:

> Oh world, I will never forget my land.
> My land is my life, my soul.
> I know all its parts.
> I know my Homeland liberated.
> I am willing to sacrifice for the sake of my
> Homeland's land.
> I am willing to sacrifice for its soil.
> I am homesick, I have nostalgia for Palestine.
>
> Oh children, and the next generation.
> You are the hope.
> Sing with us in order that we will not forget Haifa,
> Jaffa, Jerusalem, Palestine . . .

The following cartoon appeared in the Bahrain (Arab Gulf state) newspaper *Achbar Alchalig*, on May 31, 1990. It was in reaction to the Arab leaders' summit in Baghdad, May 28-30, 1990. The summit convened after the Iraqi president's threat to use chemical weapons and missiles against Israel.

APPENDIX: DOCUMENTS

AGREEMENT BETWEEN EMIR FEISAL AND
DR. CHAIM WEIZMANN, JANUARY 3, 1919

His Royal Highness the Emir Feisal, representing and acting on behalf of the Arab Kingdom of Hedjaz, and Dr. Chaim Weizmann, representing and acting on behalf of the Zionist Organisation, mindful of the racial kinship and ancient bonds existing between the Arabs and the Jewish people, and realising that the surest means of working out the consummation of their national aspirations is through the closest possible collaboration in the development of the Arab State and Palestine, and being desirous further of confirming the good understanding which exists between them, have agreed upon the following Articles:

ARTICLE I
The Arab State and Palestine in all their relations aud undertakings shall be controlled by the most cordial goodwill and understanding, and to this end Arab and Jewish duly accredited agents shall be established and maintained in the respective territories.

ARTICLE II
Immediately following the completion of the deliberations of the Peace Conference, the definite boundaries between the Arab State and Palestine shall be determined by a Commission to be agreed upon by the parties hereto.

ARTICLE III
In the establishment of the Constitution and Administration of Palestine all such measures shall be adopted as will afford the fullest guarantees for carrying into effect the British Government's Declaration of the 2d of November, 1917.

ARTICLE IV
All necessary measures shall be taken to encourage and stimulate immigration of Jews into Palestine on a large scale, and as quickly as possible to settle Jewish immigrants upon the land through closer settlement, and intensive cultivation of the soil. In taking such measures the Arab peasant and tenant farmers shall be protected in their rights, and shall be assisted in forwarding their economic development.

ARTICLE V
No recognition nor law shall be made prohibiting or interfering in any way with the free exercise of religion; and further the free exercise and enjoyment of religious profession and worship without discrimination or preference shall forever be allowed. No religious test shall ever be required for the exercise of civil or political rights.

ARTICLE VI

The Mohammedan Holy Places shall be under Mohammedan control.

ARTICLE VII

The Zionist Organisation proposes to send to Palestine a Commission of experts to make a survey of the economic possibilities of the country, and to report upon the best means for its development. The Zionist Organisation will place the aforementioned Commission at the disposal of the Arab State for the purpose of a survey of the economic possibilities of the Arab State and to report upon the best means for its development. The Zionist Organisation will use its best efforts to assist the Arab State in providing the means for developing the natural resources and economic possibilities thereof.

ARTICLE VIII

The parties hereto agree to act in complete accord and harmony on all matters embraced herein before the Peace Congress.

ARTICLE IX

Any matters of dispute which may arise between the contracting parties shall be referred to the British Government for arbitration.

Given under our hand at London, England, the third day of January, one thousand nine hundred and nineteen.

Chaim Weizmann.
Feisal ibn-Hussein.

RESERVATION BY THE EMIR FEISAL

If the Arabs are established as I have asked in my manifesto of January 4th addressed to the British Secretary of State for Foreign Affairs, I will carry out what is written in this agreement. If changes are made, I cannot be answerable for failing to carry out this agreement.

Feisal ibn-Hussein.

DR. CHAIM WEIZMANN'S LETTER TO WINSTON CHURCHILL REGARDING TRANSJORDAN, MARCH 1, 1921

May I bring to your attention a matter of vital importance to the economic future of Palestine and the upbuilding of the Jewish National Home. It is the question of the eastern and southern frontiers. It was assumed that so far as the territory in the east was brought within the British sphere, the needs of the Jewish National Home would be fully satisfied.

However, certain parts of the address delivered to the Sheikhs assembled at Es Salt last August, by his Majesty's High Commissioner, which might perhaps be interpreted as suggesting the possible separation of Trans-Jordania from Cis-Jordania, were the cause of some misgiving, but it was taken for granted that those remarks were not intended to foreshadow a fundamental change in the Policy of His Majesty's Government and that they were not meant to do more than adumbrate the possible division of the country for administrative purposes into two parts - Western and Eastern Palestine. It was, none the less, expected that even should this eventuate, Trans-Jordania would still fall under the general provisions of the Palestine Mandate. It is quite appreciated, however, that the administrative control of the mandatory might assume a looser form in Trans-Jordania than in Cis-Jordania, and that the local customs and institutions might be modified gradually as Zionist colonisation proceeded. The Jewish colonists, moreover, could not expect the same security for life and property in Eastern Palestine as in Western Palestine. They would, like pioneers in all countries, be expected to defend their settlements from raids and local disturbances. The opening of Eastern Palestine to Jewish colonisation would consequently, far from aggravating the military burden of the mandatory, offer the most promising prospect of its gradual reduction and ultimate surcease, for it is only through a permanent settlement of a peaceful population upon the Trans-Jordanian plateaux that the problem of the defence of the whole Jordan Valley can be satisfactorily solved.

But if it is thought advisable to provide a corridor (for the Hedjaz Railway) between Palestine and the desert, it should none the less be clearly recognised that the fields of Gilead, Moab and Edom, with the rivers Arnon and Jabbok, to say nothing to the Yarmuk, the use of which is guaranteed under the recently signed convention, are historically and economically linked to Palestine, and that it is upon these fields, now that the rich plains to the north have been taken from Palestine and given to France, that the success of the Jewish National Home must largely rest. Trans-Jordania has from earliest times been an integral and vital part of Palestine. There the tribes of Reuben, Gad and Manasseh first pitched their tents and pastured their flocks. And while Eastern Palestine may probably never have the same religious and historic significance as Western Palestine, it may bulk much larger in the economic future of the Jewish National Home. Apart from the Negeb in the south, Western Palestine has no large stretches of unoccupied land where Jewish colonisation can take place on a large scale. The beautiful Trans-Jordanian plateaux, on the other hand, lie neglected and uninhabited save for a few scattered settlements and a few roaming Bedouin tribes.

The climate of Trans-Jordania is invigorating; the soil is rich; irrigation would be easy; and the hills are covered with forests. There Jewish settlement could proceed on a large scale without friction with the local population. The economic progress of Cis-Jordania itself is dependent upon the development of these Trans-Jordanian plains, for they form the natural granary of all Palestine and without them Palestine can never become a self-sustaining, economic unit and a real National Home. The aspirations of Arab nationalism centre about Damascus and Baghdad and do not lie in Trans-Jordania.

It is confidently hoped, therefore, that there will be no thought of any further diminution of the legitimate claims of Palestine when the eastern and southern frontiers come under discussion. The unsatisfactory character of the settlement in the north makes it all the more vital that the Jewish National Home be generously dealt with on the east and south.

THE DECLARATION OF ISRAEL'S INDEPENDENCE, MAY 14, 1948

The Land of Israel was the birthplace of the Jewish people. Here their spiritual, religious and national identity was formed. Here they achieved independence and created a culture of national and universal significance. Here they wrote and gave the Bible to the world.

Exiled from Palestine, the Jewish people remained faithful to it in all the countries of their dispersion, never ceasing to pray and hope for their return and the restoration of their national freedom.

Impelled by this historic association, Jews strove throughout the centuries to go back to the land of their fathers and regain their statehood. In recent decades they returned in masses. They reclaimed the wilderness, revived their language, built cities and villages and established a vigorous and ever-growing community, with its own economic and cultural life. They sought peace yet were ever prepared to defend themselves. They brought the blessing of progress to all inhabitants of the country.

In the year 1897 the First Zionist Congress, inspired by Theodor Herzl's vision of the Jewish State, proclaimed the right of the Jewish people to a national revival in their own country.

This right was acknowledged by the Balfour Declaration of November 2, 1917, and re-affirmed by the Mandate of the League of Nations, which gave explicit international recognition to the historic connection of the Jewish people with Palestine and their right to reconstitute their National Home.

The Nazi Holocaust, which engulfed millions of Jews in Europe, proved anew the urgency of the re-establishment of the Jewish State, which would solve the problem of Jewish homelessness by opening the gates to all Jews and lifting the Jewish people to equality in the family of nations.

The survivors of the European catastrophe, as well as Jews from other lands, proclaiming their right to a life of dignity, freedom and labor, and undeterred by hazards, hardships and obstacles, have tried unceasingly to enter Palestine.

In the Second World War the Jewish people in Palestine made a full contribution in the struggle of the freedom-loving nations against the Nazi evil. The sacrifices of their soldiers and the efforts of their workers gained them the title to rank with the peoples who founded the United Nations.

On November 29, 1947, the General Assembly of the United Nations adopted a Resolution for the establishment of an independent Jewish State in Palestine, and called upon the inhabitants of the country to take such steps as may be necessary on their part to put the plan into effect.

This recognition by the United Nations of the right of the Jewish people to establish their independent State may not be revoked. It is, moreover, the self-evident right of the Jewish people to be a nation, as all other nations, in its own sovereign State.

ACCORDINGLY, WE, the members of the National Council, representing the Jewish people in Palestine and the Zionist movement of the world, met together in solemn assembly today, the day of termination of the British Mandate for Palestine, by virtue of the natural and historic right of the Jewish people and of the Resolution of the General Assembly of the United Nations,

HEREBY PROCLAIM the establishment of the Jewish State in Palestine, to be called ISRAEL.

WE HEREBY DECLARE that as from the termination of the Mandate at midnight this night of the 14th to 15th May, 1948, and until the setting up of the duly elected bodies of the State in accordance with a Constitution, to be drawn up by a Constituent Assembly not later than the first day of October 1948, the present National Council shall act as the Provisional Government of the State of Israel.

THE STATE OF ISRAEL will be open to the immigration of Jews from all countries of their dispersion; will promote the development of the country for the benefit of all its inhabitants; will be based on the precepts of liberty, justice and peace taught by the Hebrew Prophets; will uphold the full social and political equality of all its citizens, without distinction of race, creed or sex; will guarantee full freedom of conscience, worship, education and culture; will safeguard the sanctity and inviolability of the shrines and Holy Places of all religions; and will dedicate itself to the principles of the Charter of the United Nations.

THE STATE OF ISRAEL will be ready to cooperate with the organs and representatives of the United Nations in the implementation of the Resolution of the Assembly of November 29, 1947, and will take steps to bring about the Economic Union over the whole of Palestine.

We appeal to the United Nations to assist the Jewish people in the building of its State and to admit Israel into the family of nations.

In the midst of wanton aggression, we yet call upon the Arab inhabitants of the State of Israel to return to the ways of peace and play their part in the development of the State, with full and equal citizenship and due representation in all its bodies and institutions – provisional or permanent.

We offer peace and unity to all the neighboring states and their peoples, and invite them to cooperate with the independent Jewish nation for the common good of all.

Our call goes out to the Jewish people all over the world to rally to our side in the task of immigration and development and to stand by us in the great struggle for the fulfillment of the dream of generations – the redemption of Israel.

With trust in Almighty God, we set our hand to this Declaration, at this Session of the Provisional State Council, in the city of Tel Aviv, on this Sabbath eve, the fifth of Iyar, 5708, the fourteenth day of May, 1948.

THE PALESTINIAN NATIONAL COVENANT, 1968

This Covenant will be called "The Palestinian National Covenant" (*Al-Mîhâq Al-Watanî Al-Filastînî*).

ARTICLE 1
Palestine is the homeland of the Palestinian Arab people and an integral part of the great Arab homeland, and the people of Palestine is a part of the Arab Nation.

ARTICLE 2
Palestine with its boundaries that existed at the time of the British Mandate is an integral regional unit.

ARTICLE 3
The Palestinian Arab people possesses the legal right to its homeland, and when the liberation of its homeland is completed it will exercise self-determination solely according to its own will and choice.

ARTICLE 4
The Palestinian personality is an innate, persistent characteristic that does not disappear, and it is transferred from fathers to sons. The Zionist occupation, and the dispersal of the Palestinian Arab people as result of the disasters which came over it, do not deprive it of its Palestinian personality and affiliation and do not nullify them.

ARTICLE 5
The Palestinians are the Arab citizens who were living permanently in Palestine until 1947, whether they were expelled from there or remained. Whoever is born to a Palestinian Arab father after this date, within Palestine or outside it, is a Palestinian.

ARTICLE 6
Jews who were living permanently in Palestine until the beginning of the Zionist invasion will be considered Palestinians.

ARTICLE 7
The Palestinian affiliation and the material, spiritual and historical tie with Palestine are permanent realities. The upbringing of the Palestinian individual in an Arab and revolutionary fashion, the undertaking of all means of forging consciousness and training the *Palestinian*, in order to acquaint him profoundly with his homeland, spiritually and materially, and preparing him for the conflict and the armed struggle, as well as for the sacrifice of his property and his life to restore his homeland, until the liberation – all this is a national duty.

ARTICLE 8

The phase in which the people of Palestine is living is that of the national (*Watanî*) struggle for the liberation of Palestine. Therefore, the contradictions among the Palestinian national forces are of a secondary order which must be suspended in the interest of the fundamental contradiction between Zionism and colonialism on the one side and the Palestinian Arab people on the other. On this basis, the Palestinian masses, whether in the homeland or in places of exile (*Mahâjir*), organizations and individuals, comprise one national front which acts to restore Palestine and liberate it through armed struggle.

ARTICLE 9

Armed struggle is the only way to liberate Palestine and is therefore a strategy and not tactics. The Palestinian Arab people affirms its absolute resolution and abiding determination to pursue the armed struggle and to march forward toward the armed popular revolution, to liberate its homeland and return to it, [to maintain] its right to a natural life in it, and to exercise its right of self-determination in it and sovereignty over it.

ARTICLE 10

Fedayeen action forms the nucleus of the popular Palestinian war of liberation. This demands its promotion, extension and protection, and the mobilization of all the mass and scientific capacities of the Palestinians, their organization and involvement in the armed Palestinian revolution, and cohesion in the national (*Watanî*) struggle among the various groups of the people of Palestine, and between them and the Arab masses, to guarantee the continuation of the revolution, its advancement and victory.

ARTICLE 11

The Palestinians will have three mottoes: National (*Wataniyya*) unity, national (*Qawmiyya*) mobilization and liberation.

ARTICLE 12

The Palestinian Arab people believes in Arab unity. In order to fulfill its role in realizing this, it must preserve, in this phase of its national (*Watanî*) struggle, its Palestinian personality and the constituents thereof increase consciousness of its existence and resist any plan that tends to disintegrate or weaken it.

ARTICLE 13

Arab unity and the liberation of Palestine are two complementary aims. Each one paves the way for realization of the other. Arab unity leads to the liberation of Palestine, and the liberation of Palestine leads to Arab unity. Working for both goes hand in hand.

ARTICLE 14

The destiny of the Arab nation, indeed the very Arab existence, depends upon the destiny of the Palestine issue. The endeavor and effort of the Arab nation to liberate Palestine follows from this connection. The people of Palestine assumes its vanguard role in realizing this sacred national (*Qawmî*) aim.

ARTICLE 15

The liberation of Palestine, from an Arab viewpoint, is a national (*Qawmî*) duty to repulse the Zionist, imperialist invasion from the great Arab homeland and to purge the Zionist presence from Palestine. Its full responsibilities fall upon the Arab nation, peoples and governments, with the Palestinian Arab people at their head.

For this purpose, the Arab nation must mobilize its military, human, material and spiritual capabilities to participate actively with the people of Palestine. They must, especially in the present stage of armed Palestinian revolution, grant and offer the people of Palestine all possible help and every material and human support, and afford it every sure means and opportunity enabling it to continue to assume its vanguard role in pursuing its armed revolution until the liberation of its homeland.

ARTICLE 16

The liberation of Palestine, from a spiritual viewpoint, will prepare an atmosphere of tranquility and peace for the Holy Land, in the shade of which all the holy places will be safeguarded, and freedom of worship and visitation to all will be guaranteed, without distinction or discrimination of race, color, language or religion. For this reason, the people of Palestine looks to the support of all the spiritual forces in the world.

ARTICLE 17

The liberation of Palestine, from a human viewpoint, will restore to the Palestinian man his dignity, glory and freedom. For this, the Palestinian Arab people looks to the support of those in the world who believe in the dignity and freedom of man.

ARTICLE 18

The liberation of Palestine, from an international viewpoint, is a defensive act necessitated by the requirements of self-defense. For this reason, the people of Palestine, desiring to befriend all peoples, looks to the support of the states which love freedom, justice and peace in restoring the legal situation to Palestine, establishing security and peace in its territory, and enabling its people to exercise national (*Wataniyya*) sovereignty and national (*Qawmiyya*) freedom.

ARTICLE 19

The partitioning of Palestine in 1947 and the establishment of Israel is fundamentally null and void, whatever time has elapsed, because it was contrary to the wish of the people of Palestine and its natural right to its homeland, and contradicts the principles embodied in the Charter of the United Nations, the first of which is the right of self-determination.

ARTICLE 20

The Balfour Declaration, the Mandate Document, and what has been based upon them are considered null and void. The claim of a historical or spiritual tie between Jews and Palestine does not tally with historical realities nor with the constituents of statehood in their true sense. Judaism, in its character as a religion of revelation, is not a nationality with an independent existence. Likewise, the Jews are not one people with an independent personality. They are rather citizens of the states to which they belong.

ARTICLE 21

The Palestinian Arab people, in expressing itself through the armed Palestinian revolution, rejects every solution that is a substitute for a complete liberation of Palestine, and rejects all plans that aim at the settlement of the Palestine issue or its internationalization.

ARTICLE 22

Zionism is a political movement organically related to world imperialism and hostile to all movements of liberation and progress in the world. It is a racist and fanatical movement in its formation; aggressive, expansionist and colonialist in its aims; and Fascist and Nazi in its means. Israel is the tool of the Zionist movement and a human and geographical base for world imperialism. It is a concentration and jumping-off point for imperialism in the heart of the Arab homeland, to strike at the hopes of the Arab nation for liberation, unity and progress.

Israel is a constant threat to peace in the Middle East and the entire world. Since the liberation of Palestine will liquidate the Zionist and imperialist presence and bring about the stabilization of peace in the Middle East, the people of Palestine looks to the support of all liberal men of the world and all the forces of good progress and peace; and implores all of them, regardless of their different leanings and orientations, to offer all help and support to the people of Palestine in its just and legal struggle to liberate its homeland.

ARTICLE 23

The demands of security and peace and the requirements of truth and justice oblige all states that preserve friendly relations among peoples and maintain the loyalty of citizens to their homelands to consider Zionism an illegitimate movement and to prohibit its existence and activity.

ARTICLE 24

The Palestinian Arab people believes in the principles of justice, freedom, sovereignty, self-determination, human dignity and the right of peoples to exercise them.

ARTICLE 25

To realize the aims of this Covenant and its principles the Palestine Liberation Organization will undertake its full role in liberating Palestine.

ARTICLE 26

The Palestine Liberation Organization, which represents the forces of the Palestinian revolution, is responsible for the movement of the Palestinian Arab people in its struggle to restore its homeland, liberate it, return to it and exercise the right of self-determination in it. This responsibility extends to all military, political and financial matters, and all else that the Palestine issue requires in the Arab and international spheres.

ARTICLE 27
The Palestine Liberation Organization will cooperate with all Arab states, each according to its capacities, and will maintain neutrality in their mutual relations in the light of, and on the basis of, the requirements of the battle of liberation, and will not interfere in the internal affairs of any Arab state.

ARTICLE 28
The Palestinian Arab people insists upon the originality and independence of its national (*Wataniyya*) revolution and rejects every manner of interference, guardianship and subordination.

ARTICLE 29
The Palestinian Arab people possesses the prior and original right in liberating and restoring its homeland and will define its position with reference to all states and powers on the basis of their positions with reference to the issue [of Palestine] and the extent of their support for [the Palestinian Arab people] in its revolution to realize its aims.

ARTICLE 30
The fighters and bearers of arms in the battle of liberation are the nucleus of the Popular Army, which will be the protecting arm of the Palestinian Arab people.

ARTICLE 31
This organization shall have a flag, oath and anthem, all of which will be determined in accordance with a special system.

ARTICLE 32
To this Covenant is attached a law known as the Fundamental Law of the Palestine Liberation Organization, in which is determined the manner of the organization's formation, its committees, institutions, the special functions of every one of them and all the requisite duties associated with them in accordance with the Covenant.

ARTICLE 33
This Covenant cannot be amended except by a two-thirds majority of all the members of the National Council of the Palestine Liberation Organization in a special session called for this purpose.

"THE DEMOCRATIC STATE":
A SYMPOSIUM OF LEADERS OF SEVERAL FEDAYEEN
ORGANIZATIONS, MARCH 8, 1970*

MODERATOR
The main objective of the symposium is to discuss all the solutions proposed by the various groups of the resistance movement under the slogan "The Democratic Palestinian State," particularly the proposals of Fatah and the Popular Democratic Front. I omit from the discussion those solutions which were hatched up apart from the groups of the resistance movement, whether openly or secretly . . . I refer particularly to the solution adopted by the United States to establish a Palestinian State in the West Bank and the Gaza Strip, and France's proposals concerning the establishment of a Palestinian State to be connected with some Arab countries.

At the beginning of the symposium, I thus turned to the representative of the (Popular) Democratic Front for the Liberation of Palestine: I would like you to explain to us the Front's viewpoint concerning the Democratic Palestinian State on the basis of the resolution presented to the Sixth Congress of the Palestinian National Council which was convened last September.

REPRESENTATIVE OF THE DEMOCRATIC FRONT
The adoption of a particuiar slogan, in our estimation, does not stem from a subjective position or a subjective desire but from a study and analysis of the evolution of the objective situation, the objective possibilities present in society and within history – moving forces, as well as the nature of the potential evolution of these forces in the future . . .

Coexistence (*ta'ayush*) with this entity (Israel) is impossible, not because of a national aim or national aspiration of the Arabs, but because the presence of this entity will determine this region's development in connection with world imperialism, which follows from the objective link between it and Zionism. Thus, eradicating imperialist influence in the Middle East means eradicating the Israeli entity. This is something indispensable, not only from the aspect of the Palestinian people's right of self-determination, and in its homeland, but also from the aspect of protecting the Arab national liberation movement, and this objective also can only be achieved by means of armed stuggle . . .

We believe that hypothetical questions such as, what will happen if the working class or the Communist Party takes over the Government in Israel? – are irrelevant. For there are no signs indicating that the working class will be capable of taking over the Government in the near or distant future without armed struggle under the leadership of the Palestinian national liberation movement. Moreover, the status of the Israeli entity as a foreign colony implanted in the region impels the majority of the workers in the Zionist State to consolidate themselves around the ruling class, consequently obstructing the development of class war within Israel. This phenomenon is observable in the case of many colonialist settlements. This is observable in Algeria, where most of the sectors of the French colony that were Fascist and radically opposed to the Algerian revolution were from the petite bourgeoisie and the workers. Therefore, the liberation of Palestine is indisolubly linked with the victory of the Palestinian national liberation movement.

*As published in the Beirut daily *Al-Anwar*.

FARID AL-KHATIB
I don't consider my view to be identical with that of Fatah. I am a friend of Fatah, and my view is very close to its view . . .

The idea of coexistence in Palestinian State is not new. This idea was first brought up officially by Yahya Hamuda (Chairman of the Palestinian National Council) . . . Then in October, 1967, I believe, Abu Iyad (a Fatah leader) announced, at a press conference held by the Beirut newspaper *Al-Yawm*, the adoption by Fatah of the idea of the Democratic Palestinian State as a solution for the Zionist contradiction presently found on Arab soil . . .

The Democratic Palestinian State, as conceived by Fatah, I believe is as follows:

There is a basic condition for establishing the Democratic Palestinian State: the winning of victory. Otherwise it cannot be brought into effect. The slogan of the (Palestinian Democratic) State is one of struggle; it can in no way be isolated from the Palestinian national liberation movement . . .

In short, the Democratic State is linked to the Palestinian national liberation movement. I believe it is necessary to present the details of the Palestinian State gradually, for in presenting the idea Fatah wished to say to the world that the objective of the Palestinians and the Arabs is not to throw the Jews into the sea but to disband the Zionist State and establish a new one. What is sought is not the development of Israel into a form acceptable to the Arabs, as Member of Knesset Uri Avneri advocates; the objective is to disband the Zionist State and establish a new one, according to the will of the Palestinian national liberation movement and the will of the Jews who lived in Palestine originally, that is, before 1948, and those who came later . . .

There is no benefit in discussing details of the Democratic State at present, for the objective in presenting this slogan at the present stage is to leave a narrow opening for the Israeli enemy, while the resistance groups strike relentless blows at the enemy within Palestine, to the point that his military, economic and political forces are exhausted and he is sore pressed. Then the enemy will have no possibility but to look towards that narrow aperture, attempting to find an outlet. Then the Palestinian revolution can remove the veil, so that the Israeli enemy may find deliverance. Thus, it is not beneficial to remove the veil now.

THE REPRESENTATIVE OF THE ARAB
LIBERATION FRONT (a fedayeen organization of Iraqi influence)
There is no special (separate) solution for the Palestine issue. The solution must be within the framework of the Arab revolution, because the Palestine issue is not merely the paramount Arab issue but the substance and basic motivation of the Arab struggle. If the Arab nation suffers from backwardness, exploitation and disunity, these afflictions are much more severe in Palestine. That is, the Arab cause in the present historical stage is epitomized in the Palestine issue . . .

The liberation of Palestine will be the way for the Arabs to realize unity, not to set up regional State No. 15, which will only deepen disunity. The unified State will be the alternative to the Zionist entity, and it will be of necessity democratic, as long as we understand beforehand the dialectical connection between unity and Socialism. In the united Arab State all the minorities – denominational and others – will have equal rights . . .

When this slogan was put forth, it was understood that it was intended to conciliate progressive public opinion and the world leftist movement, but this cannot be accomplished with impractical slogans. The tactical nature of this slogan cannot elude public opinion . . .

The Arab Liberation Front considers the slogan of the (Democratic) Palestinian State, whether tactical or strategic, as incorrect, especially in the present situation, in which the Israeli enemy enjoys political, economic and military superiority, and settlement is liable to consecrate this superiority of the enemy . . .

The Liberation Front rejects this idea as a tactical step because if, let us assume, Israel agrees to it, the sponsors of the idea will have to accept it . . .

As I have already mentioned, the slogan of the Democratic State does not presently serve Arab interests. It is identical with what some regimes have proposed , that, since Israel has not accepted the Security Council resolution, we should accept this resolution, which consecrates the Zionist presence on Arab land.

SHAFIQ AL-HUT (a leader of the PLO and head of its Beirut office)
. . . The Palestinian problem is that of a Zionist-colonialist invasion at the expense of a land and a people known for thirteen centuries as the Palestinian Arab people . . .

I side with Farid al-Khatib in holding that there is no benefit in expatiating upon the slogan "Democratic Palestinian State." I hope the fedayeen organizations will not do so, although I would encourage discussion of it by those who are not in responsible positions. Whatever discussion of it there is on the part of the fighting groups may cause a sense of helplessness, despair or weakness . . .

As far as concerns the human situation of the Jews, which Farid al-Khatib mentioned, we should expose the Zionist movement and say to the Jew: The Zionist movement which brought you to Palestine did not supply a solution to your problem as a Jew; therefore you must return whence you came to seek another way of striving for a solution for what is called "the problem of the persecuted Jew in the world." As Marx has said, he has no alternative but to be assimilated into his society . . .

Even if we wished, by force of circumstances, a Democratic Palestinian State "period," this would mean its being non-Arab. Let us face matters honestly. When we speak simply of a Democratic Palestinian State, this means we discard its Arab identity. I say that on this subject we cannot negotiate, even if we possess the political power to authorize this kind of decision, because we thereby disregard an historical truth, namely, that this land and those who dwell upon it belong to a certain environment and a certain region, to which we are linked as one nation, one heritage and one hope – Unity, Freedom and Socialism . . .

If the slogan of the Democratic State was intended only to counter the claim that we wish to throw the Jews into the sea, this is indeed an apt slogan and an effective political and propaganda blow. But if we wish to regard it as the ultimate strategy of the Palestinian and Arab liberation movement, then I believe it requires a long pause for reflection, for it bears upon our history, just as our present and certainly our future.

I conclude with a warning, that this may be the beginning of a long dispute resulting in a substitute for the basic objective of the Palestinian revolution, which is the liberation of the Palestinian land and individual in the national sector, to which the land and the Palestinian individual are related (i.e. the pan-Arab sphere).

REPRESENTATIVE OF AL-SA'IQA (a Syrian fedayeen organization)
I agree with Shafiq al-Hut that there is no group which may determine independently the meaning of this slogan, or consent to its implementation. This problem does not belong to the Palestinians alone, because the Zionist design threatens the Arab region and not only the Palestinians, and every Arab citizen has the right to express his opinion concerning presumed or proposed solutions. Neither the Palestinian alone, nor any of the resistance movements, has the right to hold an independent view concerning the destiny of Palestine regarding the procedure to be adopted after the revolution or its victory.

It seems that this slogan has been raised prematurely, and this may be one of the principal reasons for the divergence of views concerning it. Thus, there is no consensus concerning the distinct meaning of this slogan . . .

The Jews are human beings like all others. No man can bear to live forever in tension, a state of emergency and threat. Every man searches for stability. However, the people living today in Palestine, subjected to this predicament, cannot return to the countries from which they emigrated, nor can they find an alternative to bearing arms against the Arab revolution, which continues to mean for the Jews the pulverization and ultimate liquidation of the millions living in Palestine.

I think that when we propose to those Jews a substitute for their present life, for the threat of death, we can reap benefit for our cause and make great strides on the way to victory. We cannot overlook the fact that these Jews, the majority of whom were born in Palestine, know no other homeland . . .

I was among those who thought five years ago that we must slaughter the Jews. But now I cannot imagine that, if we win one night, it will be possible for us to slaughter them, or even one tenth of them. I cannot conceive of it, neither as a man, nor as an Arab.

If so, what do we wish to do with these Jews? This is a problem for which I do not claim to have a ready answer. It is a problem which every Arab and Palestinian citizen has an obligation to express his opinion about, because it is yet early for a final, ripe formulation to offer the world and those living in Palestine.

Thus, I think that among many Jews, those living in Palestine, especially the Arab Jews, there is a great desire to return to their countries of origin, since the Zionist efforts to transform them into a homogeneous, cohesive nation have failed. There is a well-known human feeling – yearning for one's homeland, one's birthplace. There are a number of known facts concerning the Jews living in Palestine today which clearly point to this feeling among them. They desire to return to their countries of origin, especially Jews from the Arab region.

It should be made clear that the Arabs initially blocked the way for Jews to return to their countries. If the Arab Governments had treated these situations from the start, the problem would have "budged" by now. There are a number of known circumstances which point to this.

We have made the Jews think constantly for twenty years that the sea is before them and the enemy behind, and that there was no recourse but to fight to defend their lives . . .

For us, as the "Vanguards of the Popular War of Liberation," al-Sa'iqa, the slogan is not tactical but strategic. And, as I have said, we cannot imagine how it is possible to solve the problem of these Jews without permitting them to dwell either in Palestine or in another homeland they choose. My estimation is that many of them will choose to live outside Palestine, for Palestine will not be able to absorb all the Palestinians, as well as the Jews living there.

REPRESENTATIVE OF THE DEMOCRATIC FRONT

. . . The organization mentioned above (Matzpen) advocates a Socialist Palestine, in which the Arabs and Jews will live in equality, that is, having equal rights and obligations, and that it be part of a federal union in the Middle East . . . It is hard to say that there is responsiveness in Israel to the idea of a Democratic State. Although the idea of Matzpen is more acceptable from the Arab viewpoint, even that of Arab nationalism, Matzpen merely expresses the view of the Left; in fact, an insignificant minority of what is called the Israeli Left. Although it is a vocal and noisy organization, it represents but a small fraction of the Israeli Left . . .

It may be assumed that the continuing generation process, imposed upon history but actually existing, of what is called Jewish nationalism in Palestine must be terminated. This is not to be annihilation of this human group living there, because such a solution is not only inhuman, it is also impractical. It must be terminated by the victory of the Palestinian revolution. I agree with the representative of al-Sa'iqa that the slogan of the Palestinian State is not a tactical slogan in the Machiavellian sense. We adopt this slogan not simply in order to win world public opinion, or to deceive the Jews regarding their destiny. This slogan must be presented clearly and with intellectual honesty. It should be stated that Zionism must cease to exist in Palestine, but this does not necessitate the human liquidation of the Israeli community living in Palestine . . .

We do not adopt this slogan because we are weak, with the intention of changing when we become strong. The matter must be explained otherwise. Our struggle must have a clear objective based on actual reality, not on our desires and wishful thinking . . .

As for the question concerning what will happen if Israel agrees to our impractical assumptions on which we base a political position, the answer is: Israel will not agree to this slogan, and it is impossible for Israel to agree, because it means elimination of the State of Israel and all the class interests on which Israel is based. There has never been in history a class, social, or political power which has consented to its own elimination . . .

MODERATOR

. . . Can we consider the Kurdish problem and the manner of its solution as similiar to the Jewish problem and its solution under the heading of the slogan of one Democratic State? . . .

REPRESENTATIVE OF THE LIBERATION FRONT
Our view of the subject of Kurdish national rights follows from objective and historical considerations which substantially contradict the nature and objectives of the Zionist movement. The Kurds comprise a nationality having a distinct, well-known historical, geographical and human dimension . . .

In this connection, we must not forget the historical, religious and social ties that have bound Kurdish-Arab brotherhood for centuries. Salah al-Din al-Ayyubi (who was a Kurd) was the one who led the struggle against the foreign presence in the Arab region a number of centuries ago.

FARID AL-KHATIB
I agree with the view of the representative of the Democratic Popular Front, namely, if a group of people lives together for a long time in a homeland, they become a nationality, as has happened in America. But it seems that calling the Jewish denomination a nationality is premature . . .

The Jews are a denomination associated with more than one people; the Arabs are a people which embraces more than one religion . . .

As far as the Arab character of the Democratic State is concerned, the Jews in Palestine have the right to express their view concerning the Arab character of the Democratic State in a democratic manner. And although it is possible to say that the Democratic State is Arab, and to say furthermore that it is a union, it is advisable to hold back additional information until the appropriate stages in the evolution of the resistance are reached. When the Zionist movement came to Palestine, it first sought a refuge, afterwards a homeland, and then a State; and now it is striving to build an empire within and outside Palestine (i.e. Zionism also disclosed its objectives in stages).

There is nothing to be gained by summoning the Jews in the Zionist State to join national liberation movement, as Shafiq al-Hut proposed, when he advocated convening the unified State at once. This will not convince the Jews of the world and world public opinion.

As far as concerns the number of Palestinians, all those who emigrated to Latin America in the nineteenth century, and those who live in the desert, in exile, under conquest, or in prison, all are citizens in the State. For example: the number of Bethlehemite residents living in South America exceeds the number of those Bethlehemites living in occupied Palestine, and the combined total (of all Palestinians) is not less than that of the Jews not living in the Zionist State . . .

SHAFIQ AL-HUT
First, how can Farid (al-Khatib) think that the Jews and Zionists who came to set up an empire in our country have the privilege to express their democratic right in the Palestinian State? Second, how can he claim that it is difficult to convince Jewish citizens to join the liberation movement?

FARID AL-KHATIB
I think that most of the Jews living in Palestine are groups of people who were deceived by the Zionist movement and the world imperialist movement. And the Jew, as a man, has the right to express his opinion in a democratic manner regarding his future life after the collapse of the Zionist State, which is opposed

to the Democratic State insofar as it discriminates between the Eastern Jew and the Western Jew and the Circassian Jew.

The second point: The greatest ambition of the revolution is to polarize Jews of the Zionist State into the ranks of the resistance movement . . . But what I wanted to say is that it is difficult to persuade the Jews to join the resistance movement because its immediate objective is to dissolve the Zionist contradiction within the Zionist State . . .

REPRESENTATIVE OF THE DEMOCRATIC FRONT

It seems to me that many of the disagreements that exist concerning this idea can be traced to some manner of misunderstanding or lack of communication . . . This state is not bi-national in the sense that there would be two national States joined together in one form or another. This solution must be rejected, not only because it is inconsistent with our own desire, but also because it is not a true democratic solution. It is rather a solution that will represent the continuation of the national conflict which exists between the Jews and Arabs, not a solution of this conflict. It is impossible to speak of a democratic solution if it is powerless to eliminate the conflict between the different denominations and peoples within the Democratic State. When we speak of democracy it must be clear that we do not mean liberal democracy in the manner of "one man, one vote." We mean a people's democratic regime, which will put to an end the social basis upon which Zionism rests, and will consequently settle the class conflicts, and then those among the denominations and peoples.

THE REPRESENTATIVE OF AL-SA'IQA

The struggle is a protracted and very bitter one, and I think that adopting the slogan of the Democratic State at this early stage is premature, and that the Palestinian revolution should persevere in the way of the people's war of national liberation.

SHAFIQ AL-HUT

I agree with the representative of al-Sa'iqa, and I believe we are on the same wave-length.

REPRESENTATIVE OF THE DEMOCRATIC FRONT

I support what the representative of al-Sa'iqa says.

FARID AL-KHATIB

I also.

TEXT OF POLITICAL PLAN APPROVED BY THE PLO COUNCIL, JUNE 8, 1974*

On the basis of the National Palestinian Covenant and the PLO's political plan as approved at the 11th session (6-12 January 1973); and in the belief that a just and lasting peace in the region is impossible without restoration of the full national rights of the Palestinian nation, and first and foremost the right of return and self-determination on the homeland's soil entire; and after having studied the political circumstances as they developed during the period between its previous and its present session - the Council resolves as follows:

1. Emphasis of the PLO's position with relation to Security Council Resolution 242, which overlooks the national rights of our nation and approaches the Palestinian issue as a refugee problem.
   The Council therefore rejects any action on that basis on any level of Arab and international operation, including the Geneva Conference.
2. The PLO is fighting by every means, and primarily by the armed struggle, to free the Palestinian land and establish a national, independent and fighting government over every part of the soil of Palestine to be freed. This calls for a considerable change in the balance of forces, for the good of our nation and its struggle.
3. The PLO objects to any plan for a Palestinian entity at the price of recognition, peace (*sulh*), secure boundaries, surrender of national rights and deprivation of our nation's prerogative of return and of self-determination in its homeland.
4. Any step of liberation is a link in realizing the strategy of the PLO for the establishment of a Palestinian-democratic State, as resolved by the previous Councils.
5. It is necessary to struggle alongside the national Jordanian forces for the establishment of a national Jordanian-Palestinian front, with the purpose of forming a national democratic government in Jordan that will safeguard solidarity.
6. The PLO struggles to unify the efforts of the two nations and all the forces of the Arab liberation movements which subscribe to this plan.
7. In view of this plan, the PLO fights to strengthen national unity and raise it to a height where it will be capable of fulfilling its national missions.
8. After its establishment, the national Palestinian government will fight for the unity of the countries of confrontation, to complete the liberation of all the Palestinian land and as a step in the direction of overall Arab unity.
9. The PLO fights to strengthen its solidarity with the Socialist countries and the forces of liberation and progress, to frustrate all the Zionist reactionary and imperialist plans.
10. On the basis of this plan, the leadership of the revolution will formulate tactics that will enable these objectives to be realized.

*Broadcast on Saut Falastin Radio, Egypt.

RESOLUTION 242,
ADOPTED BY THE UNITED NATIONS SECURITY
COUNCIL, NOVEMBER 22, 1967

The Security Council,

Expressing its continuing concern with the grave situation in the Middle East,

Emphasizing the inadmissibility of the acquisition of territory by war and the need to work for a just and lasting peace in which every State in the area can live in security,

Emphasizing further that all Member States in their acceptance of the Charter of the United Nations have undertaken a commitment to act in accordance with Article 2 of the Charter,

1. *Affirms* that the fulfilment of Charter principles requires the establishment of a just and lasting peace in the Middle East which should include the application of both the following principles:

(i) Withdrawal of Israeli and armed forces from territories occupied in the recent conflict;

(ii) Termination of all claims or states of belligerency and respect for and acknowedgement of the sovereignty: territorial integrity and political independence of every State in the area and their right to live in peace within secure and recognized boundaries free from threats or acts of force;

2. *Affirms further* the necessity

(a) For guaranteeing freedom of navigation through international waterways in the area;

(b) For achieving a just settlement of the refugee problem;

(c) For guaranteeing the territorial inviolability and political independence of every State in the area, through measure including the establishment of demilitarized zones;

3. *Requests* the Secretary-General to designate a Special Representative to proceed to the Middle East to establish and maintain contacts with the States concerned in order to promote agreement and assist efforts to achieve a peaceful and accepted settlement in accordance with the provisions and principles in this resolution;

4. *Requests* the Secretary-General to report to the Security Council on the progress of the efforts of the Special Representative as soon as possible.

Resolution 242 (1967) was adopted *unanimously.*

THE CAMP DAVID ACCORDS, SEPTEMBER 17, 1978

Following are the texts of the two Agreements reached at the Camp David Summit and signed September 17 at the White House.

Mohammed Anwar Al-Sadat, President of the Arab Republic of Egypt, and Menachem Begin, Prime Minister of Israel, met with Jimmy Carter, President of the United States of America, at Camp David from September 5 to September 17, 1978, and have agreed on the following framework for peace in the Middle East. They invite other parties to the Arab-Israel conflict to adhere to it.

The search for peace in the Middle East must be guided by the following:

- The agreed basis for a peaceful settlement of the conflict between Israel and its neighbors is United Nations Security Council Resolution 242, in all its parts.
- After four wars during thirty years, despite intensive human efforts, the Middle East, which is the cradle of civilization and the birthplace of three great religions, does not yet enjoy the blessings of peace. The people of the Middle East yearn for peace so that the vast human and natural resources of the region can be turned to the pursuits of peace and so that this area can become a model for coexistence and cooperation among nations.
- The historic initiative of President Sadat in visiting Jerusalem and the reception accorded to him by the Parliament, Government and People of Israel, and the reciprocal visit of Prime Minister Begin to Ismailia, the peace proposals made by both leaders, as well as the warm reception of these missions by the peoples of both countries, have created an unprecedented opportunity for peace which must not be lost if this generation and future generations are to be spared the tragedies of war.
- The provisions of the Charter of the United Nations and the other accepted norms of international law and legitimacy now provide accepted standards for the conduct of relations among all states.
- To achieve a relationship of peace, in the spirit of Article 2 of the United Nations Charter, future negotiations between Israel and any neighbor prepared to negotiate peace and security with it, are necessary for the purpose of carrying out all the provisions and principles of Resolutions 242 and 338.
- Peace requires respect for the sovereignty, territorial integrity and political independence of every state in the area and their right to live in peace within secure and recognized boundaries free from threats or acts of force. Progress toward that goal can accelerate movement toward a new era of reconciliation in the Middle East marked by cooperation in promoting economic development, in maintaining stability, and in assuring security.
- Security is enhanced by a relationship of peace and by cooperation between nations which enjoy normal relations. In addition, under the terms of peace treaties, the parties can, on the basis of reciprocity, agree to special security arrangements such as demilitarized zones, limited armaments areas, early warning stations, the presence of international forces, liaison, agreed measures for monitoring, and other arrangements that they agree are useful.

FRAMEWORK

Taking these factors into account, the parties are determined to reach a just, comprehensive, and durable settlement of the Middle East conflict through the conclusion of peace treaties based on Security Council Resolutions 242 and 338; in all their parts. Their purpose is to achieve peace and good neighborly relations. They recognize that, for peace to endure, it must involve all those who have been most deeply affected by the conflict. They therefore agree that this framework as appropriate is intended by them to constitute a basis for peace not only between Egypt and Israel, but also between Israel and each of its other neighbors which is prepared to negotiate peace with Israel on this basis. With that objective in mind, they have agreed to proceed as follows:

A. West Bank and Gaza

1. Egypt, Israel, Jordan and the representatives of the Palestinian people should participate in negotiations on the resolution of the Palestinian problem in all its aspects. To achieve that objective, negotiations relating to the West Bank and Gaza should proceed in three stages:

(a) Egypt and Israel agree that, in order to ensure a peaceful and orderly transfer of authority , and taking into account the security concerns of all the parties, there should be transitional arrangements for the West Bank and Gaza for a period not exceeding five years. In order to provide full autonomy to the inhabitants, under these arrangements the Israeli military government and its civilian administration will be withdrawn as soon as a self-governing authority has been freely elected by the inhabitants of these areas to replace the existing military government. To negotiate the details of a transitional arrangement, the Government of Jordan will be invited to join the negotiations on the basis of this framework. These new arrangements should give due consideration both to the principle of self-government by the inhabitants of these territories and to the legitimate security concerns of the parties involved.

(b) Egypt, Israel, and Jordan will agree on the modalities for establishing the elected self-governing authority in the West Bank and Gaza. The delegations of Egypt and Jordan may include Palestinians from the West Bank and Gaza or other Palestinians as mutually agreed. The parties will negotiate an agreement which will define the powers and responsibilities of the self-governing authority to be exercised in the West Bank and Gaza. A withdrawal of Israeli Armed Forces will take place and there will be a redeployment of the remaining Israeli forces into specified security locations. The agreement will also include arrangements for assuring internal and external security and public order. A strong local police force will be established, which may include Jordanian citizens. In addition, Israeli and Jordanian forces will participate in joint patrols and in the manning of control posts to assure the security of the borders.

(c) When the self-governing authority (administrative council) in the West Bank and Gaza is established and inaugurated, the transitional period of five years will begin. As soon as possible, but not later than the third year after the beginning of the transitional period, negotiations will take place to determine the final status of the West Bank and Gaza and its relationship with its neighbors, and to conclude a peace treaty between Israel and Jordan by the end of the transitional period. These negotiations will be conducted among Egypt, Israel, Jordan, and the elected representatives of the inhabitants of the West Bank and Gaza. Two separate but related committees will be convened, one committee, consisting of representatives of the four parties which will negotiate and agree on the final status of the West Bank and Gaza, and its relationship with its neighbors, and the second committee, consisting of representatives of Israel and representatives of Jordan to be joined by the elected representatives of the inhabitants of the West Bank and Gaza, to negotiate the peace treaty between Israel and Jordan, taking into account the agreement reached on the final status of the West Bank and Gaza. The negotiations shall be based on all the provisions and principles of U.N. Security Council Resolution 242. The negotiations will resolve, among other matters, the location of the boundaries and the nature of the security arrangements. The resolution from the negotiations must also recognize the legitimate rights of the Palestine people and their just requirements. In this way, the Palestinians will participate in the determination of their own future through: (1) The negotiations among Egypt, Israel, Jordan and the representatives of the inhabitants of the West Bank and Gaza to agree on the final status of the West Bank and Gaza and other outstanding issues by the end of the transitional period. (2) Submitting their agreement to a vote by the elected representatives of the inhabitants of the West Bank and Gaza. (3) Providing for the elected representatives of the inhabitants of the West Bank and Gaza to decide how they shall govern themselves consistent with the provisions of their agreement. (4) Participating as stated above in the work of the committee negotiating the peace treaty between Israel and Jordan.

2. All necessary measures will be taken and provisions made to assure the security of Israel and its neighbors during the transitional period and beyond. To assist in providing such security, a strong local police force will be constituted by the self-governing authority. It will be composed of inhabitants of the West Bank and Gaza. The police will maintain continuing liaison on internal security matters with the designated Israeli, Jordanian, and Egyptian officers.

3. During the transitional period, representatives of Egypt, Israel, Jordan, and the self-governing authority will constitute a continuing committee to decide by agreement on the modalities of admission of persons displaced from the West Bank and Gaza in 1967, together with necessary measures to prevent disruption and disorder. Other matters of common concern may also be dealt with by this committee.

4. Egypt and Israel will work with each other and with other interested parties to establish agreed procedures for a prompt, just and permanent implementation of the resolution of the refugee problem.

B. Egypt-Israel

1. Egypt and Israel undertake not to resort to the threat or the use of force to settle disputes. Any disputes shall be settled by peaceful means in accordance with the provisions of Article 33 of the Charter of the United Nations.

2. In order to achieve peace between them, the parties agree to negotiate in good faith with a goal of concluding within three months from the signing of this framework a peace treaty between them, while inviting the other parties to the conflict to proceed simultaneously to negotiate and conclude similar peace treaties with a view to achieving a comprehensive peace in the area. The

framework for the conclusion of a peace treaty between Egypt and Israel will govern the peace negotiations between them. The parties will agree on the modalities and the timetable for the implementation of their obligations under the treaty.

C. Associated Principles

1. Egypt and Israel state that the principles and provisions described below should apply to peace treaties between Israel and each of its neighbors – Egypt, Jordan, Syria and Lebanon.

2. Signatories shall establish among themselves relationships normal to states at peace with one another. To this end, they should undertake to abide by all the provisions of the Charter of the United Nations. Steps to be taken in this respect include:

(a) Full recognition;

(b) Abolishing economic boycotts;

(c) Guaranteeing that under their jurisdiction the citizens of the other parties shall enjoy the protection of the due process of law.

3. Signatories should explore possibilities for economic development in the context of final peace treaties, with the objective of contributing to the atmosphere of peace, cooperation and friendship which is their common goal.

4. Claims Commissions may be established for the mutual settlement of all financial claims.

5. The United States shall be invited to participate in the talks on matters related to the modalities of the implementation of the Agreements and working out the timetable for the carrying out of the obligations of the parties.

6. The United Nations Security Council shall be requested to endorse the peace treaties and ensure that their provisions shall not be violated. The permanent members of the Security Council shall be requested to underwrite the peace treaties and ensure respect for their provisions. They shall also be requested to conform their policies and actions with the undertakings contained in this framework.

FRAMEWORK FOR THE CONCLUSION OF A PEACE TREATY BETWEEN EGYPT AND ISRAEL

In order to achieve peace between them, Israel and Egypt agree to negotiate in good faith with a goal of concluding within three months of the signing of this framework a peace treaty between them. It is agreed that:

The site of the negotiations will be under a United Nations flag at a location or locations to be mutually agreed.

All of the principles of U.N. Resolution 242 will apply in this resolution of the dispute between Israel and Egypt.

Unless otherwise mutually agreed, terms of the peace treaty will be implemented between two and three years after the peace treaty is signed.

The following matters are agreed between the parties:

(a) The full excercise of Egyptian sovereignty up to the internationally recognized border between Egypt and mandated Palestine;

(b) The withdrawal of Israeli Armed Forces from the Sinai;

(c) The use of airfields left by the Israelis near El Arish, Rafar, Ras en Naqb, and Sharm el Sheikh for civilian purposes only, including possible commercial use by all nations;

(d) The right of free passage by ships of Israel through the Gulf of Suez and the Suez Canal on the basis of the Constantinople Convention of 1888 applying to all nations; the Strait of Tiran and the Gulf of Aqaba are international waterways to be open to all nations for unimpeded and nonsuspendable freedom of navigation and overflight;

(e) The construction of a highway between the Sinai and Jordan near Eilat with guaranteed free and peaceful passage by Egypt and Jordan; and

(f) The stationing of military forces listed below.

Stationing of Forces

a. No more than one division (mechanized or infantry) of Egyptian Armed Forces will be stationed within an area lying approximately 50 kilometers (KM) east of the Gulf of Suez and the Suez Canal.

b. Only United Nations Forces and civil police equipped with light weapons to perform normal police functions will be stationed within an area lying west of the international border and the Gulf of Aqaba, varying in width from 20 km to 40 km.

c. In the area within three km east of the international border there will be Israeli limited military forces not to exceed four infantry battalions and United Nations observers.

d. Border patrol units, not to exceed three battalions, will supplement the civil police in maintaining order in the area not included above.

The exact demarcation of the above areas will be as decided during the peace negotiations.

Early warning stations may exist to insure compliance with the terms of the agreement.

United Nations forces will be stationed: (a) in part of the area in the Sinai lying within about 20 km of the Mediterranean Sea and adjacent to the intenational border, and (b) in the Sharm el Sheikh area to ensure freedom of passage through the Strait of Tiran; and these forces will not be removed unless such removal is approved by the Security Council of the United Nations with a unanimous vote of the five permanent members.

After a peace treaty is signed, and after the interim withdrawal is complete, normal relations will be established between Egypt and Israel, including: full recognition, including diplomatic, economic and cultural relations; termination of economic boycotts and barriers to the free movement of goods and peoples; and mutual protection of citizens by the due process of law.

Interim Withdrawal
Between three months and nine months after the signing of the peace treaty, all Israeli forces will withdraw east of a line extending from a point east of El Arish to Ras Muhamad, the exact location of this line to be determined by mutual agreement.

ISRAEL'S AUTONOMY PROPOSALS, 1978

In the Camp David Agreement signed on 17 September 1978 between Egypt and Israel, with the United States signing as a witness, agreement was reached on a plan for the solution of the problem of the Palestinian Arabs, that includes a proposal for full autonomy for the Palestinian Arabs living in Judea, Samaria and Gaza. The manner of establishing this autonomy, as well as its powers, were to be determined in negotiations between the signatories (Jordan was invited to participate, but did not respond). It was Israel that first raised the idea of autonomy that was later to serve as the basis of the Camp David agreement. For the first time in the history of the Palestinian Arab inhabitants of Judea- Samaria and the Gaza district, they were offered an opportunity of this kind to conduct their own affairs by themselves. Since 1979, talks have been held for the implementation of this agreement; there were intermissions in the negotiations, but talks were resumed intensively in the summer of 1981, leading to thorough-going clarification of the positions of the parties. At these talks Israel put forward its proposals with regard to the self-governing authority (administrative council), its powers, responsibilities and structure as well as other related issues. The main points of Israel's proposals, as submitted in the course of the negotiations were as follows:

SCOPE, JURISDICTION AND STRUCTURE OF
THE SELF-GOVERNING AUTHORITY
(ADMINISTRATIVE COUNCIL):

1. The Camp David accords set forth the establishment of a self-governing authority (administrative council) that will comprise one body representing the Arab inhabitants of Judea, Samaria and the Gaza district, who will choose this body in free elections, and it will assume those functional powers that will be transferred to it. Thus the Palestinian Arabs will for the first time have an elected and representative body, in accordance with their own wishes and free choice, that will be able to carry out the functions assigned to it as an administrative council.

2. The members of the administrative council will be able, as a group, to discuss all subjects within the council's competence, apportioning among themselves the spheres of responsibility for the various functions. Within the domain of its assigned powers and responsibilities, the council will be responsible for planning and carrying out its activities.

POWERS OF THE SELF-GOVERNING AUTHORITY
(ADMINISTRATIVE COUNCIL):

1.a. Under the terms of the Camp David agreement, the parties have to reach an agreement on the powers and responsibilities of the authority. Israel's detailed proposals include a list of powers that will be given to the authority and that, by any reasonable and objective criterion, represent a wide and comprehensive range of fields of operation. Without any doubt, the transferring of these powers constitutes the bestowal of full autonomy - in the full meaning of that term.

b. The powers to be granted the authority, under these proposals, are in the following domains:

1. *Administration of Justice*: Supervision of the administrative system of the courts in the areas; dealing with matters connected with the prosecution system and with the registration of companies, partnerships, patents, trademarks, etc.

2. *Agriculture*: All branches of agriculture and fisheries, nature reserves and parks.

3. *Finance*: Budget of the administrative council and allocations among its various divisions; taxation.

4. *Civil Service*: Appointment and working conditions of the Council's employees. (Today, the civil service of the inhabitants of Judea-Samaria and Gaza, within the framework of the Military Government's Civilian Administration, numbers about 12,000 persons.)

5. *Education and Culture*: Operation of the network of schools in the areas, from kindergarten to higher education; supervision of cultural, artistic and sporting activities.

6. *Health*: Supervision of hospitals and clinics; operation of sanitary and other services related to public health.

7. *Housing and Public Works*: Construction, housing for the inhabitants and public works projects.

8. *Transportation and Communications*: maintenance and coordination of transport, road traffic, meteorology; local postal and communications services.

9. *Labour and Social Welfare*: Welfare, labour and employment services, including the operation of labour exchanges.

10. *Municipal Affairs*: Matters concerning municipalities and their effective operation.

11. *Local Police*: Operation of a strong local police force, as provided for in the Camp David agreement, and maintenance of prisons for criminal offenders sentenced by the courts in the areas.

12. *Religious Affairs*: Provision and maintenance of religious facilities for all religious communities among the Arab inhabitants of Judea-Samaria and the Gaza district.

13. *Industry, Commerce and Tourism*: Development of industry, commerce, workshops and tourist services.

2. The council will have full powers in its spheres of competence to determine its budget, to enter into contractual obligations, to sue and be sued and to engage manpower. It will, moreover, have wide powers to promulgate regulations, as required by a body of this kind. In the nature of things, in view of the free

movement that will prevail between Judea-Samaria and the Gaza district and Israel and for the general welfare of the inhabitants, arrangements will be agreed upon in the negotiations, in a number of domains, for cooperation and coordination with Israel. The administrative council will, hence, have full scope to exercise its wide-ranging powers under the terms of the autonomy agreement. These powers embrace all walks of life, and will enable the inhabitants in the areas concerned to enjoy full autonomy.

3. Size: The size of the administrative council must reflect its functions and its essential purpose: it is an administrative council, whose representative character finds expression in its establishment through free elections, by the Arab inhabitants of Judea, Samaria and Gaza. Clearly, the criterion for determining the number of its members must be the functions that the council is empowered to perform. We propose, therefore, that the number of members will conform with the functions listed above.

4. Free Elections: Elections to the administrative council, under Israel's proposals, will be absolutely free, as stipulated in the Camp David agreement. Under the terms of the agreement, the parties will agree upon the modalities of the elections; as a matter of fact, in past negotiations a long list of principles and guidelines has already been prepared tn this matter. In these free elections, all the rights pertaining to a peaceful assembly, freedom of expression and secret balloting will be preserved and assured, and all necessary steps will be taken to prevent any interference with the election process. The holding of an absolutely free and unhampered election process will thus be assured in full, under the law, and in keeping with the tradition of free elections practiced in democratic societies. These elections will, in many respects, constitute a new departure in the region around us which in most of its parts is not too close to the ways of democracy, and in which free elections are a rare phenomenon. It is of some interest, therefore, to note that Judea-Samaria and Gaza, under Israel's Mllitary Government since 1967, have exemplified the practical possibility of totally free elections in these areas. In 1972, and again in 1976, Israel organized free elections in these areas based on the tradition and model of its own democratic and liberal tradition and custom; voters and elected officials alike concede that these were free elections in the fullest sense. The elections in the administrative council will be organized and supervised by a central elections committee whose composition has been agreed upon by the parties.

5. Time of elections and establishment of the self-governing authority (administrative council): The elections will be held as expeditiously as possible after agreement will have been reached on the autonomy. This was set forth in the joint letter of the late President Sadat and of Prime Minister Begin to President Carter, dated 26 March 1979, setting forth the manner in which the self-governing authority (administrative council) is to be established, under the terms of the Camp David agreement.

6. Within one month following the elections, the self-governing authority (administrative council) is to be established and inaugurated, and at that time the transitional period of five years will begin – again, in conformity with the Camp David agreement and the joint letter.

7. Hence, every effort will be made to hold elections without delay, once an agreement is reached, to be followed by the establishment of the self-governing authority (administrative council).

8. Following the elections and the establishment of the self-governing authority (administrative council) the military government and its civilian administration will be withdrawn, a withdrawal of Israeli armed forces will take place, and there will be a redeployment of the remaining Israeli forces into specified security locations, in full conformity with the Camp David agreement. Israel will present to the other parties in the negotiations the map of the specified security location of the redeployment. It goes without saying that all this will be done for the purpose of safeguarding the security of Israel as well as of the Arab inhabitants of Judea-Samaria and Gaza and of the Israeli citizens residing in these areas.

9. All of the above indicates Israel's readiness to observe the Camp David agreement fully and in every detail, in letter and spirit, while safeguarding the interests of all concerned.

ISRAEL'S PEACE INITIATIVE, APRIL 1989

Prime Minister Shamir's visit to the United States (April 4-14) and his discussions with President Bush and Secretary of State Baker have opened a new opportunity for advancing the peace process between Israel and its Arab neighbors. Speaking on the White House lawn on April 6 after his talks with the President, Prime Minister Shamir publicly presented his 4-point peace initiative for which the Bush Administration has expressed support.

The peace initiative focuses on the following key elements:

- ◆ The Camp David partners' reaffirmation of their commitment to the Accords and peace;
- ◆ Negotiations and cooperation with the Arab countries;
- ◆ A multinational effort to solve the Arab refugee problem;
- ◆ Free democratic elections in Judea-Samaria and the Gaza District as a stepping-stone to peace.

THE FOUR POINTS – AS PRESENTED BY
PRIME MINISTER SHAMIR

1. Reaffirmed Commitment to the Camp David Accords.
". . . we propose an effort to make the existing peace between Israel and Egypt, based on the Camp David Accords, a cornerstone for expanding peace in the region. We call upon the three signatories of the Camp David Accords, at this 10th anniversary of the Treaty of Peace, to reaffirm indeed their dedication to the Accords."

2. Negotiations for Peace with the Arab Countries.
". . . we call upon the United States and Egypt to make it clear to the Arab governments that they must abandon their hostility and belligerency towards Israel. They must replace political warfare and economic boycotts with negotiations and cooperation."

3. A Solution to the Arab Refugee Problem.
". . . we call for a multinational effort, under the leadership of the U.S. and with substantial Israeli participation, to finally solve the Arab refugee problem, perpetuated by Arab governments, while Israel absorbs hundreds of thousands of Jewish refugees from Arab countries. All these refugees should have decent housing and live in dignity. This process does not have to await a political solution or to substitute for it."

4. Free Democratic Elections in Judea-Samaria and the Gaza District.
"...in order to launch a political negotiating process, we propose free democratic elections, free from an atmosphere of PLO violence, terror and intimidation, among the Palestinian Arabs of Judea, Samaria and Gaza. Their purpose is to produce a delegation to negotiate an interim period of a self-governing administration. The shape of modalities and participation in the elections will have to be discussed, The interim phase is to provide a vital test of coexistence and cooperation. It will be followed by negotiations for a permanent agreement. All proposed options will be examined during these negotiations."

STEPS TOWARDS ELECTIONS IN THE TERRITORIES
The details of the Prime Minister's proposal to hold elections among the Palestinian Arabs of the territories have still to be developed and elaborated: a working group within the Israel Government will be established, further discussions will be held with the United States, and agreement will be sought with the Palestinian Arabs of the territories.

The favorable U.S. response to the proposal is highly encouraging. Moreover, the Palestinian Arabs in Judea-Samaria and the Gaza District have shown some signs of interest in the possibility of elections, notwithstanding the negative reaction by Arafat and other leading figures in the PLO. The PLO's attitude shows that it is interested only in imposing its own will on the Palestinian Arab residents of the territories, and not in giving them the opportunity to express themselves in a manner which would serve their own interests.

Israel is hopeful that the Palestinian Arabs in Judea-Samaria and the Gaza District will grasp the opportunity offered them. PLO intimidation and violence should be recognized for the anti-peace and anti-democratic danger that it is. The PLO's aim is to obstruct and undermine, not to build. The Palestinian Arabs should be given full encouragement to withstand such pressures.

THE PRIME MINISTER'S PROPOSALS IN
THE BROADER CONTEXT
The Government of Israel will make every effort to achieve peace through direct negotiations with its Arab neighbors, including the Palestinian Arabs of Judea-Samaria and the Gaza District. Elections in the territories and an interim phase are not an end in themselves, but a stepping-stone on the way to a final settlement which would be mutually acceptable to both sides, thus ensuring a genuine and lasting peace.

Israel recognizes that countries must take risks for peace. So Israel did. This was demonstrated by the sacrifices made by Israel within the framework of the Camp David Accords and the Treaty of Peace with Egypt. However, Israel cannot be expected to take steps that would endanger its security and very existence. With the exception of Egypt, the main threat faced by Israel remains the Arab states which reject Israel's right to exist. In an interview in *Time* magazine on April 3, Syria's President Assad made his intentions vis-à-vis Israel quite clear when he said, ''The Israelis are an alien people with another heritage and another history. They are antagonistic to this area.'' Syria and other Arab countries have amassed enormous quantities of sophisticated conventional arms, as well as chemical weapons the likes of which Iraq and Libya have already used against innocent civilians. Israel must contend with the reality of a region where extremism and militant fundamentalism is prevalent. A Palestinian state between Israel and Jordan would add to the danger, for in keeping with the PLO's ''Phased Program'' doctrine, its ultimate purpose would be to trigger a general war against Israel.

For movement towards peace, Israel needs bona fide peace partners. The involvement of both Jordan and the Palestinian Arabs of Judea-Samaria and the Gaza District in negotiations must be an integral part of the peace process for it to succeed. Israel believes that a mutually acceptable peace settlement is possible, and that a process of dialogue, negotiations, and movement towards coexistence will ensure this. Although much attention has focused on the subject of elections in the territories, it should be stressed that the Prime Minister's initiative contains FOUR points, all essential to the promotion of the peace process. Prime Minister Shamir's 4-point initiative creates a new opportunity for progress.

BIBLIOGRAPHY

Before listing, below, the specific works consulted, it should be mentioned that a variety of other works and publications have been used. These include the Holy Bible (both Old and New Testaments), The Koran, and other scriptural writings, plus various publications of the Israel Foreign Office (Information Department), of the Palestine Liberation Organization, of the Anti-Defamation League, of the World Organization of Jews from Arab Countries (WOJAC), and of course many newspapers and journals. ("Dry Bones" cartoons are from the *Jerusalem Post*.)

Akram, Zaitar, *Attawra Al Arabia* (The Palestinian Revolution), Cairo, 1965

Al-Husseini, Amin, *Khakaik An Kadiat Filastin* (The Truth About the Palestinian Problem), Cairo, 1954

Alsakakini, Halil, *Al Nahda Al Ortodoxia Fi Filastin* (The Orthodox Awakening in Palestine), Beirut, 1939

American-Israel Friendship League, *The Birth of Two Nations,* New York, 1985

Aruri, Naseer H., *Palestinians in Jordan: Two Nations and One State,* Southeastern Massachusetts University, Unpub. disser., 1973

Aumann, Moshe, *The Palestinian Labyrinth – A Way Out,* Jerusalem, 1985

Ben-Gad, Yitschak, *Palestinian Arab National Movement 1929-1939,* Unpub. disser., 1975

Bentwich, Norman, *England in Palestine,* London, 1932

Blum, Yehuda Z., *For Zion's Sake,* Herzl Press, New York, 1987

Cohen, Aharon, *Yisrael Vehaolam Ha'aravi* (Israel and the Arab World), Xerjavoa, 1964

Davis, Leonard J., *Myths and Facts, 1989,* Washington, D.C., 1989

Democratic Front, The, *Harakat Al-Muqawama Al-Filastiniyya Fi Waqi'Ikha Al-Rahin,* Dar Al-Tali'a, Beirut, 1969

Eilat, Eliahu, *Haj Mohammed Amin Al Husseini, The Mufti of Jerusalem,* Tel Aviv, 1968

Gibb, H. R., *The Arabs,* New York, 1940

Harkavi, Yehoshafat, *Emdat Ha'aravim Besichsuch Yisrael – Yisrael-Arav* (The Arab Position in the Arab-Israeli Conflict), Tel Aviv, 1967

Harkavi, Yehoshafat, *Ben Yisrael Learav* (Between Israel and the Arabs), Tel Aviv, 1968

Harkavi, Yehoshafat, *Three Articles on the Slogan of the Democratic State*, booklet in English translated from *Ma'ariv*, April 3, 1970-April 17, 1970

Harkavi, Yehoshafat, *Yesodot Besichsuch Yisrael Arav,* Publishing Service of the Ministry of Defense, 1971

Issat, Tannous, *The Enraging Story of Palestine,* New York, 1968

Jewish Agency, *Zionism and the Arab World,* Jerusalem, 1946

Kadi, Leila S., *Basic Political Documents of the Armed Palestinian Resistance Movement,* PLO Research Center, Beirut, 1969

Katinka, B., *Meaz Vead Henna* (From Then Till Now), Jerusalem, 1961

Khurshid, Ghazi, *Dalil Harakat Al-Muqawama Al-Filastiniyya Markaz Al-Abhath,* Beirut, March 1971

Kimche, Jon, *The Second Arab Awakening,* New York, 1970

Laffin, J., *Fedayeen – The Arab Israeli Dilemma,* Cassel, London, 1973

Laquer, Walter, *The Arab-Israeli Reader,* New York, 1968

Ma'oz M., *Soviet and Chinese Relations with the Palestinian Guerilla Organizations,* The Leonard Davis Institute for International Relations, Jerusalem Papers on Peace Problems, No. 4, March 1974

Mushin, Zuhayr, *Al-Thawra Al-Filastiniyya Bayn Al-Fakr Wal Mumasara Al-Sa'Ikqa,* Damascus, August 1972

Nagi, Allush, *Al Masra Ila Filastin* (The Campaign to Palestine), Beirut, 1964

Nisan, Mordechai, *The Arab-Israeli Conflict,* Attali Printing Services, Jerusalem, 1977

Nisan Mordechai, *The Palestinian Features of Jordan,* paper reprinted from *Judea, Samaria and Gaza: Views on the Present and Future,* Edited by Daniel Elazar, American Enterprise Institute, Washington, D.C.

Olmert, Yosef, *Between Arab and Jew – Unraveling the Knot,* Hadassah Study Series, 1989

Parkes, James, *History of Palestine from 135 AD to Modern Times,* London, 1949

Patai, Raphael, *The Arab Mind,* Scribners, New York, 1976

Pearlman, Maurice, *Mufti of Jerusalem,* London, 1947

Peretz, Don, *Israel and the Palestinian Arabs,* Washington D.C., 1958

PLO, *Al Muqawama Al Arabia Fi Filastin 1914-1948* (The Arab Opposition in Palestine), Beirut, 1967

Popular Front, The, *Nahwa Hall Dimurgrati,* n.d.

Porat, Y., *The Emergence of the Palestinian-Arab National Movement 1918-1929,* London, 1974